Franz von Benda-Beckmann,
Keebet von Benda-Beckmann

Social Security Between Past and Future

ETHNOLOGIE
Forschung und Wissenschaft

Band 13
LIT

Franz von Benda-Beckmann,
Keebet von Benda-Beckmann

Social Security Between Past and Future

Ambonese Networks of Care and Support

LIT

Gedruckt auf alterungsbeständigem Werkdruckpapier entsprechend
ANSI Z3948   DIN ISO 9706

Bibliographic information published by the Deutsche Nationalbibliothek
The Deutsche Nationalbibliothek lists this publication in the Deutsche Nationalbibliografie; detailed bibliographic data are available in the Internet at http://dnb.d-nb.de.

ISBN 978-3-8258-0718-4

A catalogue record for this book is available from the British Library

© LIT VERLAG Dr. W. Hopf Berlin 2007
Auslieferung/Verlagskontakt:
Fresnostr. 2   48159 Münster
Tel. +49 (0)251–620320   Fax +49 (0)251–231972
e-Mail: lit@lit-verlag.de   http://www.lit-verlag.de

Distributed in the UK by: Global Book Marketing, 99B Wallis Rd, London, E9 5LN
Phone: +44 (0) 20 8533 5800 – Fax: +44 (0) 1600 775 663
http://www.centralbooks.co.uk/acatalog/search.html

Distributed in North America by:

Transaction Publishers
New Brunswick (U.S.A.) and London (U.K.)

Transaction Publishers
Rutgers University
35 Berrue Circle
Piscataway, NJ 08854

Phone: +1 (732) 445 - 2280
Fax: + 1 (732) 445 - 3138
for orders (U. S. only):
toll free (888) 999 - 6778
e-mail:
orders@transactionspub.com

To Bas and Sander

List of Maps, Plates, Tables and Figures

Maps

4.1	Hila, village core with types of houses
9.1	Housing areas and land use in Hila

Plates

3.1	The trunk pieces of the sago palm have been split open
3.2	The pith dust is sieved in the tub
3.3	Villager carrying two tumang
3.4	Great quantities of sago are produced by larger teams in masohi cooperation as provision for the fasting month
4.1	Village house, built for permanent residence
4.2	Modern house with zinc roof and stone and concrete construction, built by Ambonese family living in the Netherlands
4.3	A fishing team drawing the net in
4.4	A roof is thatched in masohi cooperation
5.1	Ruin of Fort Amsterdam in Hila, built in the early 17th century
5.2	Fort Amsterdam in 1996 after its restauration
5.3	Fifth page of the testament of Hasan Suleiman of 1700
6.1	The village midwife
7.1	Yearly distribution of goods at the widows' shop
9.1	Temporary house of Butonese fishermen
9.2	A Butonese bagan fishing boat
11.1	The 18th century Emanuel church in Hila, the oldest church in the Moluccas, before its destruction

Tables

4.1	Composition of Ambonese and Butonese houses
6.1	Zakat distribution in Hila 1985 and 1986
6.2	Zakat given to the poor and needy
6.3	Concentration of zakat

Figures

3.1　　The Tree of Haji Abbas
4.1　　Kinship diagram of the Patti family
5.1　　Diagram of kinship relevant in the Lating property affairs

Contents

	Acknowledgements	xi
1	Social Security between Past and Future: Introduction	1
2	Coping with Insecurity	25
3	Sago, Law and Food Security on Ambon	59
4	Houses, People and Residence: The Fluidity of Ambonese Living Arrangements	91
5	Texts in Context: Historical Documents as Political Commodity on Islamic Ambon	137
6	Islamic Law and Social Security in an Ambonese Village	159
7	Social Security and Small-scale Enterprises in Islamic Ambon	185
8	Where Structures Merge: State and Off-State Involvement in Rural Social Security on Ambon Indonesia	205
9	Ambonese Adat as Jurisprudence of Insurgency and Oppression	235
10	Developing Families: Moluccan Women and Changing Patterns of Social Security in the Netherlands	257
11	Law, Violence and Peace Making on the Island of Ambon	281
	References	299

Acknowledgements

This book would not have been possible without the help of many people and organisations that helped us in our research on Ambon and in the processes of analysing and discussing our ideas. We gratefully remember the late H. Mohammad Galna (Mat) Ohorella, Raja (village head of the village) of Tulehu on Ambon and Senior Lecturer in Adat Law at Hasanuddin University in Makassar with whom Franz made a preliminary visit to Ambon in 1983 to convince him that Ambon was an exciting place to do research. His enthusiasm and this visit seduced us to plan our field research there and was the beginning of a long friendship that ended with his too early demise.

We chose the village of Hila as the location of our research. We lived there for a total of eleven months in 1984 and 1985 with our two children Bas and Sander who not only came to enjoy village life, but also enabled us to generate insights we would not have had had we lived there without them. After having returned to the Netherlands, they regretted that they could not live in two places at the same time. We want to express our gratitude to the people in Hila who accepted us in their midst. We are in particular grateful to Salma Moni and Haji Ismael Launuru and their family for their warm support and help. Nurya and Aida Launuru not only helped us by cleaning and cooking, they also were the cheerful, warm and caring minders for Bas and Sander. They contributed decisively to the social security of our family. Without them we could not have carried out our research. In the Netherlands, Haji Taha Launuru (a member of the few Islamic Ambonese soldiers brought to the Netherlands after Indonesia's independence) and his family gracefully offered us their house in Hila, in which we lived for 11 months. They had built the house for their own security in old-age, and indeed moved from Ridderkerk in the Netherlands to Hila in the early 1990s.

Our research in Hila was sponsored by the Indonesian Research Institute (LIPI) and the Faculty of Law of Universitas Pattimura in Ambon city. We especially remember Mrs. mr Hannie de Fretes-Tumbalaka[*], the then Dean of the Faculty, who not only helped to ease our way through the official institutions but also became a good friend with whom we could openly discuss all practical and academic problems we encountered during our research. The use of her car to visit Ambon town once a week, allowing us to visit offices of courts and administration to collect materials and to do some necessary shopping, was a tremendous help for our family.

Our research was part of a larger project on social security issues. Annemarie van Paassen did her Masters research in the village of Tulehu on the east coast of Ambon at the same time. Her friendship in the field was of great value to us. Otto Hospes also carried out his PhD research in Tulehu. Arie

Brouwer and Tanja Taale continued our research in Hila and both wrote their Masters theses on that basis, and received us in 'our' old family when we revisited Ambon in 1996. We owe much to the countless hours of discussion with them.

In the very early planning phase we met Frank Hirtz, who worked at the Max Planck Institute for Foreign and International Social Law in Munich. Frank turned out to be a kindred spirit, whose ideas for his research on rural social security in the Philippines were very similar to ours, and our early discussions helped to shape our mutual plans. His visit to Hila was a memorable event for us and our family, and for the village who continued to speak about him for a long time. Our cooperation and friendship also led to the conference on 'Formal and informal social security' in Tutzing, Germany, which we organized together with Prof. Dr. Hans Zacher of the Max Planck Institute for Foreign and International Social Law, and the IUAES Commission on Folk Law and Legal Pluralism. The conference led to the book *Between Kinship and the State: Social Security and Law in Developing Countries* (1988).

Our research sparked off a number of PhD and post doc research projects, in which issues of social insecurity were a central issue.[1] The PhD seminars we organized and the intensive discussions with our younger colleagues led to the publication of the Special Issue of Focaal on *Coping with Insecurity: An 'underall' approach* in 1994, the introduction of which is included into this volume.

The research in Hila also led to a new research project in the Netherlands. Moluccan women's organisations had pleaded for research on issues of emancipation. The *Centrum voor Onderzoek naar Maatschappelijke Tegenstellingen* (Centre for the Study of Social Conflict) at the University of Leiden, with the financial support of the Ministry of Social Affairs, asked Frency Leatemia-Tomatala, Roos Latumahina and Keebet von Benda-Beckmann to carry out this research. This led to the publication of the book *De Emancipatie van Molukse Vrouwen in Nederland* (1992) and a number of publications in journals and book chapters, one of which is included into this volume. The lively and intensive discussions among the three researchers generated valuable comparative insights and allowed us to look at Moluccan migration from both ends.

Though we have not done new field research on social security since the early 1990s, we have continued our interest and discussions with PhD students have helped us to develop the field further. Communication with Jörg Freiberg-Strauss at the GTZ brought us into contact with Renate Kirsch, with

---

[*] mr is the abbreviation for *master in de rechten* (Master of law).
[1] Vel 1994b; De Bruijn and Van Dijk 1995; Hospes 1996; Tang 1996; Marks 2000; Walsum 2000; Biezeveld 2002; Anders 2005; Koning and Hüsken 2006; Rohregger 2006.

whom we not only developed a warm friendship but also a research project in Malawi, resulting in several Masters theses and indirectly into the PhD dissertations of Barbara Rohregger and Gerhard Anders.

We are grateful to our (then) Universities, the Erasmus University of Rotterdam and the Agricultural University of Wageningen, for consistently supporting our cooperation, which started as a very private husband and wife research project, but then developed into a number of larger cooperative inter-university projects.

When moving to the Max Planck Institute for Social Anthropology in 2000, the interest in social security quickly expanded and we are grateful for the opportunity the MPI has offered us to develop our interest in the issue further. Within the Project Group Legal Pluralism, two projects deal specifically with the topic: Tatjana Thelen has studied social security in an industrial town in the eastern part of Germany, and Anja Peleikis has studied social security in connection with issues of places of remembrance and cultural property in the Curonian Lagoon Region in Lithuania. Issues of social security now have become a major focus in the institute, leading a major EU-funded research project on *Kinship and Social Security* (KASS) and a series of research projects in China and Vietnam under the guidance of Chris Hann.

Finally, we thank Gesine Koch and Johannes Stephan for their dedication in producing this volume. We thank Oliver Weihmann and Robert Goßmann for their help with the pictures and Jutta Turner for the maps.

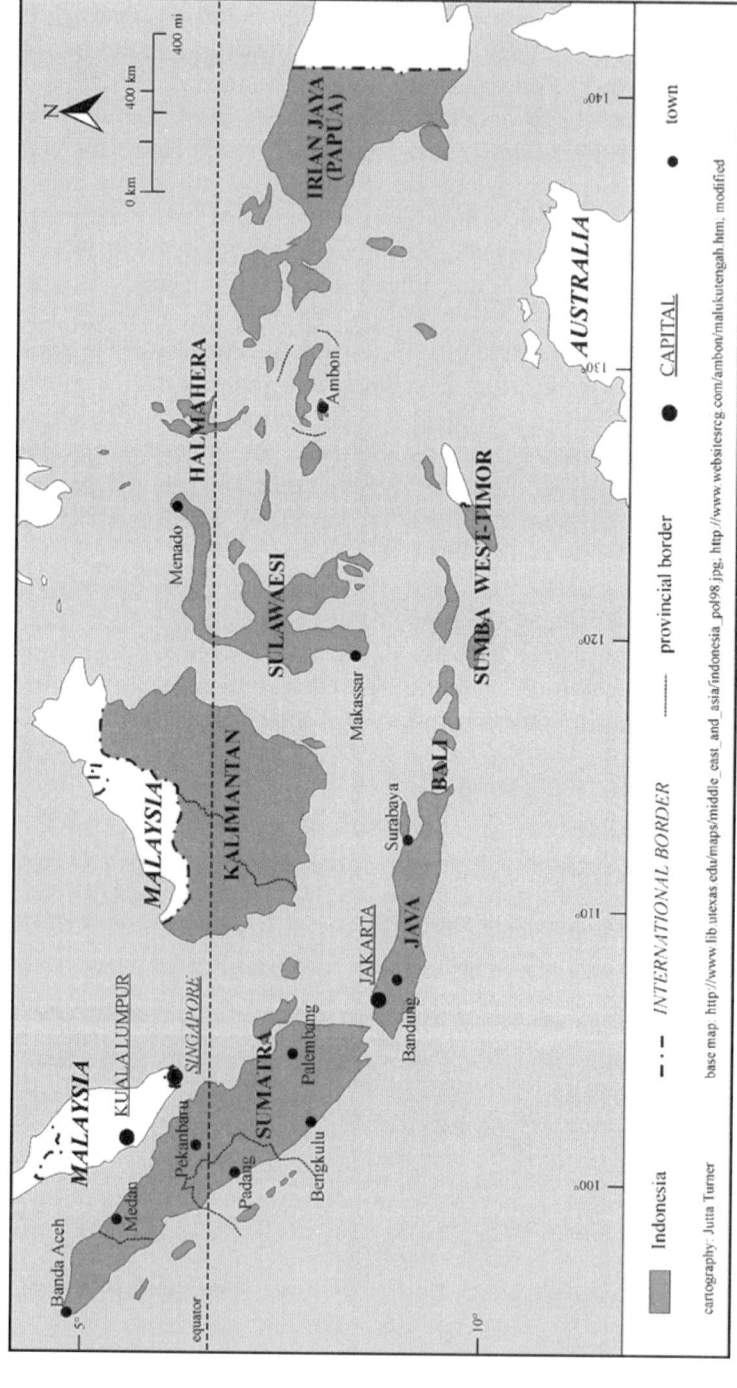

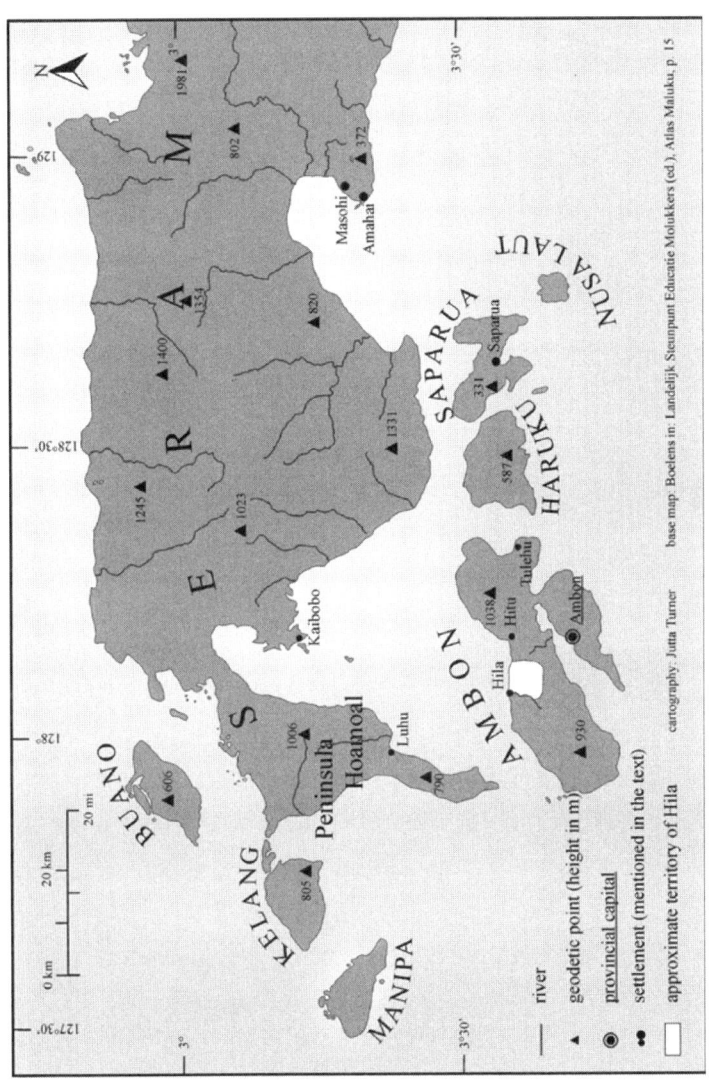

Map of West Seram and the Ambon-Lease island, with the territory of Hila.

The important cash crops of the Spice Islands

Cloves

Mace and nuts of nutmeg

Chapter 1
Social Security between Past and Future:
Eastern Indonesia
Introduction

Franz and Keebet von Benda-Beckmann

This collection of papers is the result of two research projects on social security. The research for the main project took place in the mid 1980s on the Island of Ambon. Ambon is one of the famous spice islands of the Eastern Indonesian Archipelago known as the Moluccas. It was incorporated into the Dutch East Indies in the early 17th century and after Independence in 1945 became part of the Republic of Indonesia. As a consequence of this long colonial past, over a period of four centuries the local social, political, cultural and legal organisation has been thoroughly influenced by external forces. The political organisation of the villages (*negeri*) at the coast of Ambon, land tenure, and household structures, were all largely shaped by the colonial masters. The local economy has for centuries been a mix of subsistence-oriented horticulture, in which sago and fish were the main foodstuffs, and the production of the cash-crops cloves, nutmeg and coconuts. Rice and wheat flour were not cultivated in the region, and have, again for centuries, been imported from other regions within Indonesia. The island has an ethnically and religiously heterogeneous population, half of whom are Moslems and half Christians of Calvinist provenance. With our research we wanted to contribute to the scarce ethnographic literature on the Moluccas. The few studies that had been carried out after Independence mainly dealt with the Christian part of Ambon and the surrounding islands.[1] Ethnographic material on the Moslem villages of the Central Moluccas was virtually non-existent. We chose the village of Hila on the north coast of the island for our fieldwork. Hila had a predominantly Moslem population, but there was a small Christian enclave. In addition to the Ambonese Moslem and Christian population living in the core village, there were three hamlets of Butonese, a migrant group originating from the southeast tip of Sulawesi who had settled in Hila from the late 19th century on.

Our research was centred on the question how people and organisations dealt with situations and periods of insecurity, especially in a place where the state as potential provider had little to offer. We were primarily interested in food, shelter and care. Though we did deal with access to education and medical services as important factors in the strategies of social security, the organisation

---

[1] Cooley 1961, 1962 and 1967; Van Fraassen 1972; Bartels 1978, 1989, 2003; Knaap 1987a and 1987b.

of education and medical services as such were beyond the scope of this study. Exploring the full range of relationships through which goods and services for social security were provided and received, whether based on the state, on kinship, neighbourhood, or on patron-client relationships within the village and beyond, we intended to obtain a comprehensive overview of the social security situation. We wanted to examine the functioning of the various arrangements, and the availability of material and immaterial resources that could serve social security purposes. Our legal anthropological background made us particularly interested in the plural normative structures of rights and obligations involved in social security, which comprised state law, Ambonese customary law, called *adat*, the local variety of Islamic law, and emerging new forms of self-regulation in the village. The study was set in a historical perspective which would allow us to understand changes in the mixes of social security relationships that people had, changes in the normative structure, and in the elasticity of the mechanisms of social security.

The second research project concerned Moluccans in the Netherlands and their relationships with their home villages. Ambon had been a strategically important base for the colonial government, from which it had recruited civil servants and a substantial part of the colonial army. Due to their position within the Dutch colonial army, at the end of the Indonesian War of Independence a substantial number of mainly Christian Moluccans moved to the Netherlands, where they have had a tumultuous history. This group of migrants was the subject of a study on "The Emancipation of Moluccan Women in the Netherlands" carried out in the early 1990s.[2] The issue of emancipation in many ways is related to social security and Chapter 10, in which the developing social security networks at the initial stage of migration are discussed, is based on this research.

The empirical research for this volume took place well before the turmoil started in the Moluccas in 1998, in the aftermath of the Suharto era, during which many of the tensions that had been latent during the period of our research culminated in extraordinary levels of violence, the wounds of which have not even started to heal, though the violent conflict seems to have come to an end. Chapter 11 discusses the complexity of the conflict in its historical context, and addresses the issue of why it has been so difficult to end the conflict. We have not returned to Ambon since the outbreak of violence. From what is known, it has become a very different place and the island seems to have become completely segregated, both in religious and in ethnic terms (Bartels 2003).

One may ask why one should publish a volume on social security of a place that has become so utterly insecure and that has changed so much since

---

[2] The empirical work was done in collaboration with Frency Leatemia-Tomatala and Roos Latumahina. See K. von Benda-Beckmann and Leatemia-Tomatala 1992.

the research was carried out. We think that it is important to publish this volume for a number of reasons. First, the chapters that are now collected in this volume offer a coherent representation of the complex and fragmented social security as it functioned, and did not function, in a region on which little ethnographic work has been done.[3] The volume thus contributes to the general ethnographic literature of an under-researched region of Indonesia and to the study of social security in particular.[4]

Second, though special in its own historical setting, the material from Ambon shows some general characteristics of social security of people in rural areas in developing countries that are firmly embedded in national and transnational contexts. Because of its spice production, Ambon had attracted the attention of regional and European empires during the early period of colonial expansion. Ternate, Portugal, Spain and the Netherlands had all tried to secure a foothold on the strategically important island, until it was finally colonised by the Dutch in the 17th century. As a result, the island has been embedded within the international commodity market for centuries. Developments on the world market have always had an impact on the resource base for social security (see chapter 3). The region also has a long history of in- and out-migration within and beyond Indonesia. As a result, the population is religiously and ethnically heterogeneous (see in particular chapters 9 and 11). The strong rural and urban connections within the region and the wide transnational contacts have implications for the way the Ambonese population organises its social security (see chapters 8, 10 and 11). The social security situation on Ambon is also typical for most rural regions in developing states, in that the state, with a few exceptions for military personnel and civil servants, provides little if any social security for its population, especially the poor. The majority of the population in these countries face enormous social and economic problems and depend on their own local mechanisms of security, however weak and fragile, and however threatened by political, economic and ecological conditions. Large sections of the population suffer from what Macarov (1980) called the first and second law of social welfare: *Those who need the most get the least* is the first, or so-called 'iron law' of social welfare (Macarov 1980: 47), complemented by the second: *When more welfare is possible, it does not seem to be needed, and when more welfare is needed, it does not seem to be possible* (Macarov 1980: 24).[5]

---

[3] Apart from this introduction, all chapters appeared as articles and book chapters in rather different publications and for a variety of readerships. The original sources of publication are given in the beginning of each chapter.

[4] Since we conducted our research on Ambon, studies on social security in other regions of Indonesia have been carried out, see, e.g. Dirkse et al. 1993; Vel 1994b; Nooteboom 1999; Biezeveld 2002; Keasberry 2002; Lont 2002; Marianti 2002; Koning and Hüsken 2006.

[5] Castells (1998: 162-64) recently spoke about a new fourth world, made up of multiple black holes of social exclusion throughout the planet.

Thirdly, as a result of high levels of poverty and insecurity, social security, is currently highly placed on the international agenda of policy makers. The vicious conditions so aptly characterised by Macarov continue to present challenges to state governments and donor agencies engaged in social policy aiming at improving social support to the poor. These problems are addressed under a variety of terms, such as poverty alleviation, livelihood, vulnerability, social support systems and social safety nets, all concepts closely related to the concept of social security. The challenges are particularly great in times of war or other violent conflict, ecological disasters, massive displacement and refugee streams, and epidemics. Some authors have pleaded for viewing social security as part of a wider set of issues captured under the term 'human security'.[6]

When we started our research in 1983, social scientists working in developing countries showed little interest in the subject. 'Social security' was largely associated with forms of social support regulated and provided by the state. Since the governments of developing countries did little to provide social security to the majority of their populations, the issue was considered quite irrelevant for these countries.[7] In policy discussions, the dominant view of most social policy and development economists was what we called the *no longer – not yet perspective*.[8] This evolutionary and modernisation-biased perspective was formulated in terms of the oppositions traditional/modern and informal/formal. In this view, traditional, informal systems of social security are no longer capable of protecting the rural population in developing countries from poverty, especially in those situations and periods of heightened vulnerability due to physical, mental or socio-economic conditions. Traditional social security therefore is to be replaced by modern, formal social security, to be provided by the state. However, these new forms are not yet in place and state social security cannot yet cater sufficiently for the social security needs of rural people. General social policies therefore aimed at 'extending' formal social mechanisms for security in the form of insurance schemes. Designed for the 'modern' economic sectors, they were eventually to be extended not only to wage laborers in the rural sector, but also to self-employed farmers, who were said to face the same risk as agricultural wage laborers. However, these models were all based on what Macarov (1980) called 'the unholy alliance between work and welfare'. Midgley (1984) has pointed at the fact that such schemes increase rather than decrease social inequality, as the poorest in the ab-

---

[6] For an analysis of 'human security' that combines social security and state security, see Thomas 2000. See also Commission on Human Security 2003.

[7] The 1986 symposium in Tutzing, Germany, on social security and legal pluralism organised by the Commission on Folk Law and Legal Pluralism, together with the Max Planck Institute for Foreign and International Social Law in Munich, was one of the first in which the issue was discussed in relation to developing countries. And the discussions revealed just how difficult it was to think in terms of a broader conception of social security. See F. von Benda-Beckmann et al. 1988b.

[8] Gilbert 1976: 365; Platteau 1991: 163. See also Schmidt 1992.

sence of direct taxation tend to contribute most through indirect taxation, while not profiting from state social security expenditures.

In the course of the 1990s, the trend of expanding state social security came to a halt. Social adjustment policies that put pressure on developing states to limit state expenditures also influenced the social policies propagated by donor agencies. This change was also informed by the decline of state involvement as provider (though not as regulator) of social security in European welfare states.[9] In Europe, welfare policies emphasizing state responsibility for its citizens were replaced by policies that emphasised the citizens' own responsibility. The market came to be regarded as an important provider of social security, while 'traditional' mechanisms of social security were upgraded and are no longer seen as mere relics of the past.[10] The redesigning of social security systems in Europe also revealed that the full extension of state social security along the lines of the classical European model of the welfare state was not economically feasible in developing countries. Besides, 'traditional' social security mechanisms were expected to erode further if left to themselves. Based on these insights, policies started to take local forms of social security more seriously and programmes were designed to 'strengthen' local institutions of social security and to create innovative linkages between them, as well as linkages to state- and NGO-supported forms of social security.[11]

Despite this heightened interest, dominant social science approaches and policies still lack an appropriate analytical approach that can look at the multiplicity of social security relationships and their normative regulations in conjunction. And this is the fourth reason why we think it is appropriate to publish this volume. Our empirical research in Indonesia has helped us develop and illustrate a broad conceptual framework for social security and an analytical approach that is suitable beyond the local particularities of Eastern Indonesia. In chapter 2 we outline what we call a functional and layered approach to social (in)security. We take as a point of departure a conception of social security as an abstractly, functionally defined field of problems. All over the world, social and economic conditions are such that a multitude of people suffer from insecurity: from uncertainty about whether they will have anything to eat or will be fed, whether they have a roof over their head, whether they will be cared for

---

[9] These developments are also hotly discussed in Germany. See the debates on changing solidarity and the welfare state in *Rechtsgeschichte* No. 5, 2004, and No. 6, 2005.

[10] For new approaches in social policies, see Van Ginneken 2003. For other more comprehensive accounts see Bossert 1985; Palriwala and Risseeuw 1996; Risseeuw and Ganesh 1998; De Jong et al. 2005; Pine and Haukanes 2005; Read and Thelen 2007; Thelen and Baerwolf 2007.

[11] For early attempts to create linkages, see Freiberg-Strauss and Jung 1988. See further Midgley and Kaseke 1996; Midgley and Tracy 1996; Midgley and Sherraden 1997. The GTZ, the German Technical Cooperation, also adopted such an approach; see F. von Benda-Beckmann et al. 1997; Freiberg-Strauss and Meyer 1999.

when they are ill, or be helped when they are young and old, or have money to support themselves when they have no means to earn it, and so forth. In the most general sense, social security thus refers to the efforts of individuals, groups of individuals or organisations to overcome these insecurities. The use of the term social security inevitably becomes multireferential. It refers to an abstractly conceived field of problems, and to the actual social phenomena within this field. The analytical conceptual baseline is thus dissociated from the usual efforts to define social security on the basis of institutions or policies. The concept can refer to different kinds of social phenomena and their interrelationships. In one sense, it refers to the economic and social position of actual people, and indicates a relative state of security or insecurity. It can also be used to describe the social security properties of social phenomena at different *layers* of social organisation. It thus not only refers to human interaction in which goods and services are transferred or appropriated for social security, but also to the social relationship within which such appropriation or transfer takes place. It can also refer to the institutions and regulations of social security, and finally, to the world of ideology, philosophy, and values. The approach is *functional* because, instead of looking primarily at institutions normatively or symbolically designed for social security, it also considers relationships and institutions that are not primarily designed for it, but that take on a function for social security. Moreover, the concept is not confined to any particular set of social security institutions but includes the full range of social security mechanisms, from state-provided social security, to traditional and new local modes, family and neighbourhood, and a variety of secular and religiously based forms of social security, and market mechanisms. And it caters for the sometimes intricate linkages between different kinds or 'sectors' of social security which are not captured by the oppositions within which the concept of social security is usually couched. The approach distinguishes the providers of social security from the sources of regulation of such services. This shows that the frequently used distinctions between formal and informal, between modern and traditional, and between state, market and community are not capable of capturing the complex mixes of social security relations most people have. The approach also draws attention to the potential plurality of cognitive and normative frameworks that define what is normal and what is a situation of need, who is entitled to receive, and who obliged to provide goods and services for social security. Social security more often than not involves complex normative structures, and on Ambon involved state law, (neo-) customary law, religious law, international law, and often other sets of norms that do not belong to any named legal system. Moreover, our analytical approach looks at the mechanisms of social security in conjunction with its material and immaterial resources. Such an approach thus helps to capture the complex networks of rights and obligations in which providers and recipients are connected and shape actual conditions of social security. It shows that social security is always a matter of degree, and that social security relationships are full of contradiction and ambivalence. This approach to social security certainly has something in common with livelihood, poverty and vulnerability studies. However, it is more comprehensive in bringing together conditions, practices, relationships, institutions and more general cultural and ideological notions.

Fifth, social security is a magnifying glass that helps us to understand how past, present and future are linked within a society. As we elaborate in chapter 2 and illustrate in some of the other chapters, current social security relationships are positioned between past and future in complex ways. Relationships built up and provisions given in the past create expectations and rights to be provided for when in need oneself, while care and support is given in the expectation that one will receive care in an unknown future. But the actualization of social security can only be established with certainty retrospectively. Prospectively, there is nothing more than probabilities, degrees of likelihood that particular contingencies will occur and that social security will be provided. In chapter 2, we suggest that the study of social insecurity and security requires both ex-ante and ex-post perspectives.

Finally, this volume is located between past and future in another sense: Ambon society in the 1980s in its particular historical setting bore the seeds of the violence that at the turn of the 21st century was to erupt, though no-one could predict when exactly it would happen. We have pointed at some of the tensions of the – then – present, resulting from the potentially explosive mixture of a highly volatile global market for the main export products cloves, nutmeg and coconut oil (see chapter 3), a contracting labour market, an ethnically and religiously heterogeneous population with unequal access to education, and a state administration that became less and less able to absorb the large young labour force it created with a general education of poor quality (see chapter 8). Another important factor leading to the violent conflict later was the interethnic tensions between the Ambonese majority and the immigrants, which in the mid 1980s had already led to small-scale violence and even incidental killings (chapter 9). Chapter 8 also shows that many of the tensions had a long tradition going back to colonial times. What was not clear at the time of our research was the extent to which the armed Indonesian forces would get involved officially and unofficially, and the destabilising effects of their involvement that are the subject of chapter 11.

'Ordinary' Adversity

Social security arrangements, whether provided by state agencies, insurance companies, kinsmen or neighbours, are meant for 'ordinary' adversity, paradoxical as this may sound. They aim to cover contingencies that are familiar, in some way predictable, and occur in ordinary times and life-cycles: problems with the acquisition of food and shelter, care of small children, in case of illness and old age, unemployment, and increased need of support, financially or in kind, in culturally or legally prescribed situations such as marriage ceremonies or burials. The 1980s were such an ordinary time of relative stability in Indonesia, when we did our research on Ambon. As a result, most of the chapters of this volume deal with these kinds of social security.

In ordinary life, people in situations of need and distress received help and assistance on the basis of kinship and neighbourhood relations and of mutual help. Especially important was that access to the main staple foods sago and fish was largely possible on the basis of non-commercialised mechanisms. People either had personal rights to sago or fish by virtue of being a member of their families, or could engage in share harvesting arrangements. Rice had become the preferred food, but as it was not produced on the island, money was required to obtain it, which people earned mainly with the sale of cloves and nutmeg. When spice prices were low, people reverted to locally produced sago and fish, which provide an important buffer in periods of economic hardship. Rights to sago were also important for house building, because a simple house could be built from various parts of the sago palm. This was particularly important for young married couples, who could easily build such a house and move out of their parents' home. Chapter 3 discusses the property rights to sago, its production chain, and the complex relationships of exchange, distribution and support involved in sago production. Chapter 4 discusses the social security implications of land rights for residence patterns and housing arrangements. The chapters show that the bilateral inheritance system created a relatively strong economic position for women, who had independent access to land for horticulture and housing. This had important social security implications. Widows or divorced women did not automatically become needy, as would be the case in kinship and inheritance systems in which women only have access to land on behalf of a husband, father or brother. Chapters 3 and 9 also show that Butonese migrants in Hila, due to the structure of land rights which excluded them from access to cash tree production, specialised in vegetable production and fishing. The Ambonese population had come to rely heavily on the Butonese for these foodstuffs, but when necessary they could revert to horticulture and fishing. Physical and emotional care was also mainly provided within households and among close kin and neighbours. When individuals or households needed especially large amounts of resources for marriage and burial ceremonies, this usually was provided on the basis of ad hoc action sets based on kinship, friendship and neighbourhood, and village membership. Moreover, some social security mechanisms based on religion worked at specific times, for instance at the end of the fasting months with the collection and distribution of *zakat fitrah* in the form of rice (chapter 6).

As we show in chapter 8 and elsewhere, the state did little in terms of direct social security arrangements.[12] Its general policy ideas and concrete institutionalised forms were heavily influenced by the development of the official, institutionally differentiated forms of social security which emerged in western industrialised states. In the first place, the state system offered income substitution to certain categories of the population in case of adversity. Social security long remained more or less restricted to civil servants and members of the armed forces and the police, who received comparatively good pensions in case of sickness, invalidity or after retirement at the age of 55.[13] The Ministry of Social Affairs in the 1980s also set up social security programmes for four categories of needy persons: widows, orphans, the disabled and the aged, which are described in chapter 7. These programmes were meant as a stimulus to set up projects that would become self-supporting and, after some time, which would make profits enabling participants to send their children to school. The government also financed various institutions and projects aimed at increasing the general level of income of those with a 'weak economic situation' in order to overcome some of the main risks of falling into poverty. Among them were the village cooperatives, the family welfare movement and the programme village health centres for the improvement of women's roles to achieve a healthy and prosperous family.

Different people had different mixes of social relations to other individuals, households and organisations through which they received or could mobilise support in situations or periods of need and distress. Likewise, most people were part of different relations and networks in which they acted, or were likely to act in the future, as providers of social security. As we show in chapter 8, the civil servants living in the village were involved in state-organised social security relations as well as in kinship and patron-client relations with villagers. Through these relationships and transfers of goods and services, organisational structures of social security operating at different spatial and social scales thus came together or merged in the village: the state-organised forms of social security and the local village based circles of solidarity.

These mechanisms of sharing, mutual support and help largely worked on the basis of balanced or generalised reciprocity, and these changed with the changing life-cycles of individuals and the households in which they lived in the course of their life (see especially chapter 4). Different deficits could largely be

---

[12] Joenoes 1982; ILO Report 1985; Esmara and Tjiptoherijanto 1986: 60; F. and K. von Benda-Beckmann 1995.

[13] The new schemes for the private sector that were emerging at the time of our research are of the insurance type and involve regular monthly payments by registered workers who have more or less regular work. In 1992, new and ambitious social security legislation was passed which considerably extended the coverage (see McLeod 1993; F. and K. von Benda-Beckmann 1995). However, concrete social security policies aiming at introducing social insurance schemes for the rural population are still in the planning stage.

balanced out against each other. For instance, care could be given in exchange for access to sago palms, or watching over children would be exchanged for helping with food processing, etc. This is not to say, of course, that it was predictable who would need how much care at what particular time. Nor does it mean that all members of solidarity groups and these distributive exchanges carried the same burden. Kinship and neighbourhood relationships were not always balanced, but may be characterised by political and social asymmetries and dependencies. In chapter 8 we describe the rather balanced relations between patrons and clients within kinship networks that were common in Hila, and which worked for mutual benefit. Though they also led to unequal exchanges and opportunities, this did not reach the extremely 'predatory' level of inequality that has been described for other parts of the world (Ngwira 1995). Particularly interesting were the changing dynamics and asymmetries in the networks of mutual support among the civil servants living in the village. Due to the fact that official salaries were very low, young government officials living away from home, such as teachers or young policemen in rural areas, were in need of support from their village neighbours. Should they later obtain higher positions in town, they might become important brokers and provide social security to clients and relatives. This often required more financial resources than their salary could carry. The chapter describes the 'off state' activities of civil servants which have a strong social security component, but which are only possible because of their position within the state. Thus, state and off-state structures become merged in intricate ways, and social security considerations appear to be an important factor in the dynamics of migration.

Social security arrangements do not work automatically; they require monetary or social 'premiums' to be paid by the future beneficiaries, and they require the willingness and capability of the providers to fulfill their promises and obligations. They are typically less reliable for the odd cases that do not suit the ordinary categories, rights and obligations. Not all expectations or claims for support are honoured and borderline cases may give rise to much tension and conflict. When support is asked, this is often done in the idiom of kinship and community, and kin ties are often drawn upon or constructed for that purpose. Fostering children and adoption are official ways of constructing kinship as a basis for long lasting and complex mutual obligations for support. But kinship may also be constructed in a more loose way, to indicate a close relationship in general. Successful migrants often appear to have a remarkably large number of close kin. On the other hand, if support is to be denied to a kinsman with whom one does not get along, a common strategy is to deny kinship ties to this person.[14] In Ambon, kinship alone was rarely sufficient for a strong claim for support, except for very close relatives. Usually friendship, living in the same

---

[14] Hirtz (1995: 107 ff.) has illustrated this point for the Philippines.

neighbourhood, or previous mutual support was an additional prerequisite.[15] However, neighbours and friends were only willing to support in case of minor adversities, while relatives are often the only possible supporters in severe cases of adversity. People also tried to avoid the burdens associated with the more vertical and coercive kinship and clientilist relationships and obligations. One way was to follow an illiquidity strategy and convert resources into assets that cannot be used for providing support or help to others, or to insert them in more horizontal and voluntary circles of obligation from which they cannot be withdrawn. Entering into rotating saving and credit associations (ROSCAs), or burial associations with persons of the same class, similar income and lifestyle is a well known strategy, especially among migrants.[16] ROSCAs, called *arisan* in Indonesia, were very popular indeed in Ambon (see also Hospes 1996). They also channelled resources from local village social security mechanisms that operate more on a vertical line towards one which operates horizontally and in stricter reciprocity.

As this volume shows, there is no reason for celebrating local arrangements of social security systems and circles of support, but that does not make them less important and nor does it make them necessarily less reliable than other forms of social security. Negotiation, difference of opinion, free-riding, mere neglect and attempts to cheat, as well as sanctioning those evading their obligations, are all part of the game. Despite all deficiencies, in normal times, systems of social security do operate on the basis of relatively stable circles of support, whether this is a community, a kin group, an insurance company or a national state. There is a main core of occurrences that can and will be taken care of. And they operate on relatively stable normative structures, even though these may be quite complex, as in the case of Ambon.

Social Security under Pressure

Changes in support networks, in the resource basis or in the normative structures are seen to a certain extent as normal and do not elicit anxiety or a sense of insecurity. Ambonese society and its social security systems have been remarkably resilient to such changes. The resource base has perhaps been the most volatile element of social security in Ambon. As a result of the strongly fluctuating world market of nutmeg and cloves, for centuries the Ambonese

---

[15] As Biezeveld (2002) has shown for the Minangkabau in West Sumatra, labour groups increasingly also serve for social support. Marianti (2006: 83) points at the fluid character of support relationships for widows in the east Javanese town of Malang. Koning (2006: 160) shows that fishermen in Karangrejo, in Middle Java, try to avoid having to rely on relatives for support because of the moral claims that are involved.

[16] See Lont 1999 and 2006; Biezeveld 2002. See for Malawi, Anders 2005 and Rohregger 2006.

population has been used to periods of wealth alternating with more frugal periods. This has taught them not to rely too much on their earnings from spice production as the main source of their livelihood and social security, but to keep other options open. In fact, as we explain in chapter 4, the Ambonese economy does not obtain its relative stability by each person pursuing one particular economic activity, because no single one is secure. The stability derives from a flexible combination of a wide range of activities, including subsistence horticulture and cash-crops, fishing, gathering in the forest, temporary jobs in various projects, and having access to relatives in government service. We have labelled this a '*cari* economy', because Ambonese describe their economic activities as *cari* (searching): searching for forest products, searching for jobs, searching for money. These are individual activities and decisions, and a person may drop one economic activity at any one time, seizing another opportunity whenever it presents itself. In order to keep options open, a highly individualised but extensive and labour intensive network of social relationships is required. As well, men and women have to strike a balance between individual *cari* behaviour and cooperation necessary or conducive for *cari*. Support relationships are built into this economic system. Here, too, people invest much time and energy to keep possibilities open and search for opportunities for support when needed.

In situations and times of rapid social, economic and political change, however, support mechanisms may come under pressure, and familiar mixes of economic activity and social security may fall apart. Chapter 3 discusses the dangers which commoditisation of sago production and distribution would bring for the village population, as has indeed occurred in other regions of Indonesia. Chapter 8 shows how education and migration, even to nearby Ambon town, changed the carrying capacity of support networks.[17] The strategy of sending children to school to ensure one's own social security in old age became increasingly risky, for it was not at all certain that these youngsters would obtain a permanent job, either in government service or in the private sector. The expansion of public administration that started in the 1970s had already come to a halt by the mid 1980s. Thus, resources invested in the education of children were siphoned away from the village, without any certainty that it would pay off.

As chapter 10 shows, the forced migration of Ambonese soldiers and their families to the Netherlands had an emotionally deeper impact on the support networks and expectations, rights and obligations pertaining to the social security of Moluccans, in the Netherlands as well as for the people in their home villages. Though the Moluccan migrants rejected the Dutch state in many respects for political reasons, they were deeply affected by their incorporation

---

[17] See also Marianti 2002 and 2006; De Jong et al. 2005; Hüsken and Koning (2006: 8) and footnote 15 highlighting the problems for the elderly when the support networks come under pressure.

into the Dutch welfare system. In a very fundamental way, this shaped not only their relationships among themselves and with Dutch society in the Netherlands; it also affected the mode in which they organised support to their relatives in their places of origin. Though most Moluccans had a rough time during the initial decades of their stay in the Netherlands, they had reached reasonable standards of living by the time money transfers to the Moluccas became feasible. Chapter 10 analyses the precarious support networks of the initial period of migration and the ways Moluccan migrants have developed over time into fuller support networks with a better resource basis. But along the way also the notions of appropriate support and care among Dutch Moluccans changed and were adjusted to Dutch norms of support. The relatively secure standard of living in turn enabled Moluccan migrants to provide support to their relatives and communities of origin in the Moluccas. Since the Indonesian government opened the border for Dutch Moluccans in the late 1970s, visits became more frequent, but these personal encounters revealed that the Dutch Moluccans had developed quite different norms for support than their relatives who had stayed in the Moluccas. Moreover, they were shocked to realise that the highly emotional feelings with which their support for their relatives in the Moluccas was associated were not reciprocated by their Indonesian relatives, who appeared to have a more instrumental approach to their relationship.[18] The dilemmas of solidarity deepened with the ethnic and religious clashes and the ensuing segregation resulting from the period of civil war at the turn of the 21st century on the Moluccas as described in chapter 11. The migrant community in the Netherlands found itself caught between the demands and wishes to support their relatives on Ambon, who needed support, and the knowledge that some would use this to buy weapons perpetuating the very violence that created the need for support.

Such dramatic changes in solidarity circles are a widespread phenomenon. They occur in the first place because of demographic change due to migration or violent conflict, such as in Ambon and other parts of Indonesia at the turn of the century.[19] Fundamental changes also occur as a result of changes in the resource base attributable to developments in the world market (chapter 3) or serious harvest failure or epidemics such as malaria and HIV/AIDS, both of which are rampant in large parts of Africa.[20] Thus, deep and rapid changes typically involve social and economic change and changes in complex normative structures of social security. Familiar mixtures of social security arrangements become less reliable and predictable and may even 'snap' (Agarwal 1991). These developments have important psychological implications and create an

---

[18] See for a discussion of the emotional aspects of social security, Read and Thelen 2007.
[19] See chapter 11. Koning and Hüsken 2006.
[20] See also De Bruijn 1994 and Van Dijk 1994; De Jong et al. 2005; Anders 2005; Rohregger 2006.

immense degree of insecurity and distrust. It is for such catastrophic situations that the term 'human security' has been developed: to indicate the connection between security against violence and social security (Thomas 2000; Commission on Human Security 2003).

Proximity and Distance

Though circles of support may extend beyond the confinement of local places and material support may be provided over long distances, the provision of social security is in important ways located in one place. Caring labour depends on physical proximity. One cannot feed and wash a sick person unless one is present. And though Dutch Moluccans provided much psychological care over long distance by telephone, in rural Ambon of the 1980s most forms of care could only be given in face to face situations. Social security needs resources, both material and immaterial. Where there is no food, obligations for providing food become meaningless. A kinship system with strong obligations of support does not help a person who has no relatives around. Without access to labour, land may not be made productive. In rural Ambon, a substantial proportion of social security is provided among people in face to face contact and with resources that are located in the immediate proximity. Distance of resources decreased the extent to which different resource deficits can be balanced out. In a local economy, such as in Hila, possibilities for substituting resources necessary for providing goods and services for social security were limited.

Migration changes the potential availability of resources for social security purposes. It is often a strategy to improve the economic situation of one relative who then may later be able to support the relatives back home. Families may make considerable sacrifices to allow one member to migrate, reallocating resources away from what might otherwise have been used for other social security purposes. Migration draws away resources in a two ways. Firstly, money is usually required to migrate, especially if migration is connected to education. As migrants are usually young adults, migration also draws away labour and potential caring capacity. The fruits of this sacrifice can only be reaped in a distant and uncertain future. If things turn out well, the migrant may at a later stage be able to provide financial support and mediate in important services, such as health care, access to education and the labour market. Migrants may establish an outpost to whom subsequent migrants can turn for support during the initial stages of their migration. Thus, a serious pressure on the current resource basis may be compensated by a possible but insecure increase in the resource basis in the distant future.

However, there are other reasons why the provision of support over long distances is fragile. Migration also changes the composition of and interrelations within support circles.[21] Migrants often do not leave their old support circles completely, but they take on a different position within them.[22] Such long distance networks have advantages for social security, but they also have some drawbacks. It is easier to evade the pressures for support if one is not face to face with the person asking for support. On the other hand, migrants, especially new migrants, typically have a contracted circle of potential providers of care for which physical proximity is needed, as chapter 10 demonstrates. Thus, circles of support that extend beyond face to face relationships become more differentiated, both for potential providers and for receivers of support. And while the resource base may become stronger in terms of financial resources and in brokering services, people at both ends may become more vulnerable when it comes to physical care. Over time, adjustments are made at both ends of long distance networks to redress some of these vulnerabilities, as chapter 10 shows. As well, people have to design new strategies to deal with extraordinary demands for support. Sudden, massive migration, for example under conditions of war, crop failure, and hunger, may prove particularly disruptive.[23] Relationships are cut off and bridging the distances between provider and recipient becomes impossible, at least temporarily. This shows how fragile a resource basis is when it is not in the immediate proximity of those in need. The Moluccan soldiers who were forced to migrate to the Netherlands were unable to maintain meaningful relationships with their relatives back home over a long period of time. Many higher civil servants left Ambon, while connections between the north coast of Ambon and Ambon city were blocked during the recent violent conflict. We do not know to what extent these relationships have been resumed after violence ceased, but it is reported that many who left the island have not yet returned.

Normative Notions of Social Security Obligations

The formation of circles of support, assignment of resources to social security, and the distribution of resources among the members of these circles do not happen automatically. The relationships, through which goods and services for social security are provided, however affectively loaded, are largely institutionalised and set in cognitive and normative structures that indicate under which conditions which persons are entitled to receive or to provide others with what kinds of resources. As the chapters of this volume suggest, part of the complex-

---

[21] See K. von Benda-Beckmann 1991a.
[22] See Glick Schiller 2002; Anders 2005; Rohregger 2006.
[23] See Rohregger 2006 for an analysis of social security under extreme conditions of crop failure and hunger in Malawi. It is often the young men who are most successful in opting out of obligations by moving away, while women bear the brunt of the remaining care.

ity of the social security arrangements in regions such as Ambon lies in the fact that different normative orders are involved (see chapters 5 and 6). State law, customary law, religious law, perhaps locally made new law, and increasingly international law: all have their own typical and often different sets of concepts, rules and regulations, rights, obligations, and procedures regulating under what conditions which persons or organisations are obliged to provide support or are entitled to receive it. At the time of our research, these normative structures provided a complex framework within which the actual practices of social security occurred. As in any legal structure, they did not determine behaviour but formed constraining and enabling contexts within which people operated. The chapters of this volume discuss how the population of Ambon dealt with these changing norms and how they affected their social security practices. In Ambon, *adat* law, Islamic law and government regulations each defined in their own way who a 'relative' is and what kinds of support a person may be entitled to. The legal systems also differed in their definition of who was needy. As chapter 7 shows, the Indonesian state designed social security programmes for categories of needy persons as defined by the Indonesian state and in accordance with mainstream international social policies, e.g. 'widows', without making any further qualifications. As a result, some widows who were relatively well off and needed no support according to local standards of neediness participated in the projects side by side with widows who actually were needy by local standards. These well-off widows felt obliged to participate because of their status within the village and their relations with the government, not because they were needy themselves.

Each legal system has its own ideological foundations. Most state-provided social security today is firmly based on some variety of a liberal market ideology, though they also show clear traces of the welfare state ideologies that were particularly dominant in Europe and Latin America, and became internationally influential through ILO conventions. In Indonesia, ideologies of a subsistence ethic and of paternalist and personalist governance styles have had their impact on the existing system as much as the internationally more dominant welfare and neo-liberal ideologies. Ideologies embody, among other things: notions of what ordinary behaviour is according to status, age, gender and phase in the life-cycle; what is considered a person's individual responsibility; what can be expected of individuals and communities; and what is beyond their carrying capacity.[24] The ideologies give these notions a flavour of self-evidence, of a natural way of things. The liberal ideology of the 19th century with its strong emphasis on individual responsibility for one's life resulted in very different expectations towards men, women and children than the ideology

---

[24] See, e.g. Risseeuw and Ganesh 1998 and De Jong et al. 2005 on gendered social security in Sub-Saharan Africa and South Asia. See Pine and Haukanes 2005 for a discussion of the gendered ideologies underlying social security in Central Eastern Europe.

that developed from the turn of the century onwards and which paved the way for the welfare state of the 20th century. Changes in the actual legal concepts, rules and procedures of social security reflect some of these ideological changes, but legislative inertia, the ideological patchwork due to competing and shifting ideologies, and a lack of coherence within a legal system and among legal systems create legal frameworks that only partially reflect the dominant ideology at any particular time.

Kinship and community-based social security are as much ideologically informed as state social security; ideologies that as often as not are contested and which are only partially reflected in the actual rules, rights and obligations, and procedures that make up the normative framework of social security. The fact that Ambonese have a strong community ideology does not mean that every member of the community has an equal claim for support towards all other members of a village community. However, kinship, neighbourhood and community membership do structure the rights and obligations for support. They imply notions of what can be expected of persons in the different phases of their life-cycle, and what constitutes need. They also imply rules for conditions for making legitimate claims and rules that determine who must provide what kind of support. Patterns of marriage, property relations and inheritance are of crucial importance. As chapter 7 shows, Ambonese women in rural areas usually had inherited property of their own. Divorce or the death of a husband was not unproblematic, but a widow or divorcee was not automatically considered in need of support. They became really needy only when they were physically no longer able to live without help, and if they did not have relatives to call on for assistance. Indeed, poverty on Ambon was largely social poverty, i.e., having no relatives nearby to draw upon. The chapter also shows that elderly widows were expected to care for themselves for longer than elderly widowers, who were more readily taken care of by relatives. The ideologically informed gender and age differences were played out in gendered care relationships.

Religion and religious law also provide ideologies and rules for social security. Differences among legal systems in basic notions of who is needy for what reason and who deserves support may create some room for manoeuvre for needy persons.[25] The differences between customary and Islamic law are not always clear cut, and sometimes rules of religious and customary law are combined. As is discussed in chapter 6, Ambonese Moslems combine Islamic categories of legitimate *zakat* receivers with *adat* law categories. The customary midwife and the marriage guardians are among the recognised recipients of *zakat fitrah* 'according to *adat*', although most people are quite aware of the fact

---

[25] For example, research by Adri van den Berg 1994; 1997 in northern Cameroon has shown that women who were deprived of support under customary law after becoming widows turned to Islam and with some success invoked Islamic rules for support that they otherwise would not have been entitled to. See De Bruijn 1994 for the Fulbe in Mali. See also Bowen 2003 for the Gayo Highlands in Aceh.

that they do not belong to the Koranic recipients. Support based on religious social relationships does not always constitute an alternative to other social relations such as kinship; it may also be complementary or reinforcing.

The normative structures provided a complex framework within which the actual practices of social security occurred. As in any legal structure, they do not determine behaviour but form constraining and enabling contexts within which people operate. The chapters of this volume discuss how the population of Ambon dealt with these changing norms and how they affected their social security practices.

Asymmetries in Rights and Obligations

In addition to the imbalance in contributions and benefits that we discussed before, we would like to draw attention here to asymmetries in moral and legal notions of need and obligations to help those in need that may create specific asymmetries in the relationships between provider and recipient of social security. For example, charity is based on an asymmetric morality, in which the presumed moral standing of the needy person determines whether support is to be provided or not. In 19th century Europe only the 'deserving poor' were eligible for charity. The moral obligation of the support-giver is paid into the moral account between the generous giver of alms and God. In this calculation, the recipient of charity does not have a role to play. In other words: the moral obligation of the recipient to live a moral life is not reciprocated in the support relationship by a duty of the provider towards the recipient. The recipient has no right to receive support from potential providers.[26] Modern western social security systems have taken away much of this asymmetry with its humiliating dependency on the capriciousness of the wealthy, though any person living on social assistance will agree that moral judgments still are important.[27] However, the deserving poor in Europe today at least do have the right to assistance from the state.

The asymmetry in charity relations points to a process that may have much wider implications. Charity is especially necessary where more traditional networks of support, such as kinship and neighbourhood, no longer or do not yet work, for example in times of hunger and epidemic; in situations of rapid economic or political change, or changes in production processes; or as a result of urban expansions with newly settling migrants. These changes bring with

---

[26] See Biezeveld (2002: 249f, 268) for similar asymmetric moral connotations of charity and *zakat fitrah*. Hüsken and Koning (2006: 19) show the decline in the morality of mutual help under the New Order of Suharto.

[27] See Redmond and Hutton (2000) for moral underpinnings of social security in communist countries and in the new unemployment regulations since transition.

them changes in normative frameworks, but the pace of change may not be the same for all participants of support networks. Thus, while needs and claims for support and expectations of support may remain and even intensify, potential providers start breaking away from their obligations. Migration and severing all contact may be a way to get away from obligations that are felt to be too burdensome. On the way, obligations that formerly were regarded as legal may be transformed into 'just' moral ones. While potential providers may no longer feel legally bound to support their relatives back home, these relatives often continue to pursue claims that are not reciprocated. Such shifts towards asymmetric moral norms of support may occur within just a few years, as Anders (2005) and Rohregger (2006) have shown for Malawi. Among Moluccan migrants in the Netherlands, this process took a generation. Young women explained that they felt morally obliged to support their parents, but they also felt that the parents no longer had a claim as they had in the past over their elder siblings. They designed ways of fulfilling their moral obligations while retaining maximum control over the nature and extent of the help they gave. They explained that it was especially important that their parents did not get the impression that help was automatic or that they were entitled to claim support. According to the young, the quantity, quality and the time at which support was to be extended should remain at the discretion of the provider. The change from an obligation based on Moluccan customary law as it was understood in the migrant setting of the Moluccan military barracks to an ethnic-religiously inspired moral obligation, as experienced from the side of the care provider, had taken almost a generation. For other relatives or neighbours further removed from the nuclear family, a similar shift has occurred. In the early times of their stay in the Netherlands, there were clear rules about support to all relatives and neighbours. This was presented as the customary law of the Moluccas, but in fact developed in the context of military life in the barracks. Here, too, there has been a shift: the moral obligation only extends to those who deserve care and support. But this change in obligation has a parallel on the receiving end: Moluccans in the Netherlands in the 1990s did not recognise a claim for support from anybody other than close relatives. The asymmetry that existed during the early period of transition from the barracks to Moluccan neighbourhoods had faded away by the 1990s. However, within the small circle of close relatives of the nuclear family, siblings, grandparents and grandchildren, the moral asymmetries in rights and obligations for support were a source of much anxiety.

Social Security between Past and Future

As we discuss in chapter 2, certainty and security refer also to a psychological condition, a feeling of insecurity or security at a given time. People have different dispositions for dealing with insecurity, different perceptions of situations that make these subjectively more or less secure. They also have different knowledge for making calculations about the future. This concerns the insecurities of life itself, the reliability of resources and the reliability of potential providers and of present and future expectations, promises and obligations inscribed into reciprocal relations, investments in social relationships and rights that reach into the future. In case of chronic contingencies, the future may be tomorrow and measures are needed immediately. But in general, social security provisions are planned for dealing with risks and uncertainties that lie in the more distant future. Some contingencies, such as needy old age, may be calculated with a relatively high degree of certainty. Other contingencies, such as illness or unemployment, only allow for educated guesses. Whether the resources will still be available, whether the potential or legally obliged providers will still be there and fulfil their obligations, whether the social premiums invested in the maintenance of future social security will still hold, whether the rights one has to resources that enable one to prepare for the future are provided for by others – all this will only become apparent in the future.

Providers and recipients of social security are linked in circles of support, but the participants of these networks have different time perspectives.[28] The different time perspectives of the actors involved create in times of political and social stability at best a delicate balance of trust in the relationships and resources available for social security. This does not mean that changes in circles of support, in the available resources, or in the regulations undermine trust in these support systems per se. However, when circles of support, quality and quantity of social security, and rights and obligations come under too much pressure, due to large scale migration, war or violent conflict, failing harvests, etc., this does not only weaken the trust people had in the system – it may also change the time perspective within which they organise their social security relationships. Long term reciprocal relationships give way to more immediate forms of a more strictly balanced reciprocity.[29]

A sense of security is not only determined by objective calculations of the future; it is also determined by experiences of the past. Having experienced periods of disintegration of usual social security mechanisms, or frequent changes in the past, creates a sense of insecurity. One need not go to rural areas in developing countries in order to find out how fragile the planned, institutionalised social security mechanisms and their normative promises may turn out to be, and how deeply disappointed people are when they see their past social security strategies suddenly turn out to have been in vain. When it comes to economic and political ruptures and violent upheavals, the common mechanisms of social security are stripped to their barest bones due to lack of resources and declining trust, especially if

---

[28] See Mulder 1994; Thelen and Baerwolf (2007) argue that social security relationships between relatives have different time perspectives from social security among friends.
[29] See also Palriwala and Risseeuw 1996.

the central state itself stimulates violence and retreats from providing services, and shatters social institutions. In such situations, social security reveals its most fragile side. Such experiences tend to have long-term effects. Shaken trust in the social security system at one particular moment will continue to shape the time perspective at a later stage. Thus, the feeling of insecurity may depend on the insecurities of life itself, the reliability of the resource base and of social relationships between potential providers and recipients and changes in the normative structure pertaining to these factors. Frequent and fundamental changes in one of these factors may create a sense of insecurity, even when sufficient resources are available and when circles of support in theory could fulfil the needs of their members. The evaluation of the past and future appears not to be a matter of objective calculation, but is a subjective and emotional act. Perceptions of the past and expectations of the future are important for the sense of security people have in the present.

Many factors characteristic of Ambon in the 1980s were indicative of a more insecure future. Agricultural policy was aimed at modernising and commoditising sago palm and sago production, job opportunities in the state bureaucracy were decreasing, and population pressure on the available terrestrial and marine resources was on the rise. Demographic developments and environmental degradation put increasing pressure on the quantity and quality of resources available to most villagers. Moreover, village resources, persons and money were withdrawn from local mechanisms and invested in migration and external relations.

Equally problematic were the strategies to invest in a good education for one's children in the expectation that one day they might get a salaried job, ideally within the government. In the 1970s and 1980s the provincial and municipal government in Ambon town absorbed a great number of educated young adults. Despite its low salaries, the government for a long time served as a firm anchor of job security because of its secure employment and the possibilities for employees to provide social security for their relatives. However, these benefits were not equally distributed among the whole population. Positions within the government were primarily reserved for Ambonese citizens and not for the Buginese, Butonese, and Toraja migrants. Moreover, during the colonial period the government hired mainly Christians. As we describe in chapters 8 and 11, this continued to be the case until the 1980s. During the mid 1980s two important things happened: The provincial and district administrations no longer could absorb the large numbers of university graduates, while at the same time Moslems demanded more openly a more equal share in government jobs. The Central Moluccan state administration quickly lost its function as reliable provider of job security. Access to state positions became increasingly contested between Christians and Moslems and Ambonese and immigrants, and these contests fed into the violent conflict at the end of the 20th century.

As a direct provider of social security the state was also unreliable. It did hardly anything to assist the rural or urban population in coping with their hardships. On the contrary, many economic policies such as commercialisation of subsistence crops, the monopoly on the clove trade, individualisation of land rights, etc., undermined local mechanisms of social security. Moreover, as we show in chapter 7, in the few social security programmes the Indonesian state did organise, frequent changes were endemic. The population learned not to count on the longevity of any state project and adopted a pragmatic stance. Moreover, social security funds often suffered from corruption and people were for that reason reluctant to invest in them. Too often the funds had disappeared with high officials who had siphoned off the accumulated assets into their own private pockets, while those with a legitimate claim for support remained empty handed. The planned insurance programmes for the rural population were severely criticised for their often prohibitive administrative requirements, issues of corruption, and for not taking into account differences in the social-economic positions of their clientele.[30] During the period of our fieldwork there was little trust in such schemes among the rural population and they viewed the planned extensions of insurance schemes with concern. They feared they would be forced into paying contributions into funds that would disappear into the pockets of officials.

Under these conditions, access to land, to the subsistence resources sago and fish, to housing sites and materials, to horticultural labour and to care, were the most important resources for social security in Hila. In Ambonese villages, land was in principle not marketable, and definitive transfers of land were rare. Inheritance of land, subsistence and cash trees was therefore the major way of acquiring rights. Inheritance was based on bilateral kinship relations. Through the generations, most land and trees become the inherited property of overlapping groups of heirs, creating complex structures of titles. But the system of land and tree rights, as well as processes of decision making in disputes, were also highly problematic and insecure. Most rights and transactions were based on Ambonese *adat* law, in the village understanding as well as in the state courts. But while the state courts used the *adat* law as it had become standardised through colonial writings and case law, in the village this standardised *adat* law coexisted with an older version of *adat* that still retained pre-colonial traits. Due to this difference, different social units could claim rights to large tracts of village territory.[31]

Kinship relationships, and inheritance rights based upon them, were a source of insecurity, linking past and present in characteristic ways. In Hila, the knowledge necessary to determine who may inherit was transmitted orally and kinship relationships were frequently contested. However, the relationships of

---

[30] See Esmara and Tjiptoherijanto 1986; Stamboel 1986. See also F. and K. von Benda-Beckmann 1995.

[31] See for more details Holleman 1923; F. von Benda-Beckmann and Taale 1996.

the past were not a stable given, but could be changed and retroactively given new meanings and legal consequences. Thus, monitoring the developments of rights to inherited property and reproducing and confirming the kinship relations legitimating rights through inheritance were important. As Goody (1986: 155) has pointed out, oral transmission entails the possibility of 'systematic forgetfulness' about the past which allows for redefining kinship relations. Yet though oral transmission of the knowledge relevant for inheritance and access to land dominated, written documents were not entirely absent. Since Hila had been a major stronghold from the early Dutch colonial administration on, many families were familiar with and actually possessed written documents, including testaments, sales agreements, and court decisions, some dating back to the year 1700.[32] These documents introduced an alternative logic of linking past and present. While documents highlight particular moments in the past and are intended to bind the future from a particular point in time onwards, they also induce their own kind of forgetfulness, as we show in chapter 5. They facilitate the processes of a direct line between the making of the document and the present, erasing all intermediate dealings with the property concerned. Moreover, what remains of the past are in particular the more problematic moments, in response to which documents, testaments or court decisions have been drawn up or made. Thus, documents gave a sharp edge to the keen awareness among the population of Ambon of a long and eventful history, emphasizing discontinuity, conflict, and contestation. This was especially so because the documents were used in a still predominantly oral tradition. Thus, these old documents were not only important to establish access to the resources for social security. They were also used to renegotiate kinship relations in the present, including support and caring relationships. In this respect, they were often an ambivalent source of security, if not a source of outright insecurity.

The Butonese population had a different relationship with the past. They were affected by the complexities and insecurities of rights to land and trees in a particular way, as is discussed in chapter 9. Being second class village citizens, they could acquire only temporary rights to agricultural land and cash tree cultivation and were entirely dependent on Ambonese owners for access to land and trees. The oral transactions usually included the clause that the Butonese share cropper would plant trees which would be shared among the Butonese planter and Ambonese the land owner when the tree started to produce some six years later. However, the Ambonese frequently reneged on these transactions, refusing to share and claiming the entire produce. In other cases, other claimants suddenly appeared, contesting the legitimacy of the earlier contracts. The state courts were not a great help, since they have consistently based their decisions on classical *adat* law, according to which trees and land could not be transferred

---

[32] Such a testament is reproduced and discussed in F. and K. von Benda-Beckmann 1987b.

on a permanent basis. The introduction of the Basic Agrarian Law in 1960 had brought some hope for the Butonese population of the time. The state had issued official land rights documents to some Butonese under the Sukarno regime. However, these documents were discredited under the Suharto regime as being part of a 'communist' land law and lost their value. Thus, the state legal system proved to be unable to cater for secure land rights for Butonese who were unable to secure permanent rights under *adat*. But in one way the Ambonese and Butonese shared experiences: the Indonesian judicial system was unreliable for all. Additionally, they had learned by experience that governments throughout history had repeatedly intervened in the structure of land rights. The unreliable governments of the past had continuously fed its population a sense of insecurity and distrust in the state. However, dispute management practices at village level could not serve as a reliable and fair alternative either (F. and K. von Benda-Beckmann 1994a).

Thus, the changing social security in Hila and of the migrants originating from Ambon in the Netherlands may present specific cases in terms of their constellations of social security mechanisms, the resources that could be employed for social security purposes, and the normative universe governing the provision of social security. Part of the future of the Ambon that is presented in this volume has become its past by now, highlighting both the fragility and the resilience of social security mechanisms. Yet we therefore believe that this book may illustrate more than the specifics of the island of Ambon and the village of Hila itself. This specific constellation, and the way it changes, may exemplify how rural people cope with the insecurities of life and with a government that turns into a source of insecurity rather than security for its population, and the fulfilled and disappointed expectations of care. It may help to generate a good analytical understanding of the complexity of social security mechanisms, their normative universes and the actual practices between past and future.

Chapter 2
Coping with Insecurity*

Franz and Keebet von Benda-Beckmann

Between order and chaos, between continuity and change, between harmony and conflict lies Uncertainty. Usually, the focus of anthropological and sociological studies is on social order and normality, or on its disruption, conflict, or change. However, the more basic counterpoint to social order may not be conflict or disruption, but uncertainty and insecurity Social organization, its institutions and norms, contested or not, only bring partial security and certainty; they are never more than 'islands of determinacy in a sea of indeterminacy', to use S. F. Moore's imagery (1978b: 48). Uncertainty and insecurity are notions that link the present with the past and the future. Looking at ways in which individuals or social institutions deal with indeterminacy, uncertainty and insecurity also means looking at how they deal with the future, how the future is conceptualized, and the extent to which the future is problematized.

There is tremendous variation in the extent to which the fundamental indeterminacy of social organization and life is perceived and evaluated in societies, how indeterminacy, uncertainty and insecurity are dealt with in cultural belief systems and ideologies, and to what extent social organization bears the promise of dealing satisfactorily with them. Individual people differ in their perception of uncertainty and insecurity and in their willingness and ability to live with them. This will depend on the personal economic situation of individuals and on their psychological constitution, and it will be strongly influenced by the social organization in which they live. Uncertainty and insecurity do not always have negative connotations. The future may be seen as attractive, an open world, bearing the exhilarating thrill of the unexpected, promising new opportunities and riches. Ideas of security and certainty then can have negative connotations and may almost be regarded as the antithesis to freedom and autonomy. But the future may also be seen as threatening and full of anxieties and worries.[33] The most devastating uncertainties concern people's most basic needs: food, shelter, health and care; and in connection with them the experience or expectation of destitution, of a sudden loss or severe reduction of the means of existence and of access to other people or social institutions which might provide help. When people worry about how to provide for their next

---

* First published 1994 in: F. von Benda-Beckmann, K. von Benda-Beckmann, and H. Marks (eds.), *Coping with Insecurity. An 'Underall' Perspective on Social Security in the Third World. Special Issue Focaal 22/23*, pp. 7-31. Nijmegen: Focaal.

[33] Kaufmann (1973) has provided an impressive and stimulating account of notions of (in)security and (un)certainty in Western Europe.

meal or for their children, how to survive when they fall ill or become old, certainty and security will be positively valued. But insecurity concerns not only the material aspects of life. It also, and perhaps in a more fundamental way, has to do with people's feelings of trust and existential security.[34] These cannot be reduced to a material basis.

In each social organization there is a range of more or less satisfactory ways to deal with the material and immaterial aspects of uncertainty and insecurity in problematic life-situations. Social relations and institutions and cultural or religious belief systems always, preventively or reactively, provide, or promise to provide, some help and assistance to those who are unable to help themselves. Situational, periodic or enduring disabilities that require help may result from a variety of causes. They may have their cause in people's physical characteristics – being an infant or an old and infirm person, being ill or having bodily and mental handicaps. They may result from social and economic deficits - lack of access to means for self-provision with the most basic needs such as food, shelter, care. Yet other situations of need may be constituted by the social and cultural order itself – for instance requirements to provide large quantities of material goods at socially important ceremonies, which a person or family cannot master through their own powers. Yet whatever the underlying reasons, such situations or periods of need and distress, as well as the means to overcome them, become subject to cultural constructions. These define what is 'normal' and 'abnormal' for society's members, or for specific categories of people, offer explanations of the causes of such situations and provide rationales for overcoming them. They also define social units and relations of responsibility for providing help in situations of distress, between individuals, small-scale social units such as families or households, and institutions representing and acting for 'society'. Some situations or periods of need are considered a matter which individuals have to deal with by themselves or in free cooperation with others by their own initiative. Others are made the responsibility of larger groups or categories of people or of social-political institutions.

These relationships, institutions and cultural belief systems are functional for people's social, economic and psychological security. This functional quality may be particularly stressed normatively or symbolically, and may be differentiated out of ordinary relationships as 'social security institutions', as is characteristic for contemporary welfare states. But relationships and institutions not so singled out can also provide security. The social security function can be embedded in ordinary relatively undifferentiated relationships, institutions or belief systems. Those institutions, on the other hand, to which a specific security function is attributed, may in fact not provide any security at all. Whether or not security is provided depends on actual social and psychological processes.

---

[34] Giddens (1991) speaks of 'ontological' security.

But in all cases, the security and certainty actually provided or promised for the future will inevitably be partial. Insecurity and individual, institutional and cultural- ideological mechanisms to deal with it thus are not confined to specific and specialized institutions. They are aspects of social life and organization in general. Therefore, social security is not only a very important cultural, social, economic, legal and political issue; it is an integral aspect of social and economic life and central to the understanding of social organization and change.

Themes of this Volume

This volume seeks to contribute to that understanding. The articles describe how people in different parts of the world lead their lives and deal with uncertainties and insecurities. Most of the contributions focus on the actual social insecurities of people. They adopt an 'underall view' (Rose 1989: 111) to questions of social (in)security in people's practices and in the relationships and institutions in which they are involved. A variety of topics and situations are addressed.

Changing Relations of Social Security

In the rural areas in the Third World as described in the papers, governmental regulation or provision of social security is largely absent. Whatever social security there may be for the majority of rural people is largely based upon social relations connecting a limited number of people within small-scale social organizations. Relations of kinship, friendship, common village-membership and patron-client relationships are the predominant ones. In these small-scale social security systems, a limited amount of resources is available, mainly resources bound to the locality.

Several papers examine the social security function of types of relationships and institutions. Van de Ven describes and analyzes the significance of inherited property in rice land in Kerinci in western Sumatra, showing its importance for food security. But, as he says in the title of his paper, this security is for 'members only'. Inclusion into this property complex, or exclusion from it, are disputed and negotiated affairs. Van Dijk looks at cattle transfers among pastoralists in the Hayre in Mali, to which an important social security function has often been accorded in the literature on pastoralist peoples. His conclusion is rather negative. These transfers hardly have a social security function, and their alleged historical role for social security may be more the romantic imagination of foreign anthropologists than historical truth. Mulder describes feasts among Javanese farmers in Surinam and shows us how participation in these feasts contributes in a dual manner to security. It gives the participants a feeling of being secure 'now'; at the same time, it is a way of maintaining relationships of reciprocal help and assistance that reach into the future and promise at least some security also in future situations of need. Leliveld examines the changing social security function of the Swazi homestead, which is for Swazi people, as well as for outside observers, the proverbial 'solidarity group'.

What the papers tell us about the changing social security functions of these relations differs widely Romantic visions of kinship solidarity are certainly not justified. Van Dijk's and De Bruijn's rather gruesome account of the breakdown of social relations among the Fulbe in the Hayre clearly testify to that. Under these extreme conditions, relations of mutual help 'snap', as has been observed elsewhere when people were faced with severe drought and famine (Agarwal 1991). But also the often heard complaint that 'traditional solidarity' is breaking down does not seem to be warranted. Though people may be poor, and social relations which in the past may have provided more social security have weakened, these relationships remain the main vehicle through which people in need and distress receive at least some help.

Multiplicity of Social Security Relations

In most social organizations, people will always be involved in a multiplicity of social relationships along which goods and services for their needs can, or should be, provided, at least in some phases of their lives. People usually compose a social security mix consisting of various arrangements for social security. But not everyone has the same capabilities to draw on existing resources, or to acquire new ones. People's social security mixes are specific to gender, age, class and status. The contributions describe different social security mixes of people in different regions of the world, under quite different social, economic and political circumstances. The papers of Leliveld, De Bruijn, Van Walsum and Mulder focus on the ways in which people, or specific categories like women or immigrants, try to maintain or rearrange their relations in changing circumstances, and by to maintain existing relationships or to establish new relationships, through which they hope to secure their and their children's future. They also show the changing interrelations between different relationships - such as kinship, patron-client relations, and newly established relations - and the resulting changes in their social security function. But not all the main actors described aim for more security. Vel describes young men on the island of Sumba who consciously head into insecurity, at the risk of being excluded from the existing social security arrangements.

Normative and Ideological Pluralism

In most contemporary societies there is a plurality of normative orders, each with its own definition of needs and construction of responsibilities. The plurality provides different ideas of need and help, which constitute and legitimize different relationships through which such care can or should be provided. To some extent, this widens the choices people have to change their social security relations; however constrained such choices may be by differences in social, economic and political power. De Bruijn and Van den Berg in particular show how, in situations of considerable distress, women try to mobilize, through the invocation of religion, which is an alternative ideology, the help and support that they cannot get under the dominant ideology De Bruijn describes a situation where, due to the deterioration of economic conditions in the Malian Sahel, it has become impossible to get the necessary support through the customary system. By invoking Islam, and by establishing relations with Islamic officials, it becomes possible to mobilize a geographically more widely spread set of relations that can provide at least some additional help. Van den Berg shows that it may become necessary for divorced women in northern Cameroon to turn to Islam for other reasons: not because the general socio-economic conditions are so dismal, but because the regulations of inheritance and divorce do not allow women to keep land after divorce. We here see another variation of 'therapeutic conversion' (Parkin 1972) where people are seeking to create new social relationships for social security, rather than to avoid obligations of help and assistance in their customary ones. Van Walsum shows to what extent immigration regulation imposes a patriarchal ideology upon migrants who are caught between the necessity to adjust to the state ideology of the Netherlands, and their embeddedness in the normative structure of their migrant community.

Migration

Even in the remotest areas people are somehow tied into larger support systems that surpass the locally confined support networks, and often are directly or indirectly connected to the personnel and the resources of the state system, or of nongovernmental aid institutions, or market forms of social security Among the most important ways of coupling local networks to these wider networks is temporary or permanent migration, to areas where state provisions are better accessible, or where economic opportunities are expected to be better. As the contributions of Moore, Brouwer, Van Walsum, Van Dijk and Leliveld in particular show, regional, national and transnational migration may thus be very much part of local social security mechanisms. Migration can be both a source of and a response to insecurity. Leliveld unravels the effects of male migration for the social security of those who stay behind in Swaziland. He shows that the effects differ according to the phase in the development cycle in which homesteads find themselves. Though his emphasis is on households as units, he does qualify his findings by pointing out some of the differential effects for household members. Brouwer also looks at the differential effects of the different waves and destinations of migration, for those staying behind in northern Portugal, and deals with the problems of return migration. Van Walsum and Moore focus on the position of migrants in their host country. Surinamese migrants in the Netherlands live under high pressure due to the immigration laws that shackle legitimate and illegal immigrants to each other. The situation which Moore describes for Burkina Faso is quite different. Here, the migrants in large numbers have settled on the land of the original settlers. But living together in geographical proximity does not automatically mean that social support systems develop. The immigration by large numbers of economically powerful migrants may be a source of insecurity and dispute, upsetting the fragile balance of the existing social security mechanisms, as much as migration may be a response to insecurity and (threatening) destitution.

Social Security and Resources

A number of contributions give a saddening account of people's social (in)security. The traditional arrangements, as has been frequently remarked, indeed cannot enable many, or most, rural people to provide sufficient protection against the general deterioration of their social and economic conditions, not to speak of situations of illness or physical disabilities. But the papers also show, that, more often than not, it is not so much the kind of interpersonal relationship involved which lies at the root of this lack of social security. Often, it is the material and social conditions under which people live, and the quantity and quality of resources available to them, which bring new insecurities or intensify existing ones. For the pastoralists in the Hayre in Mali, it is the great drought which has led to an almost complete breakdown of the local care arrangements (see Van Dijk and De Bruijn). In Surinam, the recent economic deterioration is putting much strain on support systems (see Mulder and Van Walsum). In several cases the absence of young men, who have temporarily or permanently migrated, creates new burdens for those who have stayed behind, as the examples from Portugal, Mali and Swaziland show (see Brouwer, De Bruijn, Leliveld), or for those whose land is occupied by migrants as in Burkina Faso (see Moore). In northern Cameroon the problems of women in maintaining access to land have less to do with a general shortage of land, than with the dilemmas posed by the kinship and land tenure system in connection with the high rate of divorce (Van den Berg).

Exclusion and Inclusion

What has been called 'the second law of welfare' (Macarov 1980: 24) seems to hold as truly for rural social organizations as for welfare in industrialized states: 'When more welfare is possible, it does not seem needed, and when more welfare is needed, it does not seem possible'. The papers also show that there is no direct relation between the availability of resources and the levels of welfare and (in)security of people. These are mediated through relations of differential allocation and (re)distribution, at whatever level of socio-economic organization. It holds true for the pooling of resources and redistribution of resources by government apparatuses, as well as for relationships and transfers in a village, or even within groups of kin. For the level of statewide social security, Midgley (1984 and 1994) has repeatedly emphasized that the extension of state regulated and subsidized forms of social insurance and assistance tends to have the effect that the economic conditions of the poorer rural people who are not included in these schemes deteriorate. Exclusion from and inclusion in social security arrangements are important topics in many of the papers. They show that more social security for one may be at the expense of less social security for another. These processes are rarely uncontested, and conflicts over resources increase (see Moore). What makes the difference is whether one is excluded from, or remains or becomes included in such systems of redistribution. Studies of social security therefore are different from poverty studies. Poverty or wealth refer to an economic condition measured by lack of ownership or command over resources and monetary incomes; social security refers to the conversion of resources into actually (un)fulfilled social security needs, or 'living standards' in Sen's (1987a) terminology, at whatever level of poverty or wealth.

Making Social (In)Security Visible

As the contributions of Midgley and Hirtz make clear, there are only very few studies that describe changes in local social organization and culture from the perspective of uncertainty and insecurity. Most literature on social security in Third World states is concerned with what state organizations do or should provide, and with the social policies required to meet such objectives. The relations and institutions described in most papers in this volume fall under the heading of what generally is called 'traditional' or 'informal' social security, which is still treated as a stepchild in social security studies. Inasmuch as rural social security in Third World countries is taken into account in social security studies, they tend to give accounts of the institutional aspects of social security organization. Very few deal with the actual social and economic condition of (in)security of local people and how their lives are affected by social security institutions. This is particularly so with respect to social policy studies and development economics which still dominate the social security literature. With this volume we want to contribute to filling this lacuna in empirical knowledge about local forms of people's social security.

But there is invisibility of social security also in another sense. Midgley and Hirtz note the lack of conceptual and analytical clarity in academic and policy debates. Midgley reviews the various debates on how social security should be conceptualized, and how different forms and sets of social security institutions should be distinguished. Hirtz notes and deplores the one-sided monodisciplinary attention which social security has received, mainly from economists and social policy scholars.[35] In our view, most of these problems derive from the institutionalist point of departure in most approaches to social security, which locates 'social security' in institutions and from the simplistic, and often misleading ways, in which the world of 'social security' is divided into 'modern' and 'traditional', or 'formal' and 'informal' social security. In this introductory essay, we shall try to develop a functional – though not functionalist – approach to social (in)security which in our view bears greater promise for a consistent description and analysis of the complexity of the ways in which the dimension of social security is manifested in different layers of social organization, and for the Study of the interrelations between these different layers (see also Partsch 1983). It should also provide a more congenial meeting ground for the various academic disciplines that deal with social security problems.

Delineating the Field of Social Security: Social Security as a Functional Aspect of Social Organization

The Limitations of Institutional Approaches

Social security is usually defined as the totality of Institutions that have been or should be set up with the specific aim to provide social security with respect to specified situations of need and distress (contingencies). The best known of such definitions is the one given by the ILO. There, social security is circumscribed as

> the protection which society provides for its members, through a series of public measures against the economic and social distress that otherwise would be caused by the stoppage or substantial induction of earnings resulting from sickness, maternity, employment injury, unemployment, invalidity old age and death; the provision of medical care; and the provision of subsidies for families with children (ILO 1984: 2-3).

---

[35] But see the multidisciplinary attempt made in F. von Benda-Beckmann et al. 1988a.

Until quite recently, 'society' and 'public measures' used to be identified with state regulation and provision of goods and services in pre-defined contingencies. Within this approach differences of opinion remain as to the scope of social security, for instance whether it should, or should not include social welfare and development programmes, or material and immaterial well-being.[36] But whatever its scope, social security was more or less identified with 'formal' or 'modern' Institutions of social security that bad been institutionally differentiated from ordinary social and economic relationships and specified by their normative and symbolic function. In the more recent past, it has been debated whether 'social security' should be limited to institutions regulated by the state. This tendency has been particularly strong in the growing literature on social security in developing countries. The state-focused definitions, still dominant in industrial societies, were seen as being too narrow for developing countries because they did not include contributions of households and communities. It was also increasingly recognized that such contributions were regulated by non-state normative orders such as folk (traditional or customary) or religious laws. An extended conceptual approach to social security issues has become increasingly popular, as is evidenced from recent academic and policy literature.[37] In countries with highly institutionalized welfare-state systems, such wider conceptual usage is gradually becoming more prominent as well. It has been realized that also in European states the provision of help on the basis of non-state or market relations constitutes a very important source of security provision, and in some sectors is even more important than what is provided by government bureaucracies or commercial enterprises.[38] It should therefore be taken into account, even though it is not registered by the 'official economy' (Rose 1989). Thus, the idea that social security includes more than what the state regulates or provides has become accepted in developing countries and industrialized states. The 'informal sector', stepchild of social security, seems to have been legitimized; but has it really?

We do not think so. In our view, the growing consensus concerning a broad definition of social security is treacherous. It suggests more unity in analytical approaches and assumptions than actually exists. There are still wide divergences in the further analysis, in theoretical explanation, and in the construc-

---

[36] See Zacher 1977: 42; Midgley 1984: 81 ff. and 1994; Getubig 1992 and Boos et al. 1993.

[37] See Partsch 1983; Bossert 1985; most contributions in F. von Benda-Beckmann et al. 1988a; particularly Woodman 1988, see further Bardhan 1988; Hirtz 1989; Ahmad et al. 1991; Burgess and Stern 1991: 44; Drèze and Sen 1991; Agarwal 1991. For policy agencies, see Getubig and Schmidt 1992; World Bank 1990; Radwan 1994 for the ILO. See also Hirtz 1994 and Midgley 1994.

[38] See Pahl 1984; Redclift and Mingione 1985; Ferman et al. 1987; Johnson 1987; Rose 1989; Wheelock 1990 and Elwert 1991.

tion of future scenarios and in policy implications. In our view, the major reason for this is that the extension to social security outside the realm of state regulation usually remains based upon an institutional point of departure which focuses attention on institutions which have been functionally differentiated and are normatively specified by their social security function. Through this the provision of social security which is embedded in other social relationships, may easily become invisible. More seriously, it leaves out social relationships and institutions which are not normatively defined as social security institutions, but do have a social security function. Moreover, institutional definitions usually comprise both the normative and symbolic constructions of social security as well as the actual functioning of these institutions. This introduces much ambiguity because the two layers of social organization are not always clearly distinguished, and normatively prescribed function and actual functioning are often conflated (see Kaufmann 1973). The focus on institutions detracts attention from the expression and functioning of social security at different layers of social organization. If, on the other hand, the distinction is made, the question of the institution's functioning is driven into the 'gap approach' in which actual functioning and effects in social life are measured against the normative function of the institution. The relative social(in)security then is easily explained by the functioning of the institutions and their regulatory framework. An institutional approach therefore reduces the scope of social security studies. It makes it difficult to grasp the multifunctionality which such institutions may have. It also does not systematically look at people's social security relationships and conditions. And it does not direct: attention at the ways in which social actors interpret, manipulate and change social relations and the normative frameworks that pertain to them (see Giddens 1984, Bourdieu 1990, F. and K. von Benda-Beckmann 1991). Finally, it also makes it difficult to deal adequately with the temporality of social security. Social security is never merely concerned with present but always with future provisions (Kaufmann 1973: 277). It links the present with the past and the future and is to be taken as a dynamic concept, allowing for the question as to how past, present and future are connected. Social security is always also a potentiality, consisting of arrangements that are to be invoked at some time in the future, as much as it is the present fulfillment of promises made in the past. For social security studies, this raises the question whether social security should be studied from an *ex post* or an *ex ante* perspective, or from both perspectives. The focus on Institutions introduces a temporality which is embodied in institutions, which may be quite different from that held by individual members of societies.[39]

These limitations have not disappeared with the extension of the concept of social security to 'informal' or 'traditional' social security On the contrary the usage of these terms and their underlying assumptions have to some

---

[39] Kaufmann (1973: 157) speaks of the 'annihilation of the temporality of the future'.

extent even intensified the problems of an institutional approach. For, in line with the intellectual history of the formal/informal distinction, the conceptualizations of these two sectors basically hinge on their normative regulation and on the rights which people have, or should have.[40] There are, of course, considerable differences in the form, formality, traditionality, scope and function of social security arrangements in different societies. It is certainly important to distinguish the sources of regulation (state or non-state regulated), the sources of provision (state bureaucracies, insurance companies, kinsfolk, patrons and friends), the scope of operation (state-wide, village community, neighbourhood or family), the potential of resources to be used in social security, and the actual efficiency of social security relations and institutions. But the common usage of expressing all these different dimensions of social security arrangements together in terms of the one-dimensional dichotomies between formal and informal or traditional and modern, conventional and unconventional or state/market) household, obscures rather than clarifies these distinctions. They particularly tend to conflate different layers of the social organization of social security: the (source of) regulation and the (source of) provision of goods and services. These concepts therefore tend to assume conceptually what should be a matter for empirical research.[41] The effects are particularly harmful, because these terms are used not only to characterize types or relations or institutions, but also to divide the whole society into two or three quite distinct sectors, creating a distorted simplicity where the elucidation of complexity is particularly called for (see K. von Benda-Beckmann 1987, F. von Benda-Beckmann 1987).

All this does not mean that the terms are useless and should, or even could be abandoned altogether. But it shows that they should be used consistently to characterize differences in organizational structures of social security, and that one should explicate carefully to what layer or aspect of social security one actually refers when using the terms.

Towards a Functional Approach

To avoid these problems and the resultant methodological shortcomings, we have to employ a conceptualization of social security which leaves room for both normative and empirical functions; which distinguishes between the differ-

---

[40] Midgley (1994) speaks of 'indigenous' or 'traditional' institutions to 'differentiate those institutionalized social support mechanisms which are sanctioned by the traditional culture, from statutory social security programmes operated by governments'. The strong emphasis on the legal dimension is also problematic in Sen's entitlement approach, see also Agarwal 1991.
[41] See F. and K. von Benda-Beckmann 1984; Connolly 1985; F. von Benda-Beckmann et al. 1988b and K. von Benda-Beckmann 1991c.

ent layers of social organization; and which allows the analysis of the interrelations between those layers. A solution to these problems in our view is only possible on the basis of an analytical approach which conceptualizes social (in)security as a field of problems, based on an abstract concept of social security functions.[42] We talk about social security as the dimension of social organization dealing with the provision of security not considered to be an exclusive matter of individual responsibility. Such a function is a theoretical construction. Social security as a component or domain of general social organization can only be isolated in a theoretical manner. Such theoretical isolation cannot be expected to have an empirical correspondence with clearly discrete social institutions. Empirically, social security refers to the social phenomena with which the abstract domain of social security is filled: efforts of individuals, groups of individuals and organizations to overcome insecurities related to their existence, that is, concerning food and water, shelter, care and physical and mental health, education and income, to the extent that the contingencies are not considered a purely individual responsibility, as well as the intended and unintended consequences of these efforts.[43]

By taking a functional point of departure, one is confronted with the potential 'infiniteness' of the scope of social phenomena which can have a social security quality (Zacher 1977: 42). This is a strength rather than a weakness, for the functional point of departure leads to the question of what ideas, relations and institutions become relevant as social security under different social, economic, political and cultural conditions. A functional approach allows us to use the words 'social security' to characterize social phenomena at different layers of social organization.

At the most general level of *cultural and religious ideals and ideologies,* ideas about social security may be expressed in different ways. These may be manifest in a 'subsistence ethic' or in its welfare-state and market equiva-

---

[42] This approach is largely influenced by Goldschmidt's *Comparative functionalism* (1966). See F. von Benda-Beckmann 1979. For an earlier functional approach to social security, see Partsch 1983. Our approach goes further than Partsch by differentiating the different layers of social security and looking at their interrelations. See also Drèze and Sen (1991) who replace the concepts of social security institutions or programmes by 'functionings and capabilities'.

[43] See F. and K. von Benda-Beckmann 1984; F. von Benda-Beckmann et al. 1988b: 10; K. von Benda-Beckmann 1994. Our approach shares the social concerns of most scholars and policy agencies in the field of social security studies, and includes what Getubig (1992: 2) calls 'first and second order insecurity'. It also resembles the broad definition of Boos et al. (1993: 6ff.), which includes both material and immaterial aspects of (in)security. But we do not follow their suggestion that responsibility needs to be assigned through legislation. In our approach this can be done on the basis of other than state institutions and state law, such as folk law, or religious law, which in their definition probably would be relegated to the sector of private security (ibid. 1993: 26-27).

lents. They may, or may not demand special tasks for governmental institutions. Such ideas may also be nearly absent, as was the case in the United States prior to the introduction of 'social security' (see Kaufmann 1973). Ideas of charity by the rich or by religious institutions may or may not be embodied in desired general states of affairs. Rather than for the presence or absence of such ideas, one would look for differences in the extent to which supra-individual moral or legal obligations to provide help and assistance to those unable to help themselves are emphasized.

The scope of the more concrete normative constructions of rights and obligations at the *level of institutional provision* of social security services typically fails short of the more general and abstract ideals. Institutional typifications of contingencies, of providers and recipients of social security transfers and their rights and obligations, will usually be more restrictive and limited than the general social ideals would suggest. This is not unusual. Ideals and social philosophy can for obvious reasons neither be fully in accordance with social life nor be fully reflected in institutions and normative regulations. Both cultural-ideological and normative institutional conceptualizations of social security are likely to differ from the *perceptions of individuals*. Individual perceptions of present or future situations of need and distress may be quite different from contingencies defined institutionally. What may be considered an undesirable risk by politicians, social security specialists and officials working in social security institutions, may be perceived by others as a normal part of fluctuating life conditions. We can assume that collective and institutionalized representations will influence individual perceptions, and vice versa; but we cannot assume the relationship to be one of identity or congruence.

Actual *social relationships* between recipients and providers of social security form another layer of social organization. They are different from the normatively typified relationships, and may have a distinct influence on people's interactions.

The *social practices* in which social security ideals and institutionalized rights and obligations are met, and in which resources are converted into actual fulfillment of needs, are another layer. Practices are also likely to be different from the general or concrete rules about such practices. Practices may or may not be influenced by the normative framework of institutions and social relations. But even where social security rules are followed, social security provisions do not necessarily prevent destitution.

There is, thus, a final level at which social security is to be studied, and that is the *social and economic consequences* of the practices mentioned above. The institutionally typified contingencies and provisions may fall short, or exceed the needs of actual people.[44]

---

[44] A retired lower civil servant living off a meagre, though full old age pension may be faced with social and economic needs much graver than the ones typified in the pension

In this perspective, studies of social security are not confined to any one of these layers of social organization. Social security is seen as a quality of social relationships and institutions, ideologies, philosophy, ethics, policy programmes and sets of rules. It can also refer to human interactions through which goods and services are transferred or appropriated to deal with insecurity or through which plans are made to have them transferred in the future. It can further be used to indicate the relative state of security, thus referring to the economic and social position of actual persons. Finally, it refers to resources used for the purpose of reducing insecurity.

This allows a much more systematic study of differences and similarities in the social organization of social security functions at different layers of social organization. It also allows us a better approach to the temporality of social security at the different layers of social organization. One does not (have to) assume that 'social security' should, or could be, 'the same' at these different layers, or that one of them would be the 'real' one.[45] Rather than deducing people's thoughts and practices from institutional or ideological constructions of security, uncertainty and contingencies or vice versa, it is more fruitful to distinguish the layers and to examine their interrelations.

The question remains whether such a broad conception of a dimension of social organization can distance itself sufficiently from the semantic power which the words 'social security' have acquired under given historical circumstances and whether we should still call it 'social security'. This kind of conceptual problem is not new, of course. It has been debated extensively with respect to other attempts to define institutions or domains of social life cross-culturally and cross- temporally, for instance in discussions about law, ownership, marriage or money (see Nader 1969, F. von Benda-Beckmann 1979). That such distancing from ethnocentric and normative meanings is difficult, and that one will ultimately remain bound by it, has to be accepted (Goldschmidt 1966: 93, Giddens 1984: 284). Yet it would also be naive to maintain that social scientists could not take distance from the meanings which have been developed in their own society, and that they would necessarily be forced to adopt (and keep running after) those institutional definitions of the social policy legislators. On the contrary, an analytic conceptualization allows us to see more clearly the nature of what has been called 'social security' since the 1930s. It also opens up the

---

laws. For a rich civil servant, who also receives an old age pension there may be no distress at all. His official social security provision may be just sufficient as pocket money for his grandchildren.

[45] There have been a number of heated debates about social security systems in economic anthropology, in which some parties either overemphasized the ideological and normative aspects of socio-economic systems, and others the actual practices and their consequences. See for instance the contributions of Scott 1976 and Popkin 1979. For a good analysis of that discussion, see Platteau 1991. See also the critique by the Alexanders of Geertz (Alexander and Alexander 1982).

question how and why certain forms of provision, of help in situations of need are, or are not, conceptualized as 'social security' in a given society. The provision of care by parents for their children, for instance, is rarely regarded as 'social security' in western industrial states – although it is, amongst others, proscribed by state law, and although it is regarded as the prototypical form of 'traditional' social security. We therefore see no reason to drop the term social security as a scientific category.[46] Moreover, finding the appropriate conceptual boundaries is a problem which institutional approaches also cannot avoid. Here as well, much wider meanings have been attached to social security than those which emerged in the United States in the 1930s. In both approaches, 'social security' cannot be more than a starting point which serves as a basis for making theoretically useful distinctions. Once one makes clear with which social security idea, rule, relationship or institution one is dealing, there should be little room for confusion. So both approaches are faced with the same problem, and the priority should be given to an approach which has greater analytical and heuristic value.

Time and Function in Social Security

Time and Insecurity

In small-scale societies in the Third World, social security institutions have rarely been differentiated to a significant degree from 'ordinary' social organization.[47] The same social and institutional relationships serve 'normal' life-situations and periods of need and distress. They are also multifunctional; the social security aspect is one of many aspects which are interwoven in many-stranded relationships. Also at the normative level, there is rarely a body of rules that is clearly set apart from general legal rules and principles for creating rights and obligations to provide help in categorically Specified situations of need. In contemporary states, in contrast, a variety of institutions have been established which are differentiated or 'externalized' (Zacher 1988) from ordinary social and economic relationships with the specific objective of providing social

---

[46] Kaufmann (1973: 29) draws the consequence that 'social security' cannot be used as a scientifically predefined concept. Observing that social security inevitably has a normative and symbolic content, he argues that normativity is certain to reappear and lead to misunderstandings, thus foiling attempts to maintain the precise definition required of a scientific concept. However, we remain in need of a scientific indication of the field of study we are concerned with. There is also the question of 'what kind of precision' should be aimed at.

[47] This is not to imply that there are no such differentiated institutions at all. See for examples Scott 1976.

security. These institutions, because of their 'social' character, to a large extent, are also largely freed from the constraints which dominate normal social and economic life.

On the basis of the considerable differences in social, economic and political organization, wide ranging consequences have been drawn for the domain of social security In fact, it has been more or less denied that 'traditional societies' had a social security function at all. Thematizing (in)security presupposes an awareness of the future as potentially dangerous, and therefore is attached to a self-understanding of people who search for security because they experience the temporality of the future as a danger (Kaufmann 1973: 169). Social security, it is said, also presupposes ideas about the future as relatively open, in which history is made reflexively, and where fate and destiny have no formal part to play (Giddens 1991: 109). These characteristics are seen to be given in modern society and held to be absent in pre-modern or traditional society. Modern society Kaufmann (1973: 31) suggests, perceives of time in a fundamentally different way than was usual before. In pre-modern society, there is little idea of a future full of problems which people could strive to overcome. On the contrary, given the rather immutable and rigid social organization, and the dominance of notions of fate and destiny, there was little perceived need to establish institutional mechanisms that would deal with insecurity and uncertainty (Giddens 1991).

Such ideal-types obscure rather than clarify important differences and similarities between societies. Kaufmann (1973: 31) writes that the idea 'that it is good at the present time to provide and prepare for the future, rather than waiting until events arise: thus one reduces the risks that can be reduced in order to have alternatives'. No doubt this has developed differently in different types of society. Yet it is highly questionable whether such thinking is typical for modern society only. Anthropological evidence, on the contrary, suggests that in 'traditional' societies there is as much regard for the flow of time and for the future, and the welfare of those living in the future. This is especially the case in societies in which descent and descent-based group formation is a major principle of social organization. Dealing with resources is dominated by the idea that they have been handed down from the past, and need to be preserved for future generations. These principles are also institutionalized in legal restrictions that counter attempts to weaken this conservation of resources for the future (see also Van de Ven 1994). In some societies, such as the Minangkabau of western Sumatra, the time perspective is one of overwhelming continuity, a temporal dimension extending into the past and into the future, leaving hardly any mom for a 'present' (see F von Benda-Beckmann 1979, 1993a). From the absence of differentiated and specialized institutions we therefore cannot conclude that there is no conception of a social security function. Neither does it follow that there are no rights and obligations concerning help for people in need of help, defining rights and obligations, the social units entitled to receive help from, and those obliged to provide help to others, the kind and amount of provisions, and the conditions under which this should or must be done. This cannot be assumed for ideal-typical 'traditional society', and it most certainly is not the case in contemporary social organizations. Mulder describes how people, who participate in feasts, may do so with the explicit purpose of strengthening social ties that may be needed in the future for care in old age. On the East-Indonesian island of Ambon people quite consciously included considerations of social security in the way they formed their social relationships, for instance when they set up small enterprises that are primarily income- and profit- oriented (K. von Benda-Beckmann 1991c). The relationships that are activated to set up such enterprises are not constituted with respect to specific, well-defined contingencies, and are invariably multi-stranded. Therefore, people do not usually employ the idiom of social security, but it is clear to all that this is an important aspect, and when asked explicitly they will explain the constellation also in terms of mutual help, care and the like.

Misunderstandings have probably arisen because often peoples in African or Asian tribal and village societies have other conceptions of the temporality of social and natural life, for instance cyclical or zigzag flows (see Leach 1961).[48] Kaufmann quotes Eliade (1966) as saying 'like the mystic and the religious person in general, primitive man lives in a permanent present' (Eliade 1966, Kaufmann 1973: 163). In this way, the antithesis of modern society is constructed: primitive society with its 'antihistoric tendency' in manifold rites of 'annihilating real time' on the one hand, against modern society with its obsession with a future can be 'colonized' (Giddens 1991: 111). But it is dangerous to simply infer the more general conceptions of time from such ceremonial occasions. One reason is that ritual and ceremonial annihilation of time is often the reversal, a mirror image of 'normal' time perceptions (Leach 1961). Such ritual preoccupation with the negation of time could more adequately be taken as a sign, that the future is perceived as highly unpredictable and dangerous. Another problem with such constructions is that perceptions of time and uncertainties, becoming manifest in rites and ceremonies, are identified with individual perceptions. But people, and especially 'traditional' people living under constant threats of erratic climatic conditions, demographic and political instabilities, have always and everywhere been concerned with the future at the level of individual behaviour, perceived the future as a danger, and have had a sense of probable events or periods bringing about need and distress, for which preventive measures could be and were taken.

---

[48] Even when cyclical notions of time dominate the way in which people conceptualize the temporality of social organization and of nature, we cannot assume that they would not have notions of a future: pre-harvest food shortages may be conceived as a recurring period of distress, but that will not stop people from worrying about the 'next' food shortage. The metaphor of a cycle should perhaps be substituted by a spiral.

The intensity of such concerns will of course have varied in earlier times, as they do in the present. To a large extent, the intensity of concerns with an uncertain and insecure future will always have been influenced by the level and stability of socio-economic conditions. But uncertainty and insecurity never fully disappear when economic conditions are relatively stable. The fact that a reasonable number of people are taken care of at present is not sufficient by itself to establish such a feeling of security. The sense of security is based on a combination of past experiences, on promises encapsulated in existing mechanisms, in entitlements and the continuing availability of resources, and on some estimation about future developments. Both repetitive unfulfilled promises in the past and expectations of profound change in the future may undermine the sense of security, even though at present the situation may be quite satisfactory. The European generation that went through two World Wars and the economic depression of the 1930s feels less secure than the generation that grew up after World War II, although they may agree about the present level of care and support, and even may not disagree about the near future. The fact that one generation experienced dramatic deterioration of living conditions and the other did not, causes a very different sense of security. The youngest generation has already become familiar with mass dismissals and with an acute sense of unfulfilled public promises for care. For that reason they probably feel less secure than the post-war generation. There is thus a different sense of security among the generations, depending on specific experiences in the past.

Moreover, one must also consider the cultural constructions of the reasons for insecurity at the individual level, and may not assume a direct relation between material conditions of life and feelings of security. In many societies, people feel constantly threatened by evil forces, like witchcraft which endanger their physical and material well-being (see De Bruijn 1994). 'Besides causing illness, death and sterility, witches are also believed to blight crops and to cause accidents, financial losses, ill-luck and disasters of all kinds' (Field 1960: 36). People's *search for security* (Field 1960) is looking for ways of dealing with these threats. Ideas about fate and destiny have certainly been prominent features of many historical cultures. But those ideas have not prevented enterprising people from conquering the future, waging wars, building empires, or trying to make the best of their lives on a more modest scale. Fate and destiny and determination played important roles, but much more as rationalization and justification for the course of events or for the impossibility of changing the course of events. And there are sufficient examples showing that people 'appropriate' and personalize fate and destiny, both in the past and in the twentieth century.

Individual and Institutional Notions of Insecurity

If we look at the great differences between 'traditional' and contemporary rural societies in Third World countries and contemporary industrialized states, we see that it is not so much the fact that in contemporary welfare states the future is being thematized or deemed dangerous. It is rather the emergence of an extensive and specialized system of social security institutions that makes social security in industrial society so different, and in connection with it the specific ways in which these institutions deal with the future. The development of insurance and the central role of bureaucratic institutions of social security have had a curious effect on perception of the future and on attempts to bring the future under control. Depending on the perspective of the perceiver, ordinary individual or insurance company the social constructions and definitions of contingencies, of risks, of certainties or uncertainties, may differ substantially. For example, what in the generalized collective typifications of insurance systems may be conceived of and treated as a calculable risk that can be adequately dealt with may be perceived as perfect uncertainty from the perspective of individual persons, such as for example the moment of death. In order to calculate the necessary funding for their obligations, insurance companies use statistical methods that abstract from the individual contingencies that are the primary concern of individuals. However, these statistical methods do have an impact on the perception of individuals, who have learned to rely to some extent on the calculated expectations. Though the time of death of an individual person is still unpredictable, it has subjectively lost some of its uncertainty by the knowledge of general life expectations. Western welfare societies since the middle of the nineteenth century have gone through remarkable changes in the perception of risks, both at the institutional and the individual level (see for example Schwitters 1991). And there are strong indications that a similar transformation is taking place as a result of manmade ecological catastrophes.[49]

Whose (In)Security?

For a specialized system of social security institutions to develop, it requires the development of a political organization with sufficient power and legitimacy to engage in such tasks, and with sufficient command over economic resources for pooling and reallocation. What is radically different from small-scale rural societies, thus above all lies in the fact that such tasks have been taken over by bureaucracies with respect to larger social aggregates. This needs political institu-

---

[49] Kaufmann 1973: 29 ff.; Beck 1988; K. von Benda-Beckmann 1994.

tions which live by defining, representing and giving institutional form to the 'general interest', and which also may in part derive their legitimation from this. Church charity is an earlier example in European history, which continues to be important for social security after states have made the regulation of social security an important task of government. But the emergence of social security services has not necessarily been motivated by charitable 'social' considerations. As De Swaan (1989) has pointed out, social security provision at a regional or larger scale has been very much induced, among urban elites, by fear and the need for control of vagrants and the poor. This has played a crucial role in the development of the modern nation state. What transpires and what can be observed in developing countries as well, is that it is less the perception of needs and insecurities by society's members at large which leads to the establishment of society-wide differentiated social security institutions, but needs and insecurities as perceived by political and economic elites. And the insecurity perceived is probably much more their own insecurity than that of the common and poorer people. It is hardly a coincidence that the earliest and best developed social security provisions have been developed for these elites and those segments of the population who were directly attached to them, their politics and economy, and which therefore had to be protected (see Mesa-Lago 1978). They were developed by those who had sufficient social power to do so, or who were in the position to use the establishing of social security institutions to gain social power. The main difference from poor and powerless people was that the elites could mobilize the resources to setup such institutions which the poor did not themselves have. But the feelings of insecurity of the poor were if anything more acute and intense than those of the elites. The masses of unemployed workers in the United States before 'social security' was introduced by the New Deal policy had an acute sense of a bleak and dangerous future. And German industrial labourers had clear perceptions of the risk of accidents, and strongly desired that something should be done about it, well before the Bismarckian social security reforms came.

The history of specialized social security institutions in industrial society points to another issue that is important for proper comparison. It makes one realize that such institutions do not merely serve one purpose, but that they are also multifunctional. There is an underlying equation which is often assumed in comparisons between traditional and modern societies: specialized and differentiated and therefore monofunctional institutions in contemporary states, in opposition to undifferentiated and therefore multifunctional ones in traditional societies. However, this is not straightforward at all. Contemporary specialized social security institutions usually also have other social, economic or political functions. Indeed, many authors have pointed to social and political control *as* an important additional function of social security.[50] As in traditional patronage relations, social security programmes may be set up predominantly to gain political or electoral support, whether by state politicians or other religious movements trying to establish their own power base (see for Egypt, Azer 1988). To understand the way these institutions provide social security, one may have to consider the other functions as well.

Moreover, social security in contemporary welfare states is not adequately characterized by its state-regulated and specialized social security institutions. For other relationships based on kinship, friendship, and patronage, though changed, have not disappeared. Rather than with simple opposite types of social security organization, we are faced with different degrees of complexity and plurality in the social organization of social security.

The Layered Fabric of Social Security

Normative and Institutional Pluralism

In most contemporary societies, in western industrialized states as well as in Third World states, social security is pluralistic in many respects (K. von Benda-Beckmann 1991c and 1994). In the realm of ideology, there is usually more than one set of notions concerning social security. A subsistence ethic may exist side by side, often in competition, with a social welfare ethic or a liberal market ethic, and with religious ideas about charity. The same goes for the institutions, definitions and norms concerning social security. Some plurality of legal constructions of social security, definitions of needs, contingencies, rights to receive and duties to provide others with goods and services, is the rule rather than an exception. Most contemporary developing countries have developed some forms of statutory social security that co-exist with normative regulations based on tradition, religion and new forms of self-regulation. Besides these general normative orders, state governments have introduced various types of programmes. They concern in the first place insurance types of programmes for civil servants, the armed forces and small parts of the modern industrial and service sector. In rural areas, the most elaborated are health and education services, although there are still severe problems of quality and accessibility. Besides there are special programmes of governments and donor agencies, aimed

---

[50] For example, some of the first social security measures in Great Britain such as the Poor Laws were set up to control vagrants, and nowadays a long- term unemployed in the Netherlands may receive social assistance, but under quite restrictive conditions that involve considerable control. In Third World countries, for example, social security and commercial credit are often combined in single programmes. See also Azer 1988 and Freiberg-Strauss and Jung 1988.

at income generating activities, often in combination with credit and extension services. What contingencies are, which social units are or should be recipients or providers of social security, what the prescribed kinds and amounts of resources to be given or received are, may be differently defined in local people's folk or traditional law, in religious laws, and in legal regulations of the state administration.

To a large extent, the different normative systems define different types of social relations through which goods and services are, or should be transferred. However, the sources of regulation (such as government law, religious law, folk law and self-regulation) cannot identified with or 'translated down' to the sources and organizational structures that provide social security. For several normative systems may at the same time define what is seen as the 'same' relationship type or institution. Obligations between kin, for instance, in the definitions of relevant relatives and the substance of their rights and obligations, are constructed differently by state civil law, by religious law and in traditional law (K. von Benda-Beckmann 1991c and 1994). On Islamic Ambon, state regulations, Islamic legal rules as well as local *adat* rules all regulate aspects of the collection and distribution of *zakat-al-fitrah,* the Islamic alms-tax given at the end of the fasting month (F. von Benda-Beckmann 1988). Thus, the 'same' source of provision may be regulated by several normative systems. And one normative system may regulate different sources of provision. The state not only creates social security relations between citizens and state bureaucracies. State regulations also lay down obligations of mutual help between relatives, and regulate the activities of commercial insurance enterprises, often even making insurance obligatory for certain categories of the population.

Plurality of Social Security Relations

We must thus distinguish the plurality of normatively typified relationships of social security from the multiplicity of relations that exist between actual recipients and providers of social security. These relations of social security always have a receiving and a providing side. Throughout their life, people act as providers and receivers of social security Different phases of the life cycle show different characteristic patterns of insecurity and need, demanding different forms of help and support. 'I'pically, therefore, people go through phases in which they tend to be recipients, while in other phases they act predominantly as providers. In most phases they are both providers and recipients, in varying constellations, of social security provisions of goods and services. Depending on the phase in the life cycle of individuals and of basic economic and consumption units, and on the constellations of relevant social units, individuals may have a heavier or lighter workload as they have to provide more or less services, and some phases tend to be more stressful than others. The contributions of Van den Berg, De Bruijn and Leliveld deal in different ways with these particularities of specific phases of vulnerability (see also Freiberg-Strauss and Jung 1988).

People, to varying degrees, have social security mixes which are based on a multiplicity of social relationships. These can be with kinsmen, friends, patrons, community functionaries, religious institutions, government bureaucracies or commercial insurance enterprises. The contributions of Leliveld, Brouwer and De Bruijn illustrate this for the people whose social security relations they describe. These papers also show that in the relationships of people or groups of people, different social security structures operating at different scales of social organization and space may merge. Religion may provide access to help over a larger geographical distance than mere kinship, as De Bruijn shows. But this may also occur on the basis of kinship. Urban migrants may send remittances to their local kin and friends (see Leliveld, Brouwer, Van Walsum). Such relationships may even be intercontinental, as is the case with people having emigrated to other countries. Oosterwijk indicates how this works in her review of Böcker's study of social security among Turkish migrants in the Netherlands (Böcker 1994, Oosterwijk 1994, see also K. von Benda-Beckmann 1991a). Moreover, a considerable number of people in rural areas profit indirectly from services provided by the state. State and other provision may come together on the basis of kinship or friendship relations or other forms of cooperation between civil servants and ordinary villagers. Civil servants, expecting to become dependent on their relatives in the future, may provide their needy relatives with help in the form of money and relationships with important services. This is not usually done on an equal footing, but usually takes on the form of patronage and brokerage. Considerable differences in economic and social status between village farmers and government officials may be involved (see F. and K. von Benda-Beckmann 1998). The new forms of social and economic integration achieved by these newly merged relationships and the changing allocation of resources which accompany them, usually also mean a disintegration of other relationships and losses in the resources available to maintain them. The withdrawal of reciprocity in networks of mutual help between herders and pastoralists in the Sahel (see Moore, Van Dijk, De Bruijn) illustrate this very clearly.[51] These changes may be a source of regionalization and social stratification of social security relationships, because the possibilities of profiting from such types of arrangements are not equally distributed among village populations, as

---

[51] In our research on rural social security on Ambon, we have described, several of such relationship sets which integrated local and state personnel and resources. See F. von Benda-Beckmann 1987; K. von Benda-Beckmann 1988 and 1991c; and F. and K. von Benda-Beckmann 1998.

Brouwer shows in his description of the effects of remittances to northern Portuguese villages. We should not assume that local people in rural areas would not have such choices in the absence of state social security in their vicinity. Within their local social organization, there is also a multiplicity of social relations that are relevant for social security. Kinship and patron-client relations often constitute different sets of relations in which people can invest for their social security (see De Bruijn 1994 and Leliveld 1994). Where the existing kinship relations offer no solace, as described by De Bruijn, people try to establish new relationships with persons or functionaries on the basis of religion, hoping to find more security for themselves or their children in this way. But also kinship should not be regarded as one unitary and clearly bounded 'mechanism'. Who the relevant relatives are is largely negotiable. Kinship also offers opportunities between relatives linked by descent or by marriage, between matrilateral or patrilateral relatives (see Vel 1994a). The relevant kinship relations may be singled out by friendship or by patron-client relations of dependence between kin.

Social Practices

Understanding the practices through which social security is provided, claimed, planned or withheld, and through which social security mixes are achieved or aspired, implies seeing them in the context of these plural normative frameworks and the multiplicity of social relationships. Social practices are structured and influenced, though not determined, by normative and regulative plurality. The existence of various types of norms and regulations can constrain people's possibilities of achieving social security. But it also offers options for choosing between, or for accumulating, different constructions of social security providers and recipients, for different rights and obligations. They may also be helpful for avoiding social security obligations (see De Bruijn 1994, Van Dijk 1994 and Van den Berg 1994).

But also where social organization and rules about help and reciprocity are relatively simple, principles of kinship and solidarity do not determine people's behaviour and their resultant security. We want to emphasize this, because one often encounters the perhaps most grave misunderstanding of 'traditional' systems of kinship and solidarity: the idea that such normative rules regarding help and support would somehow work 'automatically'. This is an echo from Durkheim's 'mechanical solidarity' and the mechanical structuralist-functionalist assumptions underlying it. It overlooks the fact that the relations of kinship and normative obligations of help do not act by themselves. They need mobilization and they will generally work selectively and differentially. And, more importantly, in order to be mobilized with a likelihood of success, these relationships must be maintained. 'The most ordinary and seemingly routine exchanges of ordinary life, like the "little gifts", that "bind friendship", presuppose improvisation, and therefore constant uncertainty' (Bourdieu 1990: 98, 99).[52]

In this volume, this point is vividly illustrated in Mulder's description and analysis of feasting among Javanese Surinamese. The strength of feasting as an institution lies in the opportunity it gives, with ongoing regularity, to exemplify, re-establish, arrange and rearrange relationships. They create a continuous test and confirmation for relationships which may have to be called upon in times of hardship and misfortune. They facilitate the realization of social security arrangements; and to a certain degree they contribute to the support of the elderly and poor in the most literal sense, by providing meals. As Mulder says, the involvement of the participants in the exchanges has consequences outside the feasts as well, making it easier to ask others for help in times of need, besides providing instances where people feel secure. She also stresses the long-term temporality involved in feasting. Recurrent feasting is essentially based upon reciprocity which in the course of years builds up a whole series of exchanges and claims. In this sense it is delayed reciprocity, stretching over the whole lifetime of participants, thereby creating bonds between the members of different generations. There is nothing automatic about feasting and people's participation in feasts. There are, as Bourdieu (1990: 99) states, no 'mechanical laws' of the 'cycle of reciprocity'.[53]

In this respect, there is no difference from social security institutions, pension funds and insurances of modern societies. Here as well, the very existence of such entrepreneurial or bureaucratic institutions as such does not provide security. In order to make the promises effective, people have to pay contributions and premiums. Who does not pay, does not receive any benefits. In one type of social organization people pay money into companies and bureaucracies, in the other they invest in attention and favours, creating social credit and debts, in the expectation that the social relationships and their normative promises will indeed work; that patrons will indeed help, that kinsmen will indeed help, even that children indeed will care for their parents. If they do not,

---

[52] 'To reintroduce uncertainty is to reintroduce time, with its rhythm, its orientation and its irreversibility, substituting the dialectic of strategies for the mechanics of the model, but without falling over into the imaginary anthropology of 'rational actor' theories' (Bourdieu 1990: 99).

[53] As Bourdieu (1990: 98) says: 'Cycles of reciprocity, mechanical interlockings of obligatory practices, exist only for the omniscient spectator, who, thanks to his knowledge of the social mechanic, is able to present the different stages of the 'cycle'. Quite apart from the trouble-makers who call into question the game itself and its apparently flawless mechanism, even when agents' dispositions are as perfectly harmonized as possible and when the sequence of actions and reactions seems entirely predictable from outside, uncertainty remains as to the outcome of the interaction until the whole sequence is completed'.

they will experience the same fate as those who have paid no insurance premiums: they will be uninsured. The story of Manu Wolu in this volume shows that a young man who is not inclined to pay his social premiums, under the conditions which Lawondanese social organization asks for, will not remain included in a system with social security functions. His price is gradual exclusion.

Social Security and Resources

Providing social security is impossible without resources. A multitude of quite different resources can be involved: natural resources, money, rights and obligations, personal relationships such as kinship, neighbourhood, and friendship as well as of nationality or citizenship, contracts with commercial enterprises, and social security institutions. Agarwal (1991) calls them 'fall-back positions'. But resources constitute a mere potential. The strongest rights to social security may turn out to be nothing more than unfulfilled promises. However promising their normative implications may be, they must be mobilized in social interaction and lead to corresponding transfers (F. von Benda-Beckmann 1987), converted into actual social security provision. This also holds true for (rights to) material resources. One cannot eat rice land, and money does not cook, as an elderly Moluccan lady once said when explaining why she hesitated to go back to the Moluccas and spend her last years there (K. von Benda-Beckmann and Leatemia 1992: 243). It is this process of conversion and the mechanisms through which this is done that we call summarily social 'security mechanisms'[54] Actually, a 'chain of conversions' is usually needed rather than one simple social security mechanism, and a multitude of different resources, relationships and interactions, before the potential of social security resources is successfully transformed into a state of security. One must have access rights and actual access to land, one must be able to command labour to cultivate and harvest, and usually one must process – or have them processed – agricultural products before one can eat them, often with the help of other natural resources, such as stoves, fuel, water, as well as social resources.

Whether and to what extent people are able to create and mobilize the various options depends on many factors. Rights and relationships (the entitlements and endowments of Sen 1981) are important elements, but such rights rarely exist without concomitant, often reciprocal obligations, which one must have fulfilled in the past, or must fulfill in the present or future. Besides, the character of the relations with potential providers of social security is important,

---

[54] In Sen's (1987b) terms, we are concerned with transformations of social security capability sets into functionings or living standards.

their affective loading, their economic dependence and power differential.[55] Another important factor is the extent to which people are successful 'forum shoppers' among institutions and relations providing for social security. This requires a sufficient command of the various 'idioms' in which requests are to be framed and entrance to the appropriate social fields is secured. Political power and influence and command over economic resources are always important factors in gaining access to existing institutions, in establishing social security relations and in emerging successfully from the struggles over resources which are necessary for this.

The transformation of resources into social security provisions presupposes the availability of material resources (land, crops, money, work power, people), and social resources (social relationships, rights, institutions, time) through which the material resources can be converted. But there is availability of resources also in a different sense, (relatively) independent from the social relationships and processes through which they can be made available for social security purposes: resources not yet used or not yet existent. We want to capture this with the words 'resource potential'. Positively expressed this refers to resource reserves which could have been used, and which may be used for social security purposes in the future, in the sense of being drawn or defined into the domain of social security It also refers to social relationships not yet existent, but which potentially can be established. Negatively expressed, it refers to the absence of resources for actualizing existing social security relationships or of the potential to create new social security relationships. Where there is no land, no houses can be built, even if kinsmen are obliged to, and willing to do so. Where there is no food, no food can be given away; where there is no money, no money can be exchanged for food; where there are no prospective spouses, marriage as a social security option falls out. The resource potential is not a mere matter of quantity, but also of their quality; whether it is natural resources (soil fertility, degradation of resources), economic resources (money, the value of money, the monetary value of agricultural products) or social relationship resources (the quality of kinship and patron-client relationships).

The transition from a relationship potential concerning social or natural resources to a social security relationship, usually means a transition from one type of relationship to another type. People having no patron may be only co-

---

[55] As Moore (1994) shows with an example from northern Burkina Faso, new economically strong migrants live very much segregated from the old settlers, so that little welfare mixing is possible among the ethnic groups. On Ambon, mixing of welfare among Butonese migrants and older Ambonese settlers very much depends on the historical development of the relations. The older migrants had far more opportunities to combine Butonese and Ambonese social security arrangements than recent migrants, who were almost totally excluded from Ambonese networks (see F. von Benda-Beckmann and Taale 1992).

villagers (or co-citizens, for that matter) and merely have a relationship potential. But the next day, he or she may actually have a patron, and from that day on claims and counterclaims can be made which were inconceivable before. For no one is such distinction more obvious than for the foreign researcher who comes to live in a village. From the starting point of having no social relationships, he has to explore the relationship potential. It is also relevant for civil servants and other strangers coming to live in a community. There is the potential to change a stranger-relationship into a foster child relationship, but only after one has been actually adopted can one start relying on the help and support that may come with a foster relationship, and it will depend on the wealth, influence and willingness of the foster family, what the level and quality of support and help will be (see for immigrants, F. von Benda-Beckmann and Taale 1992, for civil servants F. and K. von Benda-Beckmann 1998).

The distinction between conditions for social security, that is the availability of a resource potential, and the mechanisms of social security through which social security may be effectuated, may sometimes be difficult to make. Yet it is important, because the conditions for social security may be affected differently by the same factors, or affected by different factors than the mechanisms of social security. While mechanisms of social security may remain the same, the conditions may change so fundamentally, that the actual provision of social security may have deeply changed. The interrelationships between conditions for, and mechanisms of social security pose pressing questions in the study and the planning of social security.

Establishing Certainty and Security

Ex post, ex ante

The potentiality of social security reminds us how difficult it is to study social security. The problem is that the actualization of social security can only be established with certainty retrospectively. Prospectively, there is nothing more than probabilities, be they vague or approaching certainty. In case of chronic contingencies, the future may be tomorrow. But in general, social security provisions are planned for dealing with risks, uncertainties or certainties that may lie anywhere' in the future. Some may be measurable in time (like 'old' age), while others, such as illness or unemployment only allow for educated guesses.[56] One need not go to rural, areas in developing countries in order to

---

[56] Insurance companies have made such guesses into a statistical art. At the aggregate level that forms the basis of calculation by specialized social security institutions, such guesses may seem to turn into (near) certainties. But they remain thoroughly uncertain at the individual level of those who may come to suffer from a contingency.

find out how fragile the planned, institutionalized social security mechanisms and their normative promises may turn out to be, and how deeply disappointed people may be when they see their past social security strategies suddenly turn out to have been in vain.

This raises the question whether social security should be studied from an ex post perspective, looking at the 'outcome sets' (Sen 1987b), or from an *ex ante* perspective looking at people's 'opportunity sets'. The distinction between the *ex post* and the *ex ante* perspective is often neglected or theorized away. However, when dealing with uncertainty, and futures are notoriously uncertain, the distinction cannot be neglected, for they may lead to different conclusions. In our view, both perspectives are necessary and should not be confused. This is not only part of the question of how to treat time in theoretical constructions of social organization.[57] It is also relevant for policy makers and for the participants in social security themselves. Concluding from the *ex post* established degree and quality of social security to the *ex ante* likelihood of the same degree and quality is highly problematic. Yet it is in a profound way the basis of social security systems. That is, repetitive retroactively established actualization of social security provisions is the basis for probability calculations that lie in the future. *Ex ante* perspectives tend to be problematic, because probability calculations of the future tend to have a strong bias towards normative or teleological constructions. These promise a high level of certainty. In a sense, these normative and teleological constructions, however unrealistic they may be or turn out to have been, *are* security, and this holds true for individuals as well as for social policy makers.

No longer, not yet

Normative and teleological assumptions also underlie discussions in academic and policy debates on future social security. These are characterized by what we call the 'no longer - not yet perspective'. It is well captured in the following quotations:

> The continued usefulness of traditional systems as the major source of social protection has become highly problematic (Gilbert 1976: 365). One can think of a number of circumstances in which these systems need to be replaced by new social security institutions (Platteau 1991: 163).

---

[57] See Kanbur 1987: 69. In our view, there is no need to choose for one of the two perspectives, as is done in the discussions between Sen and his colleagues, see Kanbur 1987: 69, 70 and Sen 1987b: 105. See Baert 1989 over the treatment of time in sociological theories.

Many traditional village support systems entail high costs in terms of dynamic efficiency, because of their disincentive effects on work and investment efforts. If they were all to be maintained in the future, social security would be bought at the price of capital accumulation and economic growth (Platteau 1991: 161; for a similar view see Schmidt 1992: 25).

These quotations are indicative of an evolutionary and modernization oriented bias.[58] The argument runs as follows. The traditional systems of social security are no longer sufficient to protect rural people in the Third World from poverty, and particularly in those situations and periods in which they are especially vulnerable due to physical, mental or socio-economic conditions. They must therefore be replaced, or at least supplemented, by modem forms of social security, to be provided by the state or the market. However, these new forms are not yet in place, they do not yet cater sufficiently for the social security needs of rural people. The policy implications are clear: such new, modern forms have to be developed by the state and the market. The second implication is slightly different. It concerns the tension between types of social security system and economic growth (see also Hirtz 1994). Traditional social security systems must be replaced, not only because they are no longer sufficient to fulfill local social security needs, but also because, and primarily because, their maintenance hinders economic growth. Van de Ven and Mulder in particular show how these attitudes are expressed by policy makers with respect to the traditional institutions described in their papers.

These assumptions are largely due to the continued undifferentiated use which is made of the concepts of formal/informal or modern/traditional. For these implicitly, or explicitly, embody ideas of causality that link certain forms of socio-economic conditions, like poverty, to the social security structures of poor people. As Connolly (1985: 64) says, the poverty situation usually implied by informality is immediately explained by the lack of formality, while the formal presupposes a correspondence between certain production relations and 'good' employment conditions and social security services (ibid. 78). In this way, the terminology not only reinforces the mutually exclusive dichotomy between modem progress and wealth, on the one hand, and traditional backwardness and poverty on the other, it also diverts interest in the immediate causes of poverty from the modem sector to the non-modern sector (ibid.: 64, 65). This leads to the image deficiencies of the 'informal' mechanisms as being intrinsic to these mechanisms, while in fact the major reasons may be extrinsic to them.

---

[58] The evolutionary bias inherent in these discussions often comes close to what Fabian (1983) has called the denial of the coevalness of these societies.

These ideas are strengthened by other normative and teleological assumptions concerning the scope and the efficiency embodied in the formal/informal or modern/traditional dichotomies. State legal social security provision is not merely seen as the social security that is regulated by the state and under state law. It is at the same time firmly associated with the macro-space on which validity of state regulation is claimed (see Knorr-Cetina 1988, F. and K. von Benda-Beckmann 1991). It is from this 'greatness' that the superior quality of state social security is derived. Yet the evidence in Third World countries is rather the contrary; statutory social security only reaches minute segments of the population spread out very thinly over the state territory. Obviously, if one wanted to compare state social security with social security provided for instance through kinship relations, one would have to do this in the same social space: either by comparing the totality of state provisions with the totality of kinship provision, or by comparing both in a smaller social space such as a village, where state provision often is much more 'micro' than kinship provision. By creating such a distorted sense of reality and its underlying reasons, which Dove (1986) has called the 'ideological deflection of reality', these explanatory notions simultaneously outline and legitimate the road for future development, which has to lead from informal to formal in all fields of social and economic life.

Ironically enough, the debates about developing countries are a mirror image of European discussions. Considering the quotations above more closely, one discovers a striking reversal of socio-economic policy implications as they are expressed in western social policy debates. Substitute the word 'traditional' system by the words 'welfare state', and you have the contemporary discussion about the Dutch welfare state. Here, demands are being made that more social security should be provided by the family, the community, the 'traditional solidary' forms of social organization. The resurrection of these structures is seen as a precondition for economic growth, and reliance on state social security is the disincentive (see Burgess and Stem 1991: 70, with further references). No danger is seen that the desired larger role for kinship, friendship and community would be inimical to economic growth. No one is afraid that the individual would remain economically inactive in some parasitic expectation of being cared for by his or her family members and friends. On the contrary, being forced back out of the state welfare system is regarded as a force which would strongly motivate the individual to look for work seriously.

A general conclusion which can be drawn is that the recipe of full state support may not be realistic for developing countries; if not even the European industrialized states can manage to uphold it. The blooming of the welfare state in the reconstruction period after the Second World War in Europe has ceased. And there is no reason to expect that Third World countries will do better. Experiences in those Third World countries having a long history of social security institutions do not inspire much hope. Mesa-Lago's historical analysis of Latin

American states, where the social security system had been developed to a far wider extent than in most African and Asian countries, may be useful here: the pioneer states, which have the widest coverage, are the least solvent (Mesa-Lago 1991: 391). These states can no longer maintain their systems, and have to reduce it. The recent wave of structural adjustment policies has dramatically cut social policy expenditures. And given the fact that nearly 50% of the countries in the Third World are experiencing some sort of civil war, insecurity may increase dramatically for millions of people.

We certainly do not want to argue that state governments should not be active in social security policies. We also do not want to romanticize and expect too much from non-state forms of social security. As many of the papers in this volume show, there is no reason to do so.[59] But neither should we romanticize the 'modernity' or 'formality' of state regulated social security, whether they envisage state or market provisions. It is difficult to imagine how forms of social security based on kinship, friendship or village membership could be replaced by social security based upon state or market regulation. It is difficult to see why they should be an obstacle to development. On the contrary, they are in many cases the precondition for survival and development. However weak they may have become, they cannot be dispensed with. Even for those who are 'covered' by state regulated social security the actual contribution to overcome situations or periods of distress may be minimal, and they may draw more help from non-state regulated relationships. Kinship and patron-client relationships seem to be the basic relationships upon which the economic and social security of many 'modern' civil servants subsists.[60] The same can be said for other domains of social life. Without such forms of mutual assistance and redistribution, medical bills would not be paid and children could not go to school. Without the pooling of resources among relatives, village children could not attend universities. But schooling if successful and health services may improve the level and quality of social security based on kinship. Without a basis in food security

---

[59] For both European and Third World states, there are many indications that the images of 'traditional solidarity' and family care are often strongly romanticized and give a false impression of past social and economic life. From the available sources it appears that this social security was of a quality and quantity that would not stand up to contemporary standards. Life expectancy was low, infant mortality high, illness endemic, and help and support often meant suffocating dependence on the whims of providers. See Köhler 1977. See also Steinmetz 1988 on child abuse and neglect of the elderly.

[60] There never was a full replacement of earlier forms of social security in European welfare states. So-called traditional mechanisms – other than citizen-state or consumer-market relations – have always existed and continue to exist in modern economic surroundings. The idea, that even in European welfare states the state or market alone could sufficiently provide for the social security needs of most segments of the population, cannot be maintained seriously. See also Johnson 1987; Rose 1989; Elwert 1991 and others.

based upon subsistence forms of food production and distribution, villagers have no opportunity to engage in market production or wage labour.[61]

Conclusions

The difficulties with which political actions, required to achieve improvements or to stop deterioration of social security in Third World countries, are faced, are enormous (see Midgley 1984 and 1994, Drèze and Sen 1991). It is not our ambition to solve them here. But we hope to have shown that a functional approach to social security maybe helpful for providing a perspective that gives a better insight into the complexity of past and future social security than the normatively biased approaches centring on institutions. By distinguishing between the different layers of social security it also becomes possible to see where changes might be most effective. Thus it becomes clear that without drastic redistribution of resources for social security, any extension of 'coverage' of statutory schemes to those yet uncovered will remain cosmetic, hiding rather than curing social and economic problems. It throws light on the paradox that hitherto such extensions, as Midgley (1984) has shown and as is increasingly being acknowledged, have led to a transfer of resources from the poor to the better-off. Our approach also makes it easier to look for the most fruitful level of redistribution of economic and social resources and at the proper level of regulation. If interregional redistribution is preferable, then the state might be the most appropriate level to locate its regulation, because other types of social security structures operate at much smaller scales of social and economic resources (Partsch 1983, see also F. von Benda-Beckmann et al. 1988: 14). But the national level is not necessarily the most appropriate level, nor is state regulation always the preferable way to organize redistribution or social security. On the other hand, our approach also suggests that one should not merely look at the role of the state as a provider of social security. The state could play a more constructive role by supporting local mechanisms, rather than undermining them by policies that have a detrimental effect on the conditions for social security. Finally this perspective allows for a more creative and innovative way of linking and integrating indigenous and state mechanisms of social security as one of the important strategies to improve rural people's social and economic security, as is advocated by Midgley. One could think of combinations at each of the layers that we have distinguished. We hope to have shown that, while our

---

[61] See Dove 1986; F. von Benda-Beckmann 1990a for the relations between food subsistence security and agricultural market production. The same goes for wage labour. In fact, many factories on Java are subsidized by relatives of the young female employees who support them because salaries are too low even for subsistence, but also because they consider it their obligation to feed their unmarried daughters (Wolf 1992).

perspective cannot provide any answer to the political and economic policy problems, it may help to lay a better basis for policy debates and for a well-informed policy towards social (in)security.

Chapter 3
Sago, Law and Food Security on Ambon*

Franz von Benda-Beckmann

Introduction

> *In some parts of the archipelago, nature has distributed her gifts so freely that man can provide in his livelihood needs with a minimum of labour. This in particular holds true for those regions in which sago palms occur in such abundance that they provide the staple diet for the population. ... It is certain that the bad economic conditions are to a large extent due to the easy conditions of life which the Moluccans have thanks to the sago palm* (Ruinen 1921: 24).

This statement, dating from colonial times, suggests a problematic relationship between food security and economic development, development understood as modernization and commercialization of agriculture leading to higher rates of productivity. Though it may be exaggerated to infer a rigid causal connection from the quotation, the suggestion is that the ecological and economic conditions that provide the Ambonese with a carefree life, at least a life without hunger, are also responsible for the 'bad' economic conditions outside the sphere of food provision. And it is obvious that the Dutch commentator's value judgment inclines him to give priority to the improvement of the economic conditions; his further remarks on the potentials of a more commercially oriented exploitation of sago, and his references to more industrious Indonesian groups exporting sago to Singapore, make that clear enough.

Recent analyses of food security experts suggest the same problematic, albeit seen from the other end. Where there is economic development, food insecurity increases (Barraclough 1986: 15). There are numerous examples showing that rapid expansions of agriculture and agro-exports have been accompanied by a spectacular growth of the GNP, but also by food insecurity for larger sections of the population (Barraclough 1986: 12). Optimistic expectations about the general enhancement of the welfare of the poorer sections of the population through increased agricultural productivity seem to be unwarranted (ESCAP 1985). There is even evidence to show 'that malnutrition increases as cash-cropping cultivation increases and as farmers neglect subsistence food

---
* First published 1990 in: J. I. H. Bakker (ed.), *Food Security versus Economic Development. The World Food Crisis. Food Security in Comparative Perspective*, pp. 157-199. Toronto, Ontario: Canadian Scholars' Press. Inc.

production for monetary incomes' (MacPhearson and Midgley 1987: 46). Some analysts even tend to generalize 'that the food systems that have maintained humankind throughout most of its history are disintegrating before other forms of economic activity are able to offer alternative means of livelihood to the displaced peasantry' (Pearse 1980, Barraclough 1986: 15).

While the general validity of such statements may be questioned, the suggestion that subsistence food production may be an important element in food security, and of social security in a more general sense, is an important one.[62] Yet subsistence food production has not been given much attention in the context of social security and food security policies. This is largely due to two closely related reasons.

1. Problems of food security and hunger in third world countries generally are addressed retrospectively. There is hunger, there are food shortages, and appropriate measures have to be taken in order to overcome the problem. Also in the wider field of social and social security policies, the major themes discussed in the field of food security are curative measures, and most attention is given to the devising of risk prevention systems that may cover such failures (see Savy 1972, ESCAP 1985).

2. Besides, agricultural policies are heavily biased towards increasing productivity and income. The curative measures of social security policies and projects follow this trend. They are generally focussed upon income generating activities of the poor.[63] Projects are set up to overcome the thresholds of hunger and poverty by providing inputs for income generating activities for the poor (see Reidy 1980, Midgley 1984, MacPhearson and Midgley 1987, K. von Benda-Beckmann 1988). Not only are such programs oriented towards the market economy, they also contribute to an increasing monetization of the relations of production through a grand scale infusion of money through financial credit. Social security policies thus are heavily biased at raising the *general level of welfare*, and much less at redistributive activities on whichever level of welfare. Since most measures are directed at, and presuppose, persons who have sufficient physical and mental capacities to engage in income generating activities, those who lack those capacities will generally not be reached and will have to

---

[62] Looking at subsistence food economies as a form of social security has recently been advocated as an important research perspective on food security in developing countries, (see Smits 1986: 75). It is also a perspective underlying our research project on social security and law in rural areas in developing countries, (see F. and K. von Benda-Beckmann 1984).

[63] For a critique of the conventional anti-poverty strategies and an elaboration of an alternative strategy, see ESCAP 1985. The authors emphasize the need for a maximalization of labour absorption and the provision of land-based assets to ensure food security outside commercial food production.

depend on the local non-state mechanisms of (food)help and redistribution (see F. von Benda-Beckmann et al. 1988 b: 19).

Where the large scale extension of state-regulated social security schemes for the rural population is planned, the schemes also presuppose a money economy. Most social security policies, like in Indonesia, are premised upon the idea that whatever social security measures may be devised for self-employed farmers or paid agricultural workers, the costs of the system will have ultimately to be carried by them.[64]

This emphasis on income generating activities leads, in analysis and policy, to a general policy preference for market-oriented economic activities. Little attention is given to situations where current food provision is not an acute problem, but where the maintenance of subsistence activities may be an important objective of economic and social security policy. Therefore, few social security strategies, and food security strategies in particular, make the protection or development of non-market activities their primary goal. In other words, there is little attention to subsistence production as an integral part of the economy which is particularly important for social security.

These economic policy preferences also find their reflection in legal policies. Here one also finds the attempts to introduce or to expand a legal framework which is considered to be particularly appropriate for a market-oriented economy, a framework in which emphasis is accorded to individualized property relations and to the creation of property forms which can be given as securities for credit loans.[65] Legal forms, in which communality and obligations of reciprocity and redistribution are emphasized, are deemed an obstacle for market-orientated economic activities. New forms of communality and mutual help are invented which tend to stress communal forms of production and aim at raising the general level of welfare. Redistributive elements within the organization of production are then reduced to a newly created regulatory sphere of charitable matters. Social security policy becomes, as it were, the cleaning lady for the debris left by 'economic' development. Even if Macarov's motto of the 'unholy alliance between work and welfare' (1980) still may not be completely fitting the intended conditions in rural areas, we can see that the general idea is at least one of 'market production and welfare' – an alliance which may be as problematic as the coupling between wage labour and welfare schemes.

---

[64] See generally Zacher 1979; for developing countries see Midgley 1984; Fuchs 1985; F. von Benda-Beckmann et al 1988a: 19; Fuchs 1988: 46; for Indonesia, see Chhabra 1980; Joenoes 1982; Department of Social Affairs 1984; Stamboel 1986: 12.
[65] Like in Marris 1968-69; Mouton 1975: 150; ILO 1984: 2; see F. von Benda-Beckmann 1986; Woodman 1988: 85.

Sago and Food Security on Ambon

The case of food security on Ambon, which I shall discuss in this paper, is an instructive example that allows us to look at the problem of food security/insecurity from a different and more integrative perspective than is usually taken.

As the quotation above indicates, there has been little food insecurity on Ambon. The basic elements guaranteeing food security were the availability of sago and fish. This goes for the sago growing villages on the island Ambon itself, together with the availability of a huge sago reserve on the close by and sparsely populated island of Seram which has constituted the sago reservoir for the more densely populated islands of Ambon and Lease for centuries (see Ellen 1979, Krause-Katerla 1986, Knaap 1987a, Taale 1988).[66]

This is not to say that the Ambonese village economy was one of pure subsistence only. Being one of the legendary spice islands, Ambonese villages have for centuries had a mixed economy in which subsistence activities, like fishing and the exploitation of sago palms, have been 'interwoven' (Elwert 1980b) with the production of spices, cloves and nutmeg in particular, for non-regional commodity markets. The politico-legal frameworks for these productive activities have varied considerably, and so have the ways in which profits from clove production have been distributed over producers, traders, civil servants and state institutions. It has been carried out on the basis of tributary obligations, trade treaties under the monopoly of the Dutch East Indies Company, under the system of forced production and distribution *(cultuurstelsel)*, free trade and trade via state co-operatives.[67]

Neither was the Ambonese food economy purely subsistence oriented. Rice and wheat flour, for instance, have been imported for centuries. Also for centuries, the demand for sago as a foodstuff has varied considerably with the availability of alternative food, such as rice and wheat flour, and, given the commercial character of these imported foodstuffs, with the capacity of the local population to buy these food stuffs. The varying income from tree crop sales, and the price of rice, have more or less always been of influence on the level of production and consumption of sago by the local population.

Within this mixed economy, the production and distribution of sago has largely kept its subsistence character throughout the centuries. Non-monetized access to sago on the basis of ownership or share-harvesting agreements has been the rule; excess production was accidental rather than intended. But there was usually a relatively secure supply of sago above the level necessary for the

---

[66] For a discussion of the question whether sago was original to the island of Ambon or has been imported from neighbouring Seram, see Taale 1988.
[67] For historical descriptions see Knaap 1981a and b and 1987a; Chauvel 1981; Krause-Katerla 1986; Taale 1988.

consumptive needs of the direct producers which could be used to cater for the needs of the 'unproductive' members in the villages, a requirement for food security in subsistence-oriented food systems (see Schott 1988: 101). Sago trade has played a changing role in the Central Moluccan region (see Ellen 1979, Krause-Katerla 1986, Knaap 1987a). But for villages on Ambon without permanent sago self-sufficiency, access to sago gardens on Seram has been based largely on inter-village friendship/kinship bonds *(pela,* see Bartels 1978) or on large scale collective sago production expeditions of a group of villagers on the basis of share-harvesting.

In the contemporary Moluccas, sago still plays an important role as foodstuff. Recent estimates of the consumption of staple food by the Central Moluccan population give a general indication of the significance of sago in contemporary Ambon. Expressed in kg of rice equivalents per year, the per capita consumption in the Central Moluccas of 211 compares well with the average consumption in Indonesia of 187. However, of the 211 kg almost one half, i.e., 104 kg is sago (NEI 1982: 18). This level of intake is just above the minimum requirements as established by the WHO (NEI 1982: 18). Sago is rich in calories, but has hardly any protein and fats.[68] But served with other food added, fish in particular, it is no less nutritious than other food; there is no danger to the nutritional standard of the population.[69] Sago compares very well with all other crops in terms of energy produced per man-day and per hectare (LTA 72 1983: 4.3).

Except for this relevance in actual food consumption, the availability of more sago than is currently consumed still constitutes a safety-net for times in which the acquisition of other foodstuffs may be more costly and difficult.

As far as it is based upon sago, the Ambonese food system to a high degree exhibits the five characteristics of food security specified by Barraclough (1986: 16):

1. The capacity to generate sufficient internal food supply;

---

[68] According to estimations based upon the available statistical material, the per capita intake of calories in the Central Moluccas is higher than the Indonesian average, 2,469 as compared to 2,300. The protein intake, on the other hand, is lower for the Central Moluccas, 37.2 than the Indonesian average of 43.3. For the whole province of the Moluccas the average intake is 43.6 (NEI 1982: 18).

[69] Dassen 1848: 142; Deinum 1948: 618; Flach and Luning 1983: 3; Knaap 1987a: 173. According to Ellen (1978: 73, 167 and 1979: 49) the sago need per person/day is 0.55 kg, thus roughly 200 kg/year. The amount of wet sago won from individual palms varies, of course, with the lifetime etc. of the palm. In the literature, amounts ranging between 100 and 500 kg are reported, with an average of 200 kg. See also Ruinen 1921. It has been calculated that by working 80 hours, the sago need for one year could be fulfilled (Ellen 1979; Knaap 1987a: 172, 173). This comes close to our own observations in Hila.

2. Reliability, so that seasonal and cyclical variations are minimized;
3. A maximum of autonomy and self-determination, reducing its vulnerability to international market fluctuations;
4. Long-term stability; the production base – the ecosystem – must be conserved and improved;
5. The care for equity, the provision of a dependable access to adequate food by all social groups.

In my paper I shall examine the socio-economic characteristics of sago production and distribution. I shall try to pinpoint those elements in the system in which the food security is embedded. As I shall illustrate with material from the village of Hila,[70] this security lies in a specific form of subsistence production.[71] This specificity derives to some extent from the botanical and ecological character of sago and from the technology employed in sago production. But it also derives from the specific legal regime under which people have access to sago and under which sago is produced and distributed (Cf. Sen 1981). In my analysis I shall try to elucidate the relation between the elements of food security and the normative system which structures food production, processing and distribution, and discuss the question how this relation would be affected by legal, economic or technical change.

The Importance of Sago in Hila

General Socio-economic and Political Conditions

Location
Hila, the village where my wife and I carried out field research in 1985 and 1986, is situated at the northern coast of Leihitu, the northern peninsula of Ambon island.[72] The village territory comprises an area of 20 square kilometers. It

---

[70] The situation as found in Hila is, of course, not identical in all respects with the one in other Central Moluccan villages (see for information about Tulehu, Van Paassen 1987). However, for the analysis of the food security elements in sago production and its legal regulation such differences may be negligible.

[71] When I speak of subsistence production here I understood it as the production of food primarily as use value. Subsistence production does not exclude (and to some extent even presupposes) the production of a surplus; this surplus, however, is distributed by ways other than the market in which the food has a general exchange value (see Sahlins 1974a: 83; Evers et al. 1984; Krause-Katerla 1986: 13). Neither does it necessarily presuppose the identity of units of production and consumption (see Elwert 1980a and b; Evers et al. 1984; Wong 1984).

[72] The research project on law and social security on Ambon is carried out by cooperation between the Department of Agrarian Law, Agricultural University Wagenin-

includes a narrow, flat, coastal area in which the settlements are located. 2,407 ethnically Ambonese are living in the Ambonese core village, and another 1,700 Butonese immigrants[73] live in three separate settlements on the village territory (1985). In the coastal area one finds coconut and sago palms, and most of the gardens in which villagers grow vegetables, beans, cassava and groundnuts. A large part of the coastal area consists of clove tree gardens. The rest of the village territory is hilly, even mountainous, covered with secondary forest and newly cultivated gardens.

Political Organization

Ever since the Dutch East Indies Company ordered the Ambonese population living in the mountains to settle in coastal villages during the second half of the 17th century, the political organization has been an amalgam of *adat* principles and government regulations. The most influential government institutions were, and are, the *raja,* the village chief, and the *kepala soa,* the heads of the *soa* (clan associations). Traditionally, the village chief was assisted by the village council, *saniri negeri,* consisting of the *soa* and *dati* heads *(dati* being land holding clan-segments), a village secretary and some other officials such as the *kewang,* the village forest overseer. Since Indonesia's independence, various local government reforms have followed each other, introducing new governmental bodies on the village level. Following the most recent local government legislation of 1979, the LKMD *(Lembaga Ketahanan Masyarakat Desa)* was introduced as the new official village council, with the LMD (*Lembaga Masyarakat Desa*) as a sort of first chamber. The *raja* and *kepala soa* have been integrated into these new governmental bodies as chairman and members of the LMD.

Social Organization

The village organization is largely based upon kinship. Kinship is structured by the two overlapping principles of patrilinearity and bilaterality. The patrilineal principle is the dominant principle determining membership in the clan *(rumah tau* or *fam),* the *dati,* the *soa*-clan association and the village. For most other purposes, however, villagers' kinship relations are based upon bilaterality. The

---

gen, and the Department of Social Science, Faculty of Law, Erasmus University Rotterdam. Field research in Ambon was carried out for 8 months in 1985 and 3 months in 1986. Besides, three student researchers, A. van Paassen, T. Taale and A. Brouwer, were involved in the project. The field research has been done under the auspices of LIPI and with the sponsorship of Universitas Pattimura, Ambon. For earlier publications see the list of references.

[73] In this paper, I shall focus specifically on the functioning of Ambonese *adat* arrangements for the food security of the Ambonese population. For an analysis of the relationships between the Ambonese and the Butonese immigrants, see F. von Benda-Beckmann 1990a.

descendants of all four grandparents are considered to be kin. Also important, if less extended, are affinal relationships. At least one's spouse's parents and their descendants are considered to be close kin.

Co-residence is mainly based upon relations of descent and marriage. Post-marital virilocal residence is the culturally and statistically dominant form; however, residence rules and arrangements are rather flexible. The size and composition of houses vary considerably. From a series of in-depth house-interviews[74] it appeared that the number of persons living in one house varied between 2 and 17.[75] In the 48 houses chosen for in-depth interviews, the composition of inhabitants was as follows:

Composition of houses	Frequency	
	Total	Percentage
one two-generation family	24	50.0%
two two-generation families	2	4.2%
three two-generation families	1	2.1
one grandparent couple plus one two-generation family	13	27
one grandparent couple plus two two-generation families	7	14.0
two grandparent couples plus two two-generation families	1	2.1

---

[74] This series involved 48 houses with 353 inhabitants, approximately 15% of the total population of the Ambonese village of Hila, not including the residential areas of Butonese immigrants.

[75] The composition of the 48 houses was as follows:

Number of inhabitants	Frequency
2-4	8
5-7	21
8-10	9
11-13	7
14-17	3

The average is 7.3 persons per house.

Consumptive units – a group of persons who use one kitchen for the preparation of food for themselves and who eat together[76] – are in most parts formed by a nuclear – parent-children – family living in one house. Thus 24 or 50% of the houses in our sample had one kitchen.

In those cases where more than one nuclear family live together, e.g., two or more married brothers, sons and daughters with son-in-law, or married grandparents, they may or may not share one kitchen. The grandparents in those cases often share a kitchen with one of their children's nuclear family. Widowed grandparents living together with one of their children (married or unmarried) usually share their kitchen with them. Apart from close kin, foster-children, distant relatives living temporarily in the house join one of the kitchens. Of the 24 houses in which more than one nuclear family lived in one house, 8 (or 33%) had more than one kitchen: two kitchens in 6 houses and three kitchens in 2 houses.

This is, however, a static picture which only gives a general indication of house composition and kitchen structure. Both house composition and kitchen structure, the structure of consumptive units, are flexible and change with the developmental cycle of the family members, and with the quality of social relations between them. The latter aspect usually plays a role in those cases where sons get married and the question arises whether a son's mother and his daughter(s) or daughter(s)-in-law are going to share a kitchen. Having one kitchen for 15 persons, including for instance three married couples, is seen as a sign of good relations. If sisters or daughters-in-law establish their own kitchen this indicates a strained relationship.

The number of kitchens per house usually expands and contracts over time. For an illustration, take the house of our neighbours, a grandparent couple with 6 children, two of whom were just married when they moved into their newly built stone house in 1978. During the first years they had only one kitchen, and this was maintained when the sons started to get their first children. When the third son married, the daughter-in-law moved in, but she had difficulties with her mother-in-law and the wives of her husband's brothers. The young couple therefore moved out into the original family house where the couple established their own kitchen. Gradually, the two remaining daughters-in-law established their own kitchen in a new kitchen building. A new kitchen was built with two fire places; later the kitchen was divided into two by a partitioning wall. The grandmother continued to use the old kitchen building for her husband, the two unmarried sons and their unmarried daughter. During our stay, the second son moved out, since he could live temporarily in the house of a rela-

---

[76] This discussion of consumptive units is limited to the normal daily life. Much food, however, is also consumed during the ceremonies, mainly at marriage and burial ceremonies.

tive.[77] There remained two kitchens. In 1988, another son finished high school, and the daughter got married and moved to a different village. Under these circumstances it may just be a matter of time before the two kitchens are fused into one again.

Social and economic co-operation, permanent or incidental, between the persons living in one house, sharing or not sharing a kitchen, is highly variable.[78] Just to give a brief illustration. In the house just mentioned, the three older brothers often processed sago together. They, and their parents, had separate vegetable gardens but helped each other occasionally. Each of the sons and the father engaged separately in various income generating activities, like fishing, working in construction, or producing sweets. The women, too, helped each other in economic activities, but acted both separately and jointly in e.g., baking and selling sago bread, or fruit, or in making and selling coconut-rice lunches.

Economic Activities

Most Hila villagers are farmers. Cloves and nutmeg are the main cash crops. Since the early 1970s the clove price has risen dramatically and villagers had a great inflow of cash. Clove prices have dropped considerably, however, since the mid 1980s. Earnings from clove sales were for the greatest part spent on house building and extraordinary investments like the pilgrimage to Mecca, the acquisition of machines, and extra clothing. Fish has become largely commercialized during the past 10 years. Among the Ambonese population of Hila there were only a few professional fishermen who operated with teams of about 20 helpers. Vegetables and fruit are partly grown for subsistence, partly brought to the market in Ambon at a distance of 42 km, which has become more accessible for villagers since a tarred road connecting the northern coast with the city of Ambon has been built in the mid 1970s. Hila itself has no physical market. Most shopping is done in the 16 odd village stalls which sell all necessary items. Sago bread, sweets, fruit and vegetables are also sold along the road by women.

Food Acquisition

Villagers acquire food in a variety of ways. For some food there is no alternative to buying. This holds true for rice, wheat flour, salt, refined sugar. For others there is the alternative of providing them by one's own labour or the labour

---

[77] I have described the activities of some of the family members in F. von Benda-Beckmann 1987.

[78] Given the variable composition of houses, consumptive and productive units I have consciously avoided the use of the term 'household' to denote any specific social unit here, since it could only lead to confusion.

by one or more members of one's consumptive unit. The general data from the house interviews give a rough indication for the acquisition of some major non-imported food stuffs:
- Vegetables are usually cultivated or collected in the forest.
- 67% of the population stated that they regularly bought fish.
- 64.6% stated that they acquired sago exclusively through their own labour. For 78.9% own labour was the major form of acquisition. Only 15%, mainly 'modern' and richer people who ate little sago stated that they exclusively bought it.

The Significance of Sago

Sago as Food

In the Central Moluccas, sago is prepared as food in two different forms. One is as wet sago, which is made into a pudding and is eaten together with fish, or a spicy sour sauce. The other one is in baked form, as sago bread, the *roti Maluku, sago lempeng* (*B.I.*) or *paputih* (*B.H.*).[79]

Most people in Hila eat sago pudding although it is not the preferred food for all. Many people prefer rice, and some people stated that they, or their children, found it physically impossible to eat it. Most people live on a mixed diet in which sago plays a larger or smaller role, the proportion between sago, rice and cassava (*kasbi*) varying with the preferences and the availability of money to buy imported food. Often, some members of a consumptive unit would not eat sago, but the others would.

Most villagers also eat sago bread, for breakfast, or as additional food stuff at noon or at evening meals. However, rolls and sweets made from wheat flour, which are also baked and sold in the village, are preferred. At ceremonial meals accompanying marriages and burials rice is eaten but sago pudding is added to 'fill the stomachs'. Sweets and cakes which form an indispensable element in such ceremonial meals are made from wheat flour.
- for 73% of the concerned persons sago was one of the major food stuffs eaten;
- for 27% sago was the sole food;
- for 25% sago and cassava were the main food stuffs;

---

[79] Already in 1608, the first Dutch reports of the Ambonese mentioned sago as 'the flour of the Ambonese from which they bake their bread. It is rather tasteful and nutritious, and so the Dutchmen used to prefer it to ship-biscuits' (Steven van de Haghen [1608] in Knaap 1987b: 9).

- for another 21% it was sago besides rice and cassava;
- only 27% stated that their main food was rice.

Sago as a Building Material

Besides being an important foodstuff, materials from the sago palm, leafstalks of various length and thickness (*gabah2*), and leaves (*atap*) have traditionally been used for house construction on Ambon. It is possible to build a house largely from sago materials, and many people still do. It saves expenditures for wood, cement or stones, and for corrugated zinc plates for roofs.

In the meantime, stone houses with zinc roofs have become fashionable. During the 1970s a building boom began in Hila due to the rising income from clove sales. Now about a third of all residences are stone constructions. *Gabah2-houses* are looked upon as being old-fashioned and simple, but as very adequate temporary residences.

Still, even in the 1980s sago plays an important role in house constructions. In Hila, out of the 355 houses which served as living quarters, 45% were thatched with *atap* (sago leaves). Adding to these houses the 71 kitchen buildings (which often are used as sleeping quarters, too), the percentage of all houses thatched with *atap* is 54%. 55 houses (16% of the living quarters) and the 71 kitchens were more or less exclusively built from sago palm material.[80]

Houses in Hila 1985	
stone houses with zinc roofs	148
traditional/wooden houses with zinc roofs	46
stone with *atap* roof	67
traditional houses with *atap* roof	24
wooden houses with *atap* roof	15
gabah2 houses	55
Total	**355**
gabah2 kitchens	71
Total	**426**

---

[80] In the Butonese *kampung* of Hila (Tahoku, Waitomu, Mamua) there was a total of 305 residential dwellings. Out of those 165 (or 54 %) were fully made from *gabah2* and 224 (or 73 %) were thatched with *atap*.

The Production of Sago Food

The Processing of Wet Sago

Wet sago is usually produced by a team of three persons.[81] The work is usually done by younger married men, often brothers or more distant kinsmen or friends. The composition of teams varies frequently. Two of the workers are mainly concerned with the extraction of the sago pith dust from the tree, one with washing out the pith dust. After the palm has been felled and cleared of leaves and thorns, the trunk is divided into blocks of a length of 2 to 2.5 m.[82] These blocks are split open with the help of wooden wedges. The sago fibres are beaten into pith dust[83] with the sago hammer (*naning*). The pith dust is washed and sieved in a tub,[84] and the starch in the muddy reddish water is caught in a reservoir (*lehit*), an old canoe or an empty sago trunk, where it settles and sediments.[85] When there is sufficient starch in the reservoir, the water is let out, and the muddy starch is dried a bit and then put into a basket woven from sago palm leaves, the *tumang*. One basket carries approximately 20 kg of wet sago.[86]

---

[81] The way in which sago is extracted has not significantly changed during the past three and a half centuries; see for one of the earliest descriptions Gijsels [1621] in Knaap 1987b: 34.

[82] The trunk piece (*talal*) is divided from the leaf-crown piece (*uul*). If the palm is divided into more than one block, the middle block is called *etel*.

[83] The rough fibres are called *me-l*, the pith dust *ela*.

[84] The tub (*sahan-lunut*) is made from sago leafstalks. The sieve (*lulut*) is made from coconut leafstalk fibres.

[85] The used *ela* is thrown away (*esi ela*). The starch sediments are called *sisi*.

[86] In Hila, the sago palms harvested during our stay were between 6 and 38 tumang, thus roughly between 120 and 760 kg. The average was 16 tumang, approximately 320 kg. Amount of sago harvested from 34 sago palms in Hila (1985) in tumang (1 tumang app. 20 kg wet sago)

05-10 tumang	5
10-15 tumang	16
16-20 tumang	7
21-25 tumang	4
26-30 tumang	1
35-40 tumang	1

Plate 3.1: The trunk pieces of the sago palm have been split open. The pith dust is hacked with the sago hammer (naning)

Plate 3.2: The pith dust is sieved in the tub (sahane lunut)

Plate 3.3: Villager carrying two tumang

The wet sago kept in the *tumang* used for making sago pudding is called *lapiah* (B.I. *pappeda*) or *lapiah tuma'i (sago tumang)*. It can be stored for approximately 3 months. For shorter periods of time, it can be kept in the leaf baskets. If it is kept for a longer period, the wet sago is kept in *tumpayang*, large bowls. Every two to three days some water has to be added to keep it wet.

Besides for sago pudding, wet sago is used for making *sago tumbuh*, a very favourite sweet made from wet sago, red sugar and santen.

The Processing of sago lempeng

If sago bread *(sago lempeng)* is to be baked from wet sago, the wet sago is ground fine by hand and then dried above a fire. The material then is sieved and filled into the forms of the baking stones *(porna sago,* B.H. *hatu paputih, paputih* stones). These forms have the size of a large brick. The forms are first heated above the fire. Then they are allowed to cool off a bit and are cleaned. The hollow spaces are filled with sago flour, and heated stones are put on top of the filled forms. The stones then are allowed to cool off, the sago being baked in the process. The result is a very hard and tasteless sago bread, which to be eaten has to be dipped into tea, coffee or a sauce. Sago bread can easily be stored for more than three months (reports speak of storage for approximately one year).

Besides sago bread, there are some other forms of processing baked sago. These are two refined versions of sago bread in which it, fresh from the oven, is filled with red sugar *(sago gula)* or chills *(buburne)*.

Access to Sago: The Normative Framework for Production and Distribution

Sago palms, wet sago and sago bread can be acquired through various legal means, by sale, by gifts, by allocation out of a common property stock, by inheritance and by share harvesting/processing. In my description I shall mainly focus upon access to palms since it is of greatest economic importance and access to wet sago to a large extent follows from it.

Access to and control and exploitation of land and economic trees is largely structured by the local *adat* system. This is fully recognized by the state administration and judiciary (see the Moluccan legal document: Pengadilan Tinggi Maluku 1981). The land laws introduced by the various governments have either been absorbed into *adat*, or are rejected by the majority of the population. The Basic Agrarian Law and its implementing regulations are known, but there have been no registrations of agricultural land under the law nor conversions of *adat* rights into the property categories of the law.[87]

Ambonese *adat* makes a distinction between rights to land and rights to trees or gardens, and the persons or groups entitled to land and gardens can be different.[88] There are different forms of legitimate access to sago palms. One is

---

[87] More often than not, land and crop/tree transactions are concluded orally, or a written agreement is witnessed by the village chief. In rare cases, people go to the sub-district head, *Camat,* in order to make up a formal sales document *(akte jual beli)*, as provided by the legislation. But this is not taken to the Office of Agrarian Affairs *(Kantor Agraria)* in order to obtain a formal ownership title *(sertipikat)* (see F. von Benda-Beckmann 1986). The PRONA-registration programme, a programme of fast and cheap registrations by which the government wished to speed up the process of registration, has been a failure in Islamic Ambon. During our stay, the village government tried to find people who would at least have their house sites registered, but without much success.

[88] However, interpretations of *adat* law of Ambon relating to land and trees vary, on village level as well as in the courts (see F. von Benda-Beckmann 1986, 1990a). For a classical account of Ambonese *adat* law concerning land and trees see Holleman 1923.

exclusively based upon individual or shared property rights, in which the 'owner of the sago', the *tuan sago,* exploits his or her own palm. The other is based upon a *ma'anu* agreement, a form of share-harvesting.

Tuan Sago-ship

Tuan sago-ship can be acquired by different mechanisms which represent the different legal statuses of sago palms.

1. Sago palms may be the property of a clan segment (*dati* property). This concerns wild growing sago (mainly *sago tunih*) growing in gardens (*dusun*) which for generations are considered to be the common or shared property of the clan (segment). Shared ownership in the case of *dusun dati* means that all patrilineal *dati* descendants have in principle a right to exploit such trees. Female *dati* members, however, lose this right once they have married out. The allotment of individual trees is subject to the approval of the *dati* elders, in particular of the *kepala dati* whose task it is to control and administer the *dati* lands and trees. Once a tree is allotted to an individual *dati* member, there is no obligation to share the sago with the other members or branches of the clan (segment).
2. Sago palms may be the individual property of the person who has planted it. The sago then is his enterprise (*perusah*), which in most respects has the traits of private ownership, and which entitles the person to the exclusive use of the palm. After his/her death, the palm and its future off-shoots become *pusaka*, inherited property, for his/her heirs.
3. Sago trees can also be bought (*sago babalian*). In this case the buyer's right comes close to full ownership of the tree and its off-shoots. Should the bought trees not be harvested immediately – they may have been bought for future use – and the buyer/owner die, the trees become the *pusaka* of his descendants.
4. It is, however, rare that persons who have planted sago live to harvest it. It is more common that it is the generation of children or grandchildren of the original planter who want to harvest a palm planted by an ascendant, or an off-shoot of such a palm which follows the legal status of the 'mother stool'. Such palms after the planter's death become inherited property (*pusaka*) for his descendants in both lines.

In these cases, sharing is structured by inheritance rights. The *pusaka* property is controlled and administered by the elder men of the group of heirs, who in most cases belong to the generation of grandfathers. It is also on their generation level that the shares of the subgroups entitled to a part of the inheritance are determined. The general principle is that equal shares be given to the branches in the male line. Descendants of females (or females, sisters of the grandparent generation) are also seen as being entitled according to inheritance law. The actual shares given to them, however, vary. It is here that many people invoke the

Islamic law principle according to which male heirs receive twice as large a part as female ones.

The *perusah* and *pusaka* rights to trees on *dati* land pertain to the crops; the land, however, remains under the control of the *dati*. Access to land and trees thus can be subject to different rules, and via inheritance members of different clans may have rights in gardens and/or trees on other clans' *dati* lands.

Should a *dati* become extinct, according to the standard version of Ambonese *adat* (also supported by the state courts as valid *adat* law) the *dati* land falls to the village and can be newly allotted or otherwise used by the village government. Similar principles pertain to previously unexploited land held by the village *(tanah negeri)*. Once a cultivator has made a garden or planted trees, these become his or her individual property, and, after death, *pusaka*. According to classic *adat* (apparently already obsolete in the 1920s, see Holleman 1923) also in these cases the village retained a residual right to the *dati* land. However, in more recent times, *perusah* and *pusaka* come close to full ownership rights on both trees and land.

The land and trees in a sago garden thus generally have an exceedingly complex property structure. The land may be *dati* land, and some palm stools be *dati* property. A great part of the sago stools will be *pusaka*. The *pusaka*, however, will belong to different, though overlapping, groups of heirs: some stools may have been planted by a great-grandfather, and all his descendants who belong to different clans, can claim a right to those palms. Other stools may have been planted by a grandfather or father of the present oldest generation of villagers, and be the *pusaka* of their descendants only. Between the sago stools, there may also be fruit trees, like durian, manggis or langsat trees, some of which may have been given to out-marrying daughters, in the present generation or a generation ago. And some *dati* members may also have planted some clove trees on the land.

Thus, upon a relatively small piece of land, say 70 by 70 m, there may be, and usually is, a very complex set of rights to land and trees of various individuals and various groups, often partly overlapping but usually involving individuals and groups from several clans. It is not surprising that this legal system has been called 'chaotic and precarious' (Holleman 1923: 96, 97).

Share Harvesting

The other form of legitimate access to sago palms is by taking over a tree in a share harvesting arrangement, *ma'anu*, 'eating together'. The general standard for the division of the produce is the relation of 40% for the owner(s) and 60% for the workers. If owners join the workers' team they receive their owner's share as well as their share as one of the workers. The workers divide their share equally. No distinction is made between rasping and washing. Village external share harvesters usually work on a 50:50 basis.

Share-Baking

Although most women bake sago bread themselves, for consumption and for sale, share-baking also occurs. The standard division in these cases is 20% for the woman who does the work and 80% for the women who have provided the wet sago.

Access to Sago: Distribution

Access

Actual access to sago palms and wet sago is structured by this normative framework. It depends, however, on the actual accessibility of these resources. People must have control over sago palms or have to find someone who gives them access by way of *ma'anu*. As was mentioned above, most people acquire sago through their or their children's own labour, on the basis of their owner's or worker's share in *ma'anu* arrangements. Those who buy sago usually belong to those villagers who do not regularly eat sago.

Tuan Sago-ship

Access to sago palms on the basis of individual or shared ownership rights is not evenly distributed in Hila. Most sago gardens are former *dati* areas with wild growing and regenerating palms. In these areas, people have also planted new sago palms which, and the 'children' of which, become *pusaka* in the course of time. The current legal status of the *dati* areas is quite ambiguous. Some villagers maintain that most old sago gardens still have *dati* characteristics and that exploitation and cultivation rights should follow patrilineal descent and inheritance. A majority, however, declared their old sago gardens to be *pusaka*, and distinguished *pusaka* palms belonging to the whole clan (segment) and palms which had become *pusaka* through *perusah* efforts.

These old sago gardens largely belonged to the members of the clans which were regarded as the original settler clans of Hila. Newcomer clans or individual newcomers in the past were incorporated into *dati* groups or were given sago gardens as their own *dati/pusaka* property. This practice has decreased during the past 100 years, so that the more recent newcomers have little or no sago areas of significance.

Sago palms, on clan-wide *dati* or *pusaka* land, are allocated for individual/family consumptive needs by the *dati* or *pusaka* head of that clan segment. This has to occur regularly, since the palms must be harvested before they die out. There is a preference that people should harvest their own (*pusaka*) palms before they lay a claim to the clan property. The *pusaka* palms of groups of heirs are allocated by the elder men in that group.

The extent of actual property rights proved difficult if not impossible to determine during the research. From our series of house interviews it appeared that in 37 houses (78%) people claimed to have access to sago palms on the basis of ownership rights. Eighteen, nearly half of them, stated that they had 'many' sago palms or sago gardens. The reference in these cases, however, was always to *pusaka* complexes in which other persons in other houses had rights as well. In 11 cases (22%) people said that they had no sago of their own, or they evaded clear answers.

Ma'anu

Although sago palm ownership is not evenly distributed in Hila, most villagers willing to rasp sago will find an owner ready to give one or two palms for share-harvesting. Initiatives for *ma'anu* can come from both sides. Sago owners needing sago but not having the labour power, or the desire, to work sago themselves, ask their kin or acquaintances whether they would like to work one or more trees. On the other hand, persons having no, or no suitable trees at their disposal, may approach sago owners asking for a palm to be share-harvested. Most people, who could exploit sago which is not yet fully ripe, will save their own trees for exploitation in future times, when the palm gives its optimal yield and/or when they may be in more need.[89]

For both owners and non-owners, access to labour power therefore is very important, and, given the availability of sufficient sago, sufficient in order to obtain sago. The availability of labour to a large extent depends on the number of kin relations. Poverty in Hila to some extent is 'social' poverty, and persons lacking kin are considered to be poor even if they control significant material wealth (see K. von Benda-Beckmann 1988: 454, 455). If they find no one to rasp their sago trees, the palms will die before being harvested. This dependence of wealthier (in terms of sago palms) persons on labour also softens the exploitative potential inherent in palm ownership.

The sharing arrangements vary slightly. Much depends upon the circumstances of the individual arrangement (friendship, kinship, etc.). However, there seems to be no clear correlation of, e.g. larger shares for owner or workers in the case of kinship or friendship. This is also not to be expected. Giving a larger share to the workers may be considered to be a token of kinship largesse of the owner (controller of the productive resource), but so is the provision of labour for the owner whose labour power may be limited. So they can help each

---

[89] This 'security' strategy was already noted in 1621 by Gijsels. He noted that the Ambonese would use as few of their own trees as possible and would rather go to Seram where sago was abundant. Gijsels speculated that such preventive action was rooted in the wish to store resources in expectation of future warfare (Gijsels [1621] in Knaap 1987b: 35).

other in both directions. I have never heard of instances where the manner of division led to a discussion, or unfriendly comment of one of the parties.

Plate 3.4: Great quantities of sago are produced by larger teams in masohi cooperation as provision for the fasting month

Unmonetized Distribution

Primary Distribution

Most wet sago is distributed in a non-monetized way on the basis of the *pusaka* and *ma'anu* distribution rules mentioned above. If workers, or workers and owners, belong to the same consumptive unit, 'pooling' (house-holding, Polanyi 1966) takes place. Each of them brings in his sago for the shared consumption. In such cases, the *lapiah/pappeda* will be cooked and eaten together, and the sago bread is baked for the consumptive needs of all members. But this usually does not involve all the sago harvested. Each person who acquires sago could sell a basket for his own needs (cigarettes). Also, if sago bread is baked for sale, the money obtained will be kept separately by the individual women and not automatically be put into a common fund, or come under the control of a senior male or female. Even if women work together, and the earnings are shared, it will be clear to all concerned whose sago was baked into sago bread.

Secondary Distribution

Once the wet sago has been divided according to these rules, some part of it usually is further distributed to relatives, neighbours and friends on the basis of general reciprocity. One or two baskets, for instance, may be given to persons who have no right to share in the produce, although they may have stronger or weaker claims on the basis of the social relation they have with the possessor.

Such sago giving usually occurs when sago palms are harvested. But it is a particular feature of sago distribution occurring in the weeks before the fasting month. The fasting month is a period for which villagers require extra amounts of food, since more food than regularly is consumed and food production comes to a near stand still during this period. The weeks before the fasting month are used to generate a sufficient food supply, in sago and other foodstuffs like rice and flour. Thus relatively more sago is rasped during these weeks. Besides, the period before the fasting, and the holidays following the end of the fasting month (*hari raya, lebaran*) are ones in which good Muslims engage in gift giving. Of the sago rasped before fasting, gifts of sago to elderly and needy relatives and neighbours regularly occur. The obligatory alms, *zakat al fitrah*, which Muslims have to give in the night before *hari raya*, in Hila alone involves the redistribution of more than 2 tons of rice (see F. von Benda-Beckmann 1988). In the past, but also in more recent periods when rice was less available, these *zakat* food gifts were also given in the form of sago.[90]

---

[90] Apart from sago, rice and other food also is distributed by the government to civil servants. The 'dividends' of the government initiated social security projects are also distributed in the form of food (see K. von Benda-Beckmann 1988).

Food Spreading

This distribution has the effect that the produce of any single sago palm is spread over a considerable number of consumptive units. On the level of production workers, usually members of 2 or 3 different consumptive units are involved. On the level of owners, there are also usually 2 or more owners involved. It occurs, of course, that one of the owners and one of the workers are members of the same consumptive unit. But generally, the primary distribution of the wet sago will involve 4 to 6 consumptive units. In addition, one or two consumptive units will receive sago through the processes of secondary distribution.

The distribution of sago over consumptive units thus is rather complex. As an illustration, I shall give a (quit e typical) example of the family of our n eighbours already mentioned earlier.

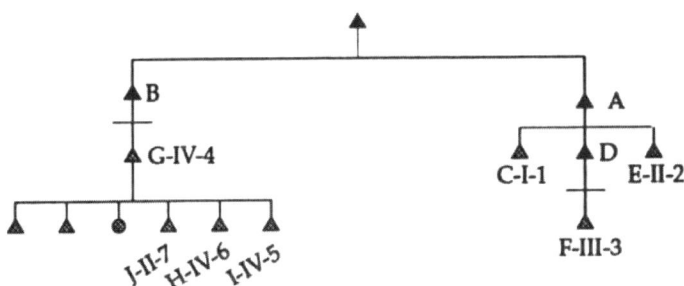

Figure 3.1: The Tree of Haji Abbas: Diagram of the Relationships

A-J = persons involved in production and sharing
(B = Hadi; A = Haji Abbas)
I-IV = houses (*e.g.* House I)
1-7 = kitchens/consumptive units involved (*e.g.* Kitchen 1)

The three brothers H, I, and J had worked a sago palm which had originally been owned by their grandfathers the father of A and B. He had divided the sago palms between his sons A and B. During the period of the study, C controlled the palms of their descent line. E was too old and weak to do so. The three brothers, C, E, G, harvested 15 baskets. Of these, 6 were for the owners, two each for the two sons of A and for D, their deceased brother's son F, H, I, and J received 9 baskets, three each. They each gave one to their father G. Thus the sago of a single palm was distributed among 7 consumptive units and over 4 houses.

Sago in Monetized Exchange

Not all sago is distributed in this way. Some wet sago is also bought and sold within Hila. The standard price during our stay was 2.000 rupiah per basket of about 20 kg. Sago is not offered was 2.000 rupiah per basket of about 20 kg.[91] Sago is not offered publicly for sale. People ask you when you are busy processing sago or when you come home with sago, whether they can buy some. Or the fact that some surplus sago is for sale is made known among friends or neighbours. It is not brought to the market in Ambon.[92] There are different types of monetized transfer:

Accidental Excess

It is quite normal that excess sago not needed for one's own consumptive needs is sold. Often when the number of baskets cannot be divided in a way that everyone gets an even share, the excess is sold for '*uang rokok*', to buy cigarettes. Excess baskets are also sold on a somewhat larger scale to obtain some extra money. However, in both such situations the sago has been primarily produced for one's own consumption.

Wet Sago as Petty Commodity

This is different, however, in those cases in which sago is produced for obtaining a money income. In contemporary Hila, only a few men make the production and sale of sago one of their main sources of income. During our stay in 1985 and 1986, there were only two of such teams. One team consisted of three brothers, who regularly bought the trees. The other team consisted of two brothers and a friend or kinsman, who preferred share-harvesting. Both teams were rather permanent.

The degree to which villagers engage in sago production as one of their main income generating activities has varied historically, and also varies now. In contemporary Hila, it seems to flourish only in times of relative prosperity. When in 1986 clove prices decreased and people saw their actual or prospective money income from clove production dwindle, the sago producers were out of work. Nobody wanted to buy sago anymore. People went themselves to produce sago.

Sago Bread

Not all sago harvested and distributed is used for sago pudding. In nearly every consumptive unit, sago bread also is baked, for one's own consumption and for sale. Most village women bake their own sago bread. However, women of

---

[91] 1 kg of rice at that time cost 350 to 400 rupiah.
[92] During our stay in 1985 and 1986 there was only one stand at the Ambon market where *sago tumang* was sold (from Tulehu).

higher social and economic status often ask other women to bake sago bread for them.

Sago bread is sold in the village along the road. Sometimes, women bake more and bring it to the market in Ambon city. Here, the sago bread made from one basket (money value 2,000 rupiah) yields approximately 5,000 rupiah (in 1985 and 1986). Going to Ambon, however, involved 1,400 rupiah in bus fares, 500 rupiah for the bus transport, 100 rupiah in market dues and another 100 for the boy who would carry the sago bread to the market place.

Analysis

Sago and Food Security

Let me now return to the characteristics of food security mentioned earlier and try to show how the Ambonese mode of producing and distributing sago relates to them.

The Ambonese food economy is a mixed economy. Within this encompassing system, the production and distribution of sago for the greatest part are still oriented toward livelihood and not to profit, and come close to what Sahlins calls the 'domestic mode of production' (1974a: 83), in which the producers' relation to the production process is one of use values, even though exchange may be involved (see also Krause-Katerla 1986). While the scope of subsistence production is largely influenced by the 'rest' of the economy – the availability and prices of other foodstuff, the money resources of villagers, the availability and value of labour – neither the production nor the exchange of sago or sago products is commoditized to a significant degree.

Sago still plays a significant role in the system of food provision and housing. Apart from the actual use in contemporary Hila, the flexibility of sago provides a safety-net for unmonetized access to food and house construction material should the provision of these requirements be threatened. Sago can be used to substitute for rice and wheat flour on a much larger scale than is done now. The same goes for house building materials. When people no longer can afford the ever rising expenditures for wood, cement, zinc, they can fall back on sago. *Gabah2* houses can serve as semi-permanent housing for young married couples and as cheap housing for the poorer section of the population.

The relative high degree of food security is maintained by a number of closely interrelated factors.

The absence of a commodity market for sago within and outside the Ambon-Seram region is, in more or less direct ways, important for the characteristics of food security mentioned by Barraclough. It gives the sago producers and consumers a high degree of autonomy and self-determination over these food resources by making access to the resources independent from external market fluctuations. This is also important for the reliability of the foodstuff. Sago is, by virtue of its botanical nature, available all year round and not subject to seasonal variations. Ambonese villagers are therefore less threatened by the *musin paceklik,* the pre-(rice)harvest period in which villagers in rice producing areas are faced with food shortage. Within the village contexts, there are cyclical deficit phases, but they can be overcome relatively easily by going to Seram, as long as the sago resources there remain accessible on a non-commoditized basis, and as long as no incentives channel them out of the region.

Since the demand for sago is determined by the flexible consumptive needs within the region, the dangers to the ecosystem are minimal, and the long term stability of the ecosystem used for sago production can be maintained. This also is relevant for the ecosystem surrounding the sago areas. As long as Ambonese eat much sago, the less new forest land has to be taken in shifting cultivation for other food crops like cassava which would lead to an increase of erosion and soil degradation.

Given the general accessibility of sago in the region, the relative dependable access to the sago resources and forms of rather equitable distribution are made possible through the legal regulations concerning property and labour relations. The provision of dependable access to sago, and the relatively high degree of equity in its distribution derive from the absence of large scale concentration of sago resources in the hands of a small number of small social units. This also enhances the relative autonomy and self-determination of the Central Moluccans over production and distribution of sago.

Saying that it is subsistence production and its legal regulation and/or the absence of a sago market which contributes to food security in the Central Moluccas comes dangerously close to a tautology. It therefore is important to see that it is not 'subsistence production' or 'legal regulation' as such which are relevant. Rather, it is the specific nature of the production process of a specific food crop and its specific regulation which exhibits those characteristics of food security. For our analysis of the present situation and for our consideration of its implications for future scenarios we must therefore take a closer look at the interrelatedness of the type of food, the technology employed and the legal regime under which production and distribution take place.

Subsistence and Property Law

It is specific for sago production that a) the produce of any single harvested sago palm supplies sufficient food for several consumptive units for about three months, the period in which wet sago can be stored rather unproblematically, and b) that the legal status of the resource and of the labour process ensures that the produce of any single palm is indeed distributed over a large number of consumptive units. It is this specific interrelation of property and labour in the process of production and economic transfers which gives sago subsistence production its distinctive character.

In this, we see a threefold distributive mechanism at work:

1. The employed simple technology and the hard physical work which sago production involves lead to the involvement of three labourers who, given the social organization of residence and consumption, tend to belong to different consumptive units.
2. Since sago property is controlled by older persons, and the labour is done by younger men, the production tends to lead regularly to a division between owners/controllers and workers.
3. Since most sago property is *pusaka*, there is usually also a division on the level of the owners/controllers.

Given the sporadic and ad hoc character of sago production, the configurations of owners and labourers also tend to be different, so no really permanent arrangements come into existence.

In case of clan-wide *dati* or *pusaka* property, the last distributory mechanism does not occur, yet the other two still would ensure that the harvested sago be spread over several consumptive units.

Besides this primary relation of production and distribution, secondary forms of distribution take place. Since the access to sago is relatively easy, there regularly is some excess sago, and since there is neither a market nor a commodity ideology for sago, people find it quite easy to give some part of their harvested sago to friends or kinsmen who would not be entitled to this purely on the basis of the distribution rules.

I emphasize these points since the specificity of sago subsistence elements cannot be adequately analysed in terms of the conventional categories which have been developed by economic anthropologists (see Polanyi 1966, Sahlins 1974a, Elwert 1980a, b). Nor do they fit the general image in which property law is related to economic activities.

Usually it is assumed that in subsistence, productive and consumptive unit coincide. However, sago subsistence production is not based upon units of production which are identical with units of consumption (or 'households'). However such units – household, houses, or consumptive units – may be defined, the production of sago, whether seen as organized input of labour, or as the combination of owners and workers, always involves members of several of such units. The Ambonese case, thus, is another example showing that the analysis of subsistence economic activities should not proceed from such assumptions, a point which has been made cogently by Elwert (1980a, b), Evers et al. (1984), and Wong (1984).[93]

Sago production on Ambon can best be seen as an ad hoc cooperation which integrates members of different consumptive units in a joint productive effort, and in which sharing is prescriptive. This structure of cooperation and distribution cannot be fitted into the conventional categories of reciprocities or pooling. One cannot say that the sago share of owners or workers is 'temporarily withdrawn from one's own sphere of consumption' (Elwert 1980a: 683) because it has never been in that sphere. Elwert's conception of traditional solidarity[94] or reciprocity, like Sahlins before him, involves the stipulation of two sides, social duality and symmetry, two distinct economic interests (Sahlins 1974a: 189). Reciprocity, as Sahlins states, can establish solidarity in social relations, insofar as the material flow suggests assistance or mutual benefit, yet the social fact of sides is inescapable (1974a: 189). Although some sago transfers based upon reciprocal social relations occur, the core of sago distribution according to *pusaka* rules is not found in such type of 'between' relation (1974a: 88).

Ambonese sago production can neither be accommodated in terms of the categories of 'pooling', or of 'house-holding' (Polanyi) as a specific type of pooling. Pooling and house-holding of sago occur in Ambonese villages, when owners and production workers bring in their sago share into their consumptive unit. But again this is secondary. 'The production process and the spreading of sago do not involve a centralized collection and redivision within a group' (Sahlins 1974a: 188-190).[95]

---

[93] As a consequence of the assumed coincidence of productive and consumptive units, cooperation and sharing *between* consumptive units have rarely been considered systematically as an element in the relations of production. Elwert in particular has argued that non-monetized production and transfers of goods (and services) on the basis of reciprocal inter-household relations or 'traditional solidarity' should be considered to be part of the production relations. He argues that 'where subsistence production still determines the economy and where consequently traditional solidarity still exists, there are obligations to divide and transfer goods which systematically distribute a part of the produced goods beyond the productive units. In the conception of people one's own need includes the need of those whom one is obliged to help (Elwert 1980b: 350, 352). In his research in Benin, he has shown the considerable redistributive effect of those transfers (1980a: 682 and 1980b: 364). In his example, 25% of maize harvested by Beninese farmers was distributed within the inter-household relations of help/solidarity.

[94] Under 'traditional solidarity' Elwert understands a system of transfers of goods and services, serving the improvement of the chances of survival and standard of living of other persons. By such transfers, goods and services are temporarily and immediately withdrawn from one's own sphere of consumption; in the long term, this also serves one's own interest (Elwert 1980a: 683, my translation).

[95] The Ambonese sago spreading is not characterized by 'centricity' or by a 'within-relation' (Sahlins 1974a: 88, 188). Pooling stipulates a social centre where the goods

This requires a closer look at the legal dimension of labour relations and property, 'this salient aspect in the organization of production and distribution' (Sahlins 1974a: 92). Sahlins assumed (and demonstrated with ethnography) that in a domestic mode of production, there is a certain autonomy in the realm of property which strengthens each household's devotion to its own interest. He asserted that this also holds in forms of property regimes which are generally called common, communal or family property/ownership, for under the level of clan/chiefly or family ownership, the individual households get usufruct rights. The communal level of property rights, Sahlins argues, is typically superimposed on the family rather than interposed between the family and its means of production. While a household in tribal society is usually not the exclusive owner of its resources, it retains the primary relation to productive resources (1974a: 93). Therefore, relations of reciprocity or pooling can exist also between/in social groups which are considered to be 'co-owners'.

Sahlins' observation shall not be disputed here since it does fit many property regimes that go under the name of family or common ownership.[96] However, it does not fit the structure of sago *pusaka* production and sharing, where the rules about *pusaka* co-ownership and *ma'anu* co-operation do define the primary relations of production and distribution.

Analytical and Practical Implications for Future Scenarios

From the above analysis we can also see that food security could be undermined from a number of directions:

- The commercialization of sago in a market located outside the Ambon-Seram region.
- The introduction of a more effective technology.
- The individualization and simplification of rights to sago palms.

As in the case of the current system, these factors should be viewed as interrelated and mutually reinforcing. The process of change may start in any of these factors and would lead to changes also in the others.

Thus the individualization of rights to palms would lead to a decrease of the sharing/spreading mechanisms and also weaken one of the constraints on the alienation of palms, a precondition for palm property concentration. Though not

---

meet and thence flow outwards, and a social boundary, too, within which persons or subgroups are cooperatively related (Sahlins 1974a: 188, 189).

[96] The system of property relations to inherited property in Minangkabau lineages which I have analysed in detail elsewhere (F. von Benda-Beckmann 1979) would be a good example.

a necessary condition for an increasing commercialization of sago exchange, it would most probably encourage such a development.

The introduction of a more effective technology (rasping machine, semi-automatic production) would reduce the number of workers required to harvest one or a few palms. Besides, it would be an important step in the commoditization of productive inputs, likely to result in restricting the numbers of producers. Such developments would reduce sharing. For there would be fewer occasions in which the sago produce would be distributed according to the rules described earlier. Commercialization and commoditization of sago would bring with them the demand of a money input for food. Consumptive units would buy their own food supply only for themselves. One would have to expect that also the current amount of secondary distribution would decrease as a consequence, and that also the ideological framework of helping and sharing would weaken since they would be less frequently maintained through actual social activity.

It thus can be expected that efforts to commercialize sago for export on a great scale would have consequences detrimental to food security. The accessibility of sago would decrease. One could expect a concentration of sago-ownership in the hands of fewer persons, and of the control over production and distribution in the hands of even fewer. In times of bad economic conditions, people would have less money to buy food. Switching to root crops would be harmful for the ecology.

The modernization of technology and the creation of an external market for sago would therefore constitute a grave danger to the food security based upon sago. This is not pure speculation, but would be a development similar to the one which has already occurred in the sago village in Riau described by Takaya (1986). He describes the far reaching changes brought about by the introduction of a new sago processing technology, a rotary rasper driven by engine (the piring) at first, and later of sago factories, and by the commercialization of sago production (1986: 92, 93). Since the factories required a large and constant supply of sago trees, the factories bought up sago from the villagers. Those who sold their trees naturally lost the chance to process sago themselves. 'Some of them became wage labourers in the sago factories' (1986: 93). Those who did not sell were also drawn into the new system of sago production. The hand driven rasper was slow and inefficient and could not compete with the machine, and people had to give up the hand driven rasper whether they liked it or not (1986: 93). When sago business boomed in the 1960s, the cultivation area expanded. A semi-automatic factory *(pabrik)* appeared in the village in 1975. In 1984, 12 such factories were operating. All of them were Chinese owned (1986: 94). This brought with it an even greater demand for sago palms, and even more sago land was bought up (1986: 97-98). As a consequence of these developments, ownership patterns changed drastically. More than half of all sago land (59%), which formerly was rather evenly distributed among the Malayan population, is virtually in Chinese hands (1986: 96), and only 3% of all sago production are still controlled by Malayans. Many Malayans today buy sago for home consumption from Chinese shops (1986: 97).

Adat (Law) and Economic Change

Since attempts to either encourage or prevent such processes of modernization as occurred in Riau would be faced with the local legal system, it is important to look at the relations between law and economic change in the Ambonese context.

We have seen that the Ambonese law relating to control, production and distribution of sago plays an important role in food security, and helps to keep at distance the commercialization of sago. These food spreading rules are further embedded in an exceedingly complex system in which different property rights are connected to a variety of social units (individuals and groups) with respect to a differentiated set of small property units, which inhibits the isolation of differentiated property relations between a small number of producers and large amounts of productive resources.

However, it is not these legal forms, or some 'traditional' or communal character of the local law as such, which have this effect. It is the particular connection of rights to resources (property and labour), a particular form of local law tied to a particular form of production, which maintains the present system. If this connection were dissolved, a change of the local law would probably not be required in order to change the sago economy. Commercialization, individualization, and in its wake less dependable and equitable access to sago (and to productive resources in general) could occur under the present local law. Other sets of *adat* rules could structure also more commercially oriented forms of sago production. Sago trees *can* be bought in Ambonese villages. It is not obligatory to work in teams of three people. If modern technology would be employed, one person could do the work, and one of the spreading factors would fall away. There is nothing in Ambonese *adat* rules as rules, which would prevent the large scale ownership of huge sago reserves necessary for a large scale capitalist exploitation of the sago reserves. *Adat* would not prevent the emergence of the unity between individual sago palm owner and producer required for petty commodity production. It is therefore not the type of *adat* property rights which would inhibit such developments, but the complex structure in which different property rights to differentiated property objects are connected to a variety of social units.

It is thus not the law – in the sense of a body of abstract rules and principles – which would have to change, but the specific combination of certain rules to a certain mode of production. Attempts to replace the *adat* rule system with a more 'modern' law therefore are likely to be frustrated as long as sago subsistence production is continued. In fact, such introduction would not be necessary, for it already exists in the form of Indonesian agrarian legislation. The fact that no agricultural land has been transformed yet to the individualistic property rights embedded in the state-made agrarian laws is good evidence for this.

Outlook

Such a future scenario is not very appealing. One should take care not to let such developments occur before there is a realistic means of safeguarding the present degree of food security for the rural population. And there are no really feasible alternatives in view. Given the fact that on the densely populated island of Ambon population pressure is already critical, a further expansion of food crop production would be a danger to the ecology. No other food would have the combination of an ideal relation between the production of energy per man-day or hectare (Flach and Luning 1983: 13, 14) and a high degree of labour absorption (see ESCAP 1985). A reduction of unmonetized food supply in the villages would also stimulate migration into the city of Ambon, a development likely to cause (or increase) widespread urban poverty. Apart from the production of cash crops, the chances of earning money through other economic activities to enable rural people to buy imported food are dim. The high costs of transport of imported goods, 'which hold the Ambonese in a firm grip of subsistence and self-sufficiency' (Flach and Luning 1983: 12) is not likely to be broken. The development of industry as an alternative for earning money to buy food also is not very promising. So far, it has not had a visible employment effect, as the plywood factories on Ambon and Seram, show for the labour has been recruited largely from outside the province (LTA 72 1983: 5.13).

These points should be particularly emphasized since the predominant attitude of local agricultural and extension officials is strongly commodity oriented (Flach and Luning 1983: 9), and prospects for the development of sago are mainly seen in marketing prospects (NEI 1982: 4.2). Also, the proposed regionalization of the province's economic organization, in which the island of Ambon is cut loose from the sago reservoirs in Western Seram (NEI 1982: 60, 61), would negatively affect food security. As long as there are no alternatives for safeguarding food security in sight, development planners should think *preventively,* about protecting those elements of the contemporary food supply system which indeed seem to guarantee food security. They should also consider that any successful engagement of the rural population in commercial economic activities will have to be based upon food security. Instead of being a major step towards the modernization of the Ambonese economy, the commercialization of the subsistence food reservoir may turn out to destroy any prospect for such modernization.

Chapter 4
Houses, People and Residence
The Fluidity of Ambonese Living Arrangements*

Franz and Keebet von Benda-Beckmann

Introduction

Over the past 15 years the debates about 'the household' have reached a high level of sophistication. The 'black box', as the household has been described, has been opened (Niehof 1994). Its contents have proved to be a rich variety of diverse relationships, undermining the explicit or implicit assumptions that households were so uniform and homogeneous in relevant social and economic aspects that they could serve as a useful basis for scientific analysis and comparison as well as for planning. From the side of women's studies it has been pointed out that women hold a different position in households than men. There is also general consensus now that households cannot be easily separated from the social world outside because household members have diverse relationships with persons living in other houses which may be more intensive and important than contacts with the persons within the same house: The internal and external relationships of persons living together in a house thus have been submitted to intensive scrutiny.

One of the virtues of the critique of the household concept has been to show how much variation is subsumed under this term, how varied the patterns of internal and external cooperation are, and how these change over time and throughout the life-cycle. This variation is captured by distinguishing types of households in terms of composition and authority or representational structure (male- or female-headed). The explanation of the variation in the social economic functions of households then is usually sought in the composition of the household – or the hearthhold – and in economic and practical considerations (see, e.g. Finch 1989: 25). However, the conditions under which people live to-

---

* First published 2000 in: J. Koning, M. Nolten, J. Rodenburg, and R. Saptari (eds.), *Women and Households in Indonesia. Cultural Notions and Social Practices*, pp. 102-141. Richmond, Surrey: Curzon Press.

gether in houses and which underlie the variation in the composition of households as co-resident units have rarely been analysed systematically.

In this chapter we shall argue that for such an analysis it is not enough to open the 'black box' and look to see what is inside; we also have to look at the black box itself, examine its physical structure and social meaning, and question the reasons for the structure and composition of co-residing people. The physical structure and social meaning of a house itself are important explanatory factors of variation in the composition of and cooperation among inhabitants. The purpose of this chapter is to examine the relationships between houses, common accommodation and cooperation in the most important aspects of social and economic life. In particular we are interested to see the extent to which residence affects gender differences. As will become clear, residence is not merely a way of locating persons and identifying them with a certain space and house as a place of accommodation. Residence also localizes economic activities, or at least the profits of economic activities; and it is a way of localizing people's political positions, rights and obligations.[97] By shifting the focus from households as the basic social unit to co-residence, we hope to contribute to the further unravelling of the concept of the household. This perspective allows for a widening of the explanations that might account for cooperation and network formation and maintenance through shared accommodation. After a discussion of the current household critiques and the implication these critiques should have for the study of residence, we shall demonstrate our approach with an analysis of residence in the village of Hila, a Muslim village on the north coast of the island of Ambon.[98] We shall address three sets of issues which together provide an analysis of residence that takes houses as such into account.

1. Variation in the association between people and houses. We shall start by describing the variation in residential arrangements, their stability or fluidity. We shall trace groups of people through the various houses in which they live during their lifetime. And we shall also look at different types of houses, and at their social history (Appadurai 1986, Kopytoff 1986).

---

[97] In some societies, an individual's residence in these different senses may be located in different houses or different parts of the village territory. See F. and K. von Benda-Beckmann 1978 and F. von Benda-Beckmann 1979 for these different aspects of residence in Minangkabau *nagari* [village state, village].

[98] We carried out field research on rural (in)security in the Central Moluccas during 11 months in 1985 and 1986. The research was sponsored by the Faculty of Law of Universitas Pattimura and the Indonesian Institute for Scientific Research (LIPI). See for earlier publications K. von Benda-Beckmann 1988, 1991a, 1992, 1996; F. von Benda-Beckmann 1987, 1990a, 1990b; F. and K. von Benda-Beckmann 1994a, 1995, 1998; F. von Benda-Beckmann and Taale 1992, 1996.

2. The conditions of co-residence. We shall then examine the conditions under which co-residence comes about. We shall look at the legal regulations structuring co-residential arrangements, at the social structure and social relationships which lead to the formation, or termination of such arrangements and at the strategies developed to deal with these factors.

3. The significance of co-residence for social, economic, political, religious and ritual cooperation and organization. Finally we approach the question of what co-residing means: In what ways is the fact that people live together in one house important to the organization of their lives? What do they do that people not living in one house do not do? What variation do we encounter here, and what are the social, legal, cultural and ecological factors that underlie these variations?

Household Critiques and their Implications

In the recent debates about households a pragmatic-political and a theoretical line can be discerned. The pragmatic line comes first of all from politicians and administrators, from census and tax officials. The more involved the state administration became in controlling village life, the smaller the administrative units with which it dealt became. Sometimes these units had to be created in order to facilitate administration. These units were narrowed down from villages, via clans and lineages to households, i.e. a unit formed by houses and the people living in them. Like all the other units, households were seen, or deemed to be represented by a head who was typically a male, the presumed authority in the household. Indirect rule was thereby brought to the lowest level of social organization. Officials may not always have chosen the most relevant or enduring form of social organization for their administrative system. The unity of people co-residing in a house, created by this household concept, may not everywhere have been functionally very important in other social, economic, political or ritual spheres of life. Yet it was a practical choice. Households have the advantage that they tie people to territorially fixed and bounded space – thus getting rid of more or less vaguely localized and bounded units such as the family or the clan, while avoiding having to deal with each individual separately. The administrators therefore should not be reproached. They had no pretensions to elevate their pragmatic administrative unit to the analytical level. They were not concerned with theories on tribal subsistence or peasant economies or comparative analyses of co-residential units across time and space. Their task was simply to count people and to levy taxes, and the household served these purposes well. Only when they started to design economic and social policies based on the assumption of homogeneous households did they run into trouble.

Pragmatic considerations also undoubtedly played a part in the increasing popularity of the household unit for social scientists. Houses are a convenient location to gather data. Besides, the economic and political significance of more encompassing social units or categories (like lineages, clans and tribes) seemed to have faded with the increasing incorporation of local social organization into wider political and economic networks and institutions. Rather than drawing intricate genealogical diagrams or tracing spatially dispersed members of lineages or extended families, social scientists found it easier to map households, which were more readily identifiable, if only because these had been identified by the state administration as the new building-blocks of social organization. To some extent, research – and in particular development and action-oriented research carried out under time constraints of rapid rural appraisals and oriented at the objectives of development projects – simply had to adapt to such constraints, often against better judgement.

More important, however, seems to have been the other, theoretical descent line of the household. For social anthropologists, development sociologists and economic theorists of subsistence or peasant production, the household provided a recurring frame of reference and challenge, as evidenced in Sahlins' ideas of the domestic mode of production (1974a), the 'classical battle line Lenin vs. Chayanov' (Wong 1987: 15), and the assumptions and propositions of the new household economics (Ellis 1988). Although the concepts of 'peasants', 'domestic group', 'family farm' and 'household' had different connotations, the household was regarded as *the* social unit of income pooling and consumption sharing, of production and reproduction, and of joint decision-making. So strong was this functional unity of the household that it became reified and personalized: the household became an actor in that it allocated labour, it had needs and utility functions, and it pursued strategies (see Whitehead 1990).

These theories form the background against which much contemporary critical research in rural areas in developing countries has been carried out. It has given researchers concepts and propositions to test. Over the past 15 years an impressive body of ethnographical evidence and theoretical argument has been built up by social scientists and economists; researchers of gender relations in particular having made important contributions. The evidence shows convincingly that the concept of the household and the assumptions built into it were rarely empirically supported and were theoretically misleading, at best superficial. Many authors have shown that in the societies they studied, the people co-residing in a house did not always form units of income pooling, consumption and production, and they pointed at the methodological consequences for the study of production and reproduction of rural people, (e.g. Cohen 1976, Elwert 1980b, Evers et al. 1984, Wong 1984, Fapohunda 1988, Wolf 1990 and 1992). The assumptions of new household economics based on the household as an 'actor' have been convincingly criticized, (e.g. Guyer and Peters 1987, Dwyer and Bruce 1988, Folbre 1988, Guyer 1988).

Gender studies in particular have questioned these propositions and have pointed to the divisions of labour and the power relationships within households, the differential power, needs, wishes and strategies of members of a household (Whitehead 1990, Moore 1994). The external relationships of persons living together in a house thus have been submitted to intensive scrutiny. Furthermore, the relations between (members of different) households were shown to play an important role in the economic and social organization (see Elwert 1980b, Wong 1984). Consequently, it was argued, researchers must pay attention to intra-household differences and differentiation, as well as to inter-household relations and networks.[99]

What were the implications to be drawn from these critiques? One way out has been the continued search for 'fundamental' social units. If earlier understandings and definitions of the household could not be substantiated empirically and consequently flawed theories in which these understandings figured prominently, then perhaps a more narrowly defined social unit would do: the household redefined as a hearthhold, as universal social unit in which at least the most important social functions for consumption and reproduction converged (Van den Berg 1997). Others have adopted a fresh perspective on social and economic organization in which households, however defined, would not a priori play a major analytical role, but would be just one, potentially important, unit within and among the wider sets of supra-individual relationships and social institutions. As Wong has argued 'the fundamental fallacy of this approach lies in its methodology – that of an analysis built around a unit defined a priori rather than analytically derived concepts that would focus on attention on processes' (Wong 1984, see also Guyer and Peters 1987). Already in 1979 Yanagisako concluded in her review that

> it seems to be more analytically strategic to begin with the investigation of the activities that are central to the domestic relationships in each particular society, rather than with its domestic groups. If we start with identifying the important productive, ritual, political and exchange transactions in a society and only then proceed to ask what kinds of kinship or locality-based units engage in these activities, and in what manner, we decrease the likelihood of overlooking some of these salient

---

[99] The extensional character of network ties, Wong argued, is as crucial to the reproduction of the individual as the inclusion principle of bounded units (1984: 61). Alderson-Smith (1984) introduced the term 'confederation of households' to indicate the spreading of sources of livelihood over several households. In addition, it has been pointed out that households, in the sense of people with a common residence who share food and a kitchen, do not form static entities, but evolve throughout the life-cycle of its members and change in composition. See Kloek 1981: 25ff; Niehof 1985: 158; Freiberg-Strauss and Jung 1988; Wolf 1990: 43ff.

units, particularly those that do not fit our conventional notion of household (Yanagisako 1979: 186).

We certainly subscribe to such a functional approach. However, we feel that the further implications of these critiques have not been fully drawn. Despite these new approaches, the concept has shown remarkable tenacity and the most severe critics have been reluctant to discard it altogether. Through a lack of alternatives, it still seems to be taken for granted too easily that households, however generally defined, are somehow the basic units of living, however open, dynamic and stratified these units may be. They are still used as 'counting units' to forming the basis of comparisons, which begs the question of whether they are indeed the basic units or not. As long as the concept remains the point of departure for the description and analysis of social and economic life, the concept, and the empirical variations that it captures, are not made subject to systematic analysis itself.

A Residence Perspective

In the critical discussions demonstrating what households are not, too little attention has been given to what they are, namely co-residential units. While there have been many excellent studies showing the variation in co-residential units, and consequently the quite different positions which such units assume in social and economic organizations, few if any have seriously looked into the nature of the association between people and houses and asked how people find shelter, and why and under what conditions they share accommodation. To be fair, various aspects are discussed in many studies,[100] but the box itself – its size and quality, value, location and its symbolic and legal status – has remained surprisingly unproblematic. The question is what difference these characteristics could make for the constellation of people living in or moving out of the box. The house, as a spatial physical unit, is usually directly tied to and made dependent on the social boundary created by it. In most approaches, this connection is constitutive of the household as a unit of analysis, rather than becoming subject to analysis.

However, in order to study the association between people and houses, we need the analytical dissociation of houses and the people living in them. Houses are physical structures and social spaces. Houses vary in size, degree of comfort, building materials, and the amount and kind of labour required for building and maintenance. They may vary from small temporary dwellings

---

[100] See Bender 1967. Niehof (1985: 184), for example, has touched upon this subject, when discussing the reasons that may influence the decision of whether a young couple on Madura will live patri-, matri- or neolocally.

made exclusively from local materials to large modern buildings, and from individual houses to family houses. In most societies, both physical structures and the constellations of people living within them are highly variable, synchronically and diachronically. The composition of co-residing units, their stability and social and economic functions are likely to be strongly influenced by these factors. A residence perspective, moreover, should not be confined to those aspects of residence concerned with domestic and economic life. It should also take into account the socio-political aspects of residence, e.g. residence in areas with higher or lower social status, and the localization of political rights, which may be important in the residential strategies of people as motivation or constraint (F. and K. von Benda-Beckmann 1978).

These issues have to be clarified before other questions can be addressed, for example: What is the significance of co-residential groups in different domains of social organization and in comparison with other important social units? What difference does co-residence make to social organization? From this perspective, the focus is not on a predefined unit, but on variation in co-resident groups and on the explanation of this variation: on the dynamics of residential arrangements; and on the constraining and enabling conditions under which people start or stop living together, move into other houses or build new houses – conditions which also largely structure whatever social and economic significance co-residing groups have. Finally this perspective allows us to look at the problem of housing (in)security, notably of people who are particularly constrained in their access to shelter due to social, economic or physical characteristics.

Variation in Residence

Houses and Co-residing People in Hila

Variation in Houses
The village (*negeri*) of Hila is a conglomeration of settlements. Coming from the city of Ambon by road and approaching Hila by the border with the neighbouring village of Wakal, one first passes through three Butonese settlements, the *kampung* of Mamua, Waitomu and Tahoku. At the western edge of Tahoku there is a complex of new government buildings since Hila became the sub-district capital in 1980, as well as the buildings of the local clinic (PUSKESMAS), the village cooperative (KUD), a post office, and a research institute on fisheries established in the 1990s. Approaching Hila proper, the residential pattern becomes increasingly dense, particularly in the village core area. The variety of housing within and between these residential areas is striking, each type of housing providing living space of different quality and embodying

Plate 4.1: Village house, built for permanent residence. The roof is thatched with sago leaves. The upper part of the walls is made by pieces of sago leaf-stalks

Plate 4.2: Modern house with zinc roof and stone and concrete construction, built by Ambonese family living in the Netherlands

different construction materials and labour processes. The following categories can be distinguished (see Figure 4.1):

1. Houses made more or less completely from sago palm leafstalks, called *gaba-gaba*, and thatched with sago leaves called *atap*, varying considerably in size. Most separate kitchens are also of this type. Such buildings have an earthen floor, and rarely have glass windows. Sago material is available from the sago forests of Hila. Most adult men have the skills required to build this type of house, and it can be done by a small number of persons, though the erection of the building is usually done in large working parties (*masohi*).

2. Houses made from timber and thatched with sago leaves. These are also very simple houses with earthen floors, timbered walls and without glass windows. All the materials are available nearby. This housing type can be built with the same relatively small amount of labour as the first category. Wooden planks are usually sawed by local specialists.

3. Traditional permanent houses built upon a foundation of (coral) stones and plastered with *kapur*, a mixture of burnt coral stone and sand. The lower parts of the walls are made from the same material, the higher parts of the walls are made from sago leafstalks. The roof is thatched with sago leaves. These houses usually have an open veranda, with wooden pillars supporting the roof. The materials for these houses are usually available locally: from the sea, the beach, and the forest of Hila or neighbouring villages. *Kapur*-making requires a large amount of collective labour.

4. Semi-modern houses built from coral stone and half-timbered walls. Some of those have zinc plate roofs; others are thatched with sago leaves. The construction of such houses is similar to the traditional houses; zinc roofing, however, requires money.

5. Modern houses built from bricks and cement, large structures with zinc plate roofs, representing the most modern constructions. These have glass windows and often tiled floors. The materials for these buildings have to be bought and brought in from the outside. The construction of these houses also needs construction/building specialists (*tukang*), who work with three to five assistants. But many activities can be, and usually are done by unskilled labour.

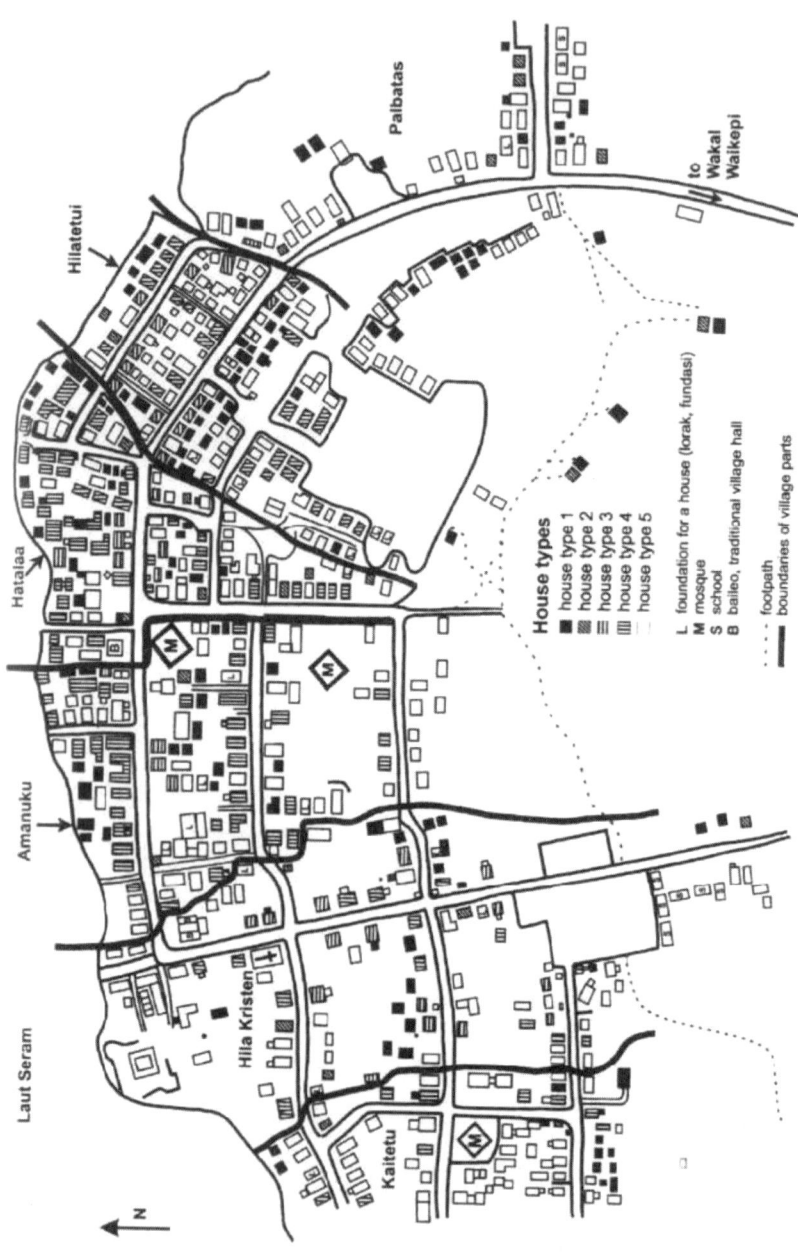

Map 4.1: Hila, village core with types of houses

Houses of the last three categories are designed as *permanent houses*, to provide enduring residential space. It is expected that they can be repaired or partially rebuilt if the physical structure should become too weak. In contrast, most houses in categories 1 and 2, built from sago and wood, are designed to be temporary or provisional houses, serving as living quarters for a limited period of time. There may be different reasons for building a temporary dwelling. A house can serve as an intermediate home, until one's new permanent house is finished, or as a temporary additional residence for an overcrowded house. A kitchen sometimes also serves as an overflow accommodation when houses are overcrowded. An entirely different category of temporary houses are the houses for 'newcomers', such as Butonese immigrants. To emphasize that residence and resident rights are provisional, and that it is still unclear whether they will be allowed to stay permanently at that site, these immigrants are not allowed to build a concrete or stone house. This explains the high percentage of sago houses in the Butonese settlements.

The distribution of house types varies considerably between and within the four settlement areas. The core village of Hila, inhabited almost exclusively by ethnic Ambonese, was in 1985 dominated by modern stone houses or modernized half-timbered houses with zinc roofs. Some 55% of all (355) houses are of this type. 15% of the living quarters and all (71) separate kitchens are wholly constructed from sago, while 45% of the houses and all kitchen buildings are thatched with sago leaves.[101] The housing situation in the Butonese *kampung* is strikingly different: 55% of the 305 residential dwellings are solely made from sago materials, and nearly 75% are thatched with sago leaves (see Figure 4.1 above) (F. von Benda-Beckmann 1990a).[102]

Variation in the Constellation of Co-residing People
According to our sample, Ambonese houses have an average of 7.35 persons, while the Butonese average is 7.23, both ranging from 2 to 17 inhabitants for Ambonese houses, and from 2 to 14 for Butonese ones. The official statistics, however, mention an average of 8.9 for Ambonese and 4.9 for Butonese houses, but the difference is almost certainly not as large as the official statistics show.[103] There is, however, a striking difference in composition between Am-

---

[101] For a more detailed description of house-types, see F. von Benda-Beckmann 1990a: 170.

[102] The house types were not equally distributed over the Butonese settlements. In Mamua, the oldest *kampung*, the houses of types 4 and 5 constituted 33.6% of all residences; in Waitomu 21.8%, and in Tahoku only 18.8%. On the variation of the relationships between the Ambonese and Butonese in these three *kampung*, see F. von Benda-Beckmann 1990b; F. von Benda-Beckmann and Taale 1992.

[103] Official statistics are notoriously unreliable. They mention 271 Ambonese houses, while we counted 355. But they mention 365 Butonese houses, while we counted only

bonese and Butonese houses. As Table 4.1 shows, Butonese live in two- or three-generation families, while married siblings or cousins do not live in the same house. Among Ambonese this is not uncommon: 20% of the houses in our sample are inhabited by more than one married couple of the same generation.

Nine out of the 22 Ambonese houses with more than one married couple have one kitchen. Of the houses with more than one kitchen, there are two kitchens in six houses, and three kitchens in two houses. All Butonese houses have one kitchen only (see Table 4.1).

The Dynamics of Residential Arrangements

The data of section 1 provide a static picture which only gives a general indication of house composition and kitchen structure. However, house composition, kitchen structure and the structure of consumptive units are flexible and change with the developmental cycle of the family members. We shall first give a brief overview of the general residence patterns during the stages of the life-cycle and then present the residential history of the family of Haji Sudin Patti and his wife Siti Manusia. If we look at individual people and families and at houses in more detail, we see considerable movement and impressive flexibility. Many people live consecutively in three or four houses in the course of their life, but may move back and forth many more times. Houses, on the other hand, see people flow through them, and in the process may change ownership and control, as will become clear from the residential history of a house described in the part entitled 'the significance of co-residence' later in this chapter.

Composition of residents	Ambonese N=48	Butonese N=13
One couple (with unmarried children)	26	8
Three generations (max. one couple per generation)	12	5
More than one couple, same generation	3	0
Three generations (more than one couple per generation)	7	0

Table 4.1: Composition of Ambonese and Butonese houses

---

305. The difference between the official statistics and our findings of Ambonese houses can probably in part be explained by the fact that many temporary buildings were not included in the official statistics, though they were used as separate living quarters. We may have missed some of the illegal Butonese houses in the hills, but that probably does not account for the total difference of 60 houses.

Life-cycle Residence Pattern

Young children. The residence of young children is determined by adults. Most young children live with their parents, but quite a few live with foster or adoptive parents. One of the reasons for the adoption or fostering of children is that they help to take care of childless old people. The child, a granddaughter or niece, may start living with the couple long before they become needy, in anticipation of future needs. Eventually the foster child may take over the house, temporarily or permanently. Orphans are usually taken in by an aunt or uncle, or come to live with the grandparents of either side. Another reason for fostering or adoption is to take away the threat of grave sickness and death from the child. It is believed that the child will thus escape the magic and spiritual danger that surrounds its parents and their house. Sometimes the child stays only for a few weeks with the foster parents, but it may last much longer, and there are examples where the child stayed and was ultimately adopted. Once they get older, the children are quite free to decide whether to stay or go back to their own families, and some children happily move back and forth between the families, belonging to both. Only formally adopted children stay with their adopted family, but formal adoption sometimes takes place many years after a child has started to live with the foster parents, and thus may be a conclusion of a long-established practice. Fostering and adoption are very common. In two-thirds of all houses included in our survey it had occurred at one time. Half of all houses had at one time had one or more close relatives from the village living in as a foster child. Almost one-third of the houses had accommodated one or more high school students.

Adolescence. Adolescent children may leave their parents' home when there is too much conflict at home and stay with grandparents, other relatives or friends. Boys move around more freely than girls at that age. Sometimes it is not clear at all where an adolescent boy lives, for he may move between two or three houses. This free period ends upon marriage. If a youngster has to move out of the home village for further education, the choice has to be made between renting a room in student housing or living with relatives. Girls expressed a far stronger preference for renting a room to living with relatives than boys, because they feared being overburdened with household chores. In practice, girls did seem to do much more chores than boys.[104] In Hila many children from surrounding villages live in foster-like arrangements with Hila families (often distant relatives) during their secondary education.

---

[104] This information is based on two surveys among third grade Lower Secondary School (SMP) students in two consecutive years. For more details, see K. and F. von Benda-Beckmann 1987a.

Marriage. Post-marital virilocal residence after an official bride-price marriage is the culturally and statistically dominant residence pattern. But in the case of a 'take-in marriage' (*kawin masuk*) the son-in-law is more or less incorporated into his wife's clan, and post-marital residence is uxorilocal (see Cooley 1962, Van Fraassen 1972). However, residence rules and arrangements are rather flexible. It also occurs in the more common marriage form that sons-in-law move in with their wives' parents, in the expectation that they will eventually build a house of their own or move into a house of their own clan. Though polygamy does not occur frequently, there are several men in Hila with more than one wife. One of them lives with his two wives in one house, but each of the women has her own section of the house and they cook separately, their husband taking his meals and sleeping in turn with each wife. All other polygamously married women live in separate houses. Some husbands rotate among their wives; others live with one and only visit the others. For polygamous men, residence cannot always unequivocally be established.

A young couple usually starts out sharing a kitchen with the parents they live with. Slowly they become more independent. Depending on the relationship between the women, they may continue to share a kitchen, or split up. But it is not uncommon that at a later stage they may combine their kitchens again. Children may eat in either kitchen.

Divorce, widowhood and remarriage. Divorce is a reason to change living quarters for at least one of the partners. The inheritance system, though basically patrilineal, has strong bilateral features allowing for considerable independence for women. A woman may move into a family fall-back house, or go back to her parents. Sometimes she has equally strong claims to the house and it happens frequently that she stays while her husband moves out. Most younger widowed and divorced persons marry again and start a new family. Although the tradition is for children of a first marriage to remain with the father, in practice they often stay with the mother. Step-parents often have a strained relationship with their step-children.

After the age of about 40 years, remarriage is no longer frequent, and a divorced or widowed person may move in with a widowed or divorced sibling, preferably of the opposite gender. The extent and mode of cooperation in such an arrangement vary widely. Generally it is valued that one is able to perform all tasks which a more conventional family also performs, while adhering to the gender-specific division of labour where necessary or convenient.

Old age. Most people expect to grow old in their own houses. For older people the amount and quality of help and care that they need and are able to mobilize is the main motivation for their decision to stay or move in with others. In order to secure minimal requirements of assistance in cooking and washing, they may take in relatives as foster children. Alternatively, though still controlling housing space, they will move voluntarily to another house if there is more congenial companionship, with a child or a younger sibling. When people get really old, they become increasingly dependent on others. Residence then follows their dependence, and they may not have much choice.

Case Study: A Residential History of a Family[105]

Sudin's parents, Daud and his wife, lived in the Patti family house (*lumaela*) of the Patti sub-clan to which Daud belonged. The oldest sons Rahmad, Bail and Abdul were born there. Daud and his wife built a new house in 1928-1930, where their younger children Sudin and Aida were born. Rahmad and Abdul lived in Daud's house until they moved away from Ambon, Rahmad joining the KNIL and later moving to the Netherlands, while Abdul as a young man migrated to Jakarta. Bail remained in Daud's house, and still lives there. But he had it rebuilt after Daud's death. Sudin and Siti Manusia married in 1950. Their oldest son Gani was born in Daud's house. But Siti did not get along with her mother-in-law, and the young couple moved out into the family house where all their other children were born. Their first two sons married there and brought their wives into the family house (see Figure 4.2).

Daud himself also moved for some time into the family house, while his wife lived in the new house with Bail and Aida. But later he moved back again into his own new house, where he died in 1967. When Aida wanted to marry, and her father opposed her marriage because she was to become the second wife of the (then) village head, she fled to the family house. She married nevertheless, and continued to live in the family house with her daughter. Her husband, who continued to live with his first wife, only visited her occasionally. After his first wife died, however, he moved in with Aida.

---

[105] All names of individual persons and their clans mentioned in this chapter have been made anonymous.

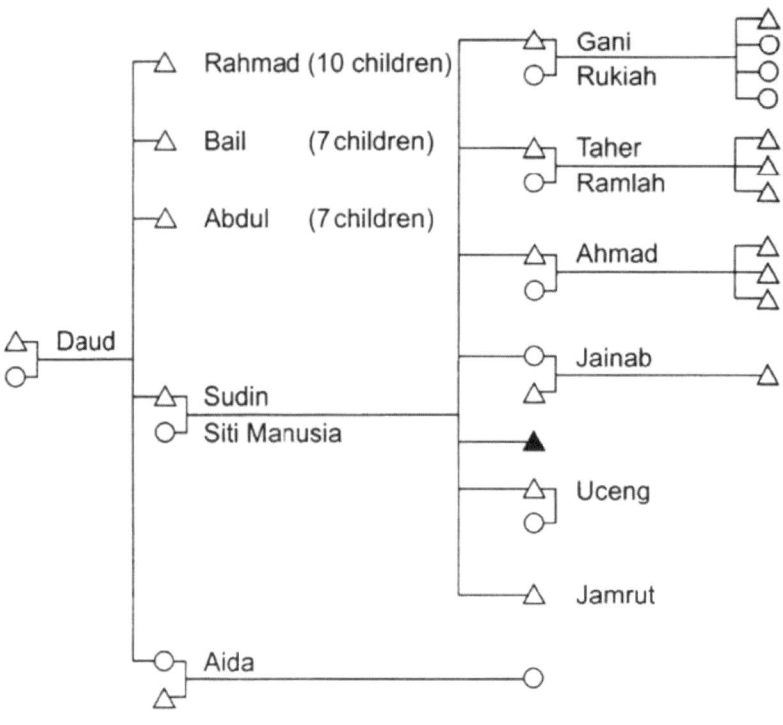

Figure 4.1: Kinship diagram of the Patti family

Sudin and Siti with all their children and two daughters-in-law moved from the family house in 1977 into their new house, built in 1977-1978. The third son Ahmad married and his wife moved in with him. The relationship between his wife and his mother was bad and in 1983 Ahmad and his wife moved into the family house where they lived until 1994. But Ahmad's eldest son frequently visited his grandparents and at times would practically live there.

In the early years in the new house, all women shared one common kitchen, Gani's wife Rukiah and Taher's (the second son's) wife Ramlah helped in the common household. Around 1980, when the first children were born, Rukiah and Ramlah established their own kitchen, built on the premises by Gani and Taher, with a separate fireplace for each of the women. Siti and her unmarried daughter Jainab continued to use the old kitchen building and cooked for Siti, Sudin and their three un-married children. Siti and Sudin together with all their children and daughters-in-law and grandchildren slept in the main house, with the exception of Ahmad and his family. In 1986, a new, bigger kitchen was built for the daughters-in-law with one compartment for each woman. Later that year Taher and Ramlah with their three children moved out into the house of a distant kinsman. Taher had helped much in the construction of the house and was asked to live there as long as the owner Dullah, a high civil servant, lived elsewhere (see F. von Benda-Beckmann 1987, F. and K. von Benda-Beckmann 1998).

In the early 1980s Gani and Taher had made plans to build their own houses. Gani had already selected a place to build a house of his own. But when he wanted to start building, his younger brother, a promising student at the teachers' training college, died, and all the money that had been saved was spent on the funeral. In 1986 Taher and Gani had again selected sites for their houses and thought of laying a foundation. The urge was temporarily toned down when Taher and his family moved into Dullah's house. Their departure made living in the house of Siti and Sudin more comfortable, because it had become less crowded. But a few years later, an aunt of Dullah's wife moved into Dullah's house. Eventually the relationship between them was troubled, and Taher together with Ramlah and their children eventually moved back to Siti and Sudin.

After early retirement in the Netherlands Rahmad, Sudin's migrant brother, and his wife frequently visited Hila. They contributed to the improvement of the house of Sudin and Siti, so that it was enlarged with a kitchen and a bathroom. However, relations between the families soon deteriorated. The 'Dutch' relatives tolerated only Sudin and Ahmad, the son who had moved into the family house. Relations with Siti and her other daughters-in-law were particularly bad. Gani was ordered to take away the kitchen he had built in 1986, and a high fence was erected between the two houses. Rukiah from then on used Siti's old kitchen. When Taher and Ramlah returned to the house, they also started using the old kitchen and for some time she and Rukiah shared one.

In 1994 the only daughter Jainab married and moved to another village, but she visited her family frequently. Her son was born in Hila. After separation, she moved back to her parents and shared a kitchen with her mother. The fourth son, Uceng, also married and lived with his wife Fitria and their child in the house of his parents-in-law where more space was available. They had hoped to move into a house belonging to Fitria's family, but for some reason it did not happen. For quite some time they moved back and forth between the houses of the respective parents and in 1996 moved in with Siti and Haji Sudin more permanently. Fitria had a separate kitchen but sometimes shared one with her mother-in-law. Jamrut, the only yet unmarried son, lived in the main house. Ahmad, the favourite of their 'Dutch' uncle and aunt, built a house with their financial support, and moved out. But he maintained good relationship with his own siblings, and his brothers and brothers-in-law and other close male relatives and affines participated in the communal work (*masohi*) to help build the house, while the female relatives prepared food for the workers. In 1994 Gani also started to build a house and moved out. The foundation was laid and a simple wooden structure was erected which was to become the kitchen but served as living quarters until they had saved enough to pay for the construction of the house.

So in a period of about 15 years, at one time the whole family lived in the same house with one kitchen; at another time they were distributed over five houses, each with a separate kitchen. Mother Siti's unit consisted of eight people in the beginning, increased to 14, then reduced to five (Sudin, Siti and three unmarried children), and then was expanded again to seven or eight, and contracted to a smaller size again. Individuals may live in three or four different houses in the course of their lives, sometimes at quite different locations in the village. Daud had moved back and forth between the family house and the house he had built himself. Gani was born in his grandfather Daud's house, moved to the family house, then to his father's house, and into his own house which may not be his last residence either. Brother Taher was born in the family house, moved into his father's house, then lived in the house of their distant kinsman Dullah, went back to live with his parents, and now eagerly waits to move into his own house. For many people it is not possible to establish unequivocally where they live during certain periods of their lives, nor is it always possible to say how many kitchens there are and who shares which kitchen. This is in particular the case for children and adolescents, but adults may also go through periods of unclear residence patterns. Polygamous men live in two or more houses. Young couples may for a considerable time move between the houses of the parents. And old widowed persons may move among relatives.

The Conditions of (Co-)Residence

Introduction

The variation in houses and residential arrangements is conditioned by a number of quite different factors which together influence the formation or termination of co-residential arrangements (see also Niehof 1985: 158). Access to houses and land for house sites has its basis in *social relationships* such as kinship, friendship, foster and child-parent relationships, often created and reinforced through marriages, in the present or earlier generations. Kinship is structured by two overlapping principles of patrilinearity and bilaterality. The patrilineal principle is the dominant one determining membership in a clan (*rumah tau* or *fam*), a landholding clan segment (*dati*), a clan association (*soa*) and the village. For most other purposes, however, villagers' kinship relations are bilateral. Also important, if less extended, are affinal relationships. The spouse's parents and their descendants are considered to be close kin. Nuclear families are called *keluarga*, this refers to parents and their children, but is also used to refer to three-generation families. These relationships, and the potential that they have for establishing residence, also have a legal basis in the *adat* of property and inheritance Apart from membership in *dati*, which is based on patrilineal descent and ceases for women upon marriage, inheritance is bilateral. Actual access to houses and house sites is also influenced by the material and economic basis of social relationships and rights or obligations. Access rights to houses fail where houses are overcrowded; plans to build new houses are unfulfilled if one cannot acquire land or the necessary money, or mobilize the labour.

In the following sections we shall go more into the details of these different constraining and enabling factors that condition residence and variation in residence. We shall first describe the legal conditions, and then discuss the social relationships and the residential strategies of people during the various phases the life-cycle. We then deal with the economic constraints which people may face, which also contribute to variation in residence. First the situation of Ambonese villagers will be discussed, followed by the conditions under which strangers acquire access to housing.

The Property Basis of Residence

Access to Residential Space

The possibilities for access to houses and rooms in houses are structured by property relationships.[106] Houses and land on which houses are to be built may have differing legal status. The legal status of houses and land defines the circle of potential claimants to housing and the circle of persons who must partake in the decisions as to who may live in an existing house, or who will be allowed to build a house and where the house will be erected. Actual access to existing housing space is largely a matter of acceptance by those living in the house. Generally speaking, upon marriage Ambonese villagers move in with close relatives. Kinship, good personal relationships with the inhabitants, as well as available space are factors that are taken into consideration. Empty houses are inherited by the descendants of the builder. If there are no immediate descendants, empty houses may also be given to more distant kin. When wanting to

---

[106] For accounts of Ambonese land law, see Van Hoëvell 1875; Holleman 1923; F. von Benda-Beckmann and Taale 1996.

build a new house, people are confronted with other problems: The need to obtain the legal right to build a house on land and the need for the materials and labour for its construction. Such land can be inherited, given or bought. Less than one-fifth of all houses and house sites in the Ambonese settlement are bought, as most are either given or inherited.

The old clan houses (*rumah pusaka*) in the village centre have been clan property for many generations, often for centuries. Important decisions as to who may live in these houses are theoretically made by all members of the clan or clan-segment, but are in practice predominantly made by the male members of the oldest living generation and the residents of the house, if there are any, in particular the women of the oldest generation. Since women do more work in house than men, and men have more possibilities to avoid each other in a house than women, the question of whether co-residing women get along with each other is more important than whether the men get along well.

A new house will obtain the status of self-made property (*perusa*) of the man or the couple for whom it is made, even though the land may be inherited property (*pusaka*). The couple may then decide who will live in the house. After their death their descendants will hold it as inherited property.

Claims to house sites depend on the status of the land. Patrilineal descent is the strongest legitimation to request allocation of a plot of land as a house site or to move into an existing occupied or empty house, but also matrifilial links are often needed to obtain permission to live in a house, as well as more distant kinship. Land and houses that have been *pusaka* for many generations have a larger circle of potential claimants than newly built houses or recently cultivated land. Usually land that is to be converted is *pusaka* of the descendants of the person who originally had brought the land under cultivation. They have to decide on such conversion and allocation. In practice the decision is taken by the men of the oldest generation. In case of *dati* land, the oldest generation male members of the *dati* group decide on actual allocation of a particular plot. Often there are trees on land envisaged as house sites. Trees may have a different legal status from the land itself; they may be the personal property of the planter (*perusa, tatanaman*) or the inherited property of a group of heirs. For example, a much valued durian tree may have been planted by the grandfather and is now *pusaka* of his male and female descendants, whereas the *pusaka* holding group of the land may go back further and is therefore much larger. As a consequence, different groups of persons may have to be involved in the decision-making process (F. von Benda-Beckmann and Taale 1996).

Conversion of agricultural land into a housing site will inevitably mean some economic loss to (some of) the larger circle of persons entitled to the proceeds of that land and the trees on it. If land is scarce in a particular lineage, permission will be given to close male relatives only. But if there is abundant land available, female lineage members and their husbands may also get permission to build a house. Conversion of home gardens in the village centre into house sites is in particular problematic for elderly women, for whom the alternative of a garden outside the residential area is too burdensome. These women have an important say in the decision about conversion, but usually they consent to the request.

In the village centre another motive for selecting a place to build a house may play a role. In former times there was a rather strict spatial division of the residential area according to the rank of clans. Members of the highest-ranking clans still consider it important to live in their section of the village, in Amanuku or Hatalaa (see Figure 4.1 above). Moving out would mean living among lower-ranking people and would cause some loss of status. In order to avoid this, the village centre has become very densely populated. However, the old status differences have lost much of their former strength, which may have made it easier for people to move out. At the same time, more people moving out, and being forced to move out, may have helped to weaken the old status differences between the areas. Many persons prefer more space, quietness and privacy, and will gladly move into an individual house in another village section, even at the cost of a slight loss of status. Besides, new criteria for residential value compete with the old status criteria. Living closer to one's gardens, to fishing places, to new economic opportunities, the road to the newly opened Higher Secondary School (SMA) and to the administrative centre and new public facilities like the Village Cooperative (KUD), the Medical Post (Puskesmas) and the post office have become more important and valued than the old criteria. Besides, new sites mostly make it possible to have a home garden close by.

Sales of housing sites among Ambonese villagers are rare in Hila, and have only started with the rapid expansion of the residential area outside the old village core and occur mainly among distant relatives.[107] Land is only sold when the buyer intends to build a *permanent* home. The sales by Ambonese which we could record involve areas in the old settlement core, which also became more crowded during the residential expansion. It involves further land which did not have *kintal* status before and was used as vegetable or tree gardens, planted with sago palms, coconut palms or clove trees. In that area, buying becomes more frequent. The area close to the road is the most desirable, and is gradually becoming very scarce (see F. von Benda-Beckmann and Taale 1996).

---

[107] The standard size was in the mid-1980s 15 x 20 m. The sale's agreement (*jual-beli*) is usually laid down in a document and sometimes the village government writes its acknowledgement on the document. Formal written sales contracts (*akte jual beli*) are rare and we have not come across one single example of a house site registered with a certificate (*sertipikat*) by the Agrarian Office. Prices vary according to the relationships between buyer and seller, and according to the location and what grows on the site. Usually, land to be converted into a housing site is cultivated with coconut palms, clove trees or sago. Trees are always compensated, but land may or may not be paid for.

An important way to gain access to residential quarters is by being 'given' (*kasih*) a house or a housing site. 'Giving' can have different meanings, and includes allocations out of a common property stock. When clans become extinct, the last living members may give the land and/or house to another person or clan. In these cases land is given on a permanent basis and cannot be withdrawn. Also newcomers are often given land for houses in perpetuity. These last type of gifts creates a special relationship between receiver (and descendants) and recipient (and descendants) which has many elements of a patron-client relationship. It entails the obligation of help towards the givers in a variety of circumstances: to come when one is called for communal labour, e.g. when houses are built and rebuilt, when roofs are thatched and when marriage or funeral meals have to be cooked and served. Such help is consciously seen and valued as recognition of the fact that 'they' have received their land/house from 'us'. It also calls for political loyalty – a loyalty often stronger than common clan membership.

Giving can also be for temporary use. The temporary character may be underlined by the fact that a house of a temporary type is built on the site. As long as people *numpang saja* [reside only temporarily in a sago house], the land can be used and usually no monetary compensation is asked. But temporariness may last a lifetime and such land may even be inherited. Transfers of given land or houses lie at the basis of many conflicts and uncertainties about its precise status (see F. von Benda-Beckmann and Taale 1996).

The Residential History of Houses

Houses and house sites therefore may have a varied property history. Successive occupants may live in a house on different legal bases. Inherited houses usually pass from the builders into *pusaka* of the descendants along patrilineal lines, but daughters are frequently allowed to remain in the house with their husbands, to be used by them and their descendants. This happens especially when there are already many ties with the family of the husband, because of earlier marriages between members of the respective families. The house is given to the couple, but it is not always made clear whether this is done only temporarily or on a permanent basis. Gradually, the house will be associated with the clan of the husband and eventually house and control over the house site pass on to his clan. In case of disagreement, the disputing families negotiate a settlement. Often such a settlement is reached by letting a boy and girl from the disputing families marry and live in the house. A brief summary of a house history may illustrate this.

Case Study: History of a House

> The Manusia house was an old house, built early in this century. It was located on a piece of land which had originally belonged to the Sama clan. When this clan was about to become extinct, the last living mal

clan member gave it to his foster child, a women from the Latu clan. She, together with her husband from a different village, lived in a house on the same site. Her daughter married Mesir Patti (Haji Sudin's father's father's brother's sister), who moved out of his father's house, and was allowed to build a house there. His wife being a Latu, he had good relations to the Latus who controlled the land. His wife, in an earlier marriage, had been married to a man from the Manusia clan and had had several children who grew up in the house of their step-father. After Mesir's death, the Patti relatives claimed the house as a Patti house. The Manusia children, adults by that time and led by Mahmud Manusia, the eldest son, refused to yield it. A compromise was reached, as is not uncommon, through marriage. Mahmud and his family would continue to live in the house, now a Manusia house. But one of his daughters would marry Haji Jamil Patti, a direct nephew (FBS) of Mesir and the major claimant. For an additional confirmation of the new relationship, Mahmud Manusia's younger daughter Siti would marry (later Haji) Sudin Patti, Haji Jamil's first cousin. The house is now considered 'a Manusia house' – it went from Sama to Latu, from Latu to Patti, from Patti to Manusia.

With the changing numbers of occupants, the social meaning of a house may also change from a regular one-family house to the family house in the sense of the centre of a larger family group. Over the years, the nuclear family for whom it was built expands and contracts, while new generations are born and start a family of their own. Sometimes the house may serve as a fall-back residence for quite distantly related individuals or nuclear families, who have not yet built their own houses, or who are unwilling to live with their parents. Sometimes temporary houses are left behind after the occupants have found a more permanent house in which to live. But house sites are becoming scarce and are not lightly given up any more. What starts out as a simple temporary house made of sago, may over time be rebuilt in wood and eventually in concrete. It may be enlarged and embellished. This process often takes decades.

Social Relationships and Residential Strategies

Apart from the rights to housing space or land, there are also obligations and standard preferences concerning residence, which vary according to gender and the phase in the life-cycle. In principle small children live with their parents; post-marital residence is viri- or neolocal in principle. But there are many examples in which these principles are not followed. Neither property rights nor residence rules and principles determine residence practices: moving in and out of houses, or building new houses, is also influenced by the nature and quality of the social relationships between people. Rules merely exclude certain options and facilitate others, leaving much room for individual choice and to negotiate agreeable living conditions.

For instance, it is an *adat* principle that the youngest son stays with his parents and takes the house over eventually, but this is not always the case. In the Patti history, the older brothers often retained or took over the house. It also depends on the status of the house. While youngest sons are supposed to take over the house, it is the task of oldest sons to represent the lineage and the lineage (segment's) property, and therefore retain control over the future of the house. As far as moving out of the house also means moving out of the area in which the clan is located (in terms of the old political system), it may be the younger sons who have to move out while the oldest remain. On the other hand, old women usually prefer to stay with a daughter.

Marriage is an important event, which makes people think of moving out. But who stays and who moves out, and when, strongly depends on the quality of the relationships between the co-residing persons, on the availability and attractiveness of living space under the control of both spouses' families, and on the possibilities to build their own house. One common problem, and perhaps the greatest potential for tensions leading to young couples moving out, is the relationship between the mother and her daughters-in-law, or between daughters-in-law. It depends very much on individual personalities and their interaction whether a mother shares one kitchen with her daughters-in-law for a long period, whether some pressure is relieved by establishing separate kitchens, or whether the relationships get so intensely conflictive that the young couple moves out. It happened twice in the case of Haji Sudin.

The decision to move out depends also on the availability of space. This is not just a matter of the size of the house which they share with their parents, but also of the availability of alternative housing, such as clan houses or 'underpopulated' or temporarily empty houses. As we have seen in the residential history of Siti and Haji Sudin, old clan houses function as a residential safety-valve if tensions within a house reach boiling-point, or if the parents' house becomes overcrowded. They also function as residential safety-net for people who have no normal family relationships, for example widowed or divorced old people. Such houses provide people with a temporary, interim residence; although they may end up living in the interim residence permanently until their death. Moving and building new houses not only occur when housing needs are imminent: people who have voluntarily emigrated to other parts of Indonesia or who have to live and work outside Hila as part of their professional tasks may build a house to live in after retirement. Plans to return are often rather vague and houses are in the first place built to keep open the option of returning to a comfortable house. The house of Taher's kinsmen mentioned earlier is such a case.

Economic Constraints for House-Building

Establishing new residence not only requires property rights to a house site; it also depends on economic possibilities and constraints. The people who build new houses are not very young and are often parents themselves. To acquire sufficient money for married couples to build a house is primarily the responsibility of the couple themselves. The cost of materials is paid either from a regular salary or wage labour such as bus driving, or from a series of good clove or nutmeg harvests. Some manage to save enough from fishing or baking bread, or from some other kind of trade. Parents will often see it as part of their obligation to help their children build a house, especially for sons. But they will usually wait until the young couple makes its own provisions, earnings and savings; then they will help (see also Hospes 1996). In families with several married sons, who are expected eventually to establish their own houses, the policy is usually that older children go before younger ones; males have priority before females, and sons before daughters. But policies may change when new circumstances call for it, for instance in the case of Taher who had the opportunity to move out to another house, or Ahmad who was supported by his Dutch relatives.

People who have selected and acquired a site for a permanent house will generally start by making the foundation upon which the later building is erected (*lorak* or *fundasi*). If there are reasons to move out quickly or before enough money is accumulated for a permanent house, a temporary house will be erected on the site. Others will wait until a permanent house can be built. There may be a period of years between laying a *fundasi* and reaching the state whereby the house is habitable. Recent increases in the price of building materials, and the drop in clove prices have greatly increased the waiting and saving period. With the village expansion well underway, people have become aware that land by the road is rapidly becoming scarcer. Many villagers secure a site by building the foundations and waiting until their financial situation improves enough to allow them to build a house. If needed, they can always, without much cost, build a temporary sago house. But for those who are absent, even a *fundasi* may not be sufficient; a complete house has to be built and some have even started to buy land to secure their position.

Temporary and permanent houses require different combinations of materials and labour. In the case of temporary houses, made from sago materials, wood and bamboo, both materials and labour can, if necessary, be acquired on a non-monetary basis. To build a temporary house, the house owner brings in his own labour force (*sendiri*), and often that of close relatives (*keluarga dekat*). Together they will prepare the required materials, sago leaf-stalks of various size, wooden poles or beams, sago-leaf roof elements, etc. To erect the house, they call in *masohi* labour, which is unpaid labour on the basis of mutual help from friends, neighbours and kinsmen, in exchange for food and cigarettes.

Skilled labour is usually not needed, except perhaps for inserting wooden beams in the front wall for door and windows. Such a professional builder (*tukang*) will be paid in cash.

In the case of permanent stone houses, most building materials have to be acquired on the open market. The construction itself requires a large amount of skilled labour which also has to be paid for. The major problem thus is acquiring sufficient money to buy materials and, to a lesser extent, paying the labour. Usually a professional builder from the village is hired to construct the building and/or to supervise and direct the building process. He has usually three or four helpers. He may build the whole house with perhaps some additional help: this is called *kontrak*. But more often, he supervises un-monetized *masohi* labour. The payment which a *tukang* receives for his services varies according to his involvement in the construction process, and according to the relationship he has with the house builders. If he is a kinsman, he will usually demand less money than otherwise.

It is rare for houses to be fully built by paid labour, but it is equally rare for houses to be built without paying any money whatsoever in labour costs. Those who can afford to have a house built entirely by professionals often hesitate to do so and make sure some *masohi* is involved to show that they take social relationships in the village seriously. Teachers and other civil servants regard physical work as incompatible with their status and also rely on *masohi* labour to some extent. Both male and female relatives are invited to help: men help with the building, while the women prepare food and drinks. All buildings thus require some money to be paid for labour services, but paid labour can to a large extent be substituted by unpaid labour – one's own and that of close friends and kinsmen. *Masohi* labour, though unpaid, does require a substantial amount of cash for food and cigarettes. It is because of the expenses involved in providing food and cigarettes that the poorest cannot afford *masohi* and prefer to build a house alone or with one or two brothers or friends only.

The Situation of 'Strangers'

These situations and conditions pertain to villagers who have been born into the village and its web of social and economic relationships, notably property relationships. It is quite different for newcomers. As has been described in more detail elsewhere (F. von Benda-Beckmann and Taale 1992), the notion of newcomer (*pendatang*) is relative, since it is recognized that more or less all people living in the coastal village have come from somewhere else in the course of history. An important distinction is whether or not newcomers are fully incorporated into the social-political *adat* constitution of Hila through membership in the clan association (*soa*), either by individually joining a clan belonging to a *soa*, through marriage, or through acceptance of their own clan as *soa* member.

In case of incorporation, land, including residential land, was in principle given for permanent use to an individual and his clan (segment). But not everybody is fully incorporated. 'Giving' of land to people not incorporated was in principle temporary and revocable, should the land need to be put to other uses. These practices continue to the present day.

An important category of newcomers is that of the civil servants. Hila, which became the sub-district capital in 1980, has seen a considerable inflow of civil servants, mainly school teachers and officials of the *Puskesmas*. They are in an especially precarious situation as they are usually young, often unmarried, and have a job that takes up most of their time and yet brings in little money. The government is expected to provide official housing for its civil servants, but does not live up to these expectations. Official housing is usually inadequate and building may take years. Civil servants therefore are largely dependent on villagers for living space. At the SMA in 1985, for instance, 23 of the 30 teachers were outsiders. Three married Hila spouses. They and three others have been incorporated into a clan association in Hila or the neighbouring village of Kaitetu, on the basis of their own or their father's marriage. Of the 30 teachers, 11 live in their own house and five live in an old school building which is no longer used. Six people live in with other families as foster children (*anak piara*, see F. and K. von Benda-Beckmann 1998). Two have acquired new housing, two have been given housing land, and four have rented a room. The difference between being a foster child and renting a room appears to lie in the degree to which the people can form an independent domestic unit. Single people are usually taken in as foster children, while married couples rather rent living space.

The situation is different for those newcomers who do not look for, or do not succeed in establishing residence on the basis of family or clan relationships. For them, there is no access to existing housing space; they need a site to build a house for themselves. Although there are some such cases in the residential area of Hila proper, by far the largest category of such newcomers is the Butonese living in the Butonese settlements as distinct residential and social groups. The early Butonese coming to live in Hila received land for temporary housing from the Ambonese landowners without a problem. Granting of temporary housing usually includes access to garden land (see F. von Benda-Beckmann and Taale 1992). Butonese may also acquire sites for permanent stone houses, in which case the land has to be bought from the Ambonese owners. The number of stone houses in the Butonese *kampung* is therefore an indication of how much housing land has been sold to Butonese. In all cases there developed patron-client relationships between the Ambonese landlords/sellers and the Butonese renters/buyers. But there is considerable variation in these relationships. The older the settlements are, and the more distant their location, the better and closer are the relationships. Not surprisingly, the oldest *kampung*

The Significance of Co-Residence

In the previous sections of this chapter we gave an account of the variation in houses and co-residing people, and of the legal, social and economic conditions that underlie these variations. On that basis we want to address several questions: What is the significance of co-residence in the economic, reproductive, ceremonial and political organization? To what extent can co-residents (or 'the household') be regarded as a stable and basic unit within these domains of social organization? In what ways and how greatly does cooperation between co-residing persons vary? In dealing with these questions, we shall roughly distinguish between different functions of social organization: the production of food and other earnings; the preparation of meals, child-rearing and care of the aged; and the ceremonial activities and the position in political and administrative organization. However crude such a categorization may be, we prefer it to the conceptual straitjacket of the conventional dichotomies such as domestic/non-domestic or domestic/public, which raise more questions than they answer.[108] We shall first give a general account of economic life and organization, and illustrate this with a picture of the family whose residential history we have described earlier. We then deal more generally with different food production and income-generating activities, horticulture, commercial fishing and sago rasping, petty trade or other business, shops and wage labour. We examine how co-residence is conducive to cooperation in each of these types of economic activities. We shall then turn to more 'domestic' activities such as food preparation and consumption, child-rearing and the care of the aged. The final part of this section deals with the public sphere, notably the socio-political organization of the village and state administration at the lowest level on the one hand, and the public celebration of religious ceremonies on the other hand. We shall see how and to what extent co-residence is important in the public and political representation within the village community, as it is defined by the public administration and by local terms.

---

[108] For an excellent analysis of the multiple meanings of the public/private distinction, including the distinction between the domestic (private) and public spheres in feminist scholarship, see Weintraub 1997.

The Economy of Cari

The Moluccan rural population earns an income from many different sources. For centuries the rural economy has been a mixed one, combining subsistence production based on sago and fish with the production of cash-crops (cloves, nutmeg, coconuts) for regional, national and international markets (Van Fraassen 1972, Krause-Katerla 1986, Knaap 1987a, F. von Benda-Beckmann l990a, Taale 1991, Hospes 1996). Most people make a living from a combination of any of the following activities: horticulture (involving sago, vegetables, tubers and root crops, fruit, coconut, cloves and nutmeg), fishing, gathering and petty trade, and miscellaneous state projects or projects set up by Moluccan migrants in The Netherlands and Java. The range of activities open to individuals is great. None of these activities alone provides for a secure and dependable income, due to fluctuations on the world market for products such as cloves, nutmeg and coconut. It also has to do with seasonal characteristics of some crops, especially of sago (F. von Benda-Beckmann 1990a, Brouwer 1990). And it has increasingly to do with the unpredictable and intermittent flow of governmental projects for infrastructure and other development programmes that come and go (see F. and K. von Benda-Beckmann 1998).

These new forms of income, at times substantial but never enduring, seem to fit perfectly into the already existing economic pattern. People speak of *cari* [searching] when going to the forest to look for forest products, as well as when looking for a temporary job in a project, or selling products to the market in order to earn some cash income. This principle permeates the whole range of economic life (see Taale 1991). We therefore propose to speak of a *cari* economy. The stable incomes of the few relatives who earn a fixed salary, as well as the relationships in which relatives in the civil service may mediate, are also an important part of the *cari* system. The result is a highly volatile economic system, in which every individual kind of activity is highly insecure, but in which a certain stability and security are sought by combining many different activities, by keeping open as many options as possible, and by seizing an opportunity whenever it presents itself (see F. and K. von Benda-Beckmann 1995). Individual persons, more than families or households, search for and develop their own set of opportunities and possibilities. In order to keep options open it is important to sustain a wide range of relationships, for it is often through relationships that opportunities come up. People in general spend considerable time and energy in maintaining social relationships. Both men and women have to find a balance between individual *cari* behaviour and cooperation that is necessary or conducive to *cari*. Husband and wife develop their own network of cooperation, of which some but not all strands overlap (see K. von Benda-Beckmann 1992). They both have a fair amount of independence. As we mentioned earlier, this is enhanced by a land tenure and inheritance system that, though basically patrilineal, has strong bilateral features. As a result, both men and women have access to land of their family on their own account. As a result of the economic system of *cari* and the bilateral features in the kinship and inheritance patterns, men and women are rather autonomous and keep open many options both for cooperation and for freedom of movement and economic behaviour. To illustrate *cari* behaviour, we shall present a case history from the family that was introduced above.

Case Study: An Illustration of *Cari* Behaviour within the Family

> Like many other women, Rukiah and Ramlah made and sold snacks at the roadside throughout most of the year. But during the fruit season, when *langsat* and *mangistan* were ripe, Ramlah took the opportunity to make more money than usual. In 1985 she made snacks to sell in the forest to those who were harvesting their trees and who were too busy to cook. From the money earned she bought fruit to sell in the market in Ambon city. However, she did not go to the market herself, for that would take at least half a day if not more and she could not spare the time, because she had to cook, do some cleaning and take care of her children when she came home. In the evening she would start making new snacks and leave in the morning for the forest on a new round of selling and buying fruit. Rukiah, who was pregnant at that time and who did not like to go to the forest as much as her sister-in-law anyway, also made snacks, but far less than Ramlah. She sold these along the roadside, to people on their way to or from the forest, and bought some fruit. She could also keep an eye on her own small children. The children of Ramlah stayed around the house under the supervision of Nurya, a niece who lived next door. Ramlah's husband Taher could not look after the children, for he was busy building a house. Besides, he had little patience and was not very dependable with his children. His sister Jainab worked for us and was not available either. Otherwise she would have taken the children under her care. Mother-in-law Siti was not available either, because she went to town to sell the fruit.
>
> Siti liked to go to town and was clever at negotiating a good price, so she usually went to the market. Rukiah, who did not like to go to Ambon at all, never went, but Ramlah did occasionally, sometimes taking along fruit for her sister as well. Usually Siti would sell the fruits she had collected plus those of her daughters-in-law. She would spend the night outside on the terrace in order not to miss the first minibus that left between 1 and 2 o'clock in the morning. If she arrived at the market before 4 o'clock, she would be able to sell the whole lot to a retailer and be back by noon. If she arrived later, she would have to spend the whole day at the market and sell the fruit herself. That would be much more tiresome and get her home by the end of the afternoon, where a hungry

son would be waiting for her to prepare an evening meal. Sometimes she would again go to the market the next day, but the regular work at home also had to be fitted into her schedule and she was not as strong as she used to be.

Ahmad, who was a good tree climber, helped his mother to pick her trees. This is men's work, although a few women claimed they could and sometimes did climb trees as well. If trees, planted by an ancestor and thus owned by the whole family, were ready to be harvested, men and women of each of the branches of descendants would go to the forest together and harvest jointly. This was always a fun occasion with a lot of laughing and screaming. Children were very keen on joining this family outing, because they were allowed to gather and sell their own fruit and keep the money. Parents would carefully keep their children's fruit apart. Rukiah, for example, sold the fruit gathered by her eldest son, together with her own, and made sure he got his money.

Men hardly participated in this fruit-selling business. They did not usually bring fruit to the market, but left this to the women. The profits were kept by the women, who were in charge of the money anyway. These weeks of harvest were extremely busy and women would only get a few hours of sleep a night. But they all felt they should not miss this opportunity, for one was never sure when the next good harvest would be, as *mangistan* and *langsat* have a cycle of three years. Though there was some variation in the season throughout the island, in the peak period the market was flooded with the same fruit, and prices would drop accordingly. The best period was when fruits were not yet ripe elsewhere or had already been harvested. In the main period, a hard day's work brought Siti a profit of no more than 2,000-3,000 *rupiah*, which represented 10-15% of the turnover. The fruit trade was relatively new, for it had only become possible to sell fruit at the market of Ambon after the road had been constructed in the 1970s and buses served as transport. Women had profited in particular from this road, since it meant they no longer had to rely on men to carry the fruit to the market. It had opened a new source of income for them.

Members of the family cooperated in various ways on other occasions as well. For example, the brothers sometimes went out to fish together. When the men caught so much fish that they could not eat or sell all of it the same day, the fish would have to be fried or smoked, so that it could be sold the next day or the day after that. The men would provide banana leaves and the sticks to spear the fish, while all women would sit together, usually with two fires, one for Siti and one for the two daughters-in-law and do the cooking. The next day each woman would sell her own portion. The times when the men would catch a great amount of fish were rare and when this occurred, everything else was put aside to prepare the fish. Ramlah, who at that time had more energy than the others, would still make her snacks at night and sell both fish and snacks the next day. These decisions are made individually, and depend on personal preferences, energy and need for cash.

Rukiah and her husband Gani together kept a vegetable garden on her family land. Her brother and sister-in-law, from the same clan as her husband, who lived next door, had a garden bordering on their garden. The men had fenced their gardens together and the women often went together to work in it or to fetch some vegetables or tubers. Ramlah and Taher did not enjoy gardening and did not have one. Siti and Haji Sudin worked a plot of land next to the house of the 'Dutch' brother, and kept a garden with ground-nuts a few kilometres further down the main road to Ambon, where Haji Sudin's family owned land.

After Ramlah and Taher moved to the house of their distant cousin Dullah, which Taher had helped to build, Ramlah stopped cooperating with her mother- and sister-in-law. From then on, Ramlah and Taher started to sell ice-sticks which they made in a refrigerator bought by Dullah (F. von Benda-Beckrnann 1987). Living in the house of Dullah meant that they were to cooperate mostly with his family, several of whom came to fetch a bucket of ice-sticks every day to sell to schoolchildren. Rukiah's eldest son Mahmud, aged 6, was also among the sellers. He was allowed to keep the money but it was agreed that he would use it for school utensils.

The example shows the variety of *cari* behaviour and the cooperation it involves. Ramlah took the opportunity to earn more than usual during the fruit season, by selling snacks and buying fruits to be resold at the market in Ambon. She did this in some form of collaboration with her mother-in-law. Building the house of Dullah had been a good opportunity for Taher to earn extra income. It also secured living quarters for him, his wife and children. But when she moved into Dullah's house, Ramlah ceased, temporarily, to cooperate closely with her mother-in-law.

The three elder brothers often processed sago together, but would take their sago into their respective kitchens. Whom they worked with largely depended on the property rights to the sago palms and the labour and sharing arrangements. They would sometimes give sago to other people living in their house, but also to relatives, friends or neighbours living in other houses (see F. von Benda-Beckmann 1990a). They would go fishing either individually, or together with friends, or join a fishing team for one or more seasons. They and their parents had separate cassava and vegetable gardens but helped each other occasionally. They helped their father with his clove trees, but had recently started to plant their own trees. Each of the sons and the father engaged separately in various other income-generating activities, working occasionally in construction, etc. The women, too, helped each other occasionally in economic activities, but usually they acted separately or together with sisters and other kin, close friends, or as in the case of Rukiah, with a befriended neighbour, baking and selling sago bread, producing sweets, or making and selling coconut-rice lunches. Each picked their own inherited clove and fruit trees together with their relatives and co-owners.

The example suggests that there is a clear tendency to have stronger and more multi-stranded relationships with persons within the same house. The example also suggests that individuals have webs of relationships with people within and outside their houses with whom they cooperate, depending on the particular kind of activity. In the section below we shall discuss briefly and more systematically the main economic activities in which men and women engage and see how cooperation is structured and to what extent living in one house is important.

Plate 4.3: A fishing team drawing the net in

Cari and Cooperation

Horticulture and Silviculture
These involve a high degree of cooperation between husband and wife. Couples who have a garden usually maintain it together. The work is highly seasonal and

most of the year this is not intensive. Gardens may be made on family land of either the husband's or the wife's family. Property rights to land therefore shape cooperation to some extent. The garden itself has the status of *perusa* [self-acquired] of the couple. As case study 7.3 illustrates, siblings or in-laws may make a garden on adjacent plots of land and help each other to fence or harvest it. The proximity of persons living together in one house or next door is conducive to such cooperation, but is not a necessary condition; personal preferences play as much a role here.

Harvesting trees may be done by husband and wife if the tree has been planted by them, but it has to be done in larger working parties if property rights in trees are vested in *pusaka*-owning units who will harvest together. Fruit trees, cloves and nutmeg may be harvested by men and women, but sago harvesting is an exclusively male job. Usually sago is rasped on an ad hoc basis. There are only a few professional raspers who work in stable working parties over longer periods of time (F. von Benda-Beckmann 1990a, Brouwer 1996 and 1998). Co-residence, other than as husband and wife, does not establish the primary social units through which this type of work is shared, but living together in one house tends to lead to increased cooperation.

Butonese, who do not own land and are not allowed to own trees, engage in a far more intensive mode of horticulture. Most of them do not have permanent houses and, as a result, they usually live in two-generation families. Cooperation in horticulture beyond that family is rarer, since they are not forced into cooperation by property relationships.

House-Building

As we have seen before, the amount and quality of cooperation in house-building depend on the type of house to be erected. If *masohi* is involved, which is the case for the great majority of houses at some stage, the husband invites the men to come and work, while his wife will invite women to help cook. Each spouse thus mobilizes his or her own network. This means that there will be a core group of couples of which both spouses will come and work, but there are also persons who are invited alone, because he or she do not belong to the network of the other partner. Selection is made on the basis of several principles. In the first place, people who share rights to the land on which a house is erected are usually invited. Property rights therefore also structure cooperation in house-building. Selection is further based on services given in the past by the hosts, or expected services in the future. A person who plans to build his or her own house in the near future or who received help in the past will be much more interested in participating in *masohi* than others. Likewise, a civil servant or wealthy person who has done someone a favour in the past will call upon that person for *masohi* when building a house. Poorer relatives will gladly participate in the hope of some service from their wealthy relatives in the future. *Masohi* is thus a means to strengthen social relationships, and to widen the scope of *cari* opportunities, in the case of house-building, all persons living in the house of the hosts participate in *masohi*. The men usually also help the house builder with other work in the house as well.

Plate 4.4: A roof is thatched in masohi cooperation

Other Traders

Only very few persons live from horti- and silviculture alone, because that does not cover all cash needs. To earn the necessary cash, people engage in all kinds of other economic activities. Here cooperation is not so much structured by property relations and other considerations dominate. Only a few have permanent specialized enterprises. There are a few shops which are all run by husband and wife, one by two brothers and their respective wives. Shopkeepers have little time for other activities. Professional builders and bus drivers also have little time for other economic activities. Apart from that there are some fishing groups, with a professional fisherman as the leader, an all-male activity. Participants are selected on the basis of kinship and friendship.

Quite a few women make snacks and sell these along the roadside. This is exclusively done by women and there is considerable cooperation among co-residing women, especially mothers with unmarried adult daughters, but also among sisters-in-law. Many women prefer to cooperate with friends who live close by, but almost invariably on an ad hoc basis. And women from one house usually do not sit on the same spot in order to avoid competition, unless they are very close and enjoy each other's company.

Working as driver or ticket collector on buses, or with a professional builder, and road building and other government building projects provide men with cash-earning opportunities, on an ad hoc or more permanent basis. Many work on such jobs for a short time, until better opportunities come up. If a working party is to be formed, one often finds men who live in one house or close friends participating. They hear of the opportunity from each other more easily than a brother who lives in another part of the village.

Civil Servants

These people have a special position in the *cari* economy. For them status and, in the case of non-villagers, the contractual basis of their living arrangements determine the extent and mode of cooperation. Status prevents them from going to the forest to rasp sago or do agricultural work, but they need more cash than ordinary villagers and salaries are often not high enough to cover all expenses. Therefore, they depend on having a set of clients who may provide them with services. Female civil servants and wives of civil servants often trade cloth and clothing, the wealthier ones in gold as well. Though the salary is used to create and maintain a stock of trading goods by the wife, her husband is reluctant to mix with her business and often has only a vague idea of the actual income of his wife. But there are examples of extremely successful economic cooperation between husbands and wives (K. von Benda-Beckmann 1992). The situation of married senior couples and young unmarried civil servants at the beginning of their career differs considerably. Senior civil servants who have no relatives in a village usually rent a house and live there with just their immediate family. But they will enter into patron-client relationships with neighbours in order to secure the necessary services and food (F. and K. von Benda-Beckmann 1995 and 1998). As we have seen, young unmarried civil servants often live as foster children with the family. They are expected to contribute financially in exchange for food and laundry and other services. Such relationships often form a curious mixture of fostering and patronage, in which the higher status of civil servant is balanced by the status of an unmarried foster child.

Household Income Management

Generally speaking, a person who earns cash is allowed to keep it for her- or himself. There is considerable but ambivalent income-pooling between husband and wife, the wife being the keeper of the couple's income. Husbands keep their money to themselves as much as they can, which is a cause of considerable tension. It is extremely rare that the husband keeps the money of the family and to do so is regarded as a ground for divorce. Husband and wife may borrow money from each other, but this is not easily done and is always a source of tension. Children who earn money often are allowed and encouraged to keep it for themselves. Adolescents keep the money they earn for themselves as much as possible, though girls find it a bit more difficult to do so.

Food Preparation, Child-Rearing and Care of the Aged

Food preparation and consumption is not necessarily done together by all persons living in one house. This section will deal with private consumption only. There are many occasions in which food is consumed in larger groups, for example when large working parties are engaged to do a major piece of work, such as house building, thatching a roof, or during wedding and funeral ceremonies. These will below be dealt with in section 6.

Almost all of the houses in which more than one adult couple live have separate kitchens. Even in those cases where, for example, sago has been rasped by co-residing men, it will often be divided when the food is prepared for consumption or storage. In the example discussed above, the three married brothers who went out to rasp sago each brought their share home and gave the main part to their spouses and a small part to needy close relatives. The processing of sago for consumption or storage is sometimes but not always done together by both husband and wife, depending on whether the individual wife sees further opportunities to make money. A woman who goes to her garden sometimes brings some vegetables for her sister-in-law or mother-in-law. The most stable consumptive units are married couples with their unmarried children, or with young married children with whom they share a kitchen, but we have seen that there is much ambiguity and fluctuation as to the precise composition of such a unit.

Cooperation in childcare has its own constraints and tensions. While economic cooperation of the type that Siti, Rukiah and Ramlah engaged in is quite common, wives of brothers do not interfere with the raising of each other's children. It is considered highly inappropriate to comment on the manners of the children of one's husband's brother and to do so would cause considerable stress in the relationships among the wives of brothers. On the other hand it is quite common and acceptable that blood relatives take an active part in the upbringing of the children in their wider family. Thus a niece, and not the sister-in-law, was assigned with the task of baby-sitting Ramlah's children. And

Siti's son had to wait until Siti came back from town before he was fed. His sisters-in-law would not feed him. Though it is quite common and accepted that the relatives of the husband's side engage actively in the upbringing of their nieces and nephews, this can at the same time be a serious cause for tension and ultimate disruption. Much of the disagreement between Siti and Ahmad's wife had to do with the upbringing of their children, as well as with Siti's bossiness and her constant complaints about the laziness of her daughter-in-law (see K. von Benda-Beckmann 1996).

When a person falls ill or becomes old, the first persons to engage in care are those living together under one roof. But relatives, neighbours and friends frequently pay visits, so that part of the caring work is shared by others who live in other houses.

As we have mentioned before, divorced and widowed men and women past the age of 40 often remain unmarried and continue to have their own garden and kitchen. If they do so, there is a tendency to live together with another widowed or divorced relative, if possible of the opposite gender. It does not necessarily mean that these families will then form one economic consumer unit. Rather, living together under one roof increases cooperation in many respects. They come to a pragmatic arrangement in which they share what is convenient and keep other things separate.

The situation becomes different when such people get old. If they have been living with married children, they will continue to do so. Otherwise they come to live with one or more children who live nearby. If there are no married children in the village, women especially will live on their own as long as they are physically able to cook. They depend on the whims of their more distant relatives for care and food. Elderly men are more easily taken up, because they are not expected to cook for themselves, even though they may be physically capable of doing so. Some elderly people visit different relatives for meals on a rotational basis, anxiously avoiding the danger that their relatives would tire of taking care of them. They belong to no single consumer unit.

Types of Houses and Economic Cooperation

We have seen that economic cooperation and the provision of care vary greatly. The question is now how this varies with the type of houses. The example of the house of Siti and Sudin is typical for larger houses in which three generations live: a (grand)parent couple with unmarried children, one or two married children with spouse and (grand)children. There is a clear division of labour and cooperation along gender lines, but married status also plays a role. For instance, the unmarried adult children of Siti and Sudin are part of Siti's kitchen, while only married couples may contemplate establishing their own kitchen.

Furthermore, in-laws cooperate economically in a way that allows for maximum independence.

The situation is different in a fall-back house such as the family house (*lumaela*), the main reason being that those living together there are more distantly related. Ahmad and his wife Jainab, and Aida and her husband live together, but each couple has its own kitchen. But Ahmad likes his aunt Aida a lot and he sometimes would pick fruit for her or coconuts to make oil. Whenever he rasps sago she gets a basket. Only in case of special affective ties may adult inhabitants decide to cooperate closely. Otherwise, each couple or single adult keeps its own kitchen, takes care of its own children, and tries to earn money on his or her own.

The extent and intensity of cooperation among people living under one roof further depend on whether close relatives and good friends live close by or not. Thus, Gani often works closely together with the brother of Rukiah, who is married to his cousin and who lives next door. They go fishing and sago rasping together and have a garden next to each other, which they fenced together. We have also seen that Taher and Gani, and Rukiah and Ramlah worked closely together as long as they lived in one house. Moving out to a house 300 metres further down the main road ended much of this cooperation; the distance had become too great.

Temporary houses made of sago leafstalks are not meant for large families. Typically a one- or two-generation family lives there and operates rather autonomously. At the same time, cooperation between husband and wife is closer and more intensive than in larger families and larger houses. In general Butonese live in small temporary houses and cooperate mainly with co-residents. Because of their status as strangers, they have no direct access to land and houses. They need an Ambonese patron with whom they maintain relationships by various forms of cooperation and services (see F. von Benda-Beckmann 1990b, F. von Benda-Beckmann and Taale 1992).

Thus, for ordinary purposes, the type of house, as well as the contractual and property relationships to a house are important factors which shape the form, intensity and extent of cooperation. People who share a house tend to have more multi-stranded relationships and tend to cooperate more intensive than with persons living in another house. Property relationships to agricultural land induce cooperation in larger (in case of *pusaka*) or smaller (in case of *perusa*) social units. Furthermore, the *cari* economy encourages men and women alike to entertain individual networks of social relationships. There is considerable individual freedom of choice regarding whom one may cooperate with: there are constraints of property relationships; there is division of labour along gender lines; and the status of civil servants poses its own constraints on cooperation. On the other hand we have seen that the type of house poses its own constraints or possibilities upon cooperation: larger houses make more diverse forms of cooperation with persons sharing the same house possible; smaller houses lead to more exclusive, multi-stranded relations among the co-residents.

Political and Administrative Organization

The political organization of Ambonese villages is based on a complex mixture of Indonesian local government principles and *adat* elements. The political structure today is a combination of state government and local political organization which, in itself, has been continuously shaped by, but is distinct from, state government. *Adat* constitutional principles for centuries have been influenced by state regulation of local government and over the centuries have incorporated many regulations emanating from the colonial government.

In terms of the *adat* constitutional principles, individuals are members of socio-political groups, the clan association (*soa*), the clan (*rumah tau*) or the *dati* group. Though these groups have lost much of their earlier political significance, they still are important principles of political organization at the village level. These groups transcend or cross-cut co-residential groups, such as the village itself, the clan association and the patri-clan or clan segment (*rumah tau* or *famili*). At the lower level of decision-making within a *soa*, clan or clan segment, the family head, *kepala keluarga*, represents his dependants in deliberations and decision-making processes within these larger units. 'Family' here usually means the family of a person in the grandfather generation. Whether he and his descendants live in one house does not matter; the responsibility remains the same. If, on the other hand, two such family heads co-reside, each is the head of his family.

According to Indonesian constitutional and administrative law, people participate in political life as individual citizens, and are also represented as individual citizens through public elections at the village, provincial and national level. But for many administrative purposes, the government deals with what it considers the fundamental social unit between individuals and villages, and that is *rumah tangga* [literally 'household']. Most planning is based on statistical data of households, meaning houses and the persons living together in houses. Census officers, whose task it is to carry out census and aggregate for the sub-district (*kecamatan*) statistics, count houses and inhabitants of houses, irrespective of internal relationships among the persons living in one house, and irrespective of systematic differences between the Butonese and Ambonese population. No distinction is made between co-residents sharing a kitchen or having separate kitchens.

In matters of land tax (IPEDA), the situation is different. Though the exact ways in which people or groups find themselves entered in the tax register cannot always be followed, the rationale is to have tax paid by persons responsible for land-holding complexes, if possible also heads of households. Property of married women and daughters-in-law is considered household property of their husbands or fathers-in-law. Sons regarded as not yet 'fully independent' are counted as members of the tax-paying unit of their fathers, whether they co-reside with their fathers or not. According to the tax register there were 132 IPEDA paying units in Hila; in the Butonese *kampung* there were altogehter 178 units; while according to the census of 1984, Hila, including the Butonese settlements, had 636 households. The tax household therefore is larger than the census household,[109] but neither corresponds with the local terms *keluarga* or *famili*.

Ceremonial Organization

The organization in the sphere of ceremonies differs both from the relatively rigid political-administrative structures and from the highly flexible, everyday life with its seasonally determined fluctuations and its many ad hoc forms of economic cooperation.

Ceremonies are always celebrated with meals and prayers. There is a general obligation for all villagers to come and help, and each house is summoned. There is a clear division of labour according to age and gender. At funerals, for instance, it is the task of young men to dig the grave and to gather the wood-blocks and stones required to close the grave. They also fetch water and firewood and erect the temporary shelters. Several men are sent out to rasp sufficient amounts of sago. Though it is said that all should come and help, there is some idea of representation by family, in the sense that it is acceptable if only one or two sons of a (grand)father come. Co-residence is not crucial, though co-residing children may be more readily induced to come and help than a child living separately. The men regarded as heads of a family are expected to accompany the corpse to the grave and attend the burial. In the evening (and on the third, seventh and ninth days after the burial) they are invited to partake in the prayers and ceremonial meal. Family heads here means men in the oldest living generation, irrespective of whether they live together with their children or not.

Women have to contribute food, cook and bake. There is a division of labour according to status (married/widowed/divorced or unmarried) and to age. Old women who are too weak to do the hard labour are especially valued guests, not so much because they represent their house or family, but because

---

[109] Though having a population twice as large as the Butonese, the Ambonese have less IPEDA paying units. On the one hand, this could be explained by the relatively large families and landowning units among the Ambonese when compared to the Butonese. On the other hand, however, it may indicate the Butonese need for government support against political domination by the Ambonese. The first are, therefore, more inclined to cooperate in paying tax.

they represent the village community as such and add to the sense of being a community. They make the intricate dishes of glutinous rice and sit and chew betel and they are the first to be served food, before anyone else is served. Healthy old women do the bulk of the work and also represent their nuclear family and house. They usually stay long and do not eat before the male heads of families have been served during the ceremonial evening meal and prayers.

The obligations to come and work are stronger, the closer people are related to the deceased and his or her family, in terms of kinship, neighbourhood, friendship or patron or clientship. Co-resident people usually have quite different relations with a deceased person. Co-residence unites ceremonial obligations only to some extent, as those of a nuclear family or of a grandfather-headed family. Thus, in ordinary cases a man and a woman of the oldest generation both represent the house, each in their gender-specific way. Depending on the personal relationships of each individual, the input of labour and cash of specific members of the house may be greater or smaller. The plate with food that each man and woman who came to help receives as a representative of a nuclear or extended family underlines this in a ceremonial manner. But in case of doubt whether or not to go to a specific ceremony, living together in a house will tip the balance in favour of going if one co-resident has a special relationship with the hosts. In general, living in a small one- or two-generation house entails fewer ceremonial obligations than living in a larger house with more than two generations.

Conclusions

We have seen that there is considerable variation, at one particular moment and over time, in the composition of the membership of houses. We have shown that this primarily has to do with a combination of the kinship and property system and the nature of social relations among family members. To some extent, variation in the composition of co-residential units also depends on the type and size of a house, and whether it is suitable for a small family only or for more than a two-generation family. As we have shown with the histories of houses and of families, co-residence rarely establishes long-term (or structural) social, economic or political units. Co-residential units thus are not necessarily economic units, nor units of production, nor even units of income pooling. In the agro-ecological and economic conditions of Hila, with a high degree of seasonality and ad hoc cooperation in specific economic activities, the economic principle of *cari* forces and allows each individual to keep as many options open as possible. Cooperation is largely based on good relationships rather than on structural lines of authority and dependence. In ceremonial and political respects, houses do not form a unit either. To some extent, social and economic cooperation is structured by property relationships. But even property relationships do not unite co-resident family members into one property-holding unit, although tax officials would be happy if they did. Concrete property rights come into existence as a consequence of individual economic activities (*perusa*) and are not automatically extended to other persons living in the house. Or they pertain to the shared inherited property of groups of heirs who usually live in several different houses. Individual residents of a house may be, and usually are, members of various productive enterprises, participating in a wide range of social and economic activities together with persons living in other houses.

This does not mean that co-residence would not shape the ways and the extent to which people living together cooperate in different spheres. There is cooperation among some co-residents, a frequent pooling of resources and mutual help arrangements. However, the nature of cooperative arrangements are rarely equally divided among all co-residents, and may be no greater than cooperation and pooling with persons with whom one does not co-reside. Gender, status and age are demarcation principles along which care and cooperation are extended. While cooperation depends on familial or other obligations, co-residence adds another strand to already multi-stranded relationships. Co-residence leads to feelings of belonging which are likely to strengthen bonds and make the intensity of their relations greater than if the same persons had not lived together. These cannot be reduced to the feelings arising from kinship relations. Also, there are constraints evolving from a stronger interdependence of the co-residents, forcing them, perhaps often against their wills, to do things together which they otherwise would not have done. People living together within one house tend to share more social strands than others, but this does not mean that these strands are the same and equally intensive for all co-residents. And each individual has more or less intensive social, economic and ceremonial relationships with people in other houses. Distance in terms of time, space and kinship are important determining factors for the intensity of each of these strands.

The very same factors, living together in multi-stranded relations in a bounded space, also have a considerable potential for tension and conflict, which may explode any existing form of cooperation of co-residents and ultimately lead to the termination of this residence pattern. Then adolescent children move out, wives go back to their families and young married couples move into temporary houses. Gender relations play an interesting role here. We have seen that individuals largely come to live together on the basis of patrilineal kin relationships and patri- and virilocal residence. But once people live under one roof, it depends mainly on the women, and the relationships between women, whether this continues or not. One of the reasons is that adult women have less opportunity to avoid each other than men because of the gender-specific division of labour, while their relationship is already more vulnerable since they are not closely related by kin and live in a house as in-laws. Their work, notably food preparation and childcare, is more directly tied to the house than that of men, whose social and economic activities take place more often outside the house, kitchen or house yard, and who more easily can find things to do away from the house if relationships at home become strained. Thus the actual place where core activities are carried out greatly influences the potential for cooperation or conflict in relationships. The spatial dimension and the ways in which relationships and activities are spatially 'grounded' thus are important aspects to consider. This is not only a matter of 'in-door' and 'out-door' activities and frequency of contact between persons. Also the physical structure of a house provides social boundaries, and within the house it makes a difference whether or not house and kitchen are in the same building. Outside the house there are also gradations of 'social spaces', the house yard, the neighbourhood,[110] the (*adat*) village section, etc.[111]

The Ambonese situation thus shows us that a description and analysis of social and economic organization can be made without taking 'households' as the point of departure. The term 'household' does not necessarily capture the most relevant property-holding units nor units of production, redistribution, care or ceremonial organization. Even at the level of government administration, household (*rumah tangga*) means different social units. The term suggests more stability and unity than is warranted. Households may be handy for aggregating population statistics, but not for more. Policies that take the household as the central unit therefore are not likely to reach the really relevant social and economic units. The emphasis which earlier household critiques have placed on the need to study inter-household relationships besides looking into internal household relationships cannot compensate for the shortcomings of the household approach. For as we have seen in the Ambonese situation, it is rarely possible, necessary or useful to speak of inter-household relationships in the sense of a relationship connecting two whole social units. Rather it is persons living in different houses, who enter into and maintain more or less intensive relationships.

Rather than giving households, which are single abstract social units, a priori a central place in one's analytical framework, it is more fruitful to ask what the relevant social units are and what significance co-residence and co-resident units have in social and economic organization. Approaching these questions from a residence perspective and looking into the relationships between people and houses helps us to gain more insight into the conditions under which co-residing units are formed and the variable and changing significance they have. An analysis in terms of networks of relationships, in which some strands are more closely knit than others and some relationships involve more

---

[110] Ambonese *adat* has rather elaborate notions about the obligations of 'neighbours' (*ahli jirah*) towards one another, and about who neighbours are.

[111] As we have shown elsewhere, this is also relevant for the relationships between Ambonese landlords and immigrant Butonese villagers which vary with spatial distance, and with the settlement pattern, depending on whether Butonese live dispersed among Ambonese or, as in Hila, in spatially segregated *kampung* (F. and K. von Benda-Beckmann 1991; F. von Benda-Beckmann and Taale 1992).

strands than others, and of which the spatial aspect, including co-residence, is one of these strands, is more appropriate for the highly volatile economic and social system we find in Hila. Of course, there may be societies with social units which can properly be labelled households. But a general methodology must be able to capture and explain cooperation in a *cari* economy. This is all the more pressing, because a *cari*-like economy may not be an idiosyncrasy of the island of Ambon, but instead quite common for poor peasants who stand with one foot in the market economy and with the other in subsistence, and who are faced with increasing government involvement and migration.

Plate 5.1.: Ruin of Fort Amsterdam in Hila, built in the early 17th century

Plate 5.2: Fort Amsterdam in 1996 after its restauration

Chapter 5
Texts in Context:
Historical Documents as Political Commodity on Islamic Ambon*

Franz and Keebet von Benda-Beckmann

Introduction

For nearly four centuries, the famous clove islands of the Central Moluccas have been in contact with, and subjected to a colonial power with an administrative system that used documents to communicate instructions and to register important social and economic events. When the Dutch East Indies Company (VOC) started governing and exploiting Ambonese villages, the villagers became acquainted with this custom, much earlier than in other regions of the Indonesian archipelago (for 19th century documents, see Leirissa et al. 1982). This was particularly so in the village of Hila, where we lived during our research in 1985 and 1986.[112] Hila had been the seat of three of the four grand leaders of the 'Golden Federation', the Uli Helawan, a political union of the clans of Hitu and Hila which had become a dominant political force on the northern coast in the 16th century (see Rumphius 1910, Manusama 1977, Knaap 1987a). It had become an important administrative and economic centre during the reign of the VOC, and also during the period in which Ambon formed part of the Dutch East Indies colony. During and after the Dutch conquest of Ambon in the course of the first half of the 17th century, the Dutch had built a stone fort at Hila which became the seat of VOC officials and later of a Dutch Assistant Resident.

      Over the centuries many documents had been drawn up and been saved carefully within the village. Most of the older documents, from the 17th, 18th

---

* First published in W. Marschall (ed.). 1994. *Texts from the Islands: Oral and Written Traditions of Indonesia and the Malay World*. Bern: Ethnologica Bernensia 4/1994: 223-243.

[112] Our research, a joint project of the Department of Agrarian Law of the Agricultural University Wageningen and the Department of Social Sciences, Faculty of Law, Erasmus University Rotterdam, focussed upon village level forms of social security. It was carried out under the auspices of LIPI with the sponsorship of Universitas Pattimura, Ambon.

and 19th century, were in the possession of members of the Lating-Nustapi clan, and had to do with their clan affairs. The Lating-Nustapi clan had been involved in the political negotiations with the VOC in the 17th and 18th century, and after the establishment of VOC rule in the wars of 1634 and 1647, had provided the local rulers *(orang kaya,* later *raja)* until the first half of the 19th century.[113] During the 19th century, the succession of Lating village heads had been broken. From the middle of the 19th century, all village heads had come from the Ollong clan, with the exception of Djapnur Lating Nustapi who had been *raja* from 1896 (or 1900) until 1917. Latings had kept the marriage and birth registers in their capacity of village heads. The younger brothers of the village heads had been *nagulschrijvers,* the administrators and registrars of cloves which the villagers had to plant for and deliver to the VOC (see Krausc-Katerla 1986, Knaap 1987a). The Latings had also been the largest property owners in the area surrounding the residential core of the village.[114] Lating property had been a subject of many disputes, between branches of the Lating clan or between descendants of Latings belonging to other clans. Many of these cases had been decided in courts, and each court case had generated new documents. Some of these disputes had kept generations busy.[115]

We first came into contact with these documents ten days after having moved to Hila. Djaplul (Tete) Lating-Nustapi came to visit us. He had brought two documents, dated 1700, which had been written in Dutch by the official of the VOC in Fort Victoria, in the present city of Ambon. Whether we could translate the texts into Indonesian? We were quite excited and gladly complied with his request. Apparently our efforts were well received, for Tete told us that our translation was correct. We then realized that he had tested us with a text

---

[113] The clan was named after the Nustapi, one of the four offices of the Uli Helawan federation. The Lating clan had been entitled to this office until it was abolished by the Dutch. Two of the others, Pati Tuban of the clan Ollong and Totohatu of Ely had also moved to Hila, the fourth, Tanehitu of the clan Peluw staying in Hitu. See Manusama 1977; Knaap 1987a.

[114] Hasan Suleiman, the most prominent member of the clan's history, and the Hila ruler around the turn of the 18th century, had been a successful political and economic entrepreneur and had also acquired land in other villages (see Knaap 1987a). Some of his and his successors' sales were documented. Between 1683 and 1706 he had made four testaments and two codicils, authorized by VOC officials (see F. and K. von Benda-Beckmann 1987b).

[115] Thus, the *Landraad* in Ambon in 1806 had given a decision about the validity of the inheritance of Yusuf Abdul Rachman, Hasan Suleiman's adoptive son. The inheritance had become a court issue again in 1900. For the past 50 years a continuous battle has been going on between two Lating branches, represented by Haji Banga and Abdul Rahman Lating, and after their death by their sons, Abdul Salam and Tete (Djaplul) Lating (see genealogy). In 1938 the case had gone to a state court. In the 1950s the parties had fought in the Islamic court, and since the 1960s three separate disputes had gone up the civil court hierarchy to the Supreme Court.

which already had been translated into Indonesian by somebody else, the notary public in Ambon, as it turned out later. Five weeks later, the Dutch Ambassador visited the village, to see the old Fort Amsterdam. Again we were approached by Tete Lating to do a job: make an inventory, in Dutch and Indonesian, of 20 assorted documents. This list then would be presented to the Ambassador, together with the request to grant the Lating family support for a local museum. Again we complied quite eagerly, and were again excited by the documents and what they told us about the regional and village history. Registrations of persons' births or marriages helped us to give the genealogies we had made on the basis of interviews some handhold in time, records of transactions of property and written accounts of property disputes provided us with historical depth for longitudinal case-studies, and provided material against which to check contemporary oral or written accounts of past events.[116] Throughout our stay in the village, our efforts to see, if possible, photocopy, and understand these documents and their role in village life became an important part of our research activities. Since we provided free translations, our services were looked for, and the documents became the subject of many discussions during interview sessions and meetings in our house.

Gradually we realized that the villagers treasure these documents as more than mere written records of past events and relationships, although some villagers recognize the historical value of the old documents. Documents are in the first place seen and used as valuable resources in efforts to establish and prove claims to property and political offices. They serve as a landmark in history through which one may legitimize one's claim to property and offices. But because of their crucial potential as evidence for such claims, they have become a scarce resource which can be sold or exchanged for other information or for political support. Documents thus became commodities, to be mobilized when deemed profitable, or to be stored to create scarcity.

We also came to realize that the documents, even though people are quite used to them, are embedded in a basically oral culture. This has specific consequences for their significance in village life. In the first place, it influences the way in which documents are interpreted. Their meaning is largely shaped

---

[116] The documents we came across during our research fell into 6 categories:
1. Documents concerning property transfers (testaments, codicils, sales contracts, donations).
2. Registers (birth and marriage registers, tax registers, a register of property holding clan segments (*dati*).
3. Documents pertaining to appointments to office (village head, and other *adat* functionaries).
4. Documents concerning the political and administrative relations between the Dutch and the Ambonese.
5. Genealogies.
6. Court decisions.

and maintained in oral transmissions, by what the documents are thought and said to contain rather than by interpretations of the actual texts. Secondly, the relevance given to the documents in property affairs is at odds with the local customary *adat* ways of dealing with property and inheritance matters: Traditionally, past events were adjusted to the present conditions through changes in oral traditions, through negotiations about and reconstructions of the past which would fit the present needs. This induced a kind of systematic forgetfulness about the past. Documents, on the other hand, highlighted, and over-dramatized a particular point in history (see Goody 1986: 155), but they induced a different kind of forgetfulness, of the processes of adjustment which occurred between the making of the document and the present.

In our paper we want to describe the meaning and role of documents in Hila. Most of our paper will focus on the use of these documents as strategic resources in property disputes. To a large extent we shall be concerned with the interpretations of the texts. Texts, however, are only one aspect of these documents. Not all villagers who regard the documents as important have ever read the text, but the documents may have meaning for them apart from any textual interpretation. And that meaning may influence their strategies related to the use of these documents. Before turning to the interpretations of the texts, we shall therefore try to give a more general picture of the meanings attributed to the documents.

The Strategic Potential of Documents

In order to illustrate the strategic potential of the documents, a brief account must be given of the complex property system in which they may become relevant.[117]

The property to which most documents relate is land (*tanah*), individual trees (*pohon*), vegetable or tree gardens (*kebun*), plantation plots (*dusun*) planted with sago palms, nutmeg or clove trees, and uncultivated forest land (*ewang*). These categories of property can be subject to different rights, held by different social units: individuals, groups of heirs, a *dati*[118], or the village.

---

[117] For accounts of Ambonese *adat law,* see in particular Holleman 1923. Further relevant information is contained in *Adatrechtbundels* 7 (1913): 215-222; 21 (1922): 13-64; 24 (1925): 354 ff. See also F. von Benda-Beckmann 1986, 1990b and F. and K. von Benda-Beckmann 1987b. For older descriptions see Van Hoëvell 1875.

[118] *Datis* were patrilineally structured clan-segments which in colonial times were used as units for administration, *corvée* labour and clove production. As compensation, the *dati* were granted land, mainly sago gardens, the so-called *tanah dati,* for the subsistence needs for the *dati* members (see Van Hoëvell 1875: 175; Holleman 1923: 56, 64, 109; Van Fraassen 1972: 39). In the Christian villages of Ambon the *dati* land system has kept much more of its force than in Islamic villages (see Holleman 1923: 110). In

Rights to land may belong to different social units than rights and to the trees or plantations on the same land. Individual property rights (*perusah*, *tatanaman*) come into existence by someone's own efforts, e.g. through cultivation or planting. They give the holders a range of freedom over their trees comparable with private ownership. Such rights also come into existence when people buy trees or *dusun* (*babalian*, 'buyings') or donations (*pemberian*, *pengasihan*).

Inherited property (*pusaka*) rights come into existence after an individual property holder dies. His *perusah* or *babalian* then become *pusaka*. Inheritance rights are in principle bilateral; however, they are often interwoven with principles of Islamic inheritance law. *Pusaka* rights entitle heirs to the exploitation of property objects, e.g. to cultivate in a *pusaka* garden or *dusun* and to share the products of *pusaka* trees.

Dati membership is established by patrifiliation, or, in the case of immigrant groups, by adoption. Membership in a *dati* gives the right to cultivate on *dati* property and to share in the *dati*-trees, mainly uncultivated sago palms and fruit trees. Access and exploitation is regulated by the *dati*-head, in consultation with the other elders of the *dati*. Female *dati* members lose their *dati*-membership and the rights based upon it through marriage. However, they may be allocated some property if they ask for it and if the *dati* elders agree.

Village rights consist of the administrative control of village land that is not privately owned, *pusaka* or *dati* land. In most Ambonese villages, villagers can freely cultivate village land subject to the permission of the village government. In Hila, such permission was not required (see already Volker 1920). Besides, the property of extinct *dati* falls under the control of the village, to be reallocated by the village government.[119]

The fact that trees, *kebun* and *dusun* with the legal status of *perusah* and *pusaka* can be, and regularly have been/are established on village and *dati*-land, makes the system of property relations are very complex, or, to use the words of a keen observer and analyst in the 1920s, 'chaotic and precarious' (Holleman 1923). The different relations of access and inheritance (patrilineal for *dati*, bilateral for *pusaka*) lead to the situation that on most plots of land a variety of individuals and groups of heirs, belonging to the same or to different clans, have rights to trees and to the land itself.

---

the years 1814 and 1824 the *dati* lands were registered by the colonial government in all Christian villages, but only in two Islamic villages, Hitu and Batu Merah. However, for the district Hila there existed a *dati*-personnel register which gave the number of *dati* per clan association (*soa*), and the numbers of people under each *dati* head. This register was in the possession of Tete Lating.

[119] This has been regarded as a residue of the formerly more comprehensive 'right of avail' ('*beschikkingsrecht*') of the village, which in the past may have had a more comprehensive character, including residual rights on *pusaka* and *perusah* land as well. About the changes in the rights of villages see Holleman 1923.

Adat legitimations of claims to property thus are based on social positions which imply rights to land, tree gardens or individual trees, individually or as a member or representative of a larger group of persons.[120] Most of these claims must be based upon social positions of earlier possessors and the relationships – common *dati*-membership or inheritance – between them and the present claimants.[121] Struggles about property and offices mainly consist of attempts to get one's own position 'in line' with the legally relevant types of positions and relationships, to establish what Bhaskar and Giddens would call 'position-practice' relations (Giddens 1984: 83). This nearly always makes a reconstruction of historical positions and relationships necessary.

The documents embody such position-practice relations at an earlier point of time. Birth and marriage registers prove persons' existence and fix them in time. They also provide concrete links in the genealogical chains relevant for inheritance claims. Transactions of property lay down relationships and transfers which have relevance for the subsequent structure of property relationships, and therefore can be used in the construction and legitimation of claims. Once these positions and relationships have been established, the temporal distance between the documented position and the one desired and claimed must be bridged on the basis of the principles of property and inheritance rules, and it must be established that the property mentioned in the document is the same as the one presently claimed.

Since most disputes are about *dati* and inherited property, they are rarely a matter of individuals only and usually involve many more people than the official parties. One claimant may represent the descendants of common ancestors two or three generations removed, perhaps 50 or 60 persons in all. In one of the Lating disputes, for example (see below), 31 members of the Lating clan had started a case, opposing a Supreme Court judgement. 'Members' in this case meant the heads of two- or three-generation families, so that at least 80 adults were directly involved. Besides, other villagers, though not claiming a right to the disputed property by way of inheritance, may have trees on the disputed land: for instance, on one of the *dusun* disputed between two Lating branches, 66 different families from various clans owned trees.

---

[120] In Giddens' terms, legal positions are 'constituted structurally as specific intersections of signification, domination and legitimation which relates to the [legally relevant] typifications of agents' (Giddens 1984: 83). A social-legal position involves the specification of a definite 'identity' within a network of social relations [of legal relevance], that identity, however, being a 'category' to which a particular range of normative sanctions [consequences] is relevant.

[121] For a detailed account of Ambonese *adat* law of land, trees and inheritance see Holleman 1923. Quite a number of interesting data and variations between Ambonese villages are contained in the *Adatrechtbundels*. For an earlier account, see Van Hoëvell 1875. Some aspects of contemporary land and tree law in Hila have been described in F. von Benda-Beckmann 1986 and 1990b.

The Meaning of Documents in Village Life

The villagers are aware of the potential value which such documents have in property affairs. However, assessments of the documents' strategic value are not always based upon the know-ledge of the documents' texts. Most documents lead a secret and mysterious life. Not many people possess documents, and those who do try to keep them secret in order to control the information embodied in them. The greater the secrecy, the more importance is accorded to them. The elusive and mysterious character of the documents is enhanced (also for the possessors themselves) by the fact that many are written in Dutch, and some in Arabic script. Villagers do not know Dutch, and only a few read Arabic script well. But also if documents are written in romanised Malay, the 18th century handwriting is difficult to read. Getting to know the texts thus means employing a translator, with the risk of loss of secrecy and of incurring expenses. People avoid this until they feel that they really have to produce the text, for instance as evidence in a court dispute. In such a case, the notary public in Ambon city is asked to make an official translation. But even then, the person who has given the order for translation may keep it for himself. And as it costs money to get a transcription or an official photocopy of a court judgement, only those prepared to share the expenses are allowed to see the written judgement. Besides, if a judgment is not favourable enough, it may not be in the interest of its possessor to make this widely known. We came across several cases in which persons who had been parties to a court case, claimed that 'they had won' although the text of the judgment revealed the contrary. People tended to consider possession of a document to be a strong indication that its content is in the possessor's favour. Unless the real text is disclosed, this belief will not be easily shaken. The revelation of the actual text therefore often leads to grave disappointments. But even if the texts are made available, the *idées fixes* associated with the documents are often stronger than the naked truth of the texts. And this may lead people to employ the documents as proof for their own claim even in situations in which it is harmful to their interests.[122] So to a large extent, the meaning of documents rests upon oral tradition, hearsay and speculation. This is particularly so in the case of the older documents whose content has been transmitted through the generations without anyone ever having read them. But it also ap-

---

[122] Our neighbour's father (Hadi Launuru, see genealogy) had been involved in the 1960s in a dispute about the Lebeapo Lating inheritance (see below). The family strengthened their claim by producing a court judgment from 1900, in which Bunga Tjaja Lating, our neighbour's grandmother, and Boki, her cousin, had claimed property from Sadja and Hajat Lating, their cousins. The *dusun* claimed in the 1960s however, had not been mentioned in the 1900 judgment. Besides, their grandmother's claim had been dismissed by lack of proof. Our neighbour still was convinced that his grandmother had won the case.

plies to more recent and contemporary documents, like the court judgments mentioned.

Since people are convinced that the documents are important for establishing and proving claims to property, possession of the documents gives the holder power, based upon promises, or threats to use the documents in other people's property affairs. Possession of documents therefore also invites suspicion, mistrust and envy by those who might be harmed by the information in them. Manipulating with documents requires strength and prudence, and strict control of their contents. Not everybody is able or willing to carry this burden. This need for control and secrecy may go so far that people who have no vested interest in the village are not allowed to see them. Thus officials of the National Archives in Jakarta who had come to Hila several times to acquire documents for the archives had been refused to see them, even though they had offered good copies and had invited the possessor to go to Jakarta. The strategic information is only made available selectively for friends or allies.

Since documents are regarded as valuable, great efforts are made to acquire them, and some people are quite inventive in exploiting such possibilities as the presence of two researchers. Since we stayed long enough in the village to give people a chance to assess our trustworthiness, and since we came in handy as free of charge translators, we could see and copy quite a number of documents. But hours and days went into our own negotiations about the documents, and into people's continuous probing of our own motives and reliability to keep the documents secret from neighbours and other villagers.[123] Often people, aware of our involvement, would incorporate us into their strategies. They offered to help us in our research, and with this as an excuse reason approached others whom they knew or expected to have documents that would be interesting for themselves, hoping to get to know the document's secrets as well.[124] People also attempted to use us directly as brokers. We, as persons without economic interest in village property affairs, should try to get copies of documents from X, and share their contents with Y in exchange for the information Y had imparted to us. Knowing the value of secrecy, we did not comply with such requests.

---

[123] We are grateful to Tete (Djaplul) Lating-Nustapi and others who allowed us to see and photocopy some documents (see note 116). They had no misgivings about us using the materials in scientific publications.The court cases mentioned and the parties involved are known to everyone and are freely discussed in the village. People were proud of their village history and their ancestors, and they would not appreciate if their clan's, ancestors' or own involvement in this history would be alienated through the anonymity of pseudonyms.

[124] Abdul Salam and our neighbours, for example, made several trips to Ambon to fetch some court judgments from a kinsman in which they had an interest. Unfortunately, their kinsman did not put their altruistic motives above the danger of losing control of the documents, and refused to produce them.

The Documents at Face Value

But even if the text of a document is known, or becomes known during a court case or in negotiations with government officials, it often creates problems and surprises. The major problem tends to be that the information in a text is often too limited to convey the full set of data, (relationships, details of a transaction, complete description of the object of a transaction) needed to establish that the documented object is identical with the presently disputed one, and to establish the relevant relation between the past owners and oneself.

In most documents, the property transferred and also sometimes the persons concerned remain rather unspecified. An early, but typical example can be found in the testament of Hasan Suleiman of 1700 (see F. and K. von Benda-Beckmann 1987b: 264). In his testament, Hasan Suleiman appointed certain people as his successors in *dati* matters, and granted them the use of all *dati* lands as well as four slaves *(lijfeigenen)* who were attached to the cultivation of the *dati* lands. However, these properties and persons were not specified since 'the testator does not deem it necessary to specify these lands and slaves by name in this testament, since they are sufficiently known by his own descendants as well as by the people of Hila.'[125]

This may have been so at that time. But nearly 300 years later, things look different. If the chain of transmitting such knowledge through the generations is broken, such textual references no longer allow the reconstruction of the lands and people. Besides, the reconstruction is made difficult because it is unclear whether 'the *dati* lands' in Hila mentioned in the testament referred to all *dati* lands of the Lating Nustapi or just to parts of the *dati* lands under the direct control of Hasan Suleiman. Moreover, whatever may have been the situation in 1700, the Lating *dati* lands have been divided in later times. Another document in the possession of the Lating clan, the *dati* personnel register of 1847, enumerates 11 *dati* heads of the Lating clan association *(soa)*[126], of whom only half belonged to the Lating clan. Although this register, too, is only of limited value because it only gives the names of the *dati* heads, and not always even their clan name, it does show that the *dati* groups have been divided.

Another complication is that plots of land *(dusun)* are commonly only identified by their name in the documents. Very often this is not sufficient to identify the exact location of disputed property. Knowledge of the actual location of the *dusun* may have been lost or weakened; the self-evident knowledge

---

[125] '... welke landerijen en slaven den testateur onnodig aght in desen bij namen te specificeren, omdat deselve, soo bij sijne namagen, als bij die van de negorij Hila, genoeg bekent sijn ...'

[126] *Soa* are associations of different clans, grouped around a major clan. *Soa* are headed by a *kepala soa,* who together with the village head were the main political offices in the local government system, a mixture of *adat,* VOC and colonial regulations.

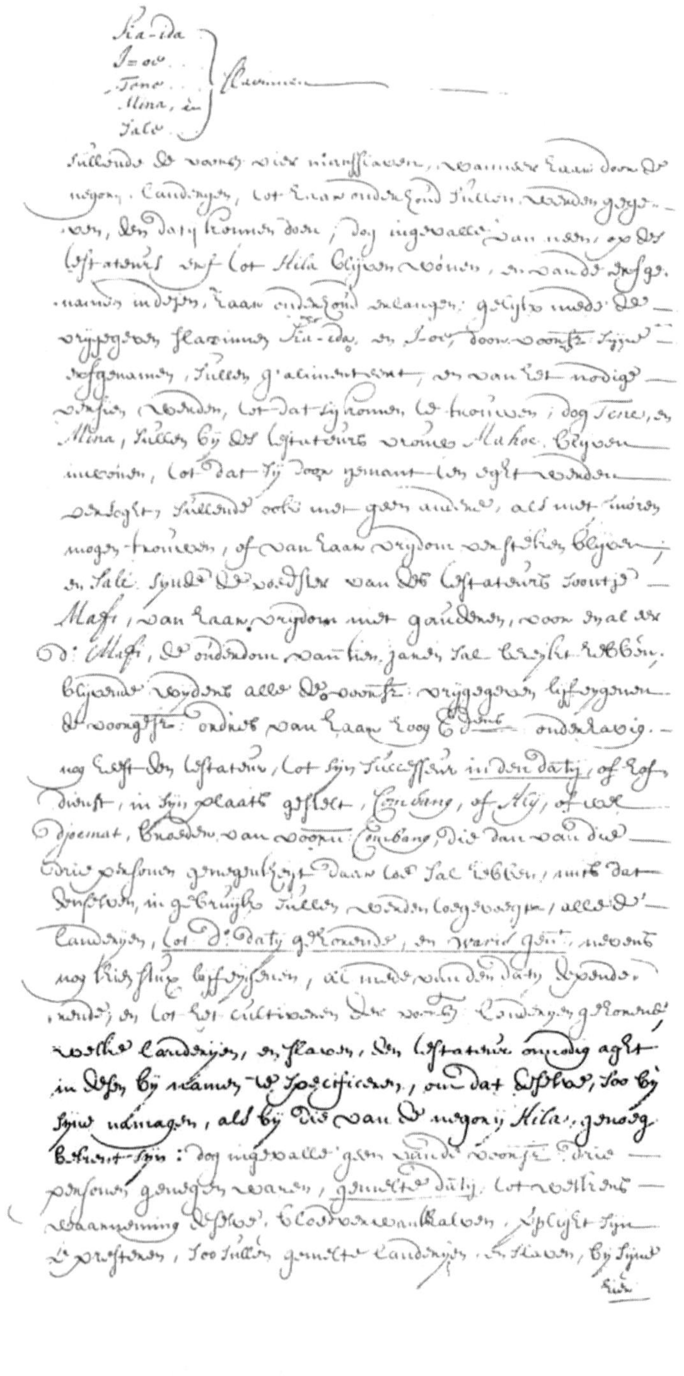

Plate 5.3: Fifth page of the testament of Hasan Suleiman of 1700. The text quoted in note 125 is highlighted

about the *dusun*'s location may have become a matter of divergent interpretations. A *dusun* named in a document may have been only part of a larger *dusun* area referred to by the same name, and *dusun* have also been renamed in the course of time.

For these reasons the use of documents may become increasingly problematic as time elapses. Relevant information that is considered to be self-evident at the time and in the context of the drafting is not included in the document for that reason. Also, means of further specification often do not endure as relevant standards throughout time. Until recently, there was no system of mapping and cadastral registration. Landmarks usually mark only larger geographical areas, rarely smaller pieces of land. Vegetation changes over time. Often, the names of the neighbouring *dusun* or tree owners are mentioned in the documents, but because of the complicated bilateral inheritance system, it will be difficult to establish after several generations who the present owners of these plots are.

This problem is not unique to documents made up under VOC or colonial rule. Theoretically, the technical means of mapping and cadastral registration of land are available now. However, in present day Hila, no agricultural land, and with a few exceptions, not even house sites, have been registered and mapped under the Basic Agrarian Law of 1960. In contemporary documents the names of the owners of land concerned are used to indicate the location of property, and the property itself is still referred to as 'a *dusun* named X' or 'a garden' or 'a piece of land'.

Strategies and Counterstrategies

Once people are convinced that documents contain relevant information with respect to contemporary claims, they have to do two things. Firstly, they have to establish that the property objects mentioned in the document and the property presently claimed are identical. Secondly, they must construct their social position in such a way that the legal consequences of the document, extended by the application of the kinship rules relevant for inheritance, lead directly to a situation which justifies their claims or counterclaims. These requirements also set the stage for counterstrategies: that the property in the document is identical with the disputed land has to be denied, and the inheritance line can be questioned. Under these circumstances, both parties try to exploit the lack of clarity in the documents.

Shifting Dusun

The information provided by the text and the inheritance right of one's opponent need not always be disputed. A claim can be made irrelevant by asserting that one talks about different objects. The troubles around the *dusun* Waisela (also written Wasela or Waesela) are a good illustration for this situation.

The first link in the chain of history was a donation of three pieces of land, documented on 23 April 1820. The text was as follows:

> 'Walida Tetuputih, head *(orang tua parenta)* of the *negeri* Senalu,[127] declared: that his deceased father, Ramalanji Tetuputij, had given to Hasang Lating, the *nagulschrijver*, three blocks of uncultivated land *(tiga pangal tanah kosong)* for him to work and make it a garden *(kebun)* by planting whatever crops.
>
> That he [Walida T.] himself now gave the pieces of land aforementioned to the *nagulschrijver* Sangkop Hitoe Lating, Hasang Lating's son, like his father had already done, because he had made already efforts in making the land into garden.
>
> He acknowledged that he had no objections that empty or garden land was included.[128]
>
> These three pieces of land, or *dusun,* were called Wasela, Tahoko, and Morol.
>
> Wasela had a length, from east to west, of 145 ells *(depa)*, and from south to north 135 ells;
>
> Tahoko a length from east to west of 113 ½ ells, from [...] to the coast 235 ½ ells, and from west to east 53 ½ ells;
>
> Morol from east to west on the land-side 33 ½ ells, and from the land to the coast 124 *depa*, and at the coast 77 ells.'

This document became an important point of reference in many disputes. In 1938, it was presented as evidence in a case between Abdul Rahman Lating, a descendant of Hasan and Sangkup Hitu Lating, and Bangsa Lating, a descendant of Hasan Lating's brother (see genealogy) about the rights to the *dusun*

---

[127] Senalu was one of the old mountain villages in the Hila area, existing well before the coastal village Hila was established. Senalu was regarded to have controlled much of the later village territory of Hila. The Senalu people moved to the coast later, together with the people from the *negeri* Marsapal, after the Lating and Ollong clans had established the coastal village. Marsapal and Senalu were only gradually incorporated into the Hila of the Uli Helawan.

[128] '... *ada mengakuw jang tiada sabarang katagahan apa turu[t] tana kosong atau kabong jang tersebut.*'

Waisela.[129] Against this evidence, Bangsa Lating did not succeed in proving his rights to the *dusun.*

In the l950s, Bangsa (now Haji Bangsa) tried again and brought a case before the Religious Court in Ambon, claiming that the disputed property was common heritage for both parties. This was confirmed by that court.[130] On appeal, however, Abdul Rahman Lating managed to convince the Court of Appeal that, notwithstanding their common descent from Yusuf Abdul Rahman, the disputed property was the one donated by Walida Teteputih, as was evident from the donation document and the 1938 judgment.[131] However, Haji Bangsa now maintained that the disputed property was not the *dusun* Waisela, but *dusun* Waipoko. While agreeing that Waisela was Abdul Rahman's *pusaka*, he contended that the disputed plot was in the *dusun* Waipoko. This was confirmed by the village government, which was anti-Lating at that time, and also by a commission headed by the chairman of the Religious Court who came to Hila to collect evidence. Armed with this evidence, Haji Bangsa brought the case about the *dusun* Waipoko to the ordinary State Court. The court dismissed the case since Abdul Rahman had proven, with the judgement of 1938 that he owned the *dusun* Waisela, which had been renamed Waipoko by Haji Bangsa.[132]

On appeal, the tide turned again. The Court of Appeal decided that the case was about the *dusun* Waipoko, and not about Waisela. It was Abdul Rahinan who had renamed the disputed *dusun*. The earlier documents concerning *dusun* Waisela therefore were irrelevant for the case. The court believed the witnesses testifying for Haji Bangsa and awarded the *dusun* to him.[133] Abdul Rahman went into cassation before the Indonesian Supreme Court, amongst others with the argument 'that he had a *dusun* document (*surat dusun*), the donation of Waisela' whereas Haji Bangsa had none. The Supreme Court, however, upheld the Court of Appeal's judgment.[134]

The Waisela/Waipoko series of disputes was not unique. Similar strategies were followed in at least two other series of disputes in the 1970s and 80s. One set of disputes concerned one of the other *dusun* mentioned in the Walida Teteputih donation of 1820, the *dusun* Tahoku:

In the 1980's, Hila had become the capital village of the new subdistrict *(Kecamatan)* Leihitu, and the offices of the *Kecamatan* were built in the Tahoku area. During our stay, a post office was to be built. The sub-district head *(Camat)* chose a site and offered to buy the land from a person who owned clove trees on it. However, Tete Lating interfered, claiming the land as his

---

[129] Landraad Ambon, case no. 65/1938.
[130] Hakim Sjara' Ambon, case no. 22/HS/56.
[131] Hakim Sjara' Propinsi Maluku, case no. 1/HSP/56.
[132] Pengadilan Negeri Ambon, case no. 281/1962 Perdata.
[133] Pengadilan Tinggi Ambon, case no. 51/1967 Perdata.
[134] Mahkamah Agung, case no. 12/K/Sip.

pusaka on the basis of the donation document. The *Camat*, unwilling to get involved in a dispute, looked elsewhere and found some undisputed land, unfortunately for the villagers at a distance of more than 2 km from the village core area.

Linking Positions to Documented Persons

Genealogies are crucial in the endeavors to establish links with persons mentioned in documents, since they lay down the lines along which property devolves. Together with documents about sales, donations, testaments or court decisions, they can mark crucial points in time where common descent ends and separate descent starts, from where inherited property, *pusaka*, belongs to one descent line only. Thus in the 1956 cases between Abdul Rahman and Bangsa Lating, Abdul Rahman Lating could establish exclusive claims for his descent line by showing with the help of the donation document that *dusun* Waisela had been given to Sankup Hitu Lating, his direct ancestor, and therefore was not part of the *pusaka* of the common ancestor Yusuf Abdul Rachman (see genealogy).

The easiest way to counter the inheritance rights of one's opponent is to question and refute the chain of descent which ties him to the person whose rights to the property are not disputed. Such manipulations of 'genealogical charters' (Bohannan) and the making of genealogies to establish legally relevant relationships to real or alleged ancestors are of course well known from anthropological accounts of tribal and village societies all over the world. But people usually have no recourse to documents which can prove, or disprove, crucial links in such charters. In Hila, much relevant information about genealogical relationships was contained in the marriage and birth registers, and also in various judgments. Such statements impose their own constraints upon later interpreters, which cannot easily be challenged. But other documents can provide information to attack the validity or relevance of such historical statements of genealogical relationships.

In the struggle over generations between the two Lating branches, whose descent lines were in principle undisputed, the parties accused each other's descent line of being blemished by illegitimate births. Sankup Hitu, so Abdul Salam Lating, the son of Haji Bangsa, had not been the real father of Hambati; even worse, it was alleged that Hambati had been the fruit of an incestuous relation. Since illegitimate children broke the line of descent, no Lating property could therefore rightfully devolve along that genealogical link. Tete Lating, Abdul Rachman's son, countered: Djamaludin was born out of wedlock, not the son of Baharudin. So no property could devolve in his opponent's line. And he supported his assertion with the birth register of Hila from the early

19th century, which showed an entrance of a child was having born out of wedlock.

Another way to change the legal relevance of the descent line is by introducing the principles of Islamic inheritance law. This must have been in the mind of Abdul Gani Lating in the suit he brought against Haji Dasna in the Religious Court in 1965, in one of the many struggles about the *pusaka* of Lebeapo and Masir Lating in which also several documents were involved.

The Lebeapo/Masir Inheritance

In 1900, Bunga Tjaya and Boki fought Hajat and Sadja Lating for property alleged to be *pusaka* of their common grandfather Lebeapo and/or Lebeapo's cousin Masir (see genealogy). Masir had died before Lebeapo. The case had been brought to the Religious Court in Ambon in 1899 where the Imam had stated that the four sons of Lebeapo were Lebeapo's heirs. This should have meant that in later property disputes, claimants would have to trace their relations to one of Lebeapo's children.[135]

In 1965, Abdul Gani Lating, the brother of Abdul Rahman, went to the Religious Court, suing Haji Dasna, in order to obtain a statement about the heirs of Masir Lating. The court stated that according to Islamic Law, only Hajat and Sadja Lating were the heirs of Masir, thus limiting the heirs to the descendants of only one of Lebeapo's children.[136]

---

[135] The *Landraad* in 1900 had dismissed the claim for lack of evidence, and the rights to the property remained unsettled. In 1961, 29 persons form the Launuru, Moni, Ely, Uluelang and Lating-Gabah2 clans, all of them descendants of Lebeapo's children, sued Abdul Rahman Lating for a *dusun* alleged to have been part of the inheritance of Lebeapo disputed already in 1900. When a closer reading of the 1900 judgement revealed that the *dusun* was not mentioned at all in the judgement, the dispute faded out.

[136] Unfortunately, we have no full documentation of these disputes, because the possessors, members of the Moni and Lating Gabah2 clans, were not willing to show us the 1965 judgment.

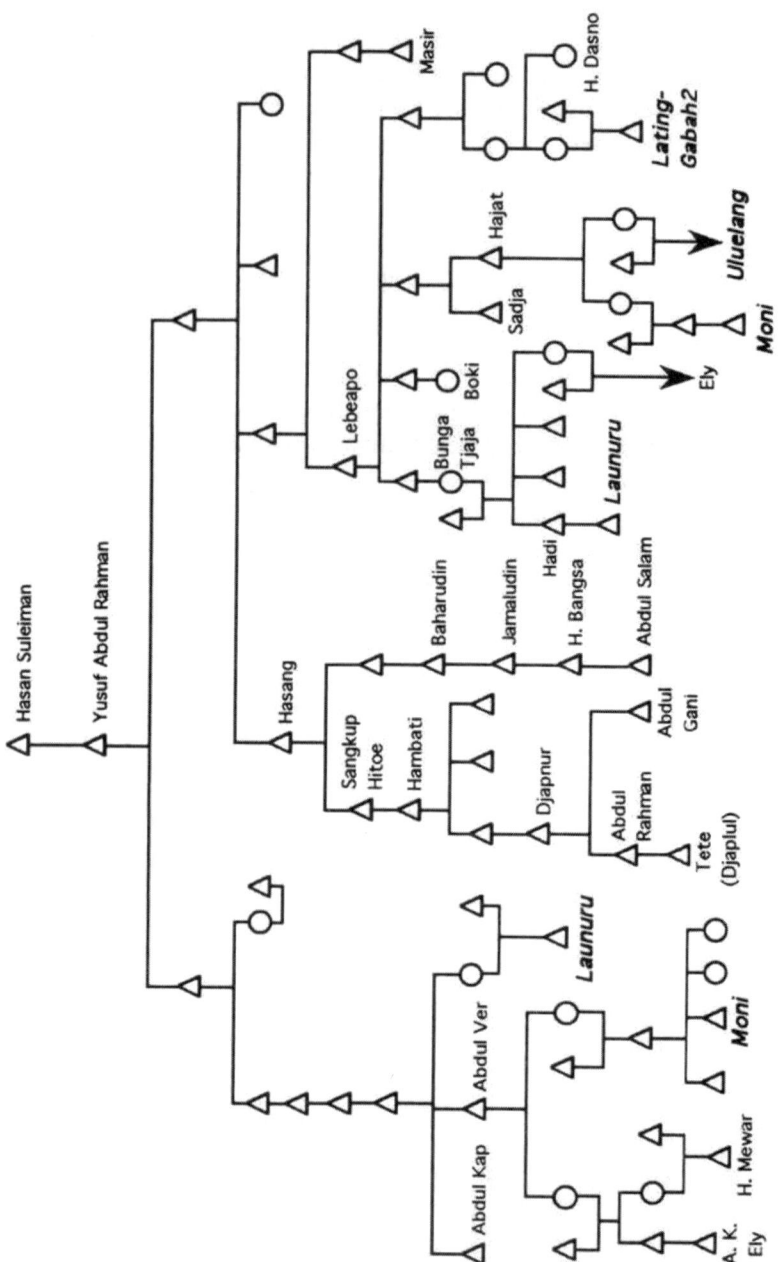

Figure 5.1: Diagram of kinship relevant in the Lating property affairs[137]

---

[137] This diagram shows the relations between the persons whose inheritances were dis-

Documents in the State Courts

The state courts play a double role with respect to documents. Firstly, they are one forum in which the validity of the documents and their relevance for presents claimants' positions can be established. Successful operation in court brings the additional advantage that, ideally at least, the sanctioning power of the state administration can be enlisted to solve property problems in the village (see K. von Benda-Beckmann 1984). But secondly, the courts are an important source of new documents which, irrespective of their short-term consequences, may become relevant for later generations as historical documents, and serve as point of reference for later readjustments of property relations, in village life and in the state courts.

Judges do not differ fundamentally from villagers in their interpretation of historical documents. However, they tend to accord court judgments a wider scope of validity than is warranted according to Indonesian legal doctrine. Formally, a judgment is only valid for the relation between the disputing parties. But in practice, courts frequently deny a later claim by a different person on the basis that the owner of the disputed property has already been established in a former dispute, to which the present claimant was not, but could have been a party (see below).

Although most villagers are not familiar with technical legal details, they clearly realize that there is a short-term and a long-term perspective on court use, and on the significance which court judgments have. Court procedures are rather risky ventures for this reason. For example, a group of heirs may push forward one claimant as their representative in a court dispute, in order to save time and expenses. The expectation is that it is so self-evident that he is only the representative of a larger group and that he will share the property if the dispute is won. However, this can easily lead to problems. For even if such an understanding works out well in the first generation, and allocations and distributions of property are made according to the general *adat* ways, problems are bound to occur later, after the persons for whom the understanding was self-evident have died. The others, or their descendants, then have no documentary proof of their rights.

Some people are well aware of these mechanisms and use them to their advantage. If one has shown that one is heir to the *pusaka* property of a distant ancestor, and has left out that many other people would likewise be entitled, one can hope to induce – at least textual – forgetfulness about these other persons. If

---

puted and the disputants. The diagram is selective and shows only the descent lines relevant for tracing inheritance rights. The actual network of kinship between the persons is much more complex since many people are additionally connected through affinal relationships on different genealogical levels. The names in bold print are clan names and do not specify individuals.

at a later time, they would put in their claims, one has a chance to refute them, because they are not mentioned in the document.[138] However, the others may be aware of this danger and devise a counter-strategy, aiming at including, themselves and their rights in the document. In both respects, state courts can be used as a strategic resource through which new documents can be produced or old documents be invalidated. The following series of disputes may illustrate this.

The Land behind the Lating Clan House Affair

The troubles began, or were rather revived, when in the 1970s the children of Haji Bangsa and Abdul Rachman, Abdul Salam and Tete Lating, had a dispute about the land behind the old Lating clan house. Tete lived in that house. The land behind the house had been settled in the 1950s and 1960s, when the residential area of the village expanded. Several families from other clans had obtained permission from Abdul Rachman Lating to build a house there. Abdul Salam claimed that this land had originally been village land and that his grandfather had brought it into cultivation and thus had exclusive rights (as his *perusah*) to it. This had been supported by a 'letter of declaration of rights', made by the village government in 1960 (by the anti-Lating village government) in which it was declared 'that the *'dusun belakang negeri'* had been empty village land, a part of which had been cleared by Djamaluddin Lating. It therefore had become his *perusah,* and after his death *pusaka* for his son Haji Bangsa Lating. Consequently, the land was now Abdul Salam's *pusaka.* Tete Lating had no rights there.' The persons who had built a house there had either to leave or to negotiate with him, Abdul Salam, about the permission.

The case had gone to the State Court in 1966 (decided in 1968), in 1969 to the Appeal Court (decided in 1973) and finally to the Supreme Court in 1973 which finally decided in 1978 that the land belonged to Abdul Salam. The dispute had then come to a dramatic climax. When in November 1978 three court officials and 18 policemen came to Hila to execute the judgment, Abdul Salam was, in their presence, attacked by kinsmen of Tete Lating and the families who were obliged to vacate their houses. Abdul Salam was stabbed and beaten up while the officers watched, and landed in hospital for three weeks. The Supreme Court judgment was not executed ... and was not yet executed in 1988!

This event brought 31 other members of the Lating clan in action. They filed suit against both Tete and Abdul Salam, claiming (very plausibly) that the disputed land around their common clan house was *pusaka* for all descendants of Yusuf Abdul Rachman Lating, the adoptive son and successor of Hasan Suleiman. Their suit was dismissed on the ground that the decision of the Supreme Court in which Abdul Salam was declared to be the rightful owner had

---

[138] When land titles in West Sumatra and Ambon are registered, some of the entitled persons are also usually excluded from the document. Registrations therefore tend to be made secretly, see F. von Benda-Beckmann 1979 and 1986. See also Goody 1986.

already the force of law. The present plaintiffs, the court argued[139], had had the chance to enter the dispute between Tete and Abdul Salam. One of them (Haji Boo Lating) had given evidence for Tete, saying that he had built his house with the consent of Tete's father. If he now claimed the land as one of the *pusaka* heirs, did he not contradict himself?

The case of the inheritance of Abdul Kap Lating is quite instructive, too.

The Inheritance of Abdul Kap Lating

In a set of complicated legal battles around the inheritance of Abdul Kap Lating (see genealogy), A.K. Ely had been able a) to prove his *pusaka* heirship and b) that he could claim by right half of the disputed land and the trees which had been planted by Haji La Djaha, one of the Butonese immigrants who had lived in Hila for several generations. Shortly afterwards, Tete Lating and other members of the Lating clan also sued Haji La Djaha for the same property. Haji Mewar and other members of descendants of Abdul Kap intervened in this dispute, claiming the *dusun* as their own *pusaka*. These two suits were dismissed, since the *dusun* had already been adjudicated the property of A.K. Ely. But so far, the judgment was in his name only. The court noted that since the Latings and Haji Mewar had not tried to assert their rights in the Ely - La Djaha case, it was too late to do so now (see also F. von Benda-Beckmann 1990b).

While court use, and the strategic deployment of documents in court procedures about property, is a well known strategy, the rules of procedure and the ways the judges interpret them are unfamiliar to villagers. Consequently, it often happens, like in the cases described above, that villagers miscalculate the timing of their interventions. What from the village point of view may be the most appropriate moment to move in with one's claims and documents may be too late to acquire legal relevance in the courts.

However, as some of the cases illustrate, the relevance of court decisions is relative. The actual consequences in social life may be quite different from those spelt out in the document/court judgment. Like in other parts of Indonesia[140], whatever happens with documents which embody important decisions or transactions is afterwards beyond the influence of the court.

It is not determined by its official legal consequences, but rather by the social field into which the document/court decision leads its further life, by the individual personalities and their social, political and economic relations in that field. In practice, thus, a more flexible situation develops than would be suggested or prescribed by the document. For instance, if one person, like A.K. Ely, who in the judgment had been exclusively declared heir to the Abdul Kap property would seriously attempt to control all this property alone, he would not

---

[139] Pengadilan Negeri Ambon, case no 437/1978/Perdata.
[140] See for Minangkabau, K. von Benda-Beckmann 1984. See also Moore 1973.

have a chance. Individual gains in court usually are, and have to be shared with others not mentioned in the document. However, the long-term perspective and relevance of the judgment/document is likely to be different again because not all the details of the property relations which would be relevant in *adat* are incorporated into the judgment at the time at which it is written. At a later historical point these may no longer be reconstructible. Then history will repeat itself. Consider (see kinship diagram) that, in the Ely - Mewar case, the present generation of disputants were already grandchildren and great-grandchildren to the last property owners. How would their own grandchildren at present aged between 1 and 6 years, establish their claims against the descendants of A.K. Ely, who could easily prove their right with the document?

Condensing the Past and Establishing Truth

In our conclusion we want to emphasize two aspects of the role of the documents in village life. Firstly, we look at the way villagers construct the relation between past and present. Secondly, we want to see in which ways the use of these documents is different from the *adat* ways in which villagers deal with property and inheritance matters.

The introduction of documents into a basically oral tradition shakes the common principles of establishing rights and truth of Ambonese villagers quite fundamentally. As we have argued in a discussion of the testaments of Hasan Suleiman (F. and K. von Benda-Beckmann 1987b: 250) the security, or certainty that rights to land and trees are recognized and devolve according to *adat* rules, was traditionally built on the basis of 'forgetfulness', in which historical 'truth' is made subject to adjustments of rights in accordance with the situation of the present, and in which the past is adjusted accordingly (see already Holleman 1923: 97, Goody 1986). The present is retrojected into the past, and past events and genealogical charters are adjusted to the present circumstances. Factors which could complicate such adjustments are 'erased' (Goody 1986: 136). The present, in a way, becomes the past, to make possible that the past can continue to have its legitimating function for the present. The construction of the past, and its legitimating power, therefore is subjected to the dominant legal and ideological principle that property rights, conflictive or not, have to be adjusted in a process of common deliberation by persons with the proper knowledge and authority.

When property rights are established with the help of documents this changes. The change is not so much in the social processes of dealing with property as such. Even in contemporary Ambon, the allocation and distribution of use and exploitation rights to land and trees are processes of constant adjustment of earlier positions, and the documents and the diverse institutions which can be strategically exploited only add to the complexity of these processes.

However, the legitimations governing these processes have changed. The historical truth of the events embodied in the documents becomes crucial for the establishment of property rights, and imposes its own constraints. It cannot be ignored, and the present claims must be in accordance with them. Genealogical charters have to be made in accordance with the documents, and contracts, transfers of land or trees, etc. may not be at odds with existing documents. In this reasoning, the documents' relevance is over-dramatized. The documented persons and objects mark the focal point in the past to which the present claimants have to relate themselves. As most of our case histories show, people do this by constructing, as directly as possible; a relation between their own position and the one laid down, or assumed to be contained, in the document. They 'shoot' their claims, as it were, through time on the lines of inheritance principles, until they reach the consequences spelt out or implied in the document. As Goody has pointed out, such recourse to written material extends the relevant facts in a legal action dramatically in time (1986: 170). However, the documents are not taken as the point of departure for tracing the subsequent legally relevant history of the disputes property through distributions and inheritances until the present situation. On the contrary, by the direct linkage the past is condensed and most transfers of property, inheritances and distribution of *pusaku dusun* and trees which have taken place in the meantime are made irrelevant.

This tendency to condense intermediate time and occurrences not only relates to the social processes dealing with property. They also occur with respect to the physical or ecological character of the property objects themselves. The troubles revolving around the donation of Walida Tetuputih are informative. In the first sentences of the donation document it was said that 'three pieces of empty land' had been given. This description was 170 years later still considered to be relevant for the ascertainment of the disputed *dusun*s Waesela and Tahoku. In several discussions about this 'alleged donation' it was repeatedly emphasized by Tete Lating's opponents that the donated land had been empty, '*kosong*' according to the document, while there were numbers of trees planted by various people on the disputed land. How could it be the land in question? Not only villagers opposing Tete Lating's claims reasoned like this. When in 1956 the chairman of the Ambonese Religious Court had come to Hila to examine the disputed property in order to find out whether it was the *dusun* Wailpoko or Waisela, he also noted 'that the information of Abdul Rahman Lating and his document, according to which the *dusun* Waisela was uncultivated land, was not true with respect to the *dusun* pointed out by Abdul Rahman Lating, since already many people, not only Haji Bangsa Lating, had trees on that *dusun*.'[141]

---

[141] In the *surat-kesaksian* of 25.9.1956 it is said: *Keterangan dari Abd. Rahman Lating seperti ternjata dalam suratnja menerangkan bahwa dusun Waisela kepunjaan mereka adalah tanah kosong akan tetapi dalam pemeriksaan karni pada waktu itu, tidak tern-*

If people would attempt to trace the physical and legal history of the *dusun* it would, of course, be obvious to everyone that there has been no empty land in that area for quite some time, and that all that had been empty in 1820 was cultivated in the course of history. It would be equally plausible that what was 'one *dusun*' in 1820, in 1960 turns out to be a *dusun* (Waipoko) where now 66 families have their own sago, clove, nutmeg and fruit trees. But in order to make a direct linkage of present claims and documented past events possible, the intermediate social and physical changes which may have gone on for longer than a century must be forgotten. Taking such changes seriously into consideration would reveal the immense complexity of property allocations, transfers and inheritances, and it would make the linkage between now and the past virtually impossible.

The main difference between situations in which no document exist and those in which there are documents thus lies in the way the relevant historical truth is constructed and can unfold its legitimating force. In situations where there are no documents, the past tends to be accommodated to the present, and truth is found in the present-day decision making. With the introduction of documents, the present has to be adjusted to the documented 'true' event in the past, and in doing so, the time lapse between the past of the document and the present shrivels to almost nothing. All documents, old or new, thus seem to have been drawn up, as A.A. Mime expressed it, 'once upon a time, a very long time ago, about last Friday'.

---

jata tanah jang ditindjuk oleh Abd. Rahman Lating menjerupai tanah kosong, tetapi tanah tsb. suddah penuh dengan pohon2 tanaman jang bukan sadja kepunjaan Haji Bangsa Lating melainkan penuh dengan pohon2 tanaman orang2 Negeri Hila lainnja.

Chapter 6
Islamic Law and Social Security in an Ambonese Village*

Franz von Benda-Beckmann

Introduction

Islamic law is pervaded by ideas of social justice and duties of assistance to the poor and needy. Several passages in the Koran refer to the desirability of charity. The most prominent institution which embodies social security and charity functions is *zakat,* the alms-tax. The giving of *zakat* is one of the five pillars of Islam. Two forms of *zakat* must be distinguished: *zakat mal,* the property *zakat,* and *zakat al fitrah,* the personal *zakat.* The *zakat mal* is a tax-like charity which Muslims are obliged to give on several forms of wealth and earnings, in particular on agricultural produce, precious metals and trade goods. The *zakat al fitrah* is a type of alms which has to be given by each living person at the end of the fasting month, in the form of a specified amount of agricultural produce. Islamic law specifies eight categories of beneficiaries of *zakat,* in which the poor and needy figure prominently.

The ways in which *zakat* has been collected and distributed has varied considerably through history and in different Muslim countries. Instances in which *zakat mal* has been given and distributed exactly in accordance with the rules of Islamic law have been rare, particularly since the rise of other taxes levied by states. There also has been great variation with respect to the degree to which individuals have in practice been allowed to give their *zakat* personally to the beneficiaries specified by law – this is in principle permitted – or *zakat* has been centrally collected into a public treasury *(bayt al mal)* and redistributed by religious or state officials. Understandably, ideas of how social justice should be achieved with the help of *zakat* revenues have differed accordingly.[142]

---

* First published 1988 in: F. von Benda-Beckmann, K. von Benda-Beckmann, E. Casiño, F. Hirtz, G. R. Woodman, and H. F. Zacher (eds.), *Between Kinship and the State: Social Security and Law in Developing Countries,* pp. 339-365. Dordrecht: Foris, Berlin: Walter de Gruyter.

[142] Islamic scholars have developed an elaborate system of rules about *zakat,* basing themselves upon several passages in the Koran and the *zakat* instructions of caliph Abu Bekr. *Zakat al mal* is obligatory only if the wealth or the earnings surpass the *nisab,* the legal minimum, which differs for the five categories of property on which *zakat* has to be paid. In the Shi'ite school of Islamic law which is generally followed in Indonesia, both *zakat mal* and *zakat fitrah* are regarded as obligatory *(wajib).* See in particular Paulus et al. 1917-1939 and Juynboll 1925: 77 ff.

In the contemporary Islamic world, there is a tendency towards increasing supervision and control of *zakat* distribution by the state. In some states *zakat* is directly linked to social security and welfare programmes. In Saudi Arabia it was decreed in 1976 that one half of the citizens' *zakat* should be collected centrally and be used to support the government's social assistance programme whereas the other half could be disposed of by individuals in the conventional way (Midgley 1984: 198). In Malaysia and Singapore also there exist state regulations under which *zakat* is paid into a General Endowment Fund out of which scholarships to further Muslim students' education or the construction of mosques are to be financed (Rosenthal 1965: 297, Siddique 1972: 89 ff).

Islamic scholars in their interpretation of *zakat* rules also give attention to the question of the ways in which *zakat* funds may be used in order to fit them into the social security schemes of modern states. Thus Farooq Hassan writes that 'there is nothing in law which prevents the use of *zakat* funds in building hospitals and schools, or in cooperative societies which can make life easier for the poorer people, or in the construction of factories which provide permanent employment to many people' (1981: 198). The category of poor and needy is seen as covering all kinds of economic disadvantage resulting from unemployment, old age, infirmity or accident (Hassan 1981: 172). In Indonesia also the distribution of *zakat* as a possible means of alleviation of the economic condition of the urban and rural poor has been given much attention by Islamic scholars in recent years (see Siddieqy 1981, Sahri 1982, Al Buny 1983). The state government, or rather the Department of Religious Affairs, is engaged in an attempt to channel parts of the *zakat* revenue into a province wide fund out of which subsidies for religious activities such as the building of mosques may be financed.

Apart from Islamic scholars, theoreticians and planners of social security have also given attention to the distribution of *zakat*. A USAID report strongly advised the Egyptian government to use *zakat* revenues, managed through Islamic banks, to reduce the poverty problem (Anon n.d.). And Midgley has recently discussed *zakat* as one of the possible innovative forms of social security in which traditional religious or social practices could be linked up with governments' attempts to extend social security to rural populations (1984: 198).

In their attempts to assess the potential of *zakat* for social justice and innovative social security schemes, Islamic scholars, government officials and theorists alike are usually hampered by their lack of knowledge about actual *zakat* practices. For Indonesia, for example, little is known about *zakat* distribution during colonial times, and even less in the period following independence (see Boland and Farjon 1983). However, in order to obtain some insight into the ways in which *zakat* might be used in supra-local distributive schemes to perform social security functions, it is necessary to study the ways in which *zakat* rules are interpreted in local communities, and the ways in which these rules are actually used and *zakat* is actually distributed. Islamic law and *zakat* rules in particular, are always operative in sociopolitical and economic contexts in which other conceptualizations of need, poverty and social justice and other normative subsystems like folk and government law pertaining to social assistance for needy persons coexist. We must expect the actual interpretations of *zakat* rules and the ways in which *zakat* is actually distributed to vary with the different ways in which people, and religious and government officials work out the relationship between these subsystems. Variations in the political organization of local Islamic communities and their integration into nation states presumably would also account for variations in *zakat* rules and practices. The chances of success in governments' and other development agents' attempts to link *zakat* practices to social security schemes are therefore likely to vary with such differences in the local organizations with which they are concerned (cf. Moore 1978a). This means that consideration of the role of *zakat* for social security should involve, as first steps, analyses of the plurality of rules pertaining to social justice and assistance prevalent in a given community, of their redistributive effects, and of the way in which *zakat* collection and distribution are related to the state.

    My paper is a modest attempt to do just this. I shall describe and analyse the ways in which *zakat* rules are conceptualized and *zakat* is distributed in Hila, an Islamic village on Ambon, one of the central islands of the Moluccas, where my wife and I are carrying out field research on law and social security.[143] I shall first give a brief description of the socio-economic and political situation of Hila and then describe the Hila *zakat* system in terms of the three aspects mentioned above: *normative pluralism, redistribution, and state intervention.* In conclusion I shall show what the case study of Hila can tell us about the more general problem of legal and social security pluralism in Third World countries.

---

[143] The research is being carried out by the Department of Agrarian Law, Agricultural University Wageningen, and the Socio-Legal Department, Faculty of Law, Erasmus University Rotterdam. The Indonesian counterpart is the legal faculty of Universitas Pattimura, Ambon. Field research in Hila (8 months in 1985 and 3 months in 1986) was carried out under the auspices of LIPI.

The Village of Hila

Economic and Social Organization[144]

The village of Hila is situated on the northern coast of Hitu, the northern peninsula of Ambon island. The village territory comprises an area of about 20 km^2. It includes a narrow, flat, coastal area in which the settlements are located. Also in the coastal area one finds coconut and sago palms, and most of the gardens in which villagers grow vegetables, beans, cassava and groundnuts. A large part of the coastal area consists of clove tree gardens. The rest of the village territory is hilly, even mountainous, covered with forest and newly cultivated gardens. The population of Hila consists predominantly of farmers. Besides agriculture, some fishing is done, and a substantial number of inhabitants also draw some income from the state, as active or retired civil or military servants. For their daily food, people live off their vegetable and sago gardens. Sago, together with fish, has for centuries been the basic staple diet of Ambonese villagers. Nowadays, rice has become increasingly popular and is also eaten by most families besides sago and roots. Rice, however, is not grown on Ambon; all rice is imported and must be paid for in money. In addition, farmers harvest fruit such as durian, langsat, mango and papaya.

Cloves and nutmeg (formerly also coconuts) are the main cash crops. Ambon is one of the famous spice islands, and through its cloves and nutmeg has been connected, in some form or other, to the world market for centuries. Since the early 1970s the price for cloves has risen dramatically and consequently villagers have grown clove trees on a larger scale. Whereas about 15 years ago cloves were of no great economic significance (Van Fraassen 1972) this now has changed dramatically, and Ambon has experienced a small economic miracle. However, since cloves only yield a full harvest every three to four years, people cannot count upon a regular income from cloves. Earnings from clove sales are usually spent on extraordinary investments such as the pilgrimage to Mecca, house building, the acquisition of machines, and extra clothing. Vegetables and fruit are partly used for subsistence, partly brought to the market.

The village consists of four settlements, totalling (in 1984) 4,186 inhabitants. The largest settlement, the actual *negeri* (village) Hila, is situated in the north-western corner of the village territory. The main settlement of *negeri* Hila is populated by 2,404 persons, of whom about 99% are ethnically Am-

---

[144] For ethnographic and historical material on Ambon, see Polman 1983. For more detailed accounts see Holleman 1923; Cooley 1961, 1967; Bartels 1978, Van Fraassen 1972. In the colonial and post-colonial literature very little attention has been given to the Islamic villages which comprise about half of the population of the island (but see Chauvel 1980).

bonese. The remaining 1,782 villagers with a few exceptions are Butonese immigrants who have left their native islands off the southeastern coast of Sulawesi to settle on Ambon. The Butonese live in three distinct settlements (*kampung*) which are situated on the coast to the east at a distance of 2, 4 and 6 km from the main village. These Butonese *kampung* have their own political and religious organization which is, however, subject to the village government of Hila in which the Butonese have no say. In the following my references to Hila will only pertain to the core-village inhabited by the Ambonese.

The population of Hila is divided into clans, called *rumah tau* or *fam*. Clan affiliation is in general patrifiliative; in addition adoption can occur. The original settler clans also form, or are subdivided into, *dati*, landholding subclans which hold parts of the village territory, mainly sago gardens used for the subsistence needs of their members. *Dati* membership is by patrifiliation; female *dati* members lose the right to share in *dati* property when they marry out of their clan. The *dati* head (*kepala dati*) is supposed to control and administer the use made of *dati* property. In principle, each *dati* member is entitled to use *dati* land for agricultural subsistence activities. However, once a *dati* member has made a garden or planted trees on *dati* property these become his property of which he can freely dispose and which after his death becomes inherited property (*pusaka*) for his heirs. Inheritance rules basically are bilateral, with a strong influence of Islamic rules which favour male over female heirs. The same rules also pertain to previously unexploited land held by the village as distinct from *dati*. Once a cultivator has made a garden or planted trees, these become his or her individual property and, after death, *pusaka* for his or her heirs. However, in the case of both *dati* and village land, the rights to the land, as distinct from the rights to the gardens and trees *on* the land, remain in the hands of the *dati* or village.

Kinship is structured by two overlapping principles, that of patrilineality and that of bilateral kinship. The patrilineal principle is the dominant principle determining membership of the clan, the *dati,* the *soa* (clan association) and the village. For most other purposes, the kinship relations of an individual villager are based upon bilaterality. The descendants of all four grandparents are considered to be 'kin'. Apart from the kin groups thus formed, each individual is also attached to the kin groups of his parents and grandparents, and thus to a large number of villagers. Also important, if less extended, are affinal relationships. At least one's spouse's parents and their descendants are considered to be close kin.

Residence is usually virilocal. However, residence and household composition are very flexible. As far as domestic and economic activities are concerned, two- or three-generation families, and the persons co-residing in one house form a multitude of social and economic units, which vary in membership with respect to different activities, such as sleeping, eating, cooking, child-care, and various economic activities.

Political and Religious Organization

Ever since the Dutch East Indies Company ordered the Ambonese population to settle in coastal villages during the second half of the 17th century, the political organization of Ambonese villages has been an amalgam of local legal (*adat*) principles and government regulations. The most influential government institutions are the *raja,* the village chief, and the *kepala soa,* the leaders of the clan associations. *Raja* and *kepala soa* are offices which are the preserve of specific clans. However, for centuries they have been officially appointed (and often also selected) by the government (Dutch East Indies Company, colonial state, independent state). Traditionally, the village chief was assisted by the village council (*saniri negeri*) consisting of the *soa* and *dati* heads, a village secretary and some other officials such as the *kewang,* the overseer of the village forest, and the *marinyo,* the village herald. Since Indonesia's independence various local government reforms have followed each other, introducing new governmental bodies at village level. Following the most recent local government laws of 1979, the LKMD (*Lembaga Kenahanan Masyarakat Desa*) was introduced as the new official village council, with the LMD (*Lembaga Masyarakat Desa*) as a sort of first chamber. The traditional functions of *raja* and *kepala soa* have been integrated into these new governmental institutions, these functionaries becoming chairman and members of the LKMD.

Since 1980, Hila has been the capital village of the newly formed sub-district (*Kecamatan*) Leihitu. The offices of *the* sub-district head, the *Camat,* and of the officials of the departments of agriculture, education etc. are located in Hila. Since 1981, Hila also has a people's clinic (*Puskesmas*). There is a number of primary schools, a lower secondary, and, since 1985, a higher secondary school.

With a few exceptions such as immigrant school teachers the population of Hila (including the Butonese immigrants) is entirely Islamic. The village has one mosque. The organization of the mosque as a village institution consists of religious and *adat* (local customary law) elements. Secular and religious spheres are clearly distinguished. There is one set of officials, the *penghulu,* whose primary tasks are to provide spiritual and religious guidance to the community and religious services at ceremonies. The head of the *penghulu* is the *Imam,* assisted by two *Chatib* and two *Modim.* But according to Hila law, the mosque is the 'property' of the *kepala soa tanah,* the 'old *soa* heads' who are regarded as *adat* functionaries. There are four of such *kepala soa tanah,* each with a title which is heritable in his sub-clan. It is their task to regulate all affairs with respect to the mosque, including the choice of the *penghulu.* They are *adat* officials, and also have to supervise *adat* ceremonial matters. '*Adat dibikin di mesjid, adat* is made in the mosque', is the characteristic way in which Hila villagers express the relationship between *adat* and Islam. The *kepala soa tanah* are assisted by a staff of 'The 12 *tukang*' (masters) whose task it is to keep the mosque in order.

Besides the mosque, the *musallah* (the women's prayer house) and religious teachers teaching the Koran (*guru mengaji*) or holding prayer sessions (*guru sembahyang*) play important roles in religious life. The *musallah* of Hila is still in the process of being constructed, and its organizational structure is still emerging. A few years ago some women *haji* initiated the building of a *musallah*. They set up an organizing committee, collected funds in the village and from emigrants and government authorities. The building is not yet finished but is already used for prayer. It has an *Imam*. Another person, the *Imam*'s brother, is regarded as a sort of '*vice-Imam*'. Like the mosque, the *musallah* is considered a public village prayer house; its status and that of its religious officials, however, is clearly lower than that of the mosque.

Besides the mosque and the *musallah* there are other places where Hila villagers, mainly women and younger men, go to pray: to the houses of their *guru sembahyang*. Such prayer rooms may be situated in large family houses. The room used for worship is given the appearance of a mosque by the painting of a mosque front on the inner wall of the room, pointing towards Mecca. Such rooms may also be found in smaller houses which serve as neighbourhood-oriented places for worship. The status and significance of such prayer houses changes with the prestige and popularity of the religious teachers. Most of the *guru sembahyang* are also religious teachers, *guru mengaji*, who instruct children and adolescents in the Koran, the Arabic script and other holy knowledge.

Social Security in Hila

Social security provision in Hila is mainly a function of local village institutions and practices, as to both the normative bases for this provision and the origins of the resources employed. On the normative level, claims, obligations and procedures with respect to the redistribution of resources are mainly rooted in *adat*. The basic institutions in which social security functions are embedded are kinship, neighbourhood and friendship. The social units which provide the individual villager, through all phases of his or her life-cycle, with most of the resources required for his or her (relative) well-being are based upon kinship. This holds true for 'normal' periods of life as well as for periods of need and crisis. In principle it generally also holds true for persons lacking the normal kinship network. Two- and three-generation households expand and contract easily. Orphaned children are easily accepted into the house of one of their father's or mother's kinsfolk. Widows and widowers usually live with one of their children or grandchildren. Old persons who can no longer farm, cook or wash by themselves are usually helped by their children, their grandchildren or the spouses of their children or grandchildren. A frequent occurrence also is the fusion of incomplete families. Thus widowed brothers and sisters, or mothers and sons may move in together, accompanied by some grandchildren, in order to give their new household the necessary man- and women-power for normal social and economic activities and the normal division of labour.

Besides the help and assistance provided by the various kinship-based units, there are other forms of mutual help, particularly for situations in which the capacity of these units is not sufficient for a particular purpose. In order to cope with the shortage of resources in such situations, Ambonese villagers through the generations have developed forms of mutual help which are generally subsumed under the concept *masohi*. The main activities in which *masohi* help is asked for and given are the ceremonies surrounding weddings and burials, house-building, clove harvesting and sago production. All *masohi* forms are conceptualized as reciprocal services, lying between generalized and balanced reciprocity (Sahlins 1974b).

From the side of the state, there is little normative interference in or practical contribution to social security in the village. There is the nationwide action-oriented PKK programme aiming to raise the welfare level of families in general, which in Hila has never really got off the ground. In 1983, the Department of Social Affairs initiated four programmes specifically aiming to strengthen the social security of widows, disabled persons, orphans and elderly. These projects are described by K. von Benda-Beckmann (1988). There are in addition state regulations about the pensions of retired civil servants and military and police officers, and 19 persons draw such pensions in Hila.

The resources employed in social security are largely derived from village-internal resources. Assistance in the form of labour is provided almost exclusively by villagers. Goods which are redistributed as social security are mainly village goods such as food, or goods obtained with income generated from village-internal resources. But the normative basis of *adat* also provides for some world-wide redistribution. Ambonese emigrants, in cities throughout Indonesia and other countries, and particularly the ex-soldiers of the Dutch colonial army and their descendants in the Netherlands, form rather close-knit associations which regard themselves as an extra-territorial extension of the village community. Three extended families originating from Hila live in the Netherlands. Although it is difficult to assess the amount of resources they transfer to their home villages, such transfers are a regularly occurring phenomenon of quite considerable importance, especially in the Christian villages. Strijbosch (1988) deals with this aspect of social security among Ambonese in the Netherlands. The resources employed by the state for the payment of pensions, the social security projects, disaster relief, etc. are also village-external resources. Although direct taxes are low, and little tax is paid by Hila villagers, they do, of course, contribute via indirect taxes to the state income.

Zakat in Hila: Legal Pluralism

Introduction

As I have briefly described above, there is a well developed system of rules and practices, grounded in *adat,* which pertains to the giving of help and assistance. The relations of kinship, friendship, neighbourhood and village membership are all pervaded, although in different degrees, by ideas of social obligation and reciprocity. Another set of rules was added to these general *adat* rules through the Islamic legal rules concerning *zakat,* although these are limited to one specific occasion for giving assistance. In fact, more than one new set has been added. For besides knowing about the *zakat* rules of Islamic school-law, Hila villagers have developed their own normative interpretations of these rules and have supplemented them by creating *zakat* beneficiaries according to *adat*.

Islamic Zakat Rules

The Islamic legal rules concerning *zakat* are of a quite different nature from the *adat* rules concerning the giving of assistance. The giving of *zakat* is a duty people have towards God. *Zakat* literally means 'that which purifies'. It is a form of sacrifice which purifies worldly goods from their worldly and sometimes impure means of acquisition, and which, according to God's wish, must be channelled towards the community. The community, *umma,* is the community of believers in which ethnic, social and spatial differences are transcended and declared irrelevant. The giving of *zakat* does not imply or presuppose any preexisting social obligation between giver and recipient. No worldly return is expected, it is in this aspect of non-reciprocity in secular terms that the great potential of *zakat* for social security purposes resides.

The categories of lawful *zakat* recipients reflect this clearly. According to Islamic law, as it has been elaborated by Islamic scholars, eight categories of persons are eligible to receive *zakat* (cf. Juynboll 1925: 86):

1. the poor and
2. the needy (*fakir miskin*),
3. the collectors of *zakat* (*amil zakat*),
4. converts to Islam, or potential allies in the cause of Islam (*mualat*),
5. slaves who have, or intended to free themselves by means of a *kitabah* contract with their master,
6. debtors who have incurred a debt for a worthy goal,
7. devout warriors who, without belonging to a salaried army, fight against the unbelievers, and
8. travellers, those who travel with a worthy goal and who cannot reach their destination without help.

According to Islam, the *zakat* revenue should be equally divided between these categories. In the legal view of the Shafi'ite school which is generally followed in Indonesia, it must be distributed equally among the remaining seven categories after a reduction in the form of a reward for the *amil*, the collectors of *zakat*. In the following section I shall describe how the *zakat* rules and categories of recipients are conceptualized by Hila villagers.

Hila Zakat Rules

The Zakat Obligation

In accordance with Islamic law, Hila villagers distinguish between *zakat mal*, in Hila called *jekat harta*, and *zakat al fitrah*, in Hila, *jekat pitrah*. They know that Islamic law gives them an option to bring their *zakat fitrah* to the mosque (i.e. the *amil*) or to give it directly to a beneficiary chosen according to their conscience (Juynboll 1925: 89). This rule is generalized to all *zakat*, which is, as far as agricultural produce is concerned, not in accordance with Islam, for Muslims are obliged to give their *zakat mal* to the *zakat* collectors if this is demanded by the government (Juynboll 1925: 88). The *zakat fitrah* obligation is taken very seriously in both theory and practice. The attitude towards the *zakat mal* obligation is somewhat ambivalent. Most villagers regard it as obligatory, too, and many know the percentages or quantities which one has to give according to Islamic law. However, it is not taken as seriously as the *zakat fitrah* obligation. It is generally recognized as permissible to meet this obligation by giving the equivalent of 'one *zakat (fitrah)*'.

Zakat fitrah in Hila is given in the form of rice. The standard amount regarded as proper is 9 (or sometimes 10) *cupak*, a corned-beef tin used as a measure generally. Pre-packed rice packs with the correct *zakat* quantity are sold in the village stores. Besides these two forms of *zakat*, people also recognize *saddakah*, non-obligatory gifts, which are also encouraged by Islam. Once *zakat* has been given and accepted, the giver has fulfilled his or her *zakat* obligation. With the exception of the *zakat* brought to the mosque which is redistributed to the poor and needy by the *penghulu*, the rice which is given as *zakat* loses its *zakat* status once it has been accepted. *Zakat* brought to the mosque in principle has to be divided between the mosque and the poor and needy. However, how much actually is redistributed depends on the amount of *zakat* brought to the mosque. The mosque officials must receive a 'decent' share first; what amounts to a decent share is not specified. For the rest no recipient of *zakat* is under any legal obligation to redistribute. However, if rich people have received *zakat* they are expected to give it away again, as *saddakah*, to the poor. With the religious teachers it very much depends on the circumstances: wealthy teachers or those who have received really 'much' should redistribute 'some', but those not particularly well-off or who have not received much can keep their *zakat* as their proper compensation for services rendered.

The Beneficiaries of Zakat according to Hila Islam
For Hila villagers it is self-evident and therefore rarely mentioned, that the circle of potential *zakat* recipients is restricted to co-villagers. Village membership and eligibility to receive *zakat* are defined in *adat* terms. This means that 'co-villagers' are those persons who, or whose ascendants, have been formally incorporated into the Hila *adat* system as full citizens, either by birth or by adoption into a clan and *soa*. Thus no one would think of giving his or her *zakat* to a poor Butonese immigrant living in one of the Butonese settlements in Hila, although according to state law the Butonese has the same political rights as a village citizen, and although he may be a devout believer. A partial exception to this rule is the convert. But converts are usually adopted into a clan at the moment of their official conversion; others residing only temporarily in the village at least stand in a foster child relationship to a Hila family.

Most villagers know that Islamic law distinguishes eight categories of beneficiaries. When restating Islamic law as such, people primarily mentioned the poor and needy (*fakir miskin*), the converts and the *amil,* or rather 'the mosque'. Travellers, slaves and holy warriors were rarely mentioned, debtors never. However, villagers usually try to give an account of all eight categories and often subdivide one of the classic categories, the poor and needy in particular, in order to reach that number. In this subsection I shall give a brief overview of how villagers think about the categories.

The Poor and the Needy
In Islamic law, *fakir miskin*, the poor and the needy, are conceived of as two categories. The distinction between *fakir* and *miskin* is not very clear and the question of whether *fakir* or *miskin* are the poorer category of persons is also disputed among Islamic scholars (see e.g. Juynboll 1925: 86). This is also the case in Hila, but people do not care very much about drawing fine distinctions. They rather think in terms of several types of poor and needy persons which are sometimes subsumed under, sometimes put outside the *fakir miskin* category. These types are:
- fatherless children (*anak yatim*)
- motherless children (*anak piatu*)
- full orphans (*anak yatim piatu*)
- widows (*janda*)
- old people (*orang tua*)

From daily conversations and formal interviews it is quite clear that villagers conceive 'poorness' and 'need' primarily in terms of incomplete kinship networks. Thus orphans or widows are poor because they lack the normal set of kin who make up the 'full' social and economic units which normally provide for their needs. The idea of being an orphan is not tied to young age or adolescence. Old people also are referred to as orphans if they have no children to support them. In that case people tend to emphasize the orphan (kinless) element over the widow characteristic. In the conceptualization of poverty and need, material poverty is seen as the consequence of social poverty. This tendency to emphasize social status over material well-being is understandable given the social and economic system of rural Ambon. Villagers depend for their economic, social and physical well-being primarily on help in the form of labour, and labour is provided by close kin. Paupers therefore are social paupers in the first place, material paupers only as a consequence.

The Mosque

Hila villagers usually speak of bringing their zakat to the mosque. They do so in the expectation that part of the *zakat* will be distributed between the mosque officials, and that the rest will be redistributed among the poor and needy. The *penghulu* are entitled to a share in the *zakat* because they provide services to the community of the faithful, according to Islam. The *kepala soa tanah* are entitled to a share because 'they own the mosque', according to *adat*. There are no clear-cut rules as to how much *zakat* should be brought to the mosque. As a general normative principle those who regularly go to pray in the mosque should bring their *zakat* there. There is a clear rule about who is entitled to make the decision about what part of the *zakat* should be redistributed: the *kepala soa tanah* as the lords of the mosque are the real *amil*; of course, they should take their decision in consultation with the religious officials, the *penghulu*. There is also a clear rule as to how the *zakat* kept in the mosque should be divided: One half should go to the *penghulu*, the other to the *kepala soa tanah* and the 12 *tukang*.

The categorization of the mosque and the *penghulu* is not consistent. Sometimes they are subsumed under the *amil* category. But villagers also rationalize the giving of *zakat* to the *penghulu* by saying that it is compensation the *penghulu* should receive for providing unsalaried services. The rationalization given by the *penghulu* themselves is similar; they see *zakat* as a partial compensation for the time they sacrifice for their fellow villagers. *Penghulu* therefore also put themselves into the *fakir miskin* category.

The Musallah and the Religious Teachers

The principle mentioned above with respect to the mosque is a general one. Unless one has a good reason to do otherwise, one should bring one's *zakat* to where one goes to pray, or where one receives religious instruction. Thus women praying in the *musallah* should bring their *zakat* to the *musallah*; others should bring it to their *guru sembahyang*. The *zakat* for children receiving religious instruction should be brought to their teacher. They 'really' should do so during the period they receive religious instruction. Continuing to bring one's *zakat* there after the instruction has finished is a good thing, too, but one may have another and better choice. As in the case of the *penghulu,* giving *zakat* to one's religious teacher expresses the intention of giving back something, a combination of respect, gratitude and material value, for services received.

Converts

The category of *mualat,* converts, denotes Christians who have become Muslims. Converts are an important category for Hila villagers, a fact which is also reflected by the way in which they treat them in the actual distribution process. In principle, converts should be given *zakat* at least during the three years following their conversion. It is especially appropriate to give them *zakat* after the fasting month directly following their conversion. Conversion is a regularly (if not frequently) occurring phenomenon on Ambon, where Islamic and Christian villages often lie adjacent to each other. The increasing inter-village mobility, and in particular the expansion of the bureaucratic apparatus, has increased the probability of Christians coming to live in Hila, to work there as teachers or in other official functions. The most frequent reason for conversions are love affairs. For a marriage between a couple of mixed religion to be concluded one of them has to change religion. Usually it is the woman who converts. But if a Christian man wants to marry an Islamic girl and thereafter live in Hila (or any Islamic village) he will change his religion. Conversion often results from a person living as a foster child *(anak piara)* in the house of an Islamic family (which often is the case with non-Islamic teachers stationed in Hila for a long period).

Converts are said to become orphans through their conversion. For such a step usually severs, at least for several years, all family relations between them and their relatives. They cannot therefore expect or demand as of right any help or material goods (not even through inheritance) from their original family. *Zakat* distribution is seen by villagers as a partial compensation for this loss.

Zakat Beneficiaries according to Adat

Besides the categories of lawful recipients of *zakat* according to Islam, village *adat* has added new categories of lawful beneficiaries. There are two categories which were always mentioned in interviews on *zakat* rules, the village midwife, *biang negeri,* and the marriage guardians, *saudara kawin.* During the research on the actual distribution it became obvious that foster parents, *orang tua piara,* were also regarded as a category of persons to whom *zakat* could and should be given. However, foster parents were not treated as a category in the general scheme; they would generally be subsumed under the Islamic *fakir miskin* category. According to some villagers the religious teachers were also included as beneficiaries according to *adat.*

The Village Midwife

The village midwife *(biang negeri)* has a high status in the village. *Biang negeri* is an *adat* office, if possible to be inherited from mother to daughter. The midwife is considered to be a member of the *saniri*, the *adat* village council. The general principle is that she should receive a *zakat* from all the children she has helped to deliver for a period of at least three years following the birth.

Plate 6.1: The village midwife

The Marriage Guardian

According to *adat,* each couple should have a marriage guardian, *saudara kawin*, who has the duties generally associated with marriage guardians elsewhere. If there is marriage trouble, he should be consulted first, and should try to mediate between the quarrelling spouses or their family members. The marriage guardian should be chosen from the bride's mother's kindred (traced in both lines). One should go back to the fourth, or at least to the third generation. This is explicitly done to reconfirm the existence of kinship relations; also, the marriage guardian should be sufficiently distant in order to be able to mediate successfully between the spouses. As a general *adat* principle, the marriage guardian is a person who must be honoured and paid respect. Giving *zakat* to him is one of the ways in which this can be done.

Zakat in Hila: Redistribution

The General Pattern of Zakat Disribution

The data on zakat distribution in Hila mainly pertain to the giving of *zakat fitrah*. The *zakat fitrah* obligation is taken very seriously. All villagers interviewed could account for their *zakat fitrah*; there were no suggestions that other people were not giving *zakat*, although in general, even in religious matters, people were not hesitant at all to make unfriendly allegations about people they did not like. *Zakat mal*, on the other hand, seems to be given only by a very few persons. Most people we talked to claimed that they did not own or earn sufficient wealth to be over the *nisab*, the level at which they would have to pay *zakat mal*. Several persons said that they would give as annual *zakat mal* 'one *zakat*', the equivalent of one *zakat fitrah,* on top of their personal *zakat*. Some rich persons were said to pay *zakat mal* in the form of money donations; we have not, however, been able to check to what degree this is done.

According to our estimate (which probably is on the cautious side) the giving of *zakat* at the end of the fasting month in Hila involves a redistribution of about 5.5 tons of rice, or a money equivalent of 2.2 million rupiah (or 2,200 US $). While this does not seem to be an impressive figure at first glance, it gains in importance if compared to other money in- and outputs. Thus the money invested on a one-time basis in the four social security projects by the Department of Social Affairs amounted only to 1.2 million rupiah. The yearly subsidy for village development received from the national government is 1.25 million rupiah. And the amount of land tax (IPEDA) paid by Hila villagers in 1985 was less than 900,000 rupiah.

The following data on the *zakat* distribution in 1985 and 1986 must be read and interpreted with caution.[145] For 1985 they are based on quite reliable

---

[145] It was not easy to get detailed information on *zakat* distribution. Many villagers did not like being questioned about the actual persons to whom they had given their *zakat*, and tended to answer by listing categories. Insisting on more precise information would often have been impolite. On the other hand villagers (except the midwife) were rather

information about the *zakat* received in the mosque, in the *musallah,* by the converts and by several religious teachers, including the most popular. In addition we can give an account of 111 (1985) and 301 (1986) instances of *zakat* given by villagers.

Category	1985	1986
poor and needy	40	30
foster parents	0	6.3
the mosque	11	12
the *musallah*	2	5.5
converts (4 persons)	21	9.3
religious teachers	20	24.5
village midwife	3	8.9
marriage guardians	3	3.5

Table 6.1: Zakat distribution in Hila 1985 and 1986 (estimated percentages)

Note: The zakat given to foster parents in 1985 is probably submerged in the poor and needy category. The drop in the amount of zakat given to the converts is explicable by the fact that their conversion increasingly becomes a past event. The 1985 estimate of the amount received by the midwife is probably much too low.

The Significance of Zakat for Social Security

In order to assess the significance of this general distribution pattern for social security, several questions must be asked. We have to know first *who* decides on the actual direction of the *zakat* flow. Do we have to do with a pattern based upon individual preferences or with a centrally directed distribution by the mosque officials? Secondly, we need to know to what degree *zakat* giving has the character of a non-reciprocal transfer and to what degree it is given in the context of a social relationship with a reciprocal character, and thus comes near to being just one pre-station in a series of reciprocal exchanges, a situation in which *zakat* may come close to a transfer of wealth which would have occurred in any case. Thirdly, and most importantly, we would like to know to what degree the giving of *zakat* is indeed channelled towards the poor, and whether it leads to an even distribution of *zakat* or to its concentration on a very limited number of persons. And finally these questions lead us to a further problem

---

open about the quantities they had received. They also talked very openly and emotionally about the question why they had, or had not, given their *zakat* to the mosque.

which is relatively independent of the actual redistributory effect of *zakat* giving: namely, whether *zakat* distribution tends to weaken other local forms of mutual help by replacing elements thereof, or whether it may strengthen or reinforce these other forms by adding another strand to an already multistranded relationship (cf. Elwert 1980a and b).

Autonomous Direction or Centralized Distribution

In 1985 and 1986 there was a strong preference among Hila villagers for deciding autonomously to whom their zakat should be given. In 1985 only 11%, in 1986 12% was given to the mosque, in the expectation that part of the zakat collected there would be redistributed by the *penghulu* to the poor and needy of whom the *penghulu* keep a register at the mosque. 89% or 88% was given directly to the personally intended beneficiaries. As I shall explain later the small quantity brought to the mosque was unusual; in former years half or even more of the total zakat revenue was given to the mosque. In 1985 and 1986 the mosque officials decided that there was not enough to redistribute among the poor and needy and divided the whole zakat amongst themselves.

The way in which *zakat* is distributed therefore is mainly determined by the villagers themselves. It is my impression that they make up their minds about the donees of their *zakat* only shortly before it is actually given. When asked some weeks before the end of the fasting month, most people we talked to stated that they did not yet know exactly to whom they would give their *zakat*. Others would start to speculate about it. In the (three-generation) family of our neighbours, the beneficiaries were discussed and decided upon in a family meeting held after dark and after the last fast had been broken. An adolescent son was then sent to the beneficiaries with the *zakat* (in packs).

Immediate Redistribution of Received Zakat

The autonomous direction of the *zakat* flow from the villagers is, however, somewhat changed through the processes of immediate redistribution of *zakat* which takes place on *hari raya,* the great holiday after the end of the fasting month. The *zakat* brought to the mosque is collected by the *penghulu* in large sacks. If the *penghulu,* after the part for the mosque officials has been laid aside, redistribute *zakat* among the poor and needy, they do this in the way which has also been reported for other areas of Indonesia (Snouck Hurgronje 1893, vol. I: 258, Juynboll 1925: 94). The *Chatib* hands over one pack of rice to the beneficiary, and then politely asks whether he may buy it back for the regular market value. He then proceeds to the next beneficiary. In this way he does not have to carry around large quantities of rice. As I have mentioned before, in 1985 and 1986 no *zakat* was redistributed since the Mosque officials divided the whole *zakat* between themselves.

The *zakat* given to the *musallah* was divided into three parts. One third each was kept by the *Imam* and the *Chatib* of the *musallah* respectively. The last third was given to the chairwoman of the committee which organized the construction of the *musallah* building. She would use it, she said, for making meals for the people coming to work at the building.

The degree to which the religious teachers (in 1985) redistributed the *zakat* they had received varied. So one, who had received 30 *zakat* from the women praying at his house, kept all for himself. Two others who had received about as much, redistributed one and two thirds respectively. The most popular religious teacher, who alone had received nearly 9% of the total *zakat* revenue, redistributed 4/5 of what he had received. When religious teachers redistribute the *zakat,* they give it, more or less without exception, to widows and orphans whom they consider to be poor and needy. In particular, they give it to the poorer women who come to pray at their house.

Zakat in the Context of Social Relations and Reciprocity

Most *zakat* is given in a context in which giver and beneficiary have multi-stranded relations of legal relevance, and these relations put their stamp upon the *zakat* distribution. On the most general level, *zakat* is given to persons who are co-villagers in terms of the *adat* political system. In 1985 and 1986 there was no exception to this rule. Within the circle of co-villagers, kinship, neighbourhood and friendship relations underlie most *zakat* transfers, no matter into which category the recipient falls. However, we can distinguish *zakat* transfers in which kinship is incidental and overlain by a different, specific sort of relationship, from those in which kinship is the underlying and dominant social relation.

1. Cases in which kinship, friendship and neighbourhood are incidental are those where *zakat* is given to the mosque, the *musallah,* a religious teacher, the village midwife or a marriage guardian. In all these cases there is a specific relationship of reciprocity between *zakat* giver and recipient. The giving of *zakat* is seen as giving a return for services rendered. People would not, of course, see such reciprocity in purely materialistic terms, and would not put *zakat* and the services given on an equal or equivalent value scale. *Zakat* given in the context of such reciprocal social relation accounts for about 39% in 1985 and for 54.4% in 1986 of the total amount. However, 10% or 12% is immediately redistributed by the religious teachers to the poor and needy. *Zakat* actually given and kept as a presentation in a specific reciprocal social relationship thus amounts to about 29% (1985) or 42% (1986).

2. The relevance of kinship can be seen if we examine more closely the recipients in the category of the poor and needy. On the basis of the sample of the *zakats* (N = 111) given in 1985 we get the following picture of the distribution. 47 *zakats* (42% of the total), were given to recipients in the poor and needy category (compare this to the 40% computed on the basis of the data on *zakat* recep-

tion, table 6.1). In 1986 90 were given to the poor and needy category, to which the 19 *zakats* given to foster parents can be added. Together they make up 36.3% of the total.

In the following table I show how the recipients of these *zakats* are related to the givers. Within this category I have distinguished the recipients according to their social status and their relational distance to the *zakat* giver: close kin (meaning the direct ascendants of one or both of the spouses and their own or their ascendants' brothers and sisters), distant kin and unrelated persons. For 1986 I have added the foster parentship relation which in the data on 1985 is subsumed under 'close kin'.

	1985 (N=47)	1986 (N=109)
close kin	42.5%	18.3%
foster parents	-	17.5%
distant kin	42.5%	28.5%
unrelated	15.00%	27.5%
unknown	-	8.2%
widows	46.8%	37.6%
orphans	10.6%	17.5%
males	38.5%	28.5%
females	51.00%	54.00%
unknown	10.5%	17.5%

Table 6.2: Zakat given to the poor and needy

Thus most of the *zakat* is given to persons with whom the giver stands in a relationship in which the obligation of mutual help and assistance as kinsfolk is an element. Secondly, it seems that poorer families in particular like to keep the *zakat* rice within the close family. However, it should be noted that, even if *zakat* is given to a widowed mother, or to a father, it is usually given to a different unit of consumption. For even if giver and recipient live together in the same house, they often have different kitchens and do not regularly eat together.

3. A distinction, however, should be made between close kin on the one hand and distant kin and unrelated persons on the other with respect to the reciprocal element in their relationship. Close kin are expected to help each other regularly. In the case of distant kin, the situation is different. Here again *zakat* is given in a situation in which parties are, in principle, obliged to help each other. However, this obligation is rather vague. As far as I could check, the relations of the recipients and their social and economic status were of a kind in which no

reciprocal services were or could be expected in practice, either from the recipients themselves or by their immediate kin. We thus can scarcely speak of reciprocal relations in these cases.

Concentration or Even Spreading

As we can see in table 6.1 the zakat is not spread evenly over the categories of beneficiaries. The four converts received a very large share in 1985 and the religious teachers in both years. If we look at the distribution pattern more closely, we see that in 1985 more than one third, and in 1986 slightly less than one third of the whole *zakat* was given to 6 persons only.

	1985	1986
The three recent converts together	20%	9.3%
The most favoured religious teacher	9%	9%
The most favoured poor person, a blind old man	3.5%	2%
The village midwife	3%	8.9%
Total	**35.5%**	**29.2%**

Table 6.3: Concentration of zakat

Zakat and Redistribution to the Poor

It is difficult to assess how much *zakat* was actually given to poor and needy persons, if we think of poverty in social and material terms and not in the categories of Islamic law as these are interpreted by Hila villagers. Based upon the samples given above, and on further information about the widows participating in the widow project described by K. von Benda-Beckmann, I would cautiously estimate that in 1985 about 55% of the *fakir miskin* recipients, or 24% of the total *zakat* recipients, were really relatively poor in terms of their social and economic situation. To these we can add the 10% immediately redistributed by the religious teachers, who tend to give their zakat to orphans and the poorer widows, mainly from among their pupils or religious clients. And we can also include the zakat given to the converts, 21%, which adds up to a total of 55%.

For 1986 my calculations come to 47.5%, consisting of 26% *fakir miskin* (90% of the *fakir miskin* category but not including foster parents), 9.3% for the converts and 12% redistributed *zakat* from the religious teachers.

Zakat and State Intervention

As I have mentioned in the introduction, the distribution pattern of Hila in 1985 was not typical. According to all the villagers, much more *zakat* had been brought to the mosque in previous years, the amount mentioned being about half of the total *zakat* given. The distribution pattern of 1985 should thus be read with caution. It probably reflects the way in which Hila villagers chose to direct the flow of their *zakat* autonomously, but apparently they could also, in the past, be content with a more centrally organized redistribution via the mosque officials. We can assume that such centralized redistribution would result in a more even spreading of *zakat* over the poor and needy – there were no complaints to be heard that in the past the *penghulu* had distributed too little or had followed their own preferences too much. However, the example of Hila shows what is likely to happen if there is external interference with the traditional *zakat* distribution regulations and practice. For it was in reaction to state intervention in *zakat* affairs that the Hila villagers drastically reduced the amount of *zakat* brought to the mosque.

When the village government was reformed in 1980, following the new legislation on village government (Law 5 of 1979; see also Unang Sunarjo 1984), the newly established LKMD, the village council, was required to establish ten sections. One of these is a section for religious matters. One of the tasks given to the religious section is the coordination of the *zakat* committee and the channelling of the *zakat* revenue to the poor and needy (*fakir miskin*).[146] At sub-district and district level, there have been established *zakat* collection committees *(badan amil zakat)*. According to instructions from the district office it is the primary task of the sub-district committee to collect and distribute the *zakat* revenue according to the following plan: 50% of the *zakat* shall be given to the poor and needy in each village; 10% to the village *zakat* committee; 5% each to the *zakat* committees on sub-district and district level; and 30% shall he transferred to the religious department at provincial level where a fund is formed out of which religious projects at a village level will be subsidized.[147]

When the Hila *zakat* committee was established, persons hitherto not entitled to any say in the distribution of the *zakat* revenue became members on the basis of their positions in the local government. The expanded *zakat* committee became one of the many arenas for political fighting, in particular over the question of who should become the new *raja*. The resulting differences between the committee members made its work impossible. Also, the villagers were quite aware of the intention that part of their *zakat* should go 'to the government'. In conversation, they were very frank about their reaction to these developments. They said that they would certainly not give their *zakat* to the mosque, for then it would find a destination outside their village. Another reason was that it was likely that part would end up in the wrong pockets, of persons who had no right to a share according to Islam or *adat*. If they had brought

---

[146] For the regulations on village government see Unang Sunarjo 1984 and Departemen Dalam Negeri 1981/1982.
[147] The provincial offices of the Department of Religion have a large autonomy to regulate *zakat* affairs. In Ambon, the provincial office gave instructions annually by circular letters (*surat edaran*) to the sub-district Offices of Religious Affairs.

a *zakat* to the mosque at all, it was only because they (generally older men) went to pray there.

Conclusions

Legal Pluralism, Zakat Distribution and Social Security in Hila

Thus we see that *zakat* distribution in Hila involves a redistribution of about 5.5 tons of rice, or a money equivalent of about 2,200 US $. About one half of the total *zakat* revenue is given to persons to whom the givers stand in social relationships which have strong elements of generalized or balanced reciprocity, and the giving of *zakat* to these persons is also consciously seen in this context by the persons involved. *Zakat* giving is embedded, or incorporated into an already existing network of multiplex relations and is largely and explicitly seen as a kind of contraprestation for services rendered or expected.

The other half of the *zakat* revenue is given to the poor in the village. *Zakat* distribution to them comes close to a situation of negative reciprocity; it concerns a prestation for which no return is or can be expected from the recipient or his or her immediate kin. This is the case with the converts, distantly related needy kinsfolk, unrelated elderly persons, and orphans. The general obligation to help such persons because they are kinsfolk in these cases does not imply reciprocity. *Zakat* is just one of the services which one may, or may not, give to distant kin. However, the *zakat* given to the poor is very unevenly spread.

In the normative system of the village the *zakat* rules of Islamic law have been adapted to the *adat* system. *Zakat* distribution has become a normative subsystem in which Islamic and *adat* rules have been integrated, without, however, losing their distinct bases of legitimacy. Moreover, the Islamic rules and categories of *zakat* recipients themselves are largely interpreted in terms of the values underlying the *adat* system concerning help and assistance.

I would say that the giving of *zakat* in principle strengthens and reinforces these social relationships. By giving *zakat* the giver recognizes the existence of a normatively conceived social relationship on the basis of which one owes 'something' 'in principle'. This may be said for relations which in everyday interaction between giver and recipient may be either reciprocal or non-reciprocal. However, *zakat* cannot be seen as a substitution for or replacement of assistance which would have been given otherwise. People do not absolve themselves from their *adat* (non-religious) obligation by giving *zakat*. Rather, *zakat* is a little extra assistance given.

The *zakat* distribution pattern is strongly influenced by this attachment to social (rather than religious) relations. In the actual distribution it is those persons who have a larger kinship network who tend to be favoured, with the exception of some particularly favoured poor and needy persons. Thus those persons most likely to be poor, socially and materially, have a small chance of receiving a significant part of the *zakat*. This was also apparent from a survey of the widows who worked in the widow project described by K. von Benda-Beckmann.

This attachment of *zakat* giving to social relationships, kinship in particular and the resultant uneven spread of *zakat* over the poor and needy is to a large extent the consequence of individual or family autonomy which allows individuals to direct the flow of *zakat* according to their personal preferences. This was clearly realized by Hila villagers. And it was one of the reasons why several villagers, notably the *penghulu,* but also others who could not be expected to be influenced by material or political considerations, complained about the fact that so little *zakat* was brought to the mosque. For the *zakat* redistributed by the *penghulu* would be distributed more evenly and fairly over the widows and orphans, the really poor and needy.

This leads me to the last point, the relation between individual autonomy and central redistribution with its state involvement. The example of Hila shows how villagers react to government intervention aiming to increase control over *zakat* collection and distribution and to draw at least part of the *zakat* revenue into a redistributive scheme operating on a higher and more inclusive level of political and territorial integration. In this case, the intervention was aimed at raising funds for religious projects such as the construction or restoration of mosques, and not for social assistance programmes. I doubt, however, whether villagers would react differently if the redistributive schemes of the government were aimed specifically at a distribution of the pooled *zakat* over the poor and needy of the whole district or province. Their *zakat* norms and practice are clearly oriented at keeping *zakat* in the village, and within the village at keeping each individual's *zakat* within the circle of people with whom the giver has social relations. I would not expect that continued exhortations by government officials – even officials of the department of religious affairs – to feed part of their *zakat* into supra-village funds would lead to different behaviour by the villagers, who would continue to direct the flow of their *zakat* autonomously. To rationalize and justify their behaviour they can easily rely on its permissibility in Islamic law.

As far as the case of Ambonese Muslims is concerned, attempts by the government to use *zakat* in redistributive schemes which would contribute to the equalization of welfare provisions between villages or larger regional units are unlikely to be successful. While there has been a quite successful integration of Islamic and *adat* ideas concerning assistance to the poor, the attempt to link this integrated scheme to government schemes has failed so far and will probably also fail in the future.

Some Wider Implications

Looking at the Hila example from a more general and comparative point of view, the question arises whether and to which degree the Hila situation can be generalized for other regions in Indonesia or even on a larger scale. Although relatively little is known about past and present *zakat* rules and practice in other parts of Indonesia and in particular hardly anything about contemporary *zakat* practices, it can probably be said that Hila is not very typical. The historical evidence from Sumatra and Java suggests a quite different picture where *zakat fitrah* and whatever was paid as *zakat mal* was mainly collected, and kept, by religious or even local government officials.[148]

However, *zakat* rules and practice in Hila, according to our preliminary analysis, fit a general pattern which is probably typical for Islamic Ambon: a rather strong and unproblematic integration of *adat* and Islamic values and institutional arrangements, and a structural opposition (not necessarily conflictive) of this integrated folk system to 'government', be it village or national government (see also F. and K. von Benda-Beckmann 1988). In the confrontation with local systems, the government is thus confronted with a block of mutually reinforcing subsystems and organizations maintaining these subsystems. The government, or supra-village planning activities associated with the government, cannot plausibly legitimate the regulations by which it aims to penetrate the local community by reference to an 'allied' normative subsystem. Another characteristic of this pattern is the wide range of autonomy recognized in village law in relation to *adat,* Islam and government law.

In these respects, Ambonese Muslim villages are certainly not representative of Islamic villages in Indonesia. Much more common are situations in which *adat* and Islam are not integrated but rather stand in a strained relation of opposition to each other, and in which either *adat* or Islamic officials are allied with supra village-government structures. Also it seems to be commoner in other parts in Indonesia, e.g. Java and Sumatra, for the range of recognized autonomy of individuals (or small kinship units) in relation to the normative subsystems to be much narrower. We would expect that *zakat* distribution, but also government intervention in the collection and distribution of *zakat*, would work out quite differently in such situations. There, the distribution of *zakat* would be most likely a 'purely' Islamic-religious affair, taking place in a discrete context of Islamic religious functionaries' competence. In such a situation the government's attempt to gain control over *zakat* would be primarily confronted by the Islamic officials in isolation, and less by the *zakat*-giving people

---

[148] See in particular the following sources: Veth 1871; Poensen 1874; Damsté 1908; Wolff van Westerrode 1901; Snouck Hurgronje 1893/94; Verkerk Pistorius 1871; Umar Junus 1966. On the relationship between *adat* and Islam see Taufik Abdullah 1966, 1972; Lev 1972; Dobbin 1983.

in general. For the people are used to seeing their *zakat* 'disappear' to higher placed officials anyway, and the shift in its direction from one set of officials to the other would not arouse great feelings of unjust suppression of autonomy. This might, on the one hand, make a partial transfer of *zakat* revenues from Islamic officials to state officials easier to accomplish. But it would probably, on the other hand, result in different defensive strategies on the part of the traditional *zakat* recipients. The religious officials and teachers, seeing themselves deprived of part of their income, would understandably not be favourably disposed towards such a change. In trying to oppose it, they would not have the option of the flexible response open to Hila villagers who can fall back upon their recognized autonomy. The only defensive strategy available to religious officials would probably be to mobilize 'pure Islam' as a legitimation of their claims. This would, of course, be a double-edged sword. For the rules of Islamic law requiring most of the *zakat* revenue to be given to the poor and needy might be easily used against them.

These considerations are, of course, highly speculative. The admittedly scant, historical evidence seems to support the hypothesis.[149] On Java and Sumatra, *zakat* was largely given to the religious officials, either to local village religious leaders *(kiyai)* or to government-installed religious functionaries (called *penghulu* on Java). The *zakat* revenue was almost entirely divided between them rather than being redistributed to the poor and needy.

Certainly much more research must be carried out into the different constellations in which *zakat* is collected and distributed. But if my analysis is correct, the case study of Hila, although limited, may indicate the kind of information necessary for an insight into the significance of *zakat* for social security, and into its potential for social security schemes linking local traditional religious practices with the state. Simultaneously it may show the possible political implications of such schemes and their possible variations. The study of *zakat* practices in Hila may thus contribute to a better understanding of some of the general problems involved in legal and social security pluralism.

---

[149] See the sources mentioned in note 148 and Hooker 1983.

Chapter 7
Social Security and Small-scale Enterprises in Islamic Ambon*

Keebet von Benda-Beckmann

Introduction

Until recently, state-provided social security in Third World countries was only for those employed by the state or in a very small part of the so-called formal sector. The needy in the informal urban sector and virtually everyone in the rural sector received almost no support from the government apart from some basic medical and educational services. In several parts of the Third World governments have now started to extend social security services to their rural populations (Reidy 1980, Midgley 1984: 164 ff). A favoured way of doing this seems to be the setting up of income-generating projects. These schemes are interesting experiments for several reasons. Unlike the various types of credit programmes, these give not loans (not even at low interest), but subsidies that do not have to be paid back. The administrative difficulties of reaching people who are not used to dealing with administrative agencies and lack the skills of such dealing seem to be reduced to a minimum. Moreover, these schemes are considered to fit better with the local forms of social security and are therefore more suitable than the various forms of pension schemes that prevail in state-provided social security. As a possible link between local and state-provided social security these schemes deserve to be studied more closely.

Indonesia has perhaps the least developed state-provided social security system in Southeast Asia. The best provisions are reserved for the military, police and civil servants. In the formal private sector also there are social security schemes. These are of the insurance type and involve regular monthly payments by registered workers who have (more or less) regular and permanent work. The programmes include widows' and orphans' pensions as well as accident pensions. Since 1983 companies with more than 25 workers and a capital of at least 1,000,000 Rupiah (Rp) have been required to participate.[150] While statistical

---

* First published 1988 in: F. von Benda-Beckmann, K. von Benda-Beckmann, E. Casiño, G. R. Woodman, and H. F. Zacher (eds.), *Between Kinship and the State: Social Security and Law in Developing Countries*, pp. 451-472. Dordrecht, Cinnaminson: Foris.

[150] Until 1983 social insurance programmes were obligatory for companies with more than 100 workers and a capital of 5,000,000 Rp. cf. Hukum Perburuhan di Indonesia

data are not available, there is no doubt that the majority of companies falling under the requirements do not in fact participate. Thus, even in the formal sector a substantial part is not actually included in the programmes.

The large majority of Indonesia's population which gains its income in the 'informal' urban and agricultural sector is altogether excluded from these types of insurance programmes. The government has now started to set up programmes for the rural destitute. They evidence part of a more general interest in and concern for the rural population, resulting in various attempts to involve peasants and their families in state activities. These programmes should therefore be studied against the background of a more generally increasing influence of the state on the rural population, secured by a combination of services provided and of governmental control exerted.

The provincial departments of social affairs are designated to select villages and set up projects for the typical categories of social security recipients: widows, handicapped, orphans and the aged. The province of the Moluccas in eastern Indonesia started a social security scheme for the rural destitute in 1983. This paper will present a description of this scheme and an analysis of its working at village level.* The village on which the analysis will be based is Hila, an Islamic village on the north coast of the island of Ambon, where four projects were set up: one for widows, one for orphans, one for handicapped and one for the aged. Of these only the first is really successful; the others either did not work at all, or worked only for a short period of time, or worked otherwise unsatisfactorily. I shall try to explain why the one was successful and the others were not and try to indicate what could and should be improved. I shall suggest that an important factor for success is the extend to which the projects' activities and their internal norms and organization correspond with the way social life is generally organized and with the kind of activities the participants carry on in daily life. Both the way people organize cooperation and the kind of activities they carry on and are expected to carry on in everyday life is different for each of the various categories for which the scheme is meant.

The paper will raise the question whether this type of scheme truly reaches the needy, what it brings the participants in terms of economic and other advantages, and whether its organization is adequate to make the participants independent of the help of others. My argument will be that the way the projects under the scheme are organized suggests that the administration is, notwithstanding the explicit goals of the programmes, not only and perhaps not mainly interested in making the participants economically self-supporting, but in keeping them under permanent control. Of course, in every social security system there is a tension between the notions of social security and of state control. The

---

1326, Instruction of the Minister of Labour, Transmigration and Cooperations number Kep.116/ MEN/1977 Section II par. 2, 1369 KEP.278/MEN/1983 Section II par. 1.

strong emphasis on state guidance and control of the Indonesian schemes tends to limit markedly the social security effects of the projects.

Social and Economic Organization

Rural Ambon is a relatively prosperous part of Indonesia. People live from gardening, fishing and cultivating cloves and nutmeg. Prices of cloves have gone up recently and as a result the island breathes modest wealth. In the northern, mainly Islamic, part the main staple food is still sago, fish, vegetables and root crops. Rice has for a long time been the main food in Christian villages and in town, as well as for civil servants and the military. It is gaining ground in the villages near the capital town Ambon as well, but on the whole sago is the basic food in the northern peninsula. In addition vegetables, groundnuts, peas and maize are grown for own consumption and for the market. These are grown in shifting cultivation in the hills behind the villages. In former times the gardens were used for three or four years. Nowadays they seem to be used longer; eight years is not uncommon. The land yields enough for the people to live on, but life is not easy. Child mortality is high and malaria and intestinal and bronchial diseases are chronic.

Approximately two thirds of the villages on the northern peninsula, amongst these Hila, stand in regular daily contact with the town Ambon. The other villages depend on irregular transport by land or small vessels by sea. The latter villages are largely self-supporting and produce little besides cloves and nutmeg for the market.

Hila is the capital of the sub-district Leihitu. The sub-district head, the head of the office of religious affairs, and the sub-district centre of the official cooperatives (KUD, *koperasi unit desa*) are all located in Hila. It has a population of 4,100 of whom 2,400 are Ambonese. The remaining 1,700 are Butonese immigrants who live in three separate settlements. There are four primary schools in Hila, and one lower secondary school. Last year a start was made with a higher secondary school. For medical services there is a small clinic with a permanent staff of three nurses and a midwife. Twice a week a doctor visits the clinic. People make frequent use of the modern medical services and regard them as a welcome addition to the traditional healing practices.

Hila has no market. Since the tarred road was finished in the late 1970s, small buses and trucks can provide services to the villagers three or four times daily in a 1½ hour drive to Ambon and its market. There are 15 small shops for the most basic needs. One or two have a somewhat more elaborate selection of goods. Some of the larger shops in Ambon maintain a regular service with the villages, sending buses or trucks to the villages to sell flour, rice, sugar, etc. at prices below those of the village shops and on credit. For the rest people have to go to Ambon to do their shopping.

Kinship is the most important basis for social relationships. It is structured by two overlapping principles, that of patrilineality and that of bilaterality. Patri-affiliation usually determines clan-membership, although adoption is widespread. Generally speaking patrilineal descent is the basis for access to clan and *dati* land.[151] However, since it is possible to establish individual rights to land through inheritance from both the paternal and maternal sides, and also through cultivation of village land, patrilineal descent has lost much of its economic importance (F. and K. von Benda-Beckmann 1985).

For most purposes kinship relations are based on bilaterality. Moreover, affinal relationships are considered very important too. People requiring assistance for ceremonies or other special occasions may thus invoke any of these principles and often more than one is applicable to the same person. Neighbours are also a source of support, even when they are not in any other way closely related.

Ambon has a complicated system of land rights of which I shall sketch the outlines only. Much of the actual farming land is either *dati*- or clan-land or communal land of the village. Individuals have the right to cultivate a garden or to plant trees, but they may not dispose of uncultivated land individually. After cultivation, however, they may dispose of the cultivated land and may sell it. Thus, access to labour is extremely important to effectuate individual rights to acquire land, either in order to cultivate it for subsistence or cash crops, or for sale. Apart from house sites, land is hardly sold as yet, but there are indications that a land market may develop rapidly in the near future. Already wealthy merchants and professionals from Ambon are showing an interest in buying uphill land to grow cloves. Several villagers have responded to this development and have started to cultivate village land in the hills, planted clove trees and made contracts with interested buyers to sell them the land as soon as the trees start to produce, which takes six years at least. If this trend develops further, communal rights to land will be transformed into individual rights. In the end the traditional land rights system will be undermined. However, for the time being it is still intact in Islamic Ambon.[152] There is no absentee landlordism on a grand scale, nor is there an autochthonous landless class. Of the Butonese immigrants only a few have been able to acquire permanent rights to land. However, although land on the whole is not scarce, it is scarce in the vicinity of the settle-

---

[151] *Dati* are parts of clans which were assigned communal land by the Dutch East Indies Company, the VOC, and had to pay services to the VOC and later the colonial administration.

[152] The situation in Christian villages in this respect seems to be quite different. There, most land was registered under the colonial administration and has acquired a much more rigid status. Moreover, land shortage is in many Christian villages a great problem.

ments. We shall see that this is a problem for widows and old and handicapped people.

The main problem on Islamic Ambon therefore is not a lack of *land*, but a lack of *labour*. People who are themselves unable to work and who have no close relatives willing to do the work cannot establish individual rights to particular plots of land. They may have inherited individual rights to land, but they cannot bring additional land under their control, because that requires personal cultivation. For elderly people this may not be too great a problem, because they will have had a garden and have planted trees in their stronger years. But the disabled, the sick, orphans and the weaker widows, who have not managed to plant trees while their husbands were still alive, are dependent on others to do the necessary labour. Labour is so important that the Ambonese use the same word for children without parents and for old people without children: both are called orphans (*anak terlantar*) and both are much pitied, for they cannot support themselves. They may be able to work the garden, but not to build and maintain a fence to keep away the wild pigs. Or they may be able to work a garden near their living quarters, but not at a three quarters of an hour's walking distance.

For special occasions, such as wedding and death ceremonies, and the building of a house, a far wider circle of relatives, friends and neighbours is called upon. There are two ways to acquire the necessary help for day-to-day work. One can always fall back on one's children, parents, grandparents, siblings or first grade nieces and nephews, aunts and uncles. If one does not have any relatives in this close circle, nor a good friend, the only other way to get the necessary help is through an important relative who can instruct others to do the work. These are usually higher (retired) civil servants or military or police officers. If one has such a person amongst one's wider circle of relatives, one may through that channel get access to the necessary labour. For those people who have no such resources there remains only one possibility: to earn some money, for example by baking bread, cookies or rice dishes and selling them to schoolchildren and people at work in the woods and gardens. This is, however, only done by women, married as well as widows. There seems to be no tradition of this type of petty trade by men and children and one never sees them doing it. It is interesting that men are usually more readily cared for by more distant relatives than women, because society expects that women can obtain food and cook for themselves unless they are completely bedridden. If they are unable to keep a garden, they are expected to engage in petty trade. Men who are unable to work in a garden have to go around and find a place to eat. This often is not easy, even though they are more readily accepted than women and some men have to look for a series of houses where they can eat in turn, until they are told to move on.

In order to avoid as far as possible the inconveniences of a widowed life, 'incomplete' households often set up a household together. Thus, one finds widows or widowers living together with their widowed mother, father, child or siblings or in-laws. Together the members of such a household can do the work which is necessary to make a living.

The Form of Social Security Schemes for the Rural Population

Under the scheme of social assistance started in the Moluccas, each village is eligible for one project for each of the four categories of needy persons (widows, orphans, disabled and the aged). The province provides a lump sum of 300,000 Rp (= US $ 300)[153], as a starting capital. This is, as far as I am aware, the first time that such projects have been set up with non-refundable subsidies rather than low-interest loans.[154] The village administration has to select a number of men of some standing who will set up the individual projects, select the participants and act as managers.

Two assumptions lie at the basis of the project's organization. One is that the participants lack the means or reserves necessary to start an enterprise. For this the administration provides a starting capital with which the project can acquire a first inventory and stock. The starting capital may be paid in money or in goods. Once the first stock is taken care of, the project should stand on its own and after some time be able to make a profit. It is left to the participants and the manager to maximize the profits. Several times a year a staff member of the department of social affairs comes to check how the project is doing and to pay some subsidy to the manager.

The second assumption is that most participants lack the training and skills to run an enterprise. Therefore the department organizes a short training programme of four days for the prospective managers. There they learn how to select the right participants and how to formulate a project, and receive some basic training in bookkeeping. They spend a considerable amount of time and energy on group-leadership and communication skills, as well as on state ideology, the social basis of cooperatives and the social functions of the state in general. After the training they go back to their villages and, together with the village administration, formulate a project, select the participants and apply for the funds. The members of each project choose their own chairperson and treasurer. Ideally these should take over the project once it has been started up, 'under the

---

[153] At the time of our first research period, in 1985, 1 U.S. $ was worth approximately 1,000 Rp. During our second field work period the Rupiah was devaluated with approximately 40%.

[154] This is perhaps a sensible response to the fact that low-interest loans especially have a notoriously bad repayment record, not only in Indonesia but also for example in the Philippines, cf. Reidy 1980.

guidance of the manager', but often the manager stays on the job. It is left to him to pass on his knowledge to the project's board or to fail to do so.

The village administration and the managers are theoretically free to choose the type of enterprise. They have to obtain the approval of the department of social affairs, but if they can show that the project has a good chance of working, the department will give its approval. In practice the diversity is very small: most projects consist of a shop.

Social Projects Initiated in Hila

Since Hila had at the time (and still has) no village head, the village secretary organized the projects. He selected eight or nine men to receive the training in Ambon and got the project started. They were mostly of some social standing, mainly because their fathers were of high standing. Of these, only one, and he the youngest, had had some experience in running a shop. He had worked for a number of years in the shop of a man of half Chinese and half Ambonese descent. The others had little or no experience at all, but they were all men in their thirties and closely associated with the village administration or with the political party, the Golkar. Of the four projects set up in Hila only one – the widows' shop described in the next section – appeared to be a success after 1½ years, and that was the one led by the only man with experience in running a shop.

The project for the (half)orphans did not even get off the ground, 30 members were selected, on what basis I do not know. Many were children of mothers who participated in the widows' project. The aim was to set up a shop. A site was selected and concrete and wood, as well as the first stock were delivered. A beginning was made with building a small shop, but the materials were not sufficient and at the instigation of the manager the project sold some of its stock to the widows who were already running their shop, so that the orphans' shop could be finished. The remaining stock was stored at the house of the village secretary. However, the project never developed beyond that stage. Shortly before the fasting month began every member received a few goods as a nominal profit, but no actual selling ever started and it was unclear what happened to the remaining stock.

For the handicapped also a small shop was built. That project did run for several months. However, as a result of internal tensions and conflicts among its 20 participants and the managers it stopped it activities. Apparently the participants did not accept the leadership of the managers and claimed that they were very well able to do it on their own, without help or guidance from others. The managers decided to let them do it, but then the members could not settle on who should act as a manager. After another two months they stopped business, closed the shop and divided the remaining goods among themselves.

A third project was set up for the aged, those of 55 years or more. The village secretary and the managers thought it unwise to start a shop for this category, because many of them were too old and weak to sit up all day and watch the store. Some members would not even be able to distinguish the different goods and prices. Instead they chose a business which people could do at home. The manager bought large drums of kerosene, and transferred the kerosene into bottles, which the participants would then sell at home. Each member would take 10 bottles home and when these had been sold, a new batch could be fetched from the manager. Although the project did exist after 1½ years, only a few of the 28 participants actually sold kerosene. The participants were nearly all women, either widows or wives of infirm men. It was the only project which was not exclusively for the Ambonese. A Butonese man married to an Ambonese wife was one of the two male participants. He died shortly after the project started and his place was taken by his Ambonese wife. Some of the participants were already too old to do even this simple work. On the whole, it can hardly be called a success. The manager sells most of the kerosene 'to help the project', but the profits are extremely marginal: once every member received rice and sugar to the value of slightly less than 5,000 Rp and once 3,500 Rp in cash.

Apart from these almost exclusively Ambonese projects, the Butonese settlements have their own. The general project manager, however, is an Ambonese, a rather unusual man who received some training in a technical school, takes a self-willed position in village politics as the head of the local section of the Islamic party, the *Partai Persatuan Pembangunan,* and is a successful entrepreneur himself. He is the only person who manages to organize a stable fishing party of approximately 20 men in the season. He lives on the fringe of the Ambonese settlement, close to the nearest Butonese settlement, with whom he maintains good relations. He set up several projects. A shop for orphans and handicapped seems to be unsuccessful, but a chicken farm for widows apparently is successful. I have no further information about these projects, nor do I have any information about projects in the other two Butonese settlements.

The Successful Social Project in Hila: The Widows' Shop

This project started with 30 women, all either widows or divorcees. After 1½ years one had remarried and had consequently had to leave the project; another had died. Their places have not been refilled. The project consists of a shop which sells the same goods as all other shops in the village: sugar, rice, flour, noodles, tea, soap, detergent, cigarettes and matches, and sweet canned milk in the beginning, adding after a year margarine, green peas, groundnuts, vinegar, palm sugar, onions, garlic and red peppers, shampoo, bandages, yarn, rubber slippers, writing utensils, kerosene and cooking oil and even canned meat. During the first 1½ years it made enough profit to enlarge the shop, creating more storage room and space for the women on duty to sleep during the night. Besides it managed to pay the participants a share in the profits, in the form of goods to a value of nearly 10,000 Rp after the first four months. A year later each member received goods and money to a total value of 30,000 Rp.

Membership

The village secretary selected the members. I have not been able to find out the exact criteria for selection other than that 'they needed it'. Rank or status hardly seems to have played a role, except for one factor: hajis, those who have made the holy pilgrimage to Mecca, do not participate, nor widows of hajis. The socially higher and lower clans of the village are about equally represented. Two thirds of the members live in the socially lower part of Hila. However, the socially higher part of the village already has a shop for orphans and the aged, set up as a private social security project with aims similar to the provincial one, by the headmaster of the secondary school. This explains why the lower part seems to be overrepresented. The lower part of the village was selected for the widows' shop because Hila has recently begun to expand to that side, whereas the higher part already has a great number of shops.

Poverty was only to a certain extent a criterion. Generally speaking, women owning many clove trees, that is, more than 100, are not selected.[155] There are at least five widows without any or with very few trees. On the other hand there are also some with quite a lot. Three claimed to have between 40 and 50 trees and two own even more than 100 trees. Eight participants mentioned an unspecified number and ten participants did not want to give any information at all. Of these 18 women some are very poor indeed, whereas others almost certainly own a considerable number of trees. Eliciting reliable information about ownership of clove trees proved to be one of the most difficult tasks of the researcher. Moreover, even with that information it is difficult to judge a person's wealth because very often the trees have not started to yield. Nonetheless there are definitely participants who are very poor and others who are fairly well off.

Other criteria were health and minimal skills in dealing with money. The very old widows, who either could not leave their houses for 24 hours continuously, or who could not manage the various goods and prices did not par-

---

[155] Hajis, having been able to finance the costly journey to Mecca, are usually wealthy. This may also be a reason why hajis or their wives do not participate in any of the social projects. One woman who participates now had owned more than 100 full-grown trees, but in the drought a few years ago her trees had died. Whilst she still owned her trees she had hoped to make the pilgrimage to Mecca, for which the harvest of three seasons would have been a solid basis. Now she has given up her plans and participates in the widows' project.

ticipate. For them the aged project was set up, but some of the very old men and women did not participate in any project at all.[156]

Business Activities and Organization

The project manager, Mansur, the son of one of the participants, is a man of about thirty years old, very modest and responsible and lacking the self-assured attitude of most other managers. He belongs to one of the chiefly clans, but to the lesser branch. The project's chairperson, Mujuna, is a forty-year-old woman from the other chiefly clan. The treasurer, Oda, also in her early forties, was formerly married to a man from a chiefly clan from a neighbouring village. Thus the central participants are of high status. But, far more important, they are all said to be good in business, especially Oda, who has an impeccable reputation in financial matters.

Whilst Mansur is the general manager of the project and does the book-keeping Oda is in charge of the money. Every day the cash register is emptied by Mujuna, who also sees to it that the shelves are refilled and the stock is replenished. She brings the money directly to Oda. When Mansur or Mujuna goes to Ambon to do the necessary shopping they ask Oda for money. All important decisions are taken by the three of them. Mansur also comes in almost every day and helps with the heavier work.

Every eight to ten days either Mujuna or Mansur goes to Ambon and does the shopping for the project. The project is a regular customer of one of the big Chinese merchants. They always pay cash except when something is needed in between trips. Then a bus-driver is asked to deliver an order at the shop and next time someone from the shop comes to Ambon the bill is paid. The shop always uses the same truck for which it pays 15,000 Rp, 2,000 Rp less than the normal fare. Every 8-10 days it spends approximately 600,000 Rp, the daily sale varying from 40,000-70,000 Rp (about 40-70 US $), although during the clove harvest it is much higher.

Apart from Mujuna, who has to come in every day to check the stock and take the money to Oda, all the widows take turns in pairs to guard the shop for 24 hours. Thus every participant is on duty once every fortnight. They come

---

[156] There seems to be an interesting pattern, although I have not yet been able to check whether it really holds, and that is membership of prayer-groups. Most women pray in a private home or a private prayer house under the leadership of a prayer leader, *guru sembahyang*. It seems that most members of the project belong to three such prayer-groups, of which there are many more. Only one or two go to the women's mosque, which has been built recently. It is situated in an area of Hila quite far from the project. But the prayer-groups involved are not all near to the shop, nor do their participants all live close to the shop or to the prayer-groups.

around nine o'clock in the evening, sleep there and stay next day until the next pair comes to replace them. When on duty, there must be one of the two widows present all the time; the shop cannot safely be left unguarded. On the rare occasion when neither is able to be there an outsider may be called in to guard the shop, usually a friend or relative who happens to be around. This does not happen often. Most women are very punctual. Only one widow does not regularly attend, because she is sick. Her only daughter, married to a teacher working in the northern Moluccas, has come to live with her mother and takes her turn in the shop. Since she has a regular income through her husband, she can afford to spend her time in the shop. She likes doing it and chatting with the customers. Sometimes, when a woman falls ill, her companion may guard the shop on her own. One woman is always alone since her companion has died.

Some women bring their own products when they are on duty, and sell these in front of the shop. However, the do not bring as much as they would try to sell on another day and the profit is not as high as on a regular vending day, because they also have to do the work in the shop. Very often a daughter or niece sells her wares in front of the shop when the mother is on duty.

Most pairs on duty are either rather close relatives or in-laws, although the only full-grade sisters do not make up pairs, but each forms a pair with an in-law or relative. As a result, there are pairs of higher and pairs of lower social standing, pairs living in the higher and the lower part of Hila, wealthier pairs and poorer pairs. There is only one 'mixed' couple, but they are first degree aunt and niece. Thus, although status and wealth might seem to play roles as criteria for the formation of pairs, they are primarily the result of selection according to kinship relations.

The women on duty are responsible for the cash, if there is a shortage; they have to make it good. They are allowed to sell goods on credit, but they have to remember to whom they sold what, so that Mujuna can check the cash at the end of the day.

Quite a few people buy on credit. In the first place these are the participants themselves. They do not have to pay interest if they pay back within a few days. All other customers have to pay interest or a fee, even if they pay the next day or a few days afterwards. Several women, who make cake, rice dishes or sweets to sell along the street, buy their supplies of rice, sugar and flour on credit. When they have used their supplies and sold the goods, they pay at the shop and get new supplies, again on credit. As long as they do not pay, they get no new supply. A third category are civil servants, especially teachers, of whom seven buy regularly at the widows' shop. Formerly they used to buy at the shop next door, but since they are notoriously poor payers, the shopkeeper refused to continue selling to them on credit. The widows' shop is still willing to grant them credit, which may run up as high as 40,000 Rp when salaries are late. Finally there are two woodcutters who come down from the hills once a fort night to sell wood and buy rice. Their credit amounts to about 20,000 Rp, but they pay regularly and are welcome customers.

Plate 7.1: Yearly distribution of goods at the widows' shop

Thus, there are about ten large creditors, and a lot of small ones whose debt hardly ever runs up higher than 1,500 Rp. Nonetheless the total amount of outstanding debts, when a calculation was made two weeks before the fasting started in 1985, was as high as 200,000 Rp. The teachers were responsible for the bulk of this sum and paid a few days later, when salaries had arrived.

The profits are divided among the members once a year, shortly before the fasting month starts. That is an expensive month in which more cash is needed than usual to make the special dishes during the month and for the feasts afterwards. In 1984 the shop had been in operation for four months when the fasts started. Every member received goods worth just under 10,000 Rp. In 1985 they each received 30 kg of rice, 7 kg sugar, 5 kg flour, 3 kg salt, one large package of tea and some other things, plus an amount of 4,000 Rp in cash, the total value being 30,000 Rp. The project manager received twice the amount of the other participants. Everybody agreed that that was a reasonable compensation for the work he does, for he comes in nearly every day, and does a substantial part of the shopping in Ambon and the bookkeeping. The social department also pays him some additional money as a subsidy. I do not know how much he actually receives. Finally, the village secretary as the general manager of all projects, and the owner of the land on which the shop stands each received 15 kg of rice in 1985. All in all, an amount of about 900,000 Rp was divided and another 900,000 Rp was kept as working capital.

An Evaluation of the Hila Projects

What Makes a Project Work?

Of course there is no single factor which alone determines whether a project works well or not. But clearly one important factor is physical and to some extent mental health. The projects are set up on the assumption that the participants can do some work; they are not meant for the completely infirm and bedridden poor. Thus it is not by chance that the widows' shop works best. Most widows are reasonably healthy and mentally fit enough to guard the shop for 24 consecutive hours and to deal with the variety of goods and prices. What I do not know is what will happen if a member falls seriously ill without having a relative to take her place. There are no built-in mechanisms to deal with such a situation and the manager could not tell what would happen.

The handicapped were usually fit enough to do the work, but in their case there were other impediments to which I shall return presently. Orphans are also healthy enough to do the work, and the reason why their project did not succeed must be sought elsewhere. The project for the aged was apparently physically or mentally too much for many participants, even though the kind of activity was easier than that of the widows.

A second criterion is good management. The only project running well is managed by a man with some experience in economic enterprises, whereas the others are managed by men selected for other qualities. I shall return to this point when discussing the relationship between the projects and the administration. However, economic skills in running a shop are not enough for such a project. It is also crucial that the manager has a good working relationship with the chairperson and secretary of the project. This is the case with the widows' shop, but not with the shop for the handicapped. The managers of the latter project not only lacked the know-how for running a shop; they were also unable to build up a good relationship with the members.

A third reason why the widows' shop runs so well is that women are used to the kind of work and cooperation that are required for the shop, whereas others are not. Most women have at some time sold food beside the road, and although this is not the same work as selling goods in a shop, it is similar. Men and children do not do such work and it is thus new to them. Moreover, handicapped persons have grown up as individualists who have to fight for themselves, for Ambonese are not soft to their handicapped. Women in general, though used to going about their own business, frequently have to cooperate, for example on the many occasions when they have to prepare ceremonial meals. It is nothing new to them to have to cooperate in the shop. Old persons, especially men, and children and handicapped persons are not used to such cooperation during the preparation of ceremonies. They are usually present at ceremonies, but do not bear the responsibilities in the way middle aged or young women do.

It is thus a combination of personal factors such as physical and mental health and abilities of the participants, managerial and business capacities of the manager, and good relationships between the manager, chairperson and treasurer, which makes a project successful. Furthermore, other social factors contribute, especially the existence of a correspondence between the activities of the various categories of participants in their regular lives and their allotted activities in the project, as well as between the ways they organize cooperation in their other social activities and in the projects.

Financial and Social Advantages of the Projects

One may ask whether the widows' project brings enough profit to make participation worth while. The answer to that question is complex. Certainly, 30,000 Rp a year is not much. Though it carries most women through the expensive fasting months, it is not nearly enough, for instance, to pay the school expenses for even one child, which is stated as one of the projects' objectives. On the other hand, the time invested is only 24 hours a fortnight and one cannot expect more than a marginal profit from a marginal input. Moreover, in an economic structure which makes it necessary for many people to seek an income from more than one occupation, it is nothing unusual that the members of such a project cannot make a living out of one kind of work (cf. Reidy 1980: 305).

Compared with what they would earn selling food along the road on a regular day, the profit from the shop is about twice as high. The shop makes a profit of around 10%, i.e. 3,000-7,000 Rp a day. If the two women who guard the shop had sold food on that day they would together have made a profit of 1,000-4,000 Rp that same day. The shop would have sold more during harvest time, but a vendor would also make higher profits during that period. Moreover, overhead costs and investments in the shop make the net profit divided among the members much lower. This may change in the future when the shop develops further, but not dramatically. On the whole, for women who sell food privately, the part of the shop's profits they can dispose of is about the same as the profits they make privately. For those who usually do not sell the advantages are obvious.

The true financial advantages lie in the fact that the members are also customers at the shop. This means that they always get a heap on top of the rice and flour measures, and the better and larger heaps of onions, garlic and peppers. Moreover, the members have a permanent source of cheap credit and that is especially attractive for women selling food. Their private economic activities are thus also supported by the project; it has, as it were, a cumulative effect, especially if they also sell products in front of the shop.

But apart from the purely economic advantages there are also social advantages. Being a member involves an obligation to help each other when that is required. One often sees members of the shop going together to cook at ceremonies. Many would have done so anyway, because they are related, but the shop definitely adds to the cohesion between the women; it makes relationships more multi-stranded. Obligations already existing between many members are more acutely felt and responded to. Moreover, the shop offers a channel through which other relatives of the widows can provide them with support. Everyday one finds different customers at the shop, who come to buy, chat, and if necessary guard the shop for a moment, or help when there are too many customers at one time. These customers are friends and relatives of one of the two widows on duty, for whom the obligation to help does not go so far that they would support the widows otherwise, but who, by becoming customers of the widows' shop and not of another shop, now can do something for these widows. If the relatives or friends live further off, they may not buy there everyday, but they will come when 'their' widows are on duty. The shop thus becomes part of the social networks of the widows, involving various degrees of obligation of support. How far relatives who would otherwise be obliged to help these widows now feel free from that obligation is difficult to judge, but the general effect seems to be positive.

Are the Needy Reached?

At the outset I stated that an important problem in designing social security programmes is to reach the very poor administratively. In this section we have to assess whether the projects in Hila have dealt effectively with this problem. Since conventional schemes of social assistance deal with clients on an individual basis, most participants would not be reached by such programmes. In the first place the administration would probably lack the manpower to deal with each person individually. Moreover, only a few would be able overcome all the administrative hurdles. Some participants cannot read or speak Malayu Ambon, the Ambonese Malay dialect, let alone Bahasa Indonesia; they only speak Bahasa Tanah, the old Ambonese language which has disappeared in the Christian villages but which is still spoken in the Islamic villages. These members hardly ever go to Ambon and have no experience with offices. Few participants would be capable of dealing with the administration, and these are the least needy in any case. However, as a group they can be reached, because the project involves a minimum of administrative involvement at the provincial level, and it does not require the potential participants to develop initiatives for which it would be necessary to apply for assistance at an office in Ambon.

The second question is whether the most needy are reached and whether they profit most from the project. Since the projects are designed for reasonably healthy persons, the very sick and infirm fail outside the scheme's reach. However, there is no doubt that some of the members of the widows' shop are very poor, unable to keep a garden and unable – or for some reason unwilling – to sell food along the road. But it has become equally clear that these members profit less from the project than the members who sell food, for the latter make more use of the credit facilities. For the former the cumulative effect described above does not work. The project thus has not been able to deal effectively with the problem of how to reach the very poor and make them profit most, for they cannot all participate and those who do participate profit less than the somewhat better off.

The last question is, whether the needy are helped in their need. That is to say: does the project help to remove the cause of their need? I have argued at the beginning that the main reason for poverty is a lack of labour. People who are themselves able to work a garden can subsist, because there is always land available. And if they can work a garden, but have no time for additional vending activities, their inability to rise above subsistence level also results from a lack of labour. It should be concluded that the project does not remove the lack of labour which is the cause of poverty, nor does it offer much of an alternative.

We can conclude that this type of project has some advantages over more conventional schemes of social security, because people are reached who would otherwise not have had access to any programme. But the projects do not reach all the poor, because the infirm and very old and feeble poor cannot participate in the kind of activities set up by the programme. Not all participants profit from the advantage of having access to cheap credit. Finally, though every participant is burdened by a chronic shortage of money and therefore finds every additional income welcome, the project does not tackle the basic problem: access to labour.

The Potentialities and Limits of the Social Projects

Potential Expansion of the Projects' Income

As long as a project is nothing more then an ordinary village shop there is no opportunity for substantial growth. There are many such shops and they have all, with the exception of one, about the same turnover and profit, which is just about enough to support one or two families. An important distinguishing feature of project shops is that they are run by larger groups, 28 persons in the case of the widows' project, whereas a regular shop is run by two to four adults. In

Hila there were two other shops also run by larger groups in 1985. One was the village shop of the local official cooperative (KUD), and the other was a private cooperative, set up by the headmaster of the secondary school as a private social security project. Both made an equally marginal profit from the shops. They were also involved in the clove trade, and this has proven to be so profitable that it has become a substantial source of income for all members. The KUD therefore was no longer interested in the shop and stopped that part of its activities.

Several people suggested that the widows should also enter into clove trade activities. However, because of recent administrative regulations, this has become increasingly difficult for others than the KUD. The KUDs have exclusively been granted tax exemption for the sale of cloves to inter-insular clove merchants who sell the spices to the cigarette factories to make the extremely popular clove cigarettes. The government had hoped that tax exemption for the KUD – and hence the possibility of offering higher prices than the Chinese merchants – would be a sufficient incentive to persuade the producers to sell their cloves to the KUD instead of to the Chinese, and that the KUD thus would become the sole intermediaries between the producing villagers and the inter-insular clove traders. It was expected that by this measure the producers in the villages would receive a larger share of the profits. (K. von Benda-Beckmann 1987)

This has not happened. Only approximately 10% of all cloves are sold to the KUD; 90% are still sold to Chinese merchants, who offer a slightly lower price than the KUD, but are considered more trustworthy buyers. Thus the margins for profits within the villages have decreased and as a result the small merchants and vendors who used to buy fresh cloves from the producers, and sold them dried to the Chinese merchants are being pushed out of business. The private cooperative which had made good profits until the new regulations were issued fell back to a yearly profit of 25,000 Rp per member in the year thereafter.[157] It is therefore doubtful whether the widows' shop could make substantial profits from the cloves trade.

The Projects as Cooperatives

The idea that the cooperative form offers the best way to organize self-help or social security prevails strongly in Indonesia. It is closely associated with the concept of mutual support (*gotong royong* in Indonesian, *masohi* in Ambonese) which plays such an important role in Indonesian political philosophy. However, formally cooperatives other than KUD are not allowed, because the government fears large organizations which it cannot directly control. The projects

---

[157] Meanwhile, I received information that the private cooperative has closed down, because of internal problems, but also because of decreasing profits from cloves.

are therefore set up in the form of cooperatives, but the term is carefully avoided, even though the government has sufficient control over them. The maximum number of members for such cooperative-like organizations is 30, but apparently the government deems it desirable that the social projects should not have less than 30 members, even though the per capita profits would have been higher had the project started with a smaller number. The handicapped started with 20, but there probably were no more participants available. Whether the social projects as they are organized presently can bring substantial improvement remains to be seen.

In the first place, there are no built-in mechanisms for continuation beyond the present membership. We have seen that the two places vacated by the women who left the project have not been taken by others. The reason is not a lack of widows who could take their place. I asked the manager whether he had given this problem any thought. He had not, and he added that if the group became too small he would have to consult the department of social affairs and ask what should be done. For the time being no new members would be admitted.[158] The project is clearly not set up as a more or less permanent provision to which women can turn if they lose their husbands. In this respect it offers no structural solution.

In the second place the project is organized in such a way that the members themselves are not supposed to run the shop on their own. The manager and not the members received a training. And, although he is called the initiator *(pembina)* and is supposed only to 'guide' the project it is nevertheless left to him whether, to what extent and to whom he chooses to pass on his knowledge and skills. Running an enterprise 'under the guidance of the manager' can mean that the manager has anything from a distant advisory role to complete control. Apparently complete self-help is deemed unrealistic, or perhaps even undesirable, so that from the outset permanent management from a non-group expert is considered necessary. And so in this respect, too, it does not structurally improve the condition of the needy in the sense that the members become self-supporting.

Thus, the cooperative form as the basic type for organizing the projects is an impediment to the achievement of economic independence and substantial profit for its members. This is not so because of any intrinsic unsuitability of cooperatives as such, but because of the ideas on which the Indonesian administration bases its cooperatives.

---

[158] The decision not to admit new members was probably made deliberately. Projects of cooperation of any kind notoriously fall apart if new members are admitted after the projects have been proven successful.

The Influence of the Administration

Throughout the world social policy has been used as an instrument of appeasement and thus of control over people who may threaten social and political stability if left to their own devices. Indonesia is no exception in this respect and it would be naive to expect the government to provide services without a certain amount of control. The way the projects are organized suggests, however, that the alleviation of the needs of the poor is not for the administration the primary objective of these social projects, and that other aspirations of the government dominate the organization of the projects.

There is at the moment a general trend towards increasing governmental influence over the private sector. The attempts often take the form of a mixture of economic and socio-political activities. Thus, the managers of the social projects were selected in the first place because of their social standing and close relationship with the village administration. The appointments seemed to have more a political than an economic nature. This impression is supported by the fact that a substantial part of the training was in state ideology and social leadership. It resembled a training for administrators rather than entrepreneurs. Reidy (1980) also draws attention to the fact that the social workers in charge of small-scale enterprise projects in the Philippines have no training in entrepreneurship. She suggests that this is a result of the idea that social assistance primarily has to deal with social rather than economic problems. Though this may also play a role in the Indonesian case, there the reason may be different.

The projects are not the only way through which the administration tries to increase its control over private citizens. The KUDs have recently come increasingly under governmental control. Moreover, the state has been undertaking various activities to mobilize private persons for state activities, many under the banner of *gotong royong,* mutual help. Recently it has started giving private persons training courses in state ideology, which used to be offered to civil servants only. Moreover, when the president's wife visited the Moluccas a few years ago every village was encouraged by her to set up a women's gardening project under the family health education programme *Pembinaan Kesejahteraan Keluarga* (PKK). The purpose remained vague: it was to serve some undefined social purpose, as well as promote better understanding between female farmers.

At the moment there is little evidence that the control extends beyond a close association between the managers and the village administration and a regular visit by officers from the social department. However, the ideas behind the projects and the general concern with the mobilization of citizens for the state result in a type of organization which inhibits the potential growth and independence of the projects.

We have seen that the preferred type of project, namely a shop, does not promise more than a marginal profit as long as the group of participants remains large. And I have shown why it has become difficult to engage in the clove trade. In this respect the governmental support for the KUD in the form of tax exemption, now turns against other groups which would deserve support themselves.

It seems that either another type of organization or another type of project or both would be required for a more than marginal relief of the needy. In the first place it will be necessary to look for managers with skills in entrepreneurship. More important, the training should be given to the members themselves, especially to the poorest ones, for only then can they become independent. Moreover, the groups are too large to make possible profits that are substantial enough to provide the members with a subsistence basis that includes such possibilities as sending their children to school, let alone more. Of course it is not feasible to break the group up into smaller groups and let them each run a shop, because, as already shown, Hila cannot support many more shops. The programme should diversify its activities. In looking for other kinds of projects, the managers should try to find those which require activities and types of organization which closely resemble activities the various groups carry out in daily life, for these have proven to be most successful. Other types of activities which would bring structural improvements would require much more input in terms of money, training and guidance than is provided in the present programmes.[159] Structural improvements that solve the lack-of-labour problem would require a completely different approach. The poorest and neediest of the villagers cannot be helped with a programme designed for healthy people. That category continues to depend fully on the local mechanism of help and support.

---

[159] See, for projects set up to help the very poor under the explicit condition that they bring about structural change in Sri Lanka, Schrijvers 1985 and Risseeuw 1980.

Chapter 8
Where Structures Merge
State and Off-State Involvement in Rural Social Security on Ambon, Eastern Indonesia*

Franz and Keebet von Benda-Beckmann

Introduction: A Perspective on the State in Society

Between 1970 and 1980, Indonesia's bureaucratic apparatus quadrupled.[160] Before, the majority of civil servants worked in the national and provincial capital towns. Only a few civil servants were stationed in sub-district capital or other villages. Nowadays, increasingly more civil servants also live in villages even in remote areas of Indonesia. The state has, in the most literal sense, moved closer to the rural population. Extension and health officers, as well as primary and secondary school teachers live in or make frequent visits to villages throughout Indonesia's archipelago and villagers are quite used to see such representatives of the state and live and interact with them. It is clear that such a vast expansion of the state bureaucracy must have profound implications for the way in which the state and rural populations are related. The spatial distribution of the institutional and personnel resources of state organisation has changed quite dramatically. More than ever, villages have become the locale in which the personal and resource structures of state apparatus and rural social and economic organisation meet and merge in new forms of integration (see F. and K. von Benda-Beckmann 1991). This integration consists of social and economic cooperation between civil servants and farmers, peasants, fishermen, and entrepreneurs in widely diverging constellations. It has a great impact upon the ways in which ordinary people in rural areas perceive and experience 'the state'. It has also led to new forms of social and economic differentiation within and between villages.

---

* Published 1998 in: S. Pannell, and F. von Benda-Beckmann (eds.), *Old World Places, New World Problems: Exploring Resource Management Issues in Eastern Indonesia*, pp. 143-180. Canberra: The Australian National University, Centre for Resource and Environmental Studies, CRES Publications.
This is a revised version of the paper presented at the Fourth International Maluku Research Conference, Universitas Pattimura, Ambon 9-13 July 1996. We thank Sandra Pannell for her many thoughtful comments. An earlier version of this paper has been presented at a conference of the EIDOS network in Amsterdam 1989.
[160] Evers and Schiel 1988: 74; Buchholt 1990.

Social security arrangements, in the sense of all those available arrangements through which people unable to acquire food, shelter, care and education for themselves, are taken care of[161], play a central role in these relationships. For it is primarily considerations of livelihood and social security which propel both civil servants and villagers into these new forms of social and economic cooperation. This is a result of the particular way in which the state apparatus of Indonesia is organized and financed and of the conditions of social (in)security in villages. For many villagers, the presence of civil servants opens up roads to outside resources to which they previously had less access. They may profit from the connections that civil servants have outside the village, or from the economic resources (salaries, project funds) that they control. Many civil servants, on the other hand, not only provide social security to the rural population in various ways, but at the same time depend upon them for their own social security. Since salaries and pensions are low, and because many expect to spend their pensioned life in their home village, civil servants have to invest in social relationships in their home villages, in order to secure the care and cooperation they will need after retirement. Thus the social security needs of both the rural population and those of civil servants lead to the establishment of closer links. It is for this reason that social security is more than just an example of social relations or policy through which the relationship between the state and the rural population can be studied. It stands at the core of this relationship.

Drawing attention to these socio-economic relationships and their social security function therefore is important, both for the analysis of the relationship between the state and village populations and the social security in rural settings. However, this is rarely perceived in both fields of study. In our view this is due to the fact that most conceptualisations of the relationship between state and civil society are based on a dichotomy through which the state and other institutions and persons tend to be distinguished, explicitly or implicitly, through distinct and mutually exclusive categories. The concept of 'state' is generally used with two different meanings. In the wider sense, it refers to a bounded entity of territory and people with a specific form of political organisation. In the narrower sense, 'state' refers to that specific political organisation, the organizational structures and institutions of which it consists, and then becomes more or less synonymous for government or state apparatus.[162] While it is acknowledged that one must distinguish between these two meanings, the implications for the analysis of the state/civil society relation are seldom spelt out systematically. When speaking of the state in the wider sense, it obviously does not make

---

[161] See F. von Benda-Beckmann et al. 1988a; and F. and K. von Benda-Beckmann 1984, 1994b and 1995.
[162] Giddens 1981, 1985; Held 1989; Melossi 1990; Elias 1982; Weber 1922; and Skocpol 1986.

sense to oppose it conceptually to civil society other than in an evolutionist or comparative framework. The state in this sense is society with a particular political organization. As such it may be compared with societies having a different political organisation, or its development may be traced through time.

In the more narrow sense, the state, as a complex organisational structure, consisting of institutions, resources and personnel, is always only part of, and socially and spatially situated within, the state in the wider sense. Here, the state apparatus cannot be identified with the encompassing entity state. Such identification can only be made in a normative, ideological way (see Knorr-Cetina 1988, F. von Benda-Beckmann 1993b). Only when discussing the state in this narrow meaning does it make sense to distinguish state organisational structures, institutions, resources and personnel from other institutions and people.

The inclination to view the relation between state and society as between distinct entities is enhanced by the frequent use of spatial metaphors such as external/internal; top/bottom; macro/micro; bridge between; encapsulation, incorporation, or interface which all imply a separation between distinct entities, of social political organizations (the state and civil society, the state and the village) or social categories (state officials, village farmers). They guide researchers to study the processes in which these spheres come together as encounters between representatives of these disparate entities, or they focus upon persons who act as middlemen or 'bridge' between them (see Rodman 1983, Long 1989). They much less help us to see and analyze the relationships, and patterns of relationships that emerge as a consequence of such interactions.[163] As Swartz says with respect to the bridge metaphor frequently used in political anthropological studies of brokers and middlemen, it forces us to ignore the social and often multiplex social ties that constitute social fields that cross-cut structurally and legally demarcated social entities. As such they are important fields of social relationships within the wider framework of society and state, although, looked at from a structural view, they also connect these entities (Swartz 1983: 275). Moreover, despite or perhaps rather due to the use of spatial metaphors, the spatial location of people who are members of social categories or even social fields, is neglected. As a consequence, the spatial distribution of the people, resources and social relationships that constitute these fields are not given sufficient consideration. As a further consequence, the actual spatial differentiation and regional differences of these newly emerging relationship patterns and their possible consequences are disregarded (F. and K. von Benda-Beckmann 1991).

Analyses of the relations between the state and civil society therefore find it often difficult to free themselves from the structuralist and institutionalist assumptions upon which this dichotomy is based, which restricts the analysis to

---

[163] See Swartz 1983; F. von Benda-Beckmann et al. 1989; and F. and K. von Benda-Beckmann 1991.

relations between what has been distinguished on the basis of these assumptions. These categories form the point of departure for the identification of social relationships between the entities, and of resources that belong to and individuals which are treated as a member or representative of one these distinctive normative-institutional categories. This tendency is strengthened by the dichotomy between 'public' and 'private' (see Rose 1987, Goodall 1990). State-citizen relationships and interactions tend to be looked for primarily in the 'public' domain, as it is defined by legal regulations. The result is that activities of civil servants are considered in relation to these regulations only. Activities not in line with the normative framework appear as 'deviations'; if completely outside the normatively defined field of functions, they are deemed irrelevant. State representatives operating in the private domain are treated as common citizens and are in that capacity put into a different category. In a way, this makes sense, of course. Civil servants *are* people and citizens. But it is frequently overlooked that those persons acting in the name of the state have multiple and ambiguous statuses and roles. They are also always part of households, kin-groups, neighbourhoods, private associations, economic complexes. Being a civil servant is only their job, and in developing countries it usually is only one of several jobs, a job they may only have during a limited number of years and for a limited number of hours per day. Our objection is not so much that they are also treated as private citizens, but that the connection between their activities as private citizens and those in their official function is not sufficiently being considered.

State and other institutions and persons therefore cannot simply be distinguished by means of a dichotomy which explicitly or implicitly is based on mutually exclusive categories. In the analysis of state/civil society relations, therefore, the primary question is to what degree state personnel, institutions and resources are interwoven with other personnel and institutions and how these relationships change over time. The study of such relations should not be restricted to the normatively defined official, public relations which state official have with other 'citizens'. The totality of their relationships and the reasons why and motives with which such relationships are forged, maintained or broken off must be studied (see also Tilly 1986). With the term 'off-state' involvement we want to draw attention to the biased analyses in which activities or impacts of 'the state' are perceived as the execution of preconceived functions, derived from the official norms regulating these activities. We are not the first ones to note that many of the so-called private activities are only possible because of a civil servant's official position in the state administration. Our point is that labelling these as private does not do justice to this intimate connection. Off-state activities are as much part of the relationship between villagers and the state as are official activities. While law, statutory duties, status and obligations are important, they are neither primary nor exclusively constitutive of these relations (Rose 1987: 74). They are the result of both private and public, 'on-state' and 'off-state' activities.

In analyzing the influence of the state, or the implementation of 'state policy' or 'intervention' in any particular sphere of life, both must be taken into consideration, irrespective of which sets of activity have officially been called 'policy' or 'intervention' in political rhetoric, policy statements, regulations and concrete directives.[164] In the policy domain of social security, for instance, we shall get a completely different picture of the significance of the state's involvement if we look only at the social security regulation and projects and their implementation, or if we also look at 'off-state' involvement, through the social security function in the multiplex social relationships between state officials and villagers.

In this paper we shall first sketch the conditions under which these new relationships emerge. We then describe some of the mechanisms in which the various links between civil servants and (other) villagers are established and maintained[165] and how state and village structures merge in 'on' and 'off-state' activities of civil servants. We shall give particular attention to the crucial role of education as a social security strategy through which villagers aim to establish new relationships with the state apparatus. In this nexus resources such as land, labour, money and connections all play a role, but they serve different purposes and have a different level of sustainability for the various actors involved. Land is important for farmers to grow crops for their own consumption and for the market, as well as for housing. Civil servants value land for housing, for crops that require little attention, such as cloves, and – increasingly – for speculation. Labour is a resource which is in particular insecure for those living far away, since it needs constant re-instatement if kin-relationships to ensure the necessary caring labour at old age. For ordinary people labour is a way to obtain access to connections that may mediate essential services. Connections are a broker's resource to obtain political loyalty and social security and care in the distant future.

The paper aims to demonstrate two interrelated points. It shows how these new relationships between state and non-state personnel and resources significantly change the relationship between the state and civil society and lead to a level of social and economic differentiation within and among villages that is new. Secondly it shows why in the field of social security the state's 'off-state' involvement may be much more important than its official social security policy measures. While our description and analysis primarily pertains to the changing relationships between the village population and the state apparatus in

---

[164] See also F. von Benda-Beckmann et al. 1989; and Goodall 1990.
[165] The empirical data are mostly drawn from the field research which we carried out in Hila on the island of Ambon, in the eastern Indonesian province of the Central Moluccas in 1985 and 1986.

a Moluccan village in Indonesia, it has wider implications for the analysis of relations between the state and civil society which in our view are still neglected in the work of most political theorists.[166]

Discontinuity in Indonesia's State Administration

Two elements in the structure of Indonesian government organization are particularly important for understanding the new linkages with which we are concerned in this paper. One is a high degree of discontinuity in allocating government resources for infrastructural facilities.[167] We call this type of government 'governing by way of projects' and sketch its basic characteristics, in order to explain the interests and needs civil servants have in their connections with the rural population. The other element is that official salaries are insufficient to support families in a manner acceptable for their position and that civil servants need additional income sources.

Governing by Way of Projects

Notwithstanding the surprising success of the Indonesian government in forging the diverse ethnic groups into one nation, the central government has to make great efforts in order to keep the nation together and fend off the ever present latent danger of regional separatism. This is difficult enough in itself. If the financial basis is weak, it becomes even more of a problem. Although Indonesia is extremely wealthy in natural resources, the state administration suffers from chronic financial shortage. In order to cope with the shortage, with the imbalances of wealth and revenue between the different regions and with the ever-threatening interregional animosity, the central government has developed a characteristic mode of administration by way of projects, which is highly distributive but which also shows a high degree of discontinuity in terms of policy implementation.[168]

Basic permanently available services, such as education and health care have been set up throughout the whole archipelago. Primary education can be found in almost every village. Health centres, however basic, are also very wide-spread throughout the country. But even some of these more permanent facilities are financed on a small project basis via the Inpres (*Instruksi Presiden*)

---

[166] For recent assessments see Giddens 1985; De Sousa Santos 1985; Skocpol 1986; Held 1989; and Melossi 1990.
[167] See Robison 1982; Hardjono 1983; Schulte Nordholt 1985; and Ravallion 1988. For Eastern Indonesia, see Azis 1996; and Sondakh 1996.
[168] See MacAndrews 1986b; Morfit 1986: 62; and Buchholt 1990.

programme which is handled by district government agencies (Hardjono 1983: 54, Morfit 1986, Ravallion 1988). Other basic facilities, such as secondary education and various extension services are distributed among the sub-district centres throughout the whole country. There is also a wide geographic coverage of official village cooperatives (*Koperasi Unit Desa,* KUD). Civil servants working in these services receive salaries and basic financial facilities are available for these services. However, these services in turn depend on projects for maintenance or extra facilities. And these are distributed on a project basis. Obtaining such funds requires intensive lobbying with patrons higher up in the administration.

The state distributes considerable resources by way of projects. Much of the infrastructure such as roads, harbours, as well as many services, are characteristically provided for in the form of projects.[169] If a certain amount of money is allocated to a region for a particular purpose, then in the next period this amount will be allocated to another region for the same purpose. Structural financing for the maintenance of such infrastructures is often not available, and when it becomes available again at the region's next turn, such works often have to begin anew. Projects thus are a major source of discontinuity in the state's involvement in rural areas. Hardjono speaks of 'badly coordinated crash-programmes' (1983: 60). The immense resources invested by foreign and international donor agencies in innumerable development projects increase this effect.

Although cyclical allotment of projects reduces the interregional competition to some extent, a fair amount of competition remains, if only because there is usually room for negotiating one's position in the sequence of allotment. The real competition is no longer located at provincial or even district level, but has been dramatically decentralized to a level that does not form a threat to central government in the way strong interregional envy would. The government tries to develop spear point centres which get a larger share of public spendings in the form of financial inputs, infrastructure, services and training programmes. Since 1969, villages directly receive a cash grant from which to finance village development projects (Hardjono 1983: 53). In addition, they may apply for money for special projects. In 1993, a massive new anti-poverty programme, the so-called IDT *Inpres Desa Tertinggal*[170] programme has been launched. The funds are largely disbursed for purposes of increasing income earning opportunities and increasing relationships with the wider economic environment. It is far too early to say much about how the programme actually will work. The first preliminary official research report points to a 'less than ac-

---

[169] See Hardjono 1983: 54; Schulte Nordholt 1985: 357; Morfit 1986; Quarles van Ufford 1987; and Buchholt 1990: 214.
[170] Presidential Decree Programme for Least Developed Villages; see Mubyarto 1994; Bambang Ismawan dan Susapto 1994; Bambang Ismawan dan Pamuji; Bappenas 1995.

curate understanding of the basic concepts of this program' (Bappenas 1995: 1). In the whole of the Moluccas, 812 out of 1,505 villages are classified as least developed (Bappenas 1995: 22).

Through this myriad of projects, regional and local government officials thus have become the major development agents (Schulte Nordholt 1985: 357). Depending largely on the relationships between village leaders and civil servants at the different levels of the state administration, some villages or sub-districts are more successful at acquiring projects than others. The most successful manage to acquire the status of a centre, securing a more permanent influx of state resources. Others may win incidental projects, but may be so successful that in effect they also receive a regular stream of state money and services. Others may profit only occasionally or hardly at all from this kind of administration.[171] Much depends on the skills and contacts of village leaders and brokers in the (sub-)district and provincial administrations.

Thus, administration by projects serves to keep the civil servants well integrated by internal patronage, while providing them with the means to develop patronage relationships outside the state apparatus.[172] Projects are lucrative for civil servants for several reasons. They mean extra income for the duration of the project; both official and unofficial (Gray 1979). Since projects are an important type of resource allocation to the rural population for which the mediation of civil servants is required, civil servants use projects to do favours to relatives, friends, neighbours and village leaders, for which they may ask favours in return. Project resource allocation is determined to a very high degree by the political and personal needs of civil servants rather than by the priorities of long- term planning.[173] Thus both villagers and civil servants from the lowest to the highest echelons each have their own interest in projects. Government by way of projects has led to income differentiation and clientelism within the state apparatus itself and to quite strong bonds between the various levels of the government and villages. It has also resulted into a degree of intra-regional differentiation that is new. Comparatively speaking, this plays a more important role in Eastern Indonesia than in other regions in Indonesia. For the allocation of *Inpres* funds per capita to Eastern Indonesia is comparatively high (Azis 1996: 98) while routine budget allocations are comparatively low (Sondakh 1996: 152).

---

[171] For a case study see Conkling 1979; and Buchholt 1990.

[172] These interrelations between politicians and bureaucrats and economic enterprises have mostly been described and analysed as they pertain to higher levels of the Indonesian political and economic organisation, see Hansen 1973; De Koninck 1983; Palmer 1978; Robison 1982, 1986; Schulte Nordholt 1985; and with particular emphasis on Java. For a detailed study of Northern Sulawesi, see Buchholt 1990.

[173] Robison 1982: 59; MacAndrews 1986b: 31; and Buchholt 1990: 244.

Low Salaries

The other element in state administration by which structural expenditures can be held low, is by paying low salaries to civil servants. Official salaries and allowances are not enough for a civil servant and his or her nuclear family to live a decent life, let alone live up to all the claims and requests for help and support from more distant relatives which civil servants are expected and pressed to comply with.[174] It is difficult to deny such requests, not only for cultural reasons, which make people feel ashamed to refuse help, or because they have to pay off moral debts because their family have made their career possible by paying for their education. An important reason for their willingness to comply with requests for help lies in their own future. Even considering the extra facilities in the spheres of housing, transport, and food (civil servants get 10 kg of rice for a family of up to three children) every civil servant has to create additional income.[175] According to MacAndrews, civil servants must augment their salaries from other sources by three to five times their basic civil service income to sustain themselves and their families (1986b: 32). In fact, each one has one or more jobs besides being a civil servant (Simanjuntak 1979; Buchholt 1990: 264).

Social security provisions for civil servants, both during and after their active service, are also insufficient, although they are more comprehensive than for any other category, with the exception of the armed forces.[176] They are entitled to sickness and disability allowances, as well as good health-care provision. After retirement, usually at the age of 55, they receive pensions which amount to 2 ½% of the basic salary per year in service, with a minimum of 40% and a maximum of 75% (Prawotosoediro 1982: 95). Given the retirement age of 55, pension payments have to be made during 20 years or more.[177]

During the period of active service civil servants therefore have to provide for the days to come, because pensions are low. The extent to which civil servants depend on such extra incomes for their basic security changes with their age and career. But 90% of all civil servants are on the lower two salary classes (Buchholt 1990: 252). Since salaries are extremely low at the beginning

---

[174] See Gray 1979; Arndt and Sundrum 1979. For teachers in particular, see Clark and Oey-Gardiner 1991.

[175] For a detailed description and analysis of civil servants' security strategies in Northern Sulawesi, see Buchholt 1990.

[176] The development of an official system of social security in Indonesia, in the sense of the ILO convention No. 102, has been relatively slow compared to other developing countries. For overviews see Mesa-Lago 1978, McGillivray 1980; Emrich 1982; Midgley 1984; Fuchs 1985; and Ahmad et al. 1991; for Indonesia see Chhabra 1980; Department of Social Affairs 1984; Esmara and Tjiptoherijanto 1986; Stamboel 1986; and F. and K. von Benda-Beckmann 1995.

[177] See for social security and pension funds Esmara and Tjiptoherijanto 1986: 60.

of a career, – particularly as one does not immediately enter into the circuit of projects or is 'close to a project' (*dekat projek,* Buchholt 1990: 259) – the period in which they can lay a basis for social security after retirement is relatively short, and some never get into the project circuit. As a result, civil servants never rely entirely upon their official salary or future state social security. Since they start with a very low salary and because they have not developed the extensive networks and the status required to operate as successful brokers, they are recipients rather than providers of social security at the beginning of their career. They must lean heavily upon other means of existence, often provided by their relatives. In the course of their career this may change, and successful civil servants may become formidable brokers who provide villagers access to state services and other services, such as treatment in private hospitals, bank loans, a place in a school, etc.[178]

After retirement, some are able to continue their position as brokers for some time, others simply remain economically independent, but with age they become increasingly dependent upon the care of others. At some point most will move back completely to being a recipient of care and help. Only the higher ranking civil servants, who have been economically successful in addition, will have sufficient means to buy the necessary help and care in old age. The majority will somehow become dependent upon social security from relatives.

Nowadays, more and more civil servants are being recruited from the rural areas, especially outside Java. These people expect to return to their home village upon retirement and know that they can expect little help if they have not supported relatives during the period in which they were able to do so. Therefore, many civil servants who live in town keep close contacts with their relatives back home and may make frequent visits to show their attachment and concern. It is for this reason that they set up forms of economic cooperation with relatives in their home village, even though it requires frequent and time-consuming visits, and perhaps means less control over the proceeds than would have been possible with an economic enterprise in town.

It is the combination of a great number of civil servants being recruited from rural areas, low salaries paid over a relatively brief period of time, and the peculiar form of government by way of projects, that creates the structure in which most civil servants have a keen and personal interest at every stage of their career in being intimately involved with the rural population. The off-state activities and the patronage relationships involved do not merely serve immediate economic gain or political support (Boissevain 1969, Breman 1971, Wolters 1979, K. von Benda-Beckmann 1988); they also serve as investments for social security of civil servants themselves, upon which they can fall back in old age.

---

[178] See also K. von Benda-Beckmann 1992; and Buchholt 1990. Arndt and Sundrum (1979) emphasize that for civil servants at the lower ranks, the advantages derived from their official position are rather limited.

Social Security Arrangements in Moluccan Villages

Being one of the legendary spice islands, Ambon-Lease was one of the first regions in the archipelago to become firmly incorporated into the colonial state and world economy. Ambonese villages have for centuries had a mixed economy in which subsistence activities, such as fishing and the exploitation of sago palms, growing of tubers, root crops and vegetables, have been interwoven (Elwert 1980a) with the production of spices, cloves and nutmeg in particular, for non-regional commodity markets.[179] The varying income from tree crop sales has more or less always been of influence on the level of production and consumption of subsistence foodstuffs. As a consequence of the clove boom in the 1970s, much money has flowed into the villages, where it has mainly been used to finance new houses, pilgrimages to Mecca, and the education of children. Rural Ambon, especially on the north coast, has no land shortage, but land belongs to the Ambonese population. Most Ambonese villagers were relatively well-off during the 1970s and 1980s, and there was little real poverty among them. Falling clove and nutmeg prices have forced many to revert to more intensive gardening and to sago as staple food. However, the Central Moluccas do not know the recurring periods of severe food shortage shortly before the rice harvest which often afflicts people in western Indonesia.[180] The availability of sago and fish as well as sufficient land provide a flexible and still well-functioning safety-net for food security.

Social security for the rural population consists of many different kinds of arrangements, and is regulated by distinct normative systems, such as *adat*, religious norms and state regulations of various kinds. Each individual develops his or her own mix of arrangements, depending on kinship, neighbourhood, village or state citizenship or religious denomination. There are few specifically differentiated institutions and regulations pertaining to social security; a largely undifferentiated social security function is embedded in relations of kinship, neighbourhood, friendship, both in the organisation of normal life and in situations or periods of need and crisis. Forms of mutual help and redistribution, particularly in the spheres of the provision of food, care and housing are still operative, though they have lost some of their former social and economic significance (F. and K. von Benda-Beckmann 1995).

An important part of the social security system is the payment of the obligatory alms-tax (*zakat al fitrah*) at the end of the fasting month. While the distribution system is adapted to *adat* and largely subordinated to kinship obli-

---

[179] See Ellen 1979; Knaap 1987a; Taale 1988, 1990; and Hospes 1996.
[180] See Alexander and Alexander 1982; Hüsken 1989. On sago production and distribution, see F. von Benda-Beckmann 1990a.

gations rather than being carried out in its pure religious law form, approximately one half of the total amount was really given to the relatively poor.[181]

Social security for orphans, and in case of illness or old age, involves both financial and labour contributions. Most villagers rely for the latter, the caring labour, on very close relatives who live nearby, parents, children, brothers and sisters, grandparents. For financial contributions they may also look for support from relatives who live further away, but have a regular income. People express it as their ideal that old people should have some children in their immediate vicinity to care for them, and in addition some in government service and some in private business as well, to contribute financially (K. von Benda-Beckmann 1996). Higher education, as a way to obtain a position in the civil or military service therefore has become an important social security strategy (see Buchholt 1990). This is not a new trend. During the colonial era children of elite families were sent to school for an education that gave entrance to the civil service. New is that higher education is now available to ordinary families. However, today there still are comparatively many persons from elite families in higher government positions. Elite families thus have consolidated their privileged position in the wider setting of state-rural population connections. The young generation has easier access to higher education, and other close relatives have better access to various kinds of resources that are mediated by their high positioned relatives. In return for their broker's activities, quite a number of these high civil services have managed to secure housing plots at privileged places in the village.

Butonese immigrants, who have settled in rural Ambon, have in many respects a different position in social security than Ambonese. Butonese are generally not allowed to own land, apart from house-plots which in exceptional cases are sold to them.[182] Though many have become involved in clove production and horticulture, they have to do so on the basis of pawning or sharecropping arrangements. While those whose relatives came to Ambon in the past century have now fully developed sets of relatives, others who came later, have to rely on a narrow circle of relatives for their social security, while they have no basis in landholding. Butonese are not considered citizens in *adat* terms. They have acquired the right to vote in the village head elections in some cases only in the mid eighties and they do not or only marginally participate in village government. In some cases Butonese settlements have acquired a status separate from the main, Ambonese, village and have been eligible for government projects themselves. Where projects are channelled through the village govern-

---

[181] See F. von Benda-Beckmann 1988: 356. In Hila, in the mid 1980s, *zakat al fitrah* involved a redistribution of about 5.5 tons of rice, or a money equivalent of 2.2 million rupiah. In comparison, the village received 1.25 million rupiah as development subsidy and 0.9 million rupiah was paid by villagers as land tax, IPEDA. See F. von Benda-Beckmann 1988: 353.

[182] See F. von Benda-Beckmann and Taale 1992; Hospes 1996.

ment, they have less easy access to them than Ambonese, especially Ambonese of the elite families.

The official state regulated social security provisions are of little direct relevance for the rural population, apart from the active and retired civil servants, who are covered by social security schemes for those in government service. The state has only gradually issued laws and regulations concerning income substitution in case of adversity for the private sector, but these are only applicable for registered workers.[183] In 1992, a new ambitious social security legislation was passed which considerably extended the coverage.[184] It includes a 'full' scale of benefits to workers, and in principle every worker is entitled to the coverage, although participation is to be phased over time.[185] 'Worker' is defined to include those who are self-employed, and would in principle also comprise the large masses of people working in what is considered to be the 'informal' sector in small enterprises and who still live without any form of insurance regulated by the state, as well as the rural population mainly engaged in agriculture as farmer or agricultural labourer. However, concrete social security policies aiming at introducing social insurance schemes for the rural population are still in the planning sphere.

But the state contributes to the social security of the rural population in several ways; through permanent facilities such as health centres, schools, village cooperatives and facilities that are provided on a project basis, such as social security projects. Health centres are wide-spread and available within a day's travelling throughout Indonesia. Every village in the Central Moluccas has a primary school and lower secondary education *(Sekolah Menengah Pertama)* is available in sub-district capitals. Higher secondary schools *(Sekolah Menengah Atas)* which until the mid-eighties only existed in district or provincial capitals are spreading in rural areas as well, though the quality of these schools is a serious problem. Furthermore, every village has a village cooperative. Apart from the more permanent services, projects have also been set up in villages. In the province of the Moluccas, a series of social security projects set up by the Ministry of Social Affairs, started in 1983 for four categories of needy persons: widows, orphans, the disabled and the aged.

---

[183] See Joenoes 1982; Esmara and Tjiptoherijanto 1986: 64; ILO Report 1985; K. von Benda-Beckmann 1988.

[184] The Jamsostek law, Undang Undang Republik Indonesia Nomor 3 Tahun 1992 tentang Jaminan Sosial Tenaga Kerja. See McLeod 1993; and F. and K. von Benda-Beckmann 1995.

[185] The benefits comprise: workers' compensation insurance for work-related accidents and illnesses, life insurance, retirement (provident funds) benefits and free health care for workers, their spouses and up to three children. For a detailed description and analysis, see McLeod 1993.

The Village as the Locale of State-Village Relationships

The village of Hila, since 1980 a sub-district capital village with a population of 4,100, of whom 1,700 are Butonese immigrants, is one of the rural centres in which the state is relatively prominently present. It has three primary schools, a lower secondary school and since 1986, a higher secondary school, which draws students from several villages on Ambon and the western part of Seram. It has a health centre with trained nurses, a trained midwife, a birth-control officer and a young doctor who visits Hila twice a week. It also has a village cooperative, its president at the same time being an officer at the Central Bureau of Cooperatives *(Pusat kooperasi unit desa, PUSKUD)* in Ambon. During the late 1980s two social security projects operated under the scheme of the Department of Social Affairs.

Together with the police, the services provided by the government form the most important link between the state and the rural population. The links are established in two distinguishable, but in practice closely intertwined ways: The connection is made through the 'street level bureaucrats' (Lipsky 1980), the staff-members of schools, medical posts, social projects and village cooperatives, in their official capacity. Children receive education, people make use of medical services, many villagers participate in the village cooperative and some in the social projects, and they do so in varying degrees of compulsion and with different intensity and varying profit. But the same staff-members also operate as individuals who do far more than fulfil their official duty. We shall first discuss two kinds of government services, the social projects and the village cooperatives and see how these organisations are encapsulated in wider arrangements of social security. Then we shall look into the ways in which civil servants operate in combination of duty and off-duty activities and see how notions of social security play a role in these activities.

Encapsulated Services

Social Projects

The Provincial Department had initiated a series of income generating projects set up by the Department of Social Affairs, which were started in 1983 for four categories of needy persons: widows, orphans, the disabled and the aged. With a non-refundable starting capital of 300,000 rupiah (then roughly US $ 300), the Department of Social Affairs intended the projects to generate enough profits to enable participants to send their children to school.[186] Two of the projects never reached an operative stage, mainly due to a lack of leadership and alleged cor-

---

[186] These projects have been described in detail by K. von Benda-Beckmann 1988.

ruption. Of the two projects that did become operative, the returns have been very modest at best. Though none of the projects fulfilled the official goal, one project provided a welcome additional income to the participants during a certain period of time and had some spin-off effects that allowed participants access to credit with which they could acquire further income. With the exception of one project coordinator, the coordinators and the village secretary used the projects for themselves, either by pocketing (part of) the subsidy, or by 'borrowing' from the shops without paying. But as the coordinators were becoming important men in the village, they used the projects to build up their clientele as well.

Strictly speaking, the village head and the secretary are not civil servants. However, they are the lowest level of state government and do get some compensation for their services. Being farmers themselves as well as in government service, they form a crucial link between the state and the rural population. All official government projects including the finances go through their hands, giving them the opportunity to become powerful patrons or brokers in government projects. They profit from such projects in various ways, from receiving a percentage of the budget or the proceeds, to asking services in return for participation or making sure that relatives participate in lucrative projects. Thus, the social projects mentioned above served the coordinators, who used the projects to build up a clientele and profited in some way personally from their projects, even though they were not successful as project managers.

Such projects are also important channels for strengthening the state ideology at village level. Coordinators and project managers, who are recruited from among the circles of young men around the village head and closely related with the leading political party Golkar, receive a training, which for a large part consists of courses in Panca Sila. They form the next generation from amongst whom at a later state the lower civil servants in the district centres are to be recruited. Two of the project managers of the mid-eighties had become a civil servant in Masohi in the early nineties.

The Village Cooperative KUD

The village cooperatives form another important link between the state and villages. Officially or ideologically their primary function is one of social security: cooperation is intended to generate income which individuals would not be able to acquire otherwise. However, the KUDs in Ambon had become more and more an instrument to regulate clove trade. As major clove traders, they bought from members and other villagers, and sold to the inter-island traders. From 1983 on the KUD had the exclusive right to auction cloves without having to pay taxes.[187] Other traders were allowed to put up auctions but they had to pay taxes. The idea was that by granting the KUD a virtual monopoly, the producers/members would profit more than if there was free trade. In fact, villagers were not very keen to sell their cloves to the village cooperative. They accused the cooperatives of tampering with the scales and complained that the cooperative too often refused to accept cloves because of alleged poor quality. They preferred to sell to local or Chinese traders, who did not pay quite as much, but who were said to be fair, reliable and to treat their clients well (K. von Benda-Beckmann 1987).

The village cooperative in Hila did not buy much directly from villagers. However, the chairman made clever deals with Chinese traders, auctioning cloves for them in the name of the village cooperative and splitting the profits. Since the turnover exceeded the total harvest of Hila in a full harvest year by several hundred percent, the profits were substantial, from which much disappeared into the pockets of the chairman. Within a few years he had become a wealthy person, married a second and a third wife, built three posh houses and had run for village head. But he was generous to the cooperative members who were willing to accept his leadership. He had managed to develop the cooperative into the wealthiest one on Ambon, using his close connections with Chinese merchants and his contacts in the provincial centre of cooperatives, where he was a civil servant. As a result, he had become one of the most important patrons in Hila, who could mobilize help and support, especially from KUD members, whenever he needed it. He channelled a considerable part of the clove profits to the members of the village cooperative, albeit according to different rules and mechanisms of unequal distribution. Some members criticized his corrupt practices and did not agree with his all too autocratic leadership, but enough members backed him, because as a patron he was successful and generous.

Both the projects and the village cooperative have been set up to serve – among other things, as social security. But they have become part of a much wider web of economic and social security relations than was originally planned.

---

[187] It had been made the task of the KUD to buy up doves by presidential decree (keputusan Presiden) No. 5/1976. This decree was implemented by *Keputusan Bersama Menteri Perdagangan, Menteri Tenaga Kerja, Transmigrasi dan Koperasi dan Menteri Dalam Negeri* of 6.6.1977. It was not until the early 1980s that the KUD was granted exclusive tax freedom. See Hospes 1996.

Off- and On-State Activities of Civil Servants

Altogether about 50 civil servants and 20 retired police and military officers[188] lived and worked permanently in the village with several more visiting frequently. Many villagers have civil servants or kinsmen in the armed forces among their immediate kin, most of whom live outside the village. Villagers are quite accustomed to including these relatives in their strategies of social security. In the following section we shall look more closely into the various constellations of relationships between villagers and civil servants in which different forms of cooperation develop, each in its own particular way geared to providing participants social security. As we have indicated at the outset, some civil servants have much more to offer than others and some are in more direct need of care and help while others seek to secure care for the far future. The specific possibilities and needs they have depend on the spatial distance to their kinsfolk and access to resources apart from their salaries, notably land. It further depends on the phase in their career, on their position in the government, on the type of work they do, and on the kinds of resources for which they may mediate the necessary connections. Roughly speaking there are four types of connections between civil servants and (other) villagers: 1. civil servants who live and work in their native village, including teachers, medical staff, extension officers, but also village heads and secretaries; 2. civil servants who live and work in a village where they have no relatives; 3. civil servants who live in town but visit their home village frequently; 4. civil servants who live far away. Each type stands in a different way in a network of relationships in which social security is a central element.

Civil Servants who Live and Work in their Native Village

Among the civil servants working in villages, teachers are the most prominent. One of the reasons is that the high value put upon education has led to a high rate of schooling, which brings virtually every family in contact with schools and teaching staff. This gives teachers a stronger position than other civil servants. We will focus on them, though much of what we write here goes for other civil servants as well.

A young teacher who has been born in the village where he or she teaches will be taken care of by close relatives, who thus subsidize the state

---

[188] Persons in active service usually are in a better position to mediate in services than retired persons, but the retired ones often have built up a financial basis which, together with their monthly pension, allows them to help poorer relatives financially. And some have enough bureaucratic skills to help less capable relatives when necessary.

educational system.[189] Most come from elite families, but as a young person they do not have a powerful position at all and they are not held in especially high regard, though they are not expected to do as much work in the household as others. Young teachers have little to offer, other than the control over the decision whether students move to a higher class at the end of the year. They stand almost completely at the receiving end of social security relationships.

This is different for senior teaching staff, especially the heads of secondary schools. They are at an age and position at which they command more respect. But their position brings with it that they are confronted with demands for financial support that are usually far beyond what they could afford on their salaries. And they often mediate in securing positions in institutions of higher education for their students. Moreover, they often have good contacts with former students in various positions of the administration as well as in the private sector and may be able to co-opt their services if necessary.

The headmaster of the lower secondary school in Hila was such a person.[190] Highly respected both by his students, their families and in the world of education, he not only managed to place former students in schools of higher education, but also provided relatives and neighbours with a wide variety of services. He and his wife, equally respected as a formidable trader and religious leader, set up a range of economic enterprises, which served as a means to earn an additional income for themselves, so that they could live up to the many demands for financial support that come with that position. But many of their activities were as much directed at providing an additional income for people who were in want of support: poorer neighbours, widows, elderly persons, etc. And they provided many villagers with credit, to be repaid in cloves when there would be a good harvest. Together they acted as powerful brokers and patrons, on whom a great number of people relied for support. Part of their services comes with the job. A headmaster is better able than anyone else to find places of higher education for former students. And the fact that his wife organized a group of women to make snacks that were sold on the premises of the school also came with their position. The headmaster was free to regulate the sale of snacks and he and his wife chose to let some of the needy women profit from this possibility.

Other activities were only remotely related to his position: the fact that he earned a relatively good salary made it possible for his wife to set up a business, which in turn allowed them to provide credit in times when ordinary farmers were in financial need. And the various cooperatives which he set up over the years were possible because of a combination of factors: the respect and authority he commanded as a good headmaster, his intimate knowledge of the vil-

---

[189] See Wolf 1990, 1992 for similar subsidizing of private factories on Java.

[190] See K. von Benda-Beckmann 1992 for a discussion of the brokerage activities of the headmaster and his wife.

lage and those in need, as well as his personal interest in being of service, and his financial means to provide a starting capital.

The headmaster and his wife were perhaps exceptional in the extent to which they cared for needy persons. But the government encourages teachers to set up 'social activities' and most heads of schools who live in their home village are more or less important brokers, though the extent of their involvement may vary. Compassion is not the only reason for their activities. To some extent they cannot avoid it: it comes with the position and it is very difficulty not to comply with the requests. But they also have a personal interest in it, for they know that they will be better taken care of in old age if they have been generous and active at the height of their career.

Civil Servants who Live and Work in a Village where they Have no Relatives

Many young teachers, extension officers, and medical staff, i.e. the majority of civil servants in villages, start their career as a single person or as a young married couple with one or two little children in a village far from home. They cannot live of their salaries and the 10 kg rice per family member which they receive in addition. They depend on the help of villagers for living space, gifts of food, a piece of land for a small vegetable garden, fuel and the care and supervision of their children. They are usually accommodated, often on the basis of rent payments, in the house of a village family. The landlord-teacher relationships with young unmarried teachers are often expressed in terms of a foster parent-child relationship (*anak piara*). The teachers may mediate between pupils or their parents within their own school if necessary, but rarely outside administrative system. In the beginning of their career, they usually receive more than they are able to give.

More senior teachers and their spouses may also use their external contacts to build up their own economic activities, such as trading clothes or gold. Mutual help relations with village women then can free them from most of the daily chores and may secure a supply of vegetables and sago, while at the same time providing them with a buyers' clientele for their goods. But only a head of a secondary school or his deputy is able to provide access to services outside the village.

The headmistress of the higher secondary school in Hila was a Christian from a distant village, without kinship connections in the village. She had only recently moved to the village and lived on the campus, at some distance from the main residential area. Asked to set up the new school until it would run smoothly, she expected to be in charge of the school for a few years only. She showed little interest in village life, and disliked what she found a backward attitude of the community. This may explain why she kept at a distance and did little to get socially and economically involved. She would try to be of help to students to go to university, but did little else besides. Would she stay longer, she might eventually become more involved, but her attitude stood in stark contrast to that of other teachers who expected to stay and felt a need to develop good relationships with neighbours and other villagers.

Villages in general and schools in particular have frequent possibilities to compete for projects. The budgets are usually calculated to include much unpaid labour. The government uses the euphemism '*gotong royong*' or the Moluccan variety '*masohi*' (see Bowen 1996). But while village governments often find it difficult to mobilize labour, schools always find parents or elder siblings of their students eager to cooperate and no payment is expected. Education is considered so important that people gladly do some extra work. When money became available to build houses for the teachers of the new SMA, hundreds of fathers and brothers came to work without complaint.

For other projects only those who expect some immediate profit or those who are clients of the project managers will be willing to do the work. Generally speaking, people do not like this type of work and consider it the new form of corvée labour that were obligatory during colonial rule.

Civil Servants who Live in a Town Close enough to Visit their Home Village Frequently

Higher civil servants who live in Ambon town also play a central role as mediators in services of various kinds, and as patrons who provide financial support to relatives back home in case of sickness, death, marriage, etc. Like the headmasters of schools they are confronted with frequent and substantial requests which they cannot possibly comply with from their salaries. But they cannot simply deny support, because they expect to return to their home village at old age. If they have not shown generosity while they were able to do so, they cannot expect to be cared for later on. Here, too, it is a combination of services that come with the position and the job, and activities that are more remotely related to the job, which characterize the network of cooperation and services. A house may be built in the village, providing work for relatives, and in which relatives may live as long as the owner is away. Often economic activities are developed with some relatives, to which the civil servant supplies the financial means and possibly relationships in town, while relatives in the village provide the labour.[191] The land that is necessary can be obtained rather easily from the family. Many civil servants manage to secure individual rights on family land. Due to their position as patron they can often pick first choice locations.

---

[191] See F. von Benda-Beckmann 1987.

Civil Servants who Live Far away and Rarely Visit their Home Village

Here the connections with relatives at home are loosest and rarely go beyond the circle of (grand-)parents - (grand-)children and brothers and sisters. Those in higher positions may contribute substantially and regularly to their old parents at home. More common is that they are asked to contribute only in cases of emergency, for example when someone has to undergo expensive and long medical treatment. Also, many hajis in rural areas have received considerable support for their journey from wealthy relatives who live far away, whether they are in government service or in private business. Some civil servants who live in one of the large cities with good educational facilities have a niece or nephew living with them to go to school or university, but this is rather the exception.[192]

The long distance prevents frequent visits and makes relationships extensive. Besides, a life away from the Central Moluccas makes a return after retirement increasingly unlikely. For those who change residence frequently and never live in one place long enough to settle, the likelihood of return to the home village is larger than for persons who settle at one place outside the Moluccas. The latter rarely return to the Moluccas and connections tend to loosen up. Since the government has a strong policy of rotation, those in government service tend to return more frequently upon retirement than people in the private sector. However, both civil servants and others living far away from the Central Moluccas usually have only relatively intensive contact with close relative only.

Education: Reallocation of Resources and Risk in Long-Term Social Security Strategies

Reallocation of Resources and Changes in the Village Social Security Potential

People realize how important and profitable it is to have contacts with civil or, preferably, military or police officials. Positions in the civil service are regarded as 'security' (*jaminan*) by most villagers (Van Fraassen 1972). A close relative in military service or with the police, whose portrait hangs prominently on the wall, may protect against simple harassment or extortion by local military or policemen. Relatives in the provincial or district administration may make it easier to obtain access to state services. And sometimes there may be special relationships with shops or clove traders through which villagers may obtain good prices or perhaps credit facilities. Furthermore, children who have become civil

---

[192] It is unclear to us whether and to what extent poor relatives are used as – underpaid – house servants.

servants or otherwise receive a regular income often let their parents take part in it. For these reasons, sending several children to secondary school, and, if possible, to university, has become one of the main social security strategies of villagers. As we shall see, it is both a risky and a costly strategy.

In general this holds true for both Ambonese and Butonese. However, there are some important differences between the two population groups. A survey we conducted in 1985, showed that of the SMP students more than 80% of the Ambonese planned to take further education that would lead to a position in the government, while only 10% (girls) and 16% (boys) wanted to go to the economic secondary school (*Sekolah Menengah Ekonomi Atas,* SMEA). Among Butonese students, 40% (boys) and 55% (girls) planned for a position in the government, while one third (boys) and one quarter (girls) opted for the SMEA. The results from the survey suggest that Ambonese and Butonese have different expectations for their future and prepare themselves through different types higher of education. Ambonese high school students generally seek employment in government service, as a teacher, a civil servant or in the armed forces. Butonese, who have few relatives employed by the government, are more directed at an education that provides entrance into the private sector. And in so far as they expect to work for the government, this will be mainly as teachers. However, for both groups education is very important and financial offers are readily made by the family.

Sending one's children to school means a significant reallocation of economic resources. Both money and labour otherwise invested in the village economy and in village forms of mutual help and social security are now invested in the children and their education. Part of this money goes into the teachers' salaries, and remains in the village in which the school is located. Since Hila draws a lot of students from outside, the school provides an inflow from other villages through food and boarding expenses for students and from the state in the form of salaries for teachers and some funds for infrastructure. But education outside Hila takes a lot of money out of the village economy. Education is expensive. The total costs for secondary education in Hila amount to approximately 55,000-70,000 rupiah a year. Going to school in Ambon, though much valued because it increases one's chances for a job in the government or a place at one of the faculties, is much more expensive. A SMA pupil or a university student in Ambon needs 400,000 to 500,000 rupiah a year for school fees, housing, clothing and food (see for similar mechanisms in Northern Sulawesi (Buchholt 1990: 250).

In addition to money, labour power is lost. Traditionally, children of school-age worked in the domestic sphere, fetching firewood, helping to weed gardens and harvest cloves, nutmeg and coconuts. As a result of their education, this labour input is dramatically reduced. Students still do some work, but far less than other children of their age. They have much less spare time and, more important, they are not expected to spend all their free time working in the house or in agriculture. Less than 20% of the boys and only 10% of the girls claimed to work in the vegetable or tree gardens. However, most girls and about half the boys had to do household chores.[193]

Labour is not only lost because children now go to school. The parents also are expected to work for the school and the teachers. When the secondary high school was built in 1985, part of the buildings, especially teachers' residences, were built by the parents or other relatives of the students. The same happened when a new school kitchen was built for one of the primary schools in 1986. Although it actually would have been the task of the government to provide these facilities, parents offered their labour, part of the material and money without grumbling, for it was for the school, their children and therefore ultimately also for themselves. The enthusiasm with which villagers respond to the call for such labour stands in striking contrast to the attempts of the village government to organize communal labour for other village projects.

Rights to land and clove or nutmeg trees may be sold in order to finance this new form of social security through the education of one's children.[194] If possible, they are sold to wealthier villagers, Ambonese or Butonese, but some land and trees have lately been sold to people from town, although this is not (yet) common practice as it has been reported from other parts of Indonesia (Buchholt 1990: 256). But also on Ambon, a tendency into that direction can be noticed (see for Tulehu, Hospes 1996). The increasing control (or appropriation) of land for housing still operates within the *adat* or Islamic law based system of inherited property where civil servants may have it easier to press claims for preferential allocation of land. This land is then withdrawn from the resource base upon which their peasant relatives have to rely (F. von Benda-Beckmann and Taale 1996).

Investment in education has various consequences. In the first place there is a general trend to increased outflow of the means of subsistence and market production, such as money and labour. Furthermore, the necessary investments strengthen tendencies towards individualization and social and economic differentiation within larger kin groups within the village. Money and labour which formerly could have been invested into forms of mutual or unilateral help, is invested in one's children, reducing the resources available for traditional forms of cooperation and redistribution with more distant kin and neighbours. Thirdly, networks of help are organized around the education of the children. Since parents alone usually cannot afford to pay all the costs, brothers and sisters, and other close kin contribute. Thus kinship-based forms of coop-

---

[193] According to our survey, more than 75% of the girls helped with cooking, sweeping and washing clothes. Of the boys, 35 % helped with cooking, 55% swept the flour and 40% washed their clothes.

[194] Compare for similar processes in Columbia, Freiberg-Strauss and Jung 1988; and for the Karo Batak in Northern Sumatra, Slaats and Portier 1988. For Tulehu, see Hospes 1996. For Northern Sulawesi, see Buchholt 1990.

eration between close kin are reinforced, while at the same time withdrawing resources away from other forms of mutual help with more distant kin and neighbours, the exception being a distantly related civil servant for those who are lucky enough to establish such a relationship.

The Risky Nature of Education as a Social Security Strategy

Investment in education carries with it increasing risks for the villagers. The period in which they are in a position to act as a provider is not very long and not everybody lives up to the expectations which their parents and close kin have invested in them. During the early years of a civil service career, civil servants still are at the receiving end of mutual help relations. Once they are in a position to be able to help at all, they will do so selectively. Most help may be expected from those who live rather close to their home village. Civil servants living on Java only rarely contribute substantially to their relatives back home.

Until the early 1980s, most students who finished their higher secondary education were fairly sure of a job in the administration. The strategy was relatively safe and many villagers have close relatives somewhere in the state apparatus, who may provide access to various resources. However, the dynamic growth of the state apparatus has come to a halt and it is already clear that many students who have had twelve years of education, will not be able to find a job with the government. This development is likely to become more dramatic in the more recent period in which structural adjustment programmes and privatization ask for a reduction of the size of the government apparatus. Besides, there is a dramatic shortage of places for secondary education. Competition for the few places at the better school in Ambon is murderous and is carried out with all available means: good marks, relations, and increasingly with outright bribes. Until 1984, the headmaster of the Hila lower secondary school had managed to find a place for all his graduates. Having served for a number of years for the United Nations as a headmaster in Irian Jaya, he was held in high esteem by the higher secondary schools in Ambon. However, in 1985 neither his own attempts nor those by other high civil servants from Hila had provided the graduates with a place in one of the Ambon higher secondary schools. Competition had become too harsh and only very few students could afford the necessary official and unofficial payments. As it turned out, the headmaster founded a higher secondary school in Hila and by far the most students remained in Hila, but on the understanding that it would be for three years only. After that, some would try to find a job, but most students would try to continue their education. The same problems will arise at the university level and many will be turned down by the state universities. They will have no other choice but to try one of the numerous private universities which are even more expensive than the state universities. Only very few will be lucky enough to have close relatives in one of the cities on Java and try to finish their education there, at yet more staggering costs.[195]

Since higher secondary and academic education is strongly geared towards white collar professions, most graduates may find it difficult to compete with more practically trained youngsters in private enterprise and technical professions. And it is even less likely that these young men and women will come back to, or stay in the village as farmers. When asked what they would do if they would not be able to continue their education beyond SMA level, only 5 % said that they would stay in Hila or go back to their home village. Around 75 % said that they would attempt to go to Ambon city to try and find a job there.[196] While the actual number of students who eventually will return to make a living in their home village will probably be larger, these data are indicative of the aspirations adolescents have.

What is intended to cover risks and provide for old age insurance thus creates serious new risks. With the closing job market, the chances that students will eventually be able to contribute substantially to the social security of relatives back home is likewise decreasing.[197] Moreover, the prospects for civil servants themselves are becoming less rosy because the expected changes in the pension schemes will increasingly shift the financial burdens for the envisaged social insurance funds to the civil servants themselves (Esmara and Tjiptoherijanto 1986: 60). This means that they have fewer funds to use for the maintenance of a social security network. The strategy of parents to send their children to school thus strongly resembles a lottery, in which they may get caught in a vicious downward spiral between the desire of sending children to school in order to have relatives in the government, and the need for relatives in the service of the government to be able to send children to school (see also Buchholt 1990: 256). Those who have invested resources such as land, labour and good relations into this lottery may later be faced with the grim truth that their aspired security will not be realized, while their village resource base for security has withered away.

---

[195] See for Northern Sulawesi, Buchholt 1990.

[196] Buchholt reports similar findings from North Sulawesi. Only 5% intend to study animal husbandry or fisheries; the important domains of agriculture in the region. 75% want to study law, social, policy or economics. Buchholt 1990: 250.

[197] See also Lundström-Burghoorn 1981: 189; MacAndrews 1986a: 15, 16; and Buchholt 1990: 255.

Conclusions

Changing Relations between the State and Rural Populations

The increase in the number of civil servants living in villages has led to new forms of linkages between the various levels of the Indonesian state and the rural populations. Governing by means of projects has led to strong networks of patronage within and outside the state apparatus that reaches in different and partly overlapping constellations and intensity from the highest levels of the national state to remote villages. These developments have changed the relationships between the state and village populations quite significantly, and they have also led to considerable changes in the constellations of social security arrangements of the village population. These developments can be interpreted as a process of de-differentiation of state and civil society, a merging of political and economic structures that continue to be embedded in spatially and organisationally distinct though connected spheres of operation, but in which political and economic resources are exchanged through the link of kinship. A process that has reached the rural areas to an unprecedented degree.

The cooperative ventures described in this paper, and the long-term security strategies through children's education, are largely based upon kinship relations. State personnel and resources become increasingly connected to village people through multiplex social ties. Although these kinship relations often mask the underlying patronage relations, they 'socialize' the relationships between villagers and the state (see Scott 1972, F. and K. von Benda-Beckmann 1987a). The single-stranded relations between civil servants and villager/citizens, as defined by the legal administrative function of civil servants, become increasingly multi-stranded through kinship and economic cooperation. 'The state', as it were, is made part of the family. This influences the villagers' perception of and their attitude towards the state. Villagers have a very ambivalent attitude towards the government. On the one hand, they are rather cynical, and nearly everyone can tell and document stories about the arbitrary, stupid, corrupt, brutal and exploitative activities of state officials, notably of the police and the military. In this respect villagers feel oppressed and exploited, and are not at all convinced by the political rhetoric of 'development' and 'social justice'. On the other hand, they will talk with appreciation and respect of their uncle, the judge, of their brother, the military officer, or dream of a career for their son in the police corps, and of the time when they will have 'the state' inside their family as a protection against 'the state'. The state with its resources is here not seen as oppressive or exploitative, but rather is regarded as a potential object of exploitation for the villagers themselves. If one hates policemen as oppressors, and yet works hard in order to facilitate one's son's career within the police, if one rejects the village cooperative as a dishonest competitor and corrupt government institution, and yet profits from it via one's uncle, then it is unlikely that an unambivalent attitude towards the state is developed (see also Scott and Kerkvliet 1973).

Socio-economic Differentiation and Regionalization

The same developments also contribute to new forms of socio-economic differentiation among villages, and within villages between larger kinship groups and even between members of larger kinship groups. The criteria on which kin may be mobilized have shifted from seniority and coercive obligation towards those of volition and equality. Villagers who have a large reservoir of kinsfolk, and especially those who already have relations with civil servants, need to invest less, and tend to profit more from recent developments than those who have not. Thus not all villagers are equally affected by these new forms of cooperation. Connections between villages and the state through higher-educated civil servants had already emerged two or three generations ago, be it on a much smaller scale. But then it was mainly the children from chiefly clans who were allowed to follow higher education, and whose descendants now have relatively more civil service connections than other villagers. It affected all villages equally. The regional differentiation which occurs now is a new development, and result from the great differences between villages in the number of civil servants and the number of projects available.

Socio-economic differentiation is enhanced by transformations of landownership. We have seen that many civil servants have acquired individual rights over good locations. These rights operate still under the *adat* or Islam based system of inherited property, but the circle of persons that will inherit these sites have become smaller than before. Socio-economic differentiation is also furthered because rights to land and clove trees are being sold to pay for education. There is a strong preference to keep such transactions within a village; it is the wealthier members of the village that will buy. Some of the wealthier Butonese, who were not allowed to own trees, have now been able to acquire trees and even land. With the traditional horizontal division between rights to the land and rights to the vegetation on the land, there is little direct transformation of land ownership, but when clove prices go down, there is bound to be more selling of land. In the mid eighties, these developments in Hila were still largely driven by social security strategies, of civil servants, but as Buchholt (1990: 247) showed for Northern Sulawesi, speculative motives may become a propelling force and that might lead to substantial changes in landholding as well. This increases the potential of severe conflicts of land, between the Ambonese villagers as well as between them and immigrants (see F. von Benda-Beckmann 1986, F. von Benda-Beckmann and Taale 1992, 1996, Mboi 1996).

The Instability of Resource Bases

One of the remarkable features of the networks cooperation that are developed is their transient nature. There is little stability over time neither in the kind of cooperation nor in the circle of participants. People move in and out as it seems fit, and 'off-state' activities of cooperation with an element of social security tend to last for a few years and then disappear. People do not like it, but have become accustomed to it and would be surprised if it were different. As long as they profit, they are willing to cooperate and regard it as a welcome source of income. This does not prevent them from being critical if some project falls flat, but they more or less expect it to happen and certainly do not reckon on permanent profit. One reason for this lies in the fact that these activities never form the main occupation nor the main source of income for those who run them.[198] Participation, in principle, is relatively voluntary, and it is relatively easy to step out of such a network. However, if the leader is a powerful broker and has access to many resources, it may be quite painful to withdraw. In general, such enterprises are in constant danger of disintegration. They share this characteristic with many government enterprises, as we have seen from social projects.

Increasing socio-economic differentiation affects the sustainability of resource basis for families differently. Those families, who have been involved in higher education for some generations, now profit more from brokers' services by higher civil servants, while they tend to have obtained individualized rights to more and better situated land than others. Thus elite families and ordinary families are differently affected, and the resource basis for Ambonese is in general more sustainable and varied that for Butonese. Few civil servants in Ambon are Butonese, which means that Butonese villagers cannot include the services of relatives in the administration in their social security strategies, but many strive successfully for a position in the private sector which does provide access to important services as well. For them education is at least as important as for Ambonese. Since Butonese usually do not own land or clove trees that can be sold, they rely on trade, fishing and horticulture of cash crops to pay for the education of their children.

---

[198] It is perhaps significant that there was only one person in Hila who managed to organize a fishing-cooperative that was active for many years, be it that the profits varied greatly. This cooperative was set up by a man who had been a civil servant for a number of years, but had quit before his pension and now lived rather quietly at some distance from the village centre. He and his men made a living from fishing and as such it had little to do with social security. However, he made sure that some people who were especially wanting received a share to sell in the village, among them the wife of a man who was jailed because he and his son had killed someone in a fight, a widow and an orphan.

Changing Social Security

The relationships between villagers and civil servants described here all have, to a different degree, a social security function, although they cannot be reduced to it. Civil servants living in villages have a keen interest in entertaining close relationships with villagers, because of their low salaries and pensions, and the uncertainties inherent in government through projects. Many villagers profit from the resources civil servants may provide. For both sides cooperation is not merely a matter of economic or political interest. Needs for social security are on both sides important incentives for setting up the kinds of cooperation described in this paper. Short- and long-term strategies on either side are interwoven in economic cooperation which lies outside the sphere of the official function of the civil servants involved. Some of the linkages described in this paper are more 'private', in the sense that some civil servants do not only bring in services directly emanating from their office as such on a structural basis. Teachers are, among other things, appreciated brokers in educational matters. In addition, the headmaster of the lower secondary school created several extra resources, e.g. by establishing a monopoly on the sale of snacks in front of his school. The young teachers make use of this resource and bring it in into their own cooperation network. The head of the KUD clearly goes over the border of legality and creates his own resources to distribute among most of the members of the village cooperative, but as personal clients, not as members.

The social security aspect works two ways: in the short-time perspective higher civil servants are providers of social security for others, relatives, neighbours, students. Young civil servants are receivers of social security far more than providers. And in the long run their own social security is at stake for all civil servants, because the quality and degree of care depends on what they offer during the height of their career.

While there is an aspect of mutual security provision in these resource exchanges, the security element seems to play a different role for civil servants and villagers. Villagers get some additional income and a claim to the services of civil servants. They aim at minimizing risks rather than maximizing profit (see Scott 1976). For civil servants, on the other hand, the temporary help and security they get is rather a means to engage in other types of activities that are profit-oriented. They recruit labour and time, drawing on the unmonetized social relations of mutual help, and use this, or their own time and labour thus made available, to operate in profit-oriented economic spheres, in which time and labour have a different value. They *want* to do this to help their relatives and clients; they also *need* to do this to live up to the demands put upon them by their clients, or else they would lose their clients and possible help and care in the further future. And they *can* do so largely on the basis of their status as civil servant and their greater ability to mobilize or create resources which are an accessory to that status, and come with 'being part of the state'. Thus state and village structures and resources are actually merged in these cooperative ventures. This merger is profitable for both civil servants and villagers, and contributes to an increase in the security of the participating villagers (compare for Northern Sulawesi, Buchholt 1990). Establishing whether and to what extent the exchanges are unequal is not easy. For one thing, villagers talk about these activities in terms of *masohi,* mutual help on the basis of equality, even though this exchange has hierarchical characteristics. The *masohi* ideology masks possible inequalities. Besides, the balance is not always easily made because the activities have different relevance and value depending on the perspective from which one makes the calculation. Moreover, it is difficult to weigh short-term against long-term profits. The fact that exchange is often unequal in favour of the civil servant, according to whatever calculation is applied, usually remains implicit in the relationship. Ideologically, it is not proper to regard the relationship as unequal (compare Scott 1985, Buchholt 1990).

Compared with what the state offers to the rural population through its social security schemes, these 'off-state' activities are far more important. The 1,200,000 rupiah invested in the social projects in Hila seem to be hardly relevant in comparison to approximately double that amount that is redistributed among villagers every year by the collection and distribution of the *zakat al fitrah* alone. People are acutely aware of how little the state has to offer by means of official permanent social security. They also experience how much of the funds leak away and little comes out of the state's promises. New schemes are being designed to expand social security for the rural population. If the plans are implemented they will probably reinforce the image of the state as an entity that tries again to get money in exchange for shallow promises. Villagers will find such investments too risky and not worth while, but they may be forced to participate (see F. and K. von Benda-Beckmann 1995).

Villagers are, on the other hand, quite willing to invest in the state through the education of their children for their own security, but outside the officially defined field of social security policy. Large amounts of economic resources are transferred out of the village economy, with serious consequences for the village since it fosters socio-economic differentiation and a weakening of relations of mutual help and redistribution between better- and worse-off villagers. Given the risky nature of such security strategies, their long-term consequences may be even more serious, because it is to be feared that many villagers will have exhausted their village-based resources for their old age security without being assured of their children's help.

Chapter 9
Ambonese Adat as Jurisprudence of Insurgency and Oppression*

Franz von Benda-Beckmann

Introduction

In August 1985, shortly before my wife and I left the village of Hila where we had been doing research, a military officer was hacked into pieces in the neighbouring village of Kaitetu. He was killed by a group of Butonese, immigrants from the Buton island group off south-east Sulawesi, who for two or three generations have lived in the village territory of Kaitetu. The killing occurred in the course of a conflict between Butonese and one of the Ambonese clans of Kaitetu, Nukuhaly, about the rights to harvest approximately 120 clove trees. The monetary value of a good harvest would at that time have been between 7 and 10 m. rupiah, approximately US $ 7,000 to 10,000. The Butonese were about to harvest the trees, the Ambonese had tried to stop them, and had asked the help of some policemen and the military officer who acted as a liaison between the sub-district police post and the villages. The officer had tried to stop the parties, about 20 men on each side, from fighting and had fired a warning shot into the air. This had been the sign for the Butonese to attack and to kill him.

This drama was the climax of a dispute which had gone on for many years and which had involved several court proceedings. In the late 1970s, the head of the Nukuhalys in Kaitetu had stated that the clove trees which had been planted by the Butonese were on their clan (*dati*) land, and that the Butonese should divide the trees or the harvest with them. According to Ambonese informants in Kaitetu, the proposal had been to come to a division which would give 70% of the trees to the Butonese, and 30% to the Ambonese. The Butonese had refused, claiming that the land had been state land (*tanah negara*) and that they had occupied it with government support in the 1960s. They further claimed that in 1965, a land reform commission had come to the village to measure the land in order to register it as their property under the provisions of the Agrarian Basic Law of 1960[199], a process which then had been stopped after the so-called communist coup in 1965.

---

* First published 1990 in: R. Kuppe, and R. Potz (eds.), *Law and Anthropology, International Yearbook for Legal Anthropology, Volume 5*, pp. 25-42. The Hague, Boston, London: Martinus Nijhoff.

[199] Undang-Undang Pokok Agraria, Law No. 5 of 1960.

In 1979 the Nukuhalys went to the State Court in Ambon, where they lost.[200] Apparently the court endorsed the opinion of the Butonese.[201] The Nukuhalys appealed, and the Appeal Court reversed the judgment of the court of first instance.[202] It declared the disputed land to be clan (*dati*) land of the Nukuhalys, and ordered the division of the harvest. If the Butonese should not accept this, they would have to evacuate the land. In addition, they were forbidden to plant any new trees on the land.

Against this judgment, the Butonese went for cassation (*kasasi*) before the Indonesian Supreme Court.[203] According to the court's findings, the Butonese had taken control of the disputed land at the direction of the government, but it turned out to be the wrong plot of land. In fact, a different piece of land should have been given to them. On this basis, the Supreme Court confirmed the judgment of the Appeal Court, stating that under these circumstances it would be just if the harvest were shared equally by the two parties.[204]

The judgment by itself did not convince the Butonese of the necessity to divide the trees. The Nukuhalys again had to go the State Court in order to obtain a decree for the execution of the judgment (case 7B/1979) which they obtained on 29.3.1985. Three times, the bailiff of the court, accompanied by the Police and the village head of Kaitetu, went to the Butonese settlement (*kampung*), the *kampung* head having been duly notified of their coming beforehand. But he and all adult members of the *kampung* could not be found. According to the bailiff's report on 13.4.1985, only two youngsters were met. However, since all formal requirements had been adhered to, it was declared on that day that the judgment had been executed. The trees were counted, and those henceforth belonging to the Nukuhalys were pointed out. The vice-village headman was

---

[200] Case 7-1979, decided on 14.3.1979.

[201] Unfortunately I have not been able to get a copy of the judgment. It is said that the court chairman was bribed by the Butonese, and was replaced afterwards when his judgment had been reversed by the Appeal Court.

[202] Case Pengadilan Tinggi Maluku 73-1979, decided on 28.12.1979.

[203] Case 2245/K/Sip/1980 Mahkamah Agung, decided on 16.4.1984. In an interim decision given on 4.11.1982, the Supreme Court ordered the Appeal Court to resume hearings about the question of whether indeed functionaries of the Department of Agrarian Affairs had already divided the land in 1965. The Appeal Court heard several witnesses on 8.4., 23.4., 20.8. and 1.6.1983.

[204] In the judgment of the Supreme Court it is said '– *bahwa walaupun para tergugat asal menempati tanah sengketa adalah atas penunjukan dari Pemerintah, namum tanah yang seharusnya diberikan pada mereka bukanlah yang terletak dalam dusun Waeyolang, akan tetapi seharusnya tanah yang berada didusun Kalauly – bahwa oleh karena para tergugat asal beradanya ditanah sengketa bukanlah karena penyerobotan, akan tetapi karena penunjukan dari Pemerintah, maka adalah adil apabila pembagian hasil atas tanah sengketa diperhitungkan sejak putusan ini mempunyai kekuatan hukum...*'

asked to notify the Butonese that these trees now were the property of the plaintiffs, and that any act violating their rights would constitute a criminal offence.

So all legal means had been used, and everybody was waiting for the harvest time, which in that year started in August. The Nukuhalys, fearing trouble, had asked the help of the police and the military in order to protect them when trying to harvest their trees, and to prevent the Butonese from harvesting all trees. After the killing, the Butonese fled into the mountains and to the island of Seram. The Ambonese of Kaitetu raided the Butonese *kampung* and burnt down 13 houses. The *kampung* then was occupied by the Mobile Brigade, looking for the killers and protecting the Butonese from further actions of revenge by the people of Kaitetu and the home villagers of the military officer. Eventually, several Butonese were caught, and sentenced to prison periods between 10 and 20 years.

The Butonese on Ambon

This tragedy is in many respects symptomatic of the political, social and economic conditions on the island of Ambon. The Butonese form a considerable part of the population in Ambonese villages, mainly in the Islamic villages in the northern peninsula Hitu. Their exact number is not known, since ethnic differences are not relevant in official Indonesian statistics. Concrete data can only be obtained in the villages themselves. In Kaitetu, roughly half of the total village population were Butonese who lived in the *kampung* Kalauly at a distance of about 3 km from Kaitetu village. In Hila, where we lived during our research, the Butonese population, living in three *kampung* numbered about 1,700 out of a total population of about 4,400.

The Butonese on Ambon generally left their home islands, off the southeast coast of Sulawesi, since the ecological and demographic conditions would not support the growing population. Many came to Ambon first as seasonal workers in the clove harvests. Some stayed on, families and friends followed; this process is still continuing. It seems that in the early settlement phases, there were hardly any problems between the Ambonese and the Butonese newcomers. They were allowed to settle, usually at a considerable distance from the Ambonese core-village, and close to the border with the neighbouring village. The Butonese *kampung* thus marked, and guarded village borders. Besides it was seen as desirable that at certain intervals there should exist new small inhabited areas along the dangerous roads or paths along the coast. Land was still plentiful, and the land in the hills originally used by the Butonese for agriculture was too far from the village centre to be of economic interest to the Ambonese. This situation changed only gradually. The increase in population in both Ambonese and Butonese settlement areas, and the continuing immigration of Butonese gradually let to greater pressure on the land which could be used for agricultural purposes. For example, the Butonese were settled along the (improved) coastal- road which tied the coastal villages to the city of Ambon, the administrative and commercial centre of the island. But the land in the hills used by the Ambonese was usually rather close to their settlements, and thus the most easily accessible from the road also for those Ambonese who wanted, or were forced to, expand their agricultural activities.

A new situation developed when in the 1970s the price for cloves started to rise dramatically, and clove tree cultivation expanded. In Hila, it seems that nobody really cared very much if the Butonese planted some clove trees in the 1950s and 1960s, since cloves did not play a great role in the Ambonese economy during these two decades (see Van Fraassen 1972). But when the clove-boom came, land suitable for clove cultivation, and land which had been planted with cloves by Butonese, became increasingly interesting. In Kaitetu, villagers or clans in Hila suddenly 'discovered' that clove trees had been planted on their land, often without 'proper' permission, and they attempted to get their share. While not all the resulting conflicts had the dimensions of the one described above, the relations between Ambonese and Butonese became increasingly strained, and are characterized by a history of disputes, fights, and the burning of houses and trees.

Legal and Political Background

Ambonese-Butonese social, economic and political relationships developed and changed in the context of a complex, and also changing, plural system of normative structures and decision making agencies. For the Ambonese, legal pluralism has a history of more than 350 years, during which different government laws (from the Dutch East Indies Company, the colonial state, and the Republic of Indonesia), Islamic law, traditional *adat* laws and various forms of self-regulation co-existed, often in legal forms which combined elements from more than one of the legal systems.[205]

Ever since the Dutch East Indies Company ordered the Ambonese population living in the mountains to settle in coastal villages during the second half of the 17th century, the political organization has been an amalgam of *adat* principles and government regulations. The most influential government institutions were, and are, the *raja,* the village chief, and the *kepala soa,* the heads of the *soa* (clan associations). *Raja* and *kepala soa* are the privileges of specific

---

[205] For historical accounts of Ambon, see Rumphius 1910, Manusama 1977, Knaap 1987a and the Dutch 17th and 18th century accounts edited by Knaap 1987b. The best colonial account of Ambonese land and tree law is Holleman 1923. See for the importance of Islamic law, F. and K. von Benda-Beckmann 1988 and F. von Benda-Beckmann 1988.

clans according to *adat*, but for centuries they have been appointed, and often also selected, by organs of the state government. Traditionally, the village chief was assisted by the village council, *saniri negeri,* consisting of the *soa* and *dati* heads – (*dati* being land holding clan-segments), a village secretary and some other officials such as the *kewang,* the village forest overseer. Since Indonesia's Independence, various local government reforms have followed each other, introducing new governmental bodies at the village level. Following the most recent local government legislation of 1979, the LKMD (*Lembaga Ketahanan Masyarakat Desa)* was introduced as the new official village council, with the LMD (*Lembaga Masyarakat Desa)* as a sort of first chamber. The *raj* and *kepala soa* have been integrated into these new governmental bodies as chairman and members of the LMD.

The population is divided into clans, called *rumah tau* or *fam.* Clan affiliation is generally patrifiliative. The original settler clans also form, or are subdivided into, *dati,* land holding subclans holding specifically marked parts of the village territory, mainly sago gardens used for the subsistence needs of their members. *Dati* membership is by patrifiliation; female *dati* members lose their right to share in the *dati* property when they marry. The *dati* head is supposed to control and administer the use made of *dati* property. In principle, each *dati* member is entitled to use *dati* land for agricultural subsistence activities. Once a *dati* member has made a garden or planted trees on *dati* land, these become his property, his *perusahan,* of which he can dispose freely and which after his death becomes inherited property, *pusaka,* for his or her heirs. Inheritance rules are basically bilateral, with a strong flavour of Islamic law which favours male over female heirs. The *pusaka* rights pertain to the crops planted on the land; the land, however, remains under the control of the *dati.* Should a *dati* become extinct, according to the standard version of Ambonese *adat* (also supported by the state courts as valid *adat* law) the *dati* land falls to the village and can be newly allotted, or otherwise used by the village government. Similar principles pertain to previously unexploited land held by the village (*tanah negeri*). Once a cultivator has made a garden or planted trees, these become his or her individual property, and, after death, *pusaka.* According to classic *adat* (apparently already obsolete in the 1920s, see Holleman 1923) also in these cases the village retained a residual right to the land. However, in more recent times, *perusahan* and *pusaka* come close to full ownership rights on both trees and land.

The *adat* law in Hila is far from being unambiguous. There are different opinions, concerning the status and scope of village land (*tanah negeri*), and the uncultivated forest land (*tanah ewang*) in particular. Since these ambiguities are relevant for the relationships between Ambonese and Butonese in Hila, I shall briefly summarize them here.

One of the ambiguities can be attributed to Hila's particular history. Hila was one of the early forts and trading posts of the Dutch East Indies Company (see Knaap 1987b). The early coastal village was first settled and dominated by the immigrant clans Lating-Nustapi and Ollong, which had formed part of the Hitu-Hila state in being (the Uli Helawan, the Golden Federation, see Rumphius 1910, Manusama 1977, Knaap 1987a). They formed the core of the two major *soa* in Hila. When they moved to Hila, however, there were still other mountain villages, Marsapal (close to the Mamua area), Ely (close to the Waitomu area) and Senalu (close to the coastal village centre) which were regarded as the 'actual' owners of the land. Voluntarily or involuntarily, these mountain people 'gave' land (and perhaps *dati*-land) to the coastal clans which dominated Hila, Hila at that time being probably much smaller than the present territory of Hila. The mountain people only gradually followed the Dutch (and Lating) demand to settle in the coastal village. The clans Tomu and Ely descended relatively early and together formed the third *soa* in Hila. This must have been later in the case of the mountain village Marsapal, where the *soa* Ukuatelu (consisting of the clans Selang, Uluelang and Pailokol) only moved to the coast after Hila proper had been founded (see the 17th century materials in Knaap 1987b).

For some time around the turn of the 17th century, the village must have been a sort of double-village, Hila (Uli Helawan) and Marsapal-Senalu, both with their own village hall *(baileo)* and mosque. It seems that during the reign of Hasan Suleiman around the turn of the 17th century, the village was centralized, the relative autonomy of Marsapal and Senalu, their *baileo* and their mosque being abolished. Ukuatelu became the fourth *soa* of Hila, and Senalu (now extinct) formed its own *soa* as well.[206] This development had the consequence that the area of Ukuatelu and Senalu in the mountains, including the *ewang* land, never was really considered to be village land, at least not by their *soa* members. It was land over which the village government of Hila had no claims; it was subject (and is now) to the control by the *soa* Ukuatelu or its constituent clans respectively.[207]

However, representatives of the village government clans (Lating) tend to uphold the village land version and the *dati* land law as it had evolved as a general *adat* law. They base their claims on an *adat* rule, also maintained by the state courts, according to which the land of extinct *dati* clans falls ('reverts' in the classic doctrine) to the village, to be allotted anew by the village govern-

---

[206] Although it is emphatically denied by many villagers that Hila ever had 5 *soa*, (Senalu being the fifth), a Dutch report from the 1920s mentions that it was unclear whether there were 4 or 5 *soa* (Adatrechtbundel 24: 369), and we have copied documents from the 19th century in which *kepala soa* of the *soa* Senalu were appointed.

[207] Already in the 1920s it was reported that in Hila (contrary to most other Islamic or Christian villages on Ambon) it was not mandatory to seek the permission of the village government if one wanted to cultivate *ewang* land (Adatrechtbundel 24: 369).

ment. In practice, however, and according to other *adat* interpretations, this is not the case.[208]

However, there are some generally acknowledged control rights over the village territory held by the village government, which may have been stronger in the Dutch time when the Dutch government strongly supported standard *adat* law. One of the traditional *adat* functionaries is the *kewang*, the village forest overseer, responsible for proper forest use and for the maintenance and control of *sasi,* a form of harvest control (see Volker 1925).

These principles of *adat* still dominate access to land and crops in contemporary Hila. This is fully recognized also by the state administration and judiciary (see Pengadilan Tinggi Maluku 1981). The land laws introduced by the various governments have either been absorbed into *adat*, or are rejected by the majority of the population. The Basic Agrarian Law and its implementing regulations are known, but there have been no registrations of agricultural land under the law nor conversion of *adat* rights into the property categories of the law.[209] More often than not, land and crop/tree transactions are concluded orally, or a written agreement is witnessed by the village chief. In rare cases, people go to the sub-district head, *Camat,* in order to make up a formal sales document (*akte jual beli*), as provided by the legislation. But this is not taken to the Office of Agrarian Affairs (*Kantor Agraria*) in order to obtain a formal ownership title (see F. von Benda-Beckmann 1986).

Ambonese - Butonese Relations

The Butonese coming to Ambon were faced with this complex legal system. For the regulation of their internal relationships, they could largely rely upon their own Butonese *adat*. However, certain types of relationships (marriage) require some intervention of state institutions like the Office of Religious Affairs (*Kantor Urusan Agama)*. Disputes within between Butonese in the Butonese *kampung* were handled within their *kampung* through their own authorities. The village government was not used as a forum for dispute settlement, and neither were the state courts.

---

[208] An example is the extinct *dati* Pai, the inheritance of which was fought for in several court disputes between the village of Hila and several Hila and Kaitetu clan-segments who traced their rights through maternal descent to the last *dati*-members. Again, in the case of the last and now extinct Senalu clan Teteputih, no Senalu lands were ever effectively claimed by the village government of Hila, and it is generally agreed that the son-in-law of the last female Teteputih member is the rightful lord of the Senalu/Teteputih lands.

[209] The Prona-registration programme, a programme of fast and cheap registrations by which the government wished to speed up the process of registration, has been a failure in Islamic Ambon.

However, in their relationships with the Ambonese villagers and village government institutions they became subject to Ambonese *adat* and to forms of self-regulation dominated by Ambonese interests. In the following I shall give a brief summary of these relations as they pertained in Hila, focusing particularly on economic relations concerning access to and exploitation of productive resources.

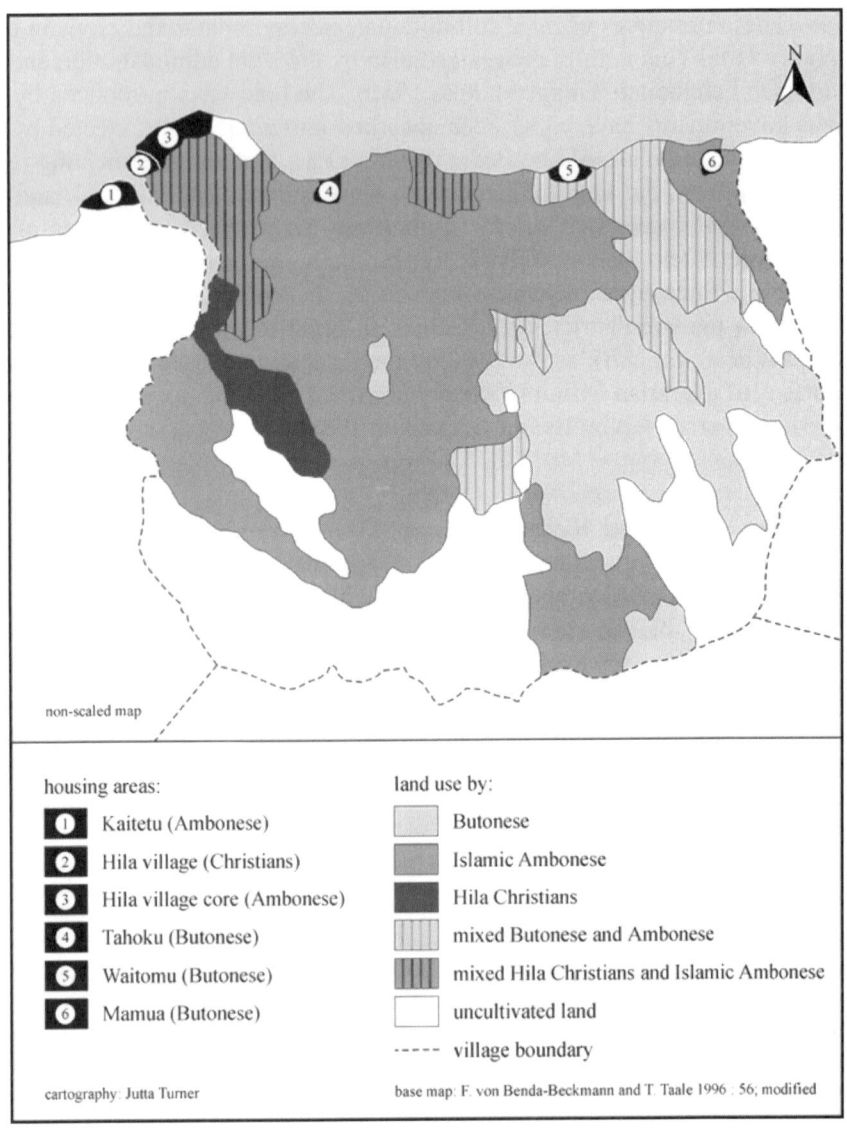

Map 9.1: *Housing areas and land use in Hila*

Socio-Spatial Relations

The three Butonese *kampung* in Hila came into existence gradually. The earliest settlers came in the late 19th century and settled in Mamua, at the border of the neighbouring village to the east, Wakal, at about 6 km distance from the settlement of Hila. In the 1930s and 1940s there was a new immigration wave, the population of Mamua grew, and a new part of the village territory was settled at Waitomu, about 4 km distance from the village. In the 1960s, three recently immigrated Butonese families started yet another settlement at Tahoku, at about 2 km distance from the village core.

In 1985, the population was distributed over the four settlement areas as follows:

negeri Hila (Ambonese) 2,404
kampung Tahoku (Butonese) 350
kampung Waitomu (Butonese) 397
kampung Mamua (Butonese) 635

The residential areas of the Butonese thus are spatially segregated. Segregation, rather than integration, also dominates most kinds of relationships which Butonese and Ambonese villagers have. There are not many social relationships between Ambonese and Butonese. Intermarriage is nearly nonexistent. Nearly all Butonese marry within their own *kampung*.[210] Two Ambonese men had married Butonese women (as first wives) but moved to their wife's *kampung* obviously they had done something that was 'not done', and said that they felt that their wives (and they themselves) would not be properly treated in the Hila core village. I have no exact data on social interaction between Butonese and Ambonese villagers outside the realm of economic affairs, but on the basis of my own observation and casual interviews it seems that there is little.

Political Relations

Politically, the Butonese are subject to the village government of Hila. However, they have some extent of formally regulated autonomy in their own *kam-*

---

[210] According to the marriages registered during the years 1982 to 1985 at the Kantor Urusan Agama of the Kecamatan Leihitu the Butonese were predominantly *kampung*-endogamous. Of the 20 marriages of Butonese men and women 17 were within the *kampung* of the spouses. There were two marriages between Butonese *kampung*, and only 1 between a Butonese and an Ambonese girl from the neighbouring village of Wakal.

pung internal affairs. The three *kampung* have their own *kepala kampung* and also their own LKMD. The *kepala kampung* represents his *kampung* population vis-à-vis the village government.

The Butonese have no representation in the Hila village government; none of the functionaries of the sections of the LKMD is Butonese. They are, in particular, not incorporated into the political *adat* constitution. Since they are not members of *soa* they cannot be represented in *adat*. Where *adat* constitutional principles do not coincide with state local government rules, until now *adat* principles have proved to be stronger.

Thus the *raja* must be chosen by the village population, and the candidate be approved and appointed by higher government authorities on district level. In the selection of possible candidates, however, *adat* descent plays a major role: the candidates must come from a *raja*-clan. In Hila, only two clans (Lating Nustapi and Ollong) are regarded as having this right. According to government law, all village residents, including the Butonese, have active voting rights. In *adat*, however, only those incorporated into the political *adat* constitution (who have been accepted as member of a *soa*) have voting rights. Until the present time, *adat* has prevailed over state law. The Butonese have not been permitted to vote in the elections of the village head (neither did they in Kaitetu). During the years 1985/86 when *raja* elections were expected to be held shortly, the sub-district heads we talked to confessed that they would not dare to let the Butonese vote because they feared the reactions of the Ambonese. This part of the state law could not yet be carried out.[211] In national elections, however, the Butonese in Hila do vote.

Religion

Both Ambonese and Butonese are Islamic. Religion, however, does not serve as a means to unify or integrate the two groups. Each settlement has its own mosque. Participation in religious rituals is generally *kampung* specific. Butonese do not participate in funerals or marriage feast of Hila villagers, except for the few occasions when it concerns their land-patrons. In the sphere of religious alms (*zakat fitrah*) collection and distribution, there are no exchanges between Ambonese and Butonese villagers (see F. von Benda-Beckmann 1988), and the respective mosque functionaries collect, keep for themselves, or redistribute *zakat* within their own territorial settlement area exclusively. A modest step was

---

[211] This changed in 1988, when one of the three *raja* candidates began mobilizing Butonese support for his candidature and the other candidates followed suit. The election committee decided, that the Butonese should have voting rights, and the Butonese voted in the election which finally took place in 1988 (A. Brouwer and T. Taale, personal communication).

made, however, when prayer groups exchanged visits between Hila proper and one of the Butonese *kampung*s.

Economic Relations

The strongest link between Ambonese and Butonese is economic. When the Butonese arrived in Hila territory, they could not claim any rights to economic resources of their own. They depended on the Ambonese for access to land, both for housing sites and for agricultural production. The following general pattern developed:

a. *Housing sites:* Butonese are obliged to ask permission of the holders of land when building a house. The permission to build *temporary* houses is invariably given, and no counterprestation has to be given by the Butonese. Temporary houses are those built with *gabah2*, the strong nerves of the sago palm leaves, and with wood. To obtain permission to build a *permanent* stone house, the land has to be bought. Nowadays, prices are considerable, varying from 300,000 to 500,000 rupiah for a plot of about 15x20 meters.[212]

Plate 9.1: Temporary house of Butonese fishermen

---

[212] In 1985 1 US $ was approximately worth 1,000 Rupiah.

Plate 9.2: *A Butonese bagan fishing boat*

b. *Gardens for vegetables, annual crops:* Again, permission must be asked from the owners. As a rule (normative and statistically) the permission is given. The right to make and to enjoy the garden is seen as temporary and subject to termination should the Ambonese owners want the land back. According to Ambonese informants, such cases occur occasionally. In the case of good relationships the Ambonese will offer the Butonese another piece of land. In cases of conflicts, however, the relationship is usually terminated. In the case of temporary gardens no counterprestation is demanded. Both Ambonese and Butonese were emphatic that nothing was ever asked or given. It is not considered obligatory for Butonese to bring a share of their produce to their Ambonese land-patrons, and apparently they rarely do so. However, when some share is demanded by Ambonese coming to the Butonese *kampung*, 'it should be given'. We and also other researchers[213] observed many instances when Ambonese passing through and stopping briefly in a *kampung*, would ask for some fruit or vegetables. This is done, but, as Butonese made clear in interviews, they resent such requests.

c. *Land/gardens for cash crops (for cloves in particular, to a much lesser extent also for nutmeg coconuts):* 'According to *adat*', Butonese could not acquire the right to plant perennials, in casu clove trees. This principle apparently used to

---

[213] A. Brouwer and T. Taale, students who did research in Hila from 1987-1988 witnessed several such cases, personal communication.

be valid in Hila, as in all other Ambonese villages. However, starting in the 1950s and 1960s, this rule lost its mandatory force.

Some general principles have developed for the arrangements between Butonese and Ambonese concerning the planting of clove trees. When an Ambonese is approached by a Butonese with the request to plant trees, consent is given. Specific and detailed agreements are rarely made. Usually it is said 'let us see and wait, and afterwards we shall divide'. 'Afterwards' usually is after several (5-7) years when the trees start to bear fruit. At that time, one knows how many trees have died out in the meantime and one can divide the exact number of healthy trees. Standards of division are flexible, and they seem to change. A division of two thirds for the Butonese, one third for the Ambonese seems to have been standard in the 1950s and 1960s, but it has gradually moved to 50:50. Some Butonese complained that 1/3:2/3 had been vaguely mentioned when they planted, but when the time of division came, division into equal parts was demanded.

A different type of arrangement has developed, apparently when during the 1970s the village government also wanted its share and asserted village rights to waste land as village land. Village land, whether village or *soa* land, is freely accessible only to Hila villagers in terms of *adat* citizen(*soa*)ship. Foreigners/outsiders do not have free access. In cases, or areas where 'village land' is concerned – the area south of the main settlement of Hila – the standard process of a Butonese starting to work and then sharing with an Ambonese – could lead to difficulties, since it could be claimed by the village government that the Butonese usurped citizen rights, clearing *ewang* without permission. In order to avoid such difficulties, smart villagers have invented the 'labour contract' version. A villager makes a labour contract with a Butonese for the planting of trees. The trees become the property (*perusahan*) of the Hila villager. When the trees start to bear fruit, the Hila villager 'sells' part of the trees to the Butonese as 'wage'.

In addition, Butonese also pledge clove trees (*sewa pohon*) from Ambonese tree owners. These arrangements are basically the same as those which obtain among Ambonese. The trees are pledged for one or more seasons (usually no longer than three seasons) for a specified amount of cash which is paid when the agreement is made. The pledgor then has the right to harvest the trees. However, only 'good' seasons are counted as seasons relevant in terms of the contract. If the trees should bear no, or very little, cloves, the harvest is not counted and is usually carried out by the tree owner.

d. *Labour relationships:* Labour relationships between Butonese and Ambonese occur in quite specific contexts. One, in conjunction with tree planting agreements, has just been mentioned. Butonese may also take over the task of watching over the trees of their land patrons in the area close to their *kampung*. Several villagers claimed that in cases of great labour demand (house building, roof thatching), activities largely carried out as *masohi,* mutual help, Butonese occasionally would participate to help their patrons; we have not, however, observed this.

Butonese also work in the clove harvest in Hila if there is sufficient labour demand. This usually is done on the basis of wage labour, not on the basis of the traditional Ambonese system of share-harvesting (*panta bakul*).

Variation and Change in Ambonese-Butonese Relations in Hila

There is considerable variation between the three Butonese *kampung*. The older the relationships between Ambonese and Butonese are, the more many stranded they are, the less they have been affected by financial-economic considerations. Thus the Butonese in Mamua, the oldest and most distant settlement, where Ambonese-Butonese inter-family relationships in many cases have already endured three generations, seem to have the least problems with their Ambonese patrons. The current prices quoted for housing sites are lower; and actual payments less frequent. In Tahoku, on the other hand, the relationships started at a time in which village economic life was already rather monetized. In these cases, Ambonese-Butonese relations did not have the time to develop into multiplex patron-client relationships; the pure financial-economic aspects dominate. Prices for hose sites are higher and commonly demanded. The permission for temporary houses is increasingly tied to the payment of *uang rokok*, 'money for cigarettes', which can run up to 15,000 rupiah. Butonese in Tahoku complain that even for the land upon which they wanted to build their mosque and that to be used for graveyards money is demanded. This is viewed as an improper thing to do in the eyes of those Ambonese who had relationships with Butonese in Mamua. Also the terms of share-planting arrangements seem to be more favourable in Mamua than they are in Waitomu or Tahoku.

Temporal distance, and the root of the relationships in a less monetized economy, here coincides with spatial distance. However, spatial distance seems to play an independent role in affecting the nature of Ambonese-Butonese relationships. Some aspects which would 'soften' the severity of the financial-economic strand of the relationship in the case of Mamua would be less strong or absent in the case of Tahoku. In the case of Mamua, the Butonese have the additional functions of border guards and of providing a welcome stop-over on the road, a place where at night lights burn and drive off bad spirits, a place to have a smoke and a chat. Besides, the land in the Mamua region is too distant to be really economically interesting. It demanded a march of an hour or an hour and a half along the coastal road. Besides, the Butonese help in protecting the trees of Ambonese against theft. In the closer Tahoku, on the other hand, the pressure on the land is much higher, both at the coast where the territorial expansion of Hila already nearly borders the settlement of Tahoku and in the cultivable hill area.

More intensive forms of social and economic cooperation with Butonese were developed by some Ambonese villagers. These were, however, 'outsiders' who led their economic and social life largely outside the purely (Ambonese) village sphere. The Ambonese men, who had married Butonese women as their first wives, went to live in their wives' *kampung*. One of the Ambonese who regularly operated a fishing team (about 20 persons) had moved to live halfway between the village core and the Butonese *kampung* Tahoku. He had several Butonese fishermen from Tahoku in his team.

The Exploitation of Dependence and Ambiguity

The Sources of Uncertainty

The Butonese in Ambonese villages thus were faced with a complex, and sometimes contradictory body of rights, with different holders of rights and village functionaries. Their own rights to land and trees are relatively unstable and uncertain. This uncertainty derives from two main sources.

- One source is the temporary nature of the rights. This goes for garden land, but it also goes for land planted with cash trees, since it is uncertain whether after the trees die out, the Butonese will be able to exercise any rights on the land. While formerly this would not have been a problem, the increasing land scarcity leads one to expect that the Ambonese will increasingly try to regain control of that land. Besides, the deferral of making a sharing agreement adds to the uncertainty, and some Ambonese exploit the weaker situation of the Butonese. In one case, a villager let a Butonese clear the ground, and then made an arrangement with a different person. The Butonese hacked down all tress in revenge.
- The other main source of uncertainty concerns the partner of the legal relationship: the question is who (are) the rightful owner(s) of the land to which the Butonese have rights. This goes for direct relations between Ambonese land holding individuals, family *(pusaka)* heads or *dati* heads, as well as for relations to land thought to be village territory and where permission had been obtained from the *raja* or by the *kewang*. Often, the two problems are entangled in relationships pertaining to the same piece of land.

There are many instances in which Butonese obtained permission from the *kewang* and *raja* to cultivate 'village land', and where later other villagers claim the same land as their own *dati* or *pusaka* land, complaining that they have never been asked permission, and demanding compensation, the division of trees, or the land back. The *raja* or *kewang* would give such permission, usually against a financial contribution. The Butonese would plant, and when his trees would start to bear fruit he would be detected by those villagers/clans who maintained that the land was theirs, that the village government had had no rights to grant any permission, and that the Butonese worked 'on their land' and therefore should divide the proceeds with them. More often than not, such instances would become public after the *raja* or *kewang* had been deposed, and everybody could put the blame upon them (this was standard practice in Hila, where the last *kewang* apparently had made a lucrative business with such land grants to Butonese, but left for Java when the thing blew up).

But the situation can be difficult enough also without the interference of the village government. Since the land usually belongs to larger family groups, and, in the case of *pusaka,* of persons of different clans, there can be a large number of different clan segments, who all may have their own ideas as to whom the land belongs, how the division of property should be done etc. And the number of claimants tends to increase with the number of trees in question. The Butonese in these cases are not just confronted with uncertainty, but also with multiple demands.

The Case of Dusun Pata

A case may illustrate several of the factors mentioned above. Haji La Djaha, a Butonese, had started to plant clove trees in the 1950s with the permission of the village government. In the beginning of the 1970s, when most trees bore cloves and the clove price raised, A.K. Ely, and with him several groups of descendants of a common Lating ancestor, claimed the land and the trees as their own property. The ensuing conflicts led to fights and the damaging of several trees, whereupon La Djaha instituted criminal proceedings against his opponents. In 1979, A.K. Ely sued La Djaha in the state court.[214] The harvest, 34 kg of cloves (at that time worth approximately US $ 600), was temporarily kept by the police in Hitu. The court decided that the disputed *dusun* was indeed, as had been claimed by the plaintiff, the *dusun* Pata which was *pusaka*, and owned (*hak milik*) by the plaintiff. The Court decided also, that, contrary to what had been stated by the plaintiff, it had been the defendant who had planted the clove trees.

The court said 'that although the trees are on the *dusun* which is the property of the plaintiff, it is felt unjust if the defendant's labour/enterprise of decades should be enjoyed by the plaintiff. Therefore it is justified (*patut*) that the defendant can enjoy the trees until the trees have died out, and that the defendant is not allowed to plant new trees afterwards, in order to avoid new disputes. The court therefore decrees

---

[214] Case Dusun Pata, Abdul Kadir Ely (Ambonese) vs. Haji la Djaha (Butonese), State Court 624/1979 PN Ambon, decided on 31.10.1981.

that there a distinction must be made between the trees and the land, since according to *adat* law trees and land can be divided from each other (*horizontale scheiding*), i.e. land and the trees on it can be owned by two different persons; that means the land is the property (*hak milik*) of the plaintiff, and the trees are the property of the defendant. Since there has never been an agreement to share between the parties, and since the plaintiff had left alone the defendant for so many years while the clove tress bore fruit, the court thinks that the plaintiff already has forfeited his rights.

N.B. It was of interest that the defendant asked that the Department of Agrarian Affairs should join the dispute and grant *hak milik* to him (since in 1965 he had already had a temporary ownership certificate (*surat hak milik sementara*). The court also ordered the Police to give the cloves back to the defendant.

The plaintiff appealed to the Appeal Court.[215] The Appeal Court confirmed the first court's finding as to the 'facts' of the case, but disagreed with the decision concerning the land and the trees:

> For if it would be allowed for the original defendant to control the land of the plaintiff until the clove trees had died, this would mean that plaintiff could not use his land for decades to come, and that would not be in line with the feeling of justice (*keadilan dan kepatutan*);
> If, on the other hand, the cloves of the defendant which already bear fruit would have to be cut down from the land of the defendant, this, too, would not be in accordance with the feeling of humanity (*perikemanusiaan*) and justice (*keadilan*). Since in the judgment of a judge the feelings of justice and humanity (*keadilan, kepatutan dan kemanusiaan*) should be mirrored, the Court therefore thinks it appropriate and just if the disputed land and the trees on it be divided in half, i.e. half of the land and the clove trees on it become the property of the plaintiff and the other half of the defendant.

The police were ordered to give one half of the cloves to each of the parties. This judgment was appealed for cassation by the original defendant, Haji La Djahs.[216] This appeal for cassation was not accepted by the Supreme Court, since the appeal had not been submitted in time.

This was not the end of it: In 1982, 12 members of the Lating clan had sued Haji La Djaha and 6 other Butonese about the same *dusun* Pata, claiming it as their own *pusaka*. Another group (the group of descendants to which also A.K. Ely belonged) then intervened in this suit, suing Haji La Djaha as well as

---

[215] Case 65/1881/PT Maluku, decided on 15.5.1982.
[216] Mahkamah Agung Reg, No. 1067/K/Sip 1983, decided on 14.6.1984.

the Latings, claiming that the *dusun* was their *pusaka,* inherited from their Lating ascendant. Both suits were refused. The court held:

> that the disputed land was the same as the one disputed between A.K. Ely and Haji La Djaha, which had already been decided. The plaintiffs (and interveners) had not tried to assert their rights then; it was too late to do so now.

It also appeared that A.K. Ely was a member of the group of heirs which had intervened, and the court stated that the interveners still had the right to assert their common ownership of the land in dispute, which so far had been represented by A.K. Ely only.

The uncertainty concerning the rights to land and trees, however, does not only operate to the disadvantage of the Butonese. It seems that they have increasingly found an answer to the second aspect of uncertainty and can exploit it to their own advantage.

In short, they avow that of course the land is not theirs and that they are prepared to divide the trees. But they demand that the question to whom the trees belong, and with whom they should share, should be sorted out first. And they exploit the trees until this problem is solved. To some extent this line is also followed with respect to housing sites for permanent homes. The more money that is involved, the greater will be the number of claimants, and the greater the probability that the claimants, as in the case of Haji La Djaha, will need much time, perhaps even a court decision, to sort out their problems. Some factors facilitate relatively successful strategies:

a. There is no 'neutral' place to store the harvest, pending the decision of a dispute settlement institution. Everybody knows that if the harvest should be stored, or publicly sold by either the village government or the police, the probability is high 'that the mice will eat', that the gains will 'somehow disappear'.

b. There is also the chance that one of the parties will seek an alliance with the Butonese which may result in a favourable settlement/division. Such alliance may be all important for the Ambonese claimant, since the outcome of the dispute may largely depend upon what the Butonese say about the origin of the relationships: who, or whose father etc., had given them oral permission etc.

c. In village border areas, such as in the area of Mamua at the border between Hila and Wakal, there is an additional aspect to be exploited, the rivalry between villages and village governments. Again the Butonese will say that they are willing to pay for the housing site, or to divide the trees, but that they do not know to which village the land belonged to, and ask that this matter be settled first. Thus they avoid paying, and have the chance that one village government will easily be inclined to waive any claims to financial compensation if their claim to village land can be supported by the Butonese. Butonese thus try to maintain and reproduce, and even actively stimulate the legal uncertainty.

The Hope on State Law

Under the legal regime dominated by Ambonese *adat*, the Butonese are embedded in relationships of political and economic subordination. Though they may try, sometimes successfully, to exploit the ambiguities of Ambonese *adat* to their own advantage, there is little in Ambonese *adat* which will give them room to improve their situation. Understandably, the Butonese try to disentangle themselves from these legally enhanced relations of subordination. One way is to engage in economic activities in which they are relatively free from the constraints of Ambonese *adat*. Fishing is one of these sectors, and the Butonese are active there. The other main way in which the Butonese search for emancipation are the government administration, and government law. It is not surprising that the Butonese vote nearly 100% for GOLKAR, the state party of functional groups – while a majority (1982) or strong minority (1987) of the Ambonese villagers support the religious opposition party (P3). 'If the government does something to help us, the only thing we can give back is our votes', as some Butonese expressed their attitude.

In the sphere of government extension and intervention in agriculture, there is also a quite different pattern of constructive cooperation with the government. In each of the Butonese *kampung*, there is a rather well functioning farmers' group (*kelompok tani*) working together with the officer of the Department of Agriculture on experimental fields. In spite of serious attempts by the agricultural officer (a Javanese who is the son-in-law of one of the *soa* heads in Hila) no such farmers' groups have been successfully established among the Ambonese. The Butonese make use of the government's credit scheme for the improvement of vegetable cultivation, and they pay back their loans. The Ambonese, on the other hand, do not want to get entangled in government credit schemes. One of the reasons is that they do not want to be dependent on the government, and submit to what they consider inappropriate constraints upon their autonomy.

In the field of law, the Butonese hope that the government will help them by making new laws in their favour, by taking its own laws seriously, or by adapting Ambonese *adat* to the specific local situation.

Thus the state law in local government grants the Butonese political rights, but they complain that the government does not 'dare' yet to implement it because it 'is still afraid' of the Ambonese.

This also applies to various aspects of agrarian law. The Butonese favour the national agrarian law. They appreciate the possibility of ownership rights of the western style and the written form of land transactions. As the case described above shows, in the 1960s there had been active attempts to get their land registered and certificated under the basic land law. But then, according to some Butonese, 'the coup [the allegedly communist attempt to take over the government which led to a massive persecution and killing of communists, and to the new Suharto government] came, and these measures were undone by the government'... which needed popular support and distrusted all too egalitarian and socialist objectives which could be, and had been, pursued in the name of the agrarian law. Although the possibility to register house sites and bought land exists now, too, most Butonese think that they are not strong enough to overcome the unwillingness of the Ambonese and the Ambonese village government, which has to cooperate in registration processes, without the help of higher government agencies.

As long as land and tree disputes still are considered to be governed by Ambonese *adat* law in state law proceedings, the Butonese wish for a change in the *adat* law which could give them more access to land: In the sharing agreements not only the trees planted could be divided, but also the land upon which the trees stand. The Ambonese on the other hand maintain the classic *adat*, in which rights to land, seen as part of earth's surface, and to the trees or other crops on the land, can be distinct, and be held by distinct persons or groups. As we have seen through the La Djaha case, in the sphere of the government courts, the dominant mode of legal interpretation is not quite clear. The state court of first instance quite explicitly restated the classic *adat* version as the valid law. The appeal court, on the other hand, decided that both trees and land should be divided, without, however, explicitly modifying the *adat* law principle. It could well be assumed that if the first court had chosen for an equal division of the trees, the Appeal Court would have confirmed the judgment. And in the Kaitetu case described in the introduction, the Appeal Court and the Supreme Court only recognized the Butonese claim to trees, and not the one to land.

Conclusions

This example shows that the relationships between state and local folk laws can be more complex than often is assumed. For descriptions and analyses of the relationships between state law and the local normative systems of rural populations usually are set into a context in which both systems are opposed to each other, and in which activities of government institutions and large-scale economic enterprises are detrimental to the economic and political interests of majority rural population groups, and are rationalized and justified in the name of state law. The local normative systems, the traditional or customary laws of the rural population groups, on the other hand are seen as expressing and regulating the political and economic interests of the rural people. Customary law, or claims for a fuller recognition of the rights embedded in customary law, often function as a kind of defensive shield against 'legal' demands and claims by the state which are not regarded as desirable or legitimate by the majority of the rural population (see F. von Benda-Beckmann 1987). This nearly prototypical constellation is well known from most former colonies which are generally referred to as the Third World. Its contours are even sharper in the so-called Fourth World, in situations where the political and economic interests governed by state law are those of a racially and culturally distinct majority, such as is the case in e.g. Canada, Australia, New Zealand (see the contributions in Morse and Woodman 1987). It is, as far as the Ambonese are concerned, certainly also the case on Ambon.

But the economic interests of governments and the dominant economic interest groups do not always fully coincide, nor need they be expressed in terms of state law. Studies critically examining local traditional laws, focusing on gender and age differences, have shown that 'folk law' often turns out to be the law of senior males, and that recourse to state law and its untraditional values can be a resource in the struggle for emancipation, although, in the long run, dominance by elder males may only be exchanged for dominance by the bureaucracy of the state (cf. Seidman 1984). State law, on the other hand, may be used to pursue local, traditional economic and political interests against the interests of parts of the state administration and 'modern' economic interest groups (see Conn and Langdon 1988).

In the case of inter-ethnic relationships, the constellation may be even more complex. I have shown how on Ambon one and the same local law, Ambonese *adat* (law) has a double function in the economic and political relationships between the Ambonese village population, Butonese immigrant groups, and the agencies of the Indonesian state. Ambonese villagers use their own law in order to shield themselves against the claims of the state for more extended control over natural and human resources. Simultaneously, Ambonese *adat* is maintained to rationalize and justify relations of dominance and oppression of the immigrant Butonese. For the Ambonese, their *adat* law is both a 'jurisprudence of insurgency and of oppression', to borrow the words of Tigar and Levy (1977). For the Butonese, on the other hand, the state and its law is one of the most promising avenues in their struggle of local economic and political insurgency, not directed at the state, but at the Ambonese, in order to obtain full political and economic rights.

Chapter 10
Developing Families: Moluccan Women and Changing Patterns of Social Security in the Netherlands*

Keebet von Benda-Beckmann

One of the recurring themes in the literature on ethnic minorities in Western Europe is individualization. Integration and adjustment to West European life seems invariably to go hand in hand with individualization. The choice for migrants, to state it crudely, is between keeping their identity or integration; between life embedded in the community of the ethnic group of origin and individualism. Not only is this the perception often expressed by authors writing about migrants, the same opinion is common among migrants themselves, who, greatly concerned about the break-down of community ties, fear a loss of ethnic identity. It is, therefore, an important issue both for members of ethnic minorities themselves and for social scientists, as well as politicians, dealing with migration. There is a great amount of literature on trends towards individualism among migrants, which seems to support this hypothesis. The development is roughly described as follows: coming from countries where individuals are firmly embedded in social networks of kinship and village communities, with strong social control and little freedom to deviate from the prevailing, traditional norms of conduct, the first generation migrants continue to live more or less according to these norms in the receiving country. Their culture prescribes that members of one's own community be supported, whether related by kinship or not. The second generation has by and large grown up with the same norms, but having been exposed to Western norms, is caught between two worlds. The majority still conforms to the old norms and traditions, but some tend to take over the culture of the receiving country. The third generation has drifted away from their cultural background and lives according to different norms. The migrant community as such means little to them and they no longer feel obliged to support the community as a whole. Instead, they feel obliged to support their relatives only. In the eyes of their grandparents – and of some researchers – this is a regrettable sign of surrender to their highly individualized West European surroundings. Very often the underlying assumptions of such analyses are that Dutch society is thoroughly atomized and individualistic. This image of Dutch society, which perhaps holds for a small, highly educated section, does not apply to the working and most of the middle classes.[217]

---

* First published 1991 in H. Claessen, M. van den Engel, and D. Plantenga (eds.), *Het Kweekbed Omheind: Opstellen Aangeboden aan Els Postel ter Gelegenheid van haar Afscheid als Hoogleraar*, pp. 35-60. Leiden: Vakgroep Culturele Antropologie en

It is probably correct that second and, even more so, third generation migrants are less concerned with the community as a whole than the first generation migrants were or are, although the trend is not necessarily linear.[218] However, the conclusion that is a sign that migrants become increasingly individualistic is perhaps too rash. Such a conclusion is based upon the assumption that in the communities of origin an individual's life was indeed subordinated to the community, that there was 'total support' from the community for each individual. The question is, whether this notion of 'Gemeinschafts'-solidarity is not simply an ideal image of a far more complex social structure. I shall argue that many interpretations are at least one-sided, based upon a shallow understanding of what community life means in social practice, and upon a disregard of developments of family networks and community life in the receiving country.

What is meant by alleged developments towards individualism, is in fact a decrease in cooperation among the members of the migrant community as a whole in the receiving country. Migrants cooperate in many different ways. Often, newcomers first live with relatives or friends and they may find work through them. But it is considered quite normal for them, after a while, to live on their own and have their own jobs. Earning an income in the rural areas of their country of origin often involved complicated arrangements of cooperation, but migrants in Europe are not expected to get their income in cooperation with other migrants. Although many find a job through fellow migrants, the jobs are individual jobs that do not necessarily depend on other migrants. Those who reside legally in Europe will also get an income from the state social security system in case of illness, unemployment or disability, adding to their independence from fellow migrants.[219] Thus, expressions of regret about perceived tendencies towards individualism thus do not usually refer to income-earning activities. However, having a guaranteed income does not mean that all the physical help

---

VENA. The research upon which this paper is based was carried out in cooperation with Roos Latumahina and Frency Leatemia.

[217] Explanations of migrants' behaviour tend to be given in cultural, rather than socio-economic terms. See for a sophisticated critique of these types of class and cultural explanations for the poor socio-economic position of Javanese migrants in Surinam, Mulder 1987: 1-25.

[218] For a very nice example of the ups and downs of integration and disintegration of Dutch migrants in Brazil, see Buysse 1984. He combines political and religious developments in his analysis with demographic, agricultural, economic and legal factors, to show that Dutch migrants over the past 140 years have known periods when the Dutch formed a more homogeneous community within Brazil, followed by periods of disintegration and adjustment to white Brazilian society, followed again by integration of the Dutch community and distancing from Brazil society.

[219] This is generally true, although access to the state social security system is much more limited for migrants than it is for the nationals of the country.

needed, or the care and support of children or assistance in times of adversity are provided for. For this, cooperation within the migrant group is a basic necessity for most migrants. Disintegration is felt most acutely in the arrangements for such informal social security. They are, as it were, the touchstone of solidarity. Individualism is, by and large, measured by the degree to which these arrangements of cooperation and mutual support lose their binding character and are no longer used or become outmoded. One useful way, therefore, to assess developments towards individualism, would be to study developments in informal social security, both at the normative level and the level of social practice.

For such an assessment two things are necessary: on the one hand a thorough understanding of non-state provided social security, in particular the role of kinship amid village-community, in the country and area of origin, and on the other, a proper understanding of developments in informal social security within the migrant community, including the role of family. Much research has already been done on the position of migrants in the labour market and in the formal educational system. More recently, as a result of the economic recession in the 1970s in Western Europe, access to and the use of state-provided social security have been studied. However, what is generally called the domestic and informal sphere of cooperation and support, or informal social security arrangements, have been severely neglected.[220] Yet, even among the Dutch, by far the most informal support is still given by and received from relatives who share a household (Tjadens and Woldringh 1989: 203).

Research has also been carried out on demographic developments. The themes that dominate in that type of research are: the decreasing size of families, the choice of spouses and the question of when adult children start to live on their own. There is much information about developments of the size of households or nuclear families, but little discussion of developments of the larger family, nor of the relationship between these demographic developments and forms of cooperation not primarily related to the family, that may have developed in the receiving country. Yet, during the first three generations, the composition of migrant communities goes through a period of rapid and fundamental change. First generation migrants live, in many respects, in a thoroughly a-normal social setting. Cut off from a wider network of kindred and other relations, they have to develop a whole new set of relations. The migrants' community as a whole often serves as a substitute for kin. After a few generations, however, migrants have a network of kin-relationships, in composition very similar to the network of kin which forms the core of social relationships in the country of origin, and the need for substitutes may decrease accordingly. There is good reason, therefore, to incorporate these demographic developments in research on forms of cooperation and support.

---

[220] But see Strijbosch 1988; Böcker 1990; K. von Benda-Beckmann et al. 1990.

A proper understanding of developments in informal social security in the receiving country requires an insight into the arrangements that were, and are, common in the country of origin. Recently, researchers have become interested in the social background of migrants and have started to do research in the country of origin.[221] There are many studies of the general economic conditions in the areas from which people migrate, but there is a remarkable lack of attention to the wider social implications of 'family' or 'village-community', two crucial concepts for an analysis of any potential tendencies towards so-called individualism. How, and to what extent, such concepts structure social life, how, and to what extent, they play a role in cooperation in various economic, social and religious sectors, very often remains unclear. This is surprising, since over the past decade and a half much anthropological work has shown that kinship may structure production, consumption, residence, religion and rituals, everyday cooperation and special occasions differentially. Such differentiations have to a large extent become common in anthropological studies of developing countries (F. von Benda-Beckmann 1990c) but seem hardly to have penetrated the literature on migrants. As a result, comparisons between the country of origin and the receiving country often lack the necessary sophistication and do not reach beyond general statements of the migrants' culture.

In this paper I will discuss the relationship between developments in family networks and arrangements for informal social security in a migrant community in the Netherlands, the Moluccan community, and compare these with the same arrangements in the country of origin. The Dutch Moluccans are, for a number of reasons, a special case. The great majority came within a period of only a few months, whereas most Turkish and Moroccan migrants, for example, have immigrated over a period of ten or more years. They came because of a military command, not from their own free will. They share a military background.[222] They did not come to seek work, as did the Turkish and Moroccan migrants, but to wait for a promised return to Indonesia as soon as the political and military situation had been settled. The Dutch government took responsibility for them from the beginning, and has only slowly withdrawn from this, whereas the government's involvement with other migrant groups only started after the economic recession when foreign labourers were dismissed en masse from their jobs. Moluccans have had a relatively long period of about ten years with hardly any contact at all with relatives in Indonesia. It was not until the mid-seventies that contacts became frequent. Turkish and Moroccan migrants have stayed in contact with their relatives back home throughout their stay in

---

[221] See, e.g. Böcker 1990. Others, such as Bartels and me, had a background in the country of origin before we started to work with migrants.

[222] A small number of Moluccans has a navy background. They form a separate community within the Moluccan community at large. Most Moluccans of the first generation grew up in the Moluccas, but there is a group that was born in the military camps, the so-called *anak kompeni*.

the Netherlands. Some have only broken off contacts since becoming unemployed. Finally, marriages with spouses from Indonesia, though they do occur in the second generation, are rare, in contrast to Turkish migrants of the second generation, for example, who frequently marry a spouse from Turkey (Böcker 1990).

These specific features will undoubtedly have an impact on the pace, degree and mode of individualization and integration into Dutch society. However, a proper understanding and evaluation of such developments in the receiving country, for any group of migrants, requires a careful comparison between the migrants' social life here and social life in the area of origin, as well as a study of demographic developments. Conclusions as to the extent of individualization will, of course, vary. But it may well be that developments that seem to be disastrous for a migrant's identity, are in fact not nearly as disastrous as they may seem to be, because they are to a large extent developments towards a more 'normal' set of social relations.

There is one major difficulty in making such a comparison: data about the Moluccas in the 1940s are not available. There have been researchers in the 1960s and 1970s, and they have written about ceremonies, but not much about daily life.[223] It was not until the mid-eighties that research on more mundane themes such as daily life and arrangements for local forms of social security was carried out by a group of researchers and students from Wageningen and Rotterdam universities.[224] We tried to find out how such arrangements have changed over the past two or three generations. My analysis will be based upon that material. Of course, we will have to take into account that the situation was different in the 1940s than people now recollect. As we shall see, people in the Moluccas offer a rather different and more differentiated picture of the past than the Dutch Moluccans. Apart from that, a comparison between the situation in the Moluccas and in the Netherlands of today is also enlightening, because it differs widely from the picture Dutch Moluccans have of life in the Moluccas. In many respects to them past and present are conflated into an ideal image of a life that probably never existed.

I shall differentiate between cooperation in everyday activities and on special celebrations. The latter involves wide participation in which various networks may be mobilized, both in the country of origin and in the Diaspora. The more daily kind of support is usually confined to a rather small circle, both in the country of origin and in the receiving country. Comparing everyday sup-

---

[223] See Kennedy 1955; Cooley 1962; Bartels 1978. These anthropologists have all devoted themselves to more traditional anthropological themes, such as the kinship system, religion, *pela*-partnership and ceremonies. Cooperation and arrangements for support have not received much attention in these works.
[224] See for example Van Paassen 1987; F. von Benda-Beckmann 1988, 1990a, b, c; K. von Benda-Beckmann 1988 and 1992.

port in the receiving country with cooperation in large celebrations in the country of origin all too easily leads to pessimistic conclusions.

The Dutch Moluccans

Moluccans came to the Netherlands in 1950 and 1951. The men had served in the Dutch colonial army. The majority had lived for many years in Dutch colonial military settlements, spread over Indonesia, but mainly on Java and Sulawesi. Some men and women of the oldest generation were even born in these settlements, but most of them grew up in the Moluccas and left their home village for the military settlements in their late teens or early twenties. Upon Indonesia's independence, the Dutch government decided that it would be too dangerous to let the Moluccans return directly to the Moluccas. Instead, they were to spend a brief period in the Netherlands, until the situation calmed down sufficiently for them to return to the Moluccas in safety. The government promised to try to create a Republic of the South Moluccas, which would become part of a federal Indonesian state. In 1950 and 1951, within a period of several months, 10,000 Moluccans arrived in the Netherlands.[225]

The Moluccans embarked under military command, but the men were demobilized on board, before they arrived in the Netherlands. Upon arrival they were put in camps, often former concentration camps, where they lived until the early sixties. In the beginning, they were explicitly forbidden to join the labour force. Food, clothing, shelter, as well as medical facilities and education were provided by the Dutch government. Each adult received a small amount of pocket money. Many, secretly, did seasonal work during harvest time. When they were caught, pocket money was cut. In 1953 the prohibition on finding paid labour was abolished. Between 1953 and 1956, 60% of the salary had to be paid to the slate, as compensation for the costs of living paid by the state.[226]

---

[225] Ethnically, the group of Moluccans consists mainly of Catholics from the Southeast Moluccas, (the Kei and Tanimbar islands) a large number of Protestants and a small number of Muslims from what is now called the Central Moluccas (Ambon Lease and Seram). Initially, they lived together, but now there are neighbourhoods with mainly Keiese and Tanimbarese, or with predominantly Protestant Central Moluccans. The very small Muslim population lives mainly in two towns. In this paper, I shall deal with Central Moluccans only. This group is also more heterogeneous than they usually present themselves. A number of men married spouses from another ethnic background on Java, Sulawesi and Sumatra. Some couples from Sulawesi have also become part of the Moluccan community. During the period immediately preceding their embarkation to the Netherlands, a number of non-Moluccan children were adopted and brought to the Netherlands. Today, many Moluccan men and women have a Dutch spouse.

[226] Veenman and Mual-Bakarbessy 1986: 35.

In 1956 Dutch policy changed to one of self-support. It became clear that the Moluccans would not return to Indonesia within the foreseeable future and it was decided that they had to provide for themselves. The men were obliged to look for a job and social allowances for those who did not find work were made dependent upon their willingness to look for a job. Since the camps were situated in rural areas where the job-market was tight, and because of a lack of formal education and command of the Dutch language, most men found work as unskilled labourers in the lowest salary scales and heaviest jobs. Many women also worked, at first temporarily in agriculture, and later in factories. The wages of their husbands were often so low that a family could hardly live on them. Those who did not find a job lived on social security (Veenman and Mual-Bakarbessy 1986: 36).

Initially, quite a number refused to work. They argued that they had been unlawfully dismissed from military service and that they were technically speaking still part of the army and that the state therefore had an obligation to provide for them. Eventually, however, most overt resistance was abandoned. The majority adjusted more or less grudgingly to the circumstances.

At present, only a minority of the men have a paid job. A considerable number live on disability allowances. Since the economic recession of the mid-seventies, unemployment has gone up as far as 40%, which is even higher than average for ethnic minorities. Among the women, unemployment rates are lower, but many of those who might like to work are not registered at the labour office, so that the hidden unemployment rate may be quite high. Many families live on unemployment allowances or social security. The oldest have now reached retirement age and many of them live solely on the state-provided old age pensions.[227]

Until the early sixties the great majority of the Moluccans lived in camps. Only a few chose to live among the Dutch and become part of Dutch society. In the late fifties, the government started to build houses for Moluccans, usually in separate housing estates, called neighbourhoods *(wijken)*, built close to or in villages and small towns. Moving to these neighbourhoods again caused a lot of trouble, because it was considered a refutation of the claim that they were still part of the army. It also meant paying rent, which the Moluccans had not paid until then. Some refused to pay rent or energy bills and lived for several months without electricity and heating. It was often due to pressure from their spouses that they gave up their resistance, found a job and started to pay rent and energy bills. Today, only one camp is still inhabited, but it has changed

---

[227] According to Veenman and Mual-Bakarbessy (1986: 51), of the Moluccan men older than 55 years, only slightly more than one quarter still had a paid job. 50% of the men had a disability pension; 10% were unemployed and 10% went on early retirement. Of the women aged between 55 and 65 years, only 8% had a paid job. 10% were disabled and 75% indicated to do the household. In the same year the general Dutch disability rates in the age category of 55 - 65 were 29% for men and 6% for women.

considerably in character over the years. From the outside it looks the same, but whereas a family used to have two rooms only, families now have several rooms and have in general the same level of comfort as people who live in the neighbourhoods.

The majority of Moluccans live in some 50 Moluccan neighbourhoods spread across the country. The houses, built in the early sixties with little modern comfort, have recently been or will shortly he renovated. Houses were designed for large families, which were standard at that time. This means that today there are individuals or young married couples without children who want to have their own apartment, but who usually have to look outside the neighbourhoods for housing facilities. The neighbourhoods, in many respects the centres of Dutch Moluccan society, have an over-representation of old people from the first generation and children, whereas the age group between 30 and 40 is under-represented.

Many Moluccans move back into a neighbourhood as soon as they find an opportunity, but an increasing minority have left the neighbourhood permanently and have no plans to return, among them most mixed Dutch-Moluccan couples. Those who move out permanently do not want to live under the permanent social control of the neighbourhood. They live in one of the larger cities, but usually maintain intensive and frequent contacts, with their relatives in the Moluccan neighbourhoods, through visits and over the telephone. Through them, people in the neighbourhoods are not as closed off from the outside Dutch world as they would seem to be (Bartels 1989: 304).

Everyday Support and Cooperation among Dutch Moluccans

During the first years of the camp period, social life had a highly communal and public character. Each family had two adjacent rooms: a living room in which the parents often also slept and a sleeping room for the children. The 'apartments' were separated by a thin wall from their neighbours, so that every word could be heard. There were communal bathing facilities which were also used to do the laundry. Food was prepared in communal kitchens. A mobile shop came to the camps once a week. There was a primary school in each camp for the younger children, so that only secondary education had to be followed elsewhere. For many people it was not necessary to leave the camp at all. Everything they needed – or could afford – could be obtained in the camp. Social control was extremely strong. Children were not only brought up by their parents, but also by neighbours, by relatives in so far as they existed, and by others. Rows between partners and parents and children were often public happenings and children were often punished in public. Those were some of the negative aspects of camp life. But people hardly had a chance to get lonely and no-one could fall ill without others knowing it. Children had lots of playmates. And

Moluccans celebrated together: baptism, confirmation, weddings and funerals were occasions in which the whole camp, and often many from other camps as well, participated. Many Moluccans look back with mixed feeling towards that period. They remember it as a difficult time, with hard labour under cold, miserable conditions, but they miss the feeling of solidarity. As an elderly lady recounted:

> In the camp the atmosphere was so much nicer. There was a sense of community and solidarity which you still find in the neighbourhood, but different in comparison to the camp. Especially in the beginning, when we lived in great uncertainty [whether and when they would go back to Indonesia] and when we were literally dependent upon each other, the common use of the kitchen made people grow towards each other. People who barely knew each other but who were thrown together by fate had to stay alive. The sense of community was much stronger than at present. In the neighbourhood everybody has their own kitchen. The sense of community only revives if people have to cooperate for some activity.

In the camps here or in the military camps in the Dutch Indies, most Moluccans had few, if any relatives, and other relationships were stressed: people who had served together in military service and who had been imprisoned by the Japanese, people who had become friends on board the ship coming from Indonesia, people from the same village, people who were related by ritual bonds called *pela*. They played a major role in celebrations. They also participated in the upbringing of each other's children. Education of children was very much oriented towards earning a living in the Moluccas, since the Moluccan community lived in the expectation and hope of returning soon. Hence they put particular emphasis on teaching their children their *adat*, the Moluccan way of life, which in some respects was a stricter version than they would have taught them in the Moluccas. Children learned to respect and obey these 'relatives', and not to refuse a request for help from family and especially not from *pela*. They were told that it was Moluccan to do so and that they distinguished themselves from the Dutch by doing so. If necessary, one could always ask kin and *pela* for help, but children also learned only to ask for support if it was really necessary. In fact, many women did not easily ask other than close kin for support.[228]

---

[228] It is a common phenomenon that migrants develop a more strict and conservative version of their culture than in the country of origin. Moluccans may have done so even more prominently than most other migrants. It is also likely that the Dutch Moluccan *adat* was stricter than in the military camps of the Dutch Indian colonial army, because they lived with members of other ethnic groups and their orientation was directed at the military situation, rather than at a living in the Moluccas. This may be an explanation

Not everybody was completely without relatives. Some families had sent all their sons to the colonial army and the daughters often married army men. These lucky few came together to the Netherlands, but the majority had few or no relatives at all. Moreover, relatives often lived in different camps. Since there was no money to travel and there were no telephones, communication remained difficult during the first years, making it out of the question for relatives to support each other in daily activities.

Over the years life in the camps life became slowly more private. When the self-support policy was introduced in 1956 and Moluccans were obliged to find a job, nuclear families became more independent. People no longer cooked meals together, but cooked in their own rooms on little stoves. Other facilities were also gradually decentralized over the barrack and apartments. And when people started to earn a salary families were able more and more to choose for themselves how to spend their sparse income. Women welcomed these possibilities to carve out some space for themselves and their families. It made life a bit easier, but they realised that it meant a decrease of community solidarity.

> In the camp there was solidarity. Of course there were difficulties, but the atmosphere was good, the way people went along with each other, together in the washing rooms or in the kitchen. When we got our own kitchen solidarity slowly lost some of its force. But I liked to have my own lavatory and kitchen.

This trend continued and accelerated when people moved to the neighbourhoods. Each family was assigned a house with a small garden. At first, the gardens were hardly separated and one could simply walk from one back-yard to the other, but slowly hedges and later walls were put up and people no longer walked freely in and out of each other's houses. Under these living conditions relationships between neighbours became less intensive, with all the positive and negative consequences. The raising of children lost much of its public character. Disagreements between husband and wife could be kept within four walls. But some people became lonely and did not get the attention that was common before. Moluccans today like to think that in former times, notably during the *tangsi* (military settlements of the Dutch colonial army in the Dutch East Indies) and the camp period, the whole community took care of everyone who needed it. If we look closer at what people tell us about that period, it was rarely the whole community that looked after everybody. The great difference with today is that the basis upon which support was given and asked for was not exclusively kin-relationship, but also friendship, *pela*, neighbourship, common descent from one village (*kumpulan*) and common background in the army. But

---

why an institution such as *pela* has obtained a wider meaning and is applied more strictly than in the Moluccas. See Strijbosch 1985; Bartels 1989: 158 ff.

several women whom we interviewed indicated that these relationships were a substitute for kin. As one woman remarked:

> In the *tangsi* you did not have your whole family nearby, but you made friends with soldiers' wives. They took on a bit the role of your family in helping with all sorts of things. Originally, for example, if you wanted to baptize your child, you chose someone from your family as godparents. In the *tangsi* you chose also relatives, if you had any, but you also chose neighbours with whom you went on patrol or with whom you went to the cadre-school.

People preferred to ask their own family for help. If other relations were asked, it was done with reluctance and great care was taken not to ask too much. One woman told us that her children used to go to a *pela* of hers to have lunch, because she worked. She always made sure that her children brought food, 'I did not want to put too much of a burden upon my *pela*', she explained. Since a *pela* may not refuse a request, it is up to the person who makes the request to be moderate. Failing to do so may lead to great distress on the side of the *pela,* as in the case where drug-addicted youths make relentless requests for financial support of their *pela* who is defenseless and has hardly any way to refuse (Bartels 1989: 161).

In the first years of their stay in the Netherlands it was hardly possible to rely exclusively on family, but nowadays close kin is so much more abundant that the other relationships have retreated into the background, at least for daily support and care. The elderly usually have one or more children either still living with them, or else close by, who look after them. Visits by children may not be frequent during some periods, but in the case of illness children may come every day or take turns. On the other hand, grandparents are the most obvious persons to take care of small children when both parents work. It is not uncommon for a granddaughter to live with her grandparents, to look after them, but also to learn to live away from home and become independent. However, not every old Moluccan has relatives living close by and there are reports of neglect. These cases have deeply shocked the Moluccan community, because they regard that as a sign that the trend towards individualism has passed a crucial stage. In some neighbourhoods small two-room houses have been built where old people can live on their own but nevertheless stay in the Moluccan community and be close to their children. However, few aged Moluccans choose actually to live there. They prefer the larger houses in which they have lived since they moved to the neighbourhoods because the whole family can be put up for the night there if necessary. These houses are also the symbolic focus of the family and are regarded as a substitute for the family houses in the Moluccas. Most of these new two-room houses are inhabited by young couples. In other neighbourhoods possibilities for creating Moluccan wings in existing old people's homes are being discussed, but the aged themselves usually indignantly refuse such a solution. 'Only the Dutch put their aged away in homes.'

Fortunately most old people are still being taken care of and cases of neglect still belong to the exceptions. That does not mean that there are no problems. It often puts a lot of strain on both the aged themselves and on the children who care for them. Many aged Moluccans wait quietly but in uncertainty for their children to come, because they consider it improper to be too much of a burden to their children. Often the aged themselves refuse to accept support, even though the children are willing to help.[229] The problems will probably increase, since the size of families is decreasing rapidly. Though most of the burden of helping is usually borne by one or two daughters only, the chance that there will be a child willing to take the task on herself, who lives close enough to her parents to do so, will be smaller in the future.

The arrangements for mutual help between grandparents, parents and (grand)children are the expression of many different things at once. They show that grandparents are still taken seriously; they express respect for parents and grandparents; they express a concern for the well-being of the aged on the side of the children and grandchildren, but also a concern for the well-being of grandchildren from the side of the grandparents; they make it possible for married women with children to participate in the labour market; on the more symbolic level, they express adherence to the Moluccan norms of mutual help and support. If for some reason there are no grandparents available to take care of small children, other close relatives are asked or may offer to take them. Mothers with small children who want to go out to work will usually stay at home if there are no close relatives nearby. Only rarely do neighbours or friends provide these services. It almost seems to be a matter of pride not to look outside your family for support. Many would be ashamed to be dependent on others and they feel they have no right to ask for help. On the other hand, asking relatives for help, especially close relatives, is regarded as normal. One does not need a further legitimation; it is quite appropriate to do so. What is more, even when one does not have a good relationship with one's parents or sisters, one may still ask them for help and expect them to comply with such a request. Thus, a woman with small children who was applying for a job said she would only take the job if her mother would take care of her children. This same woman had told me how poorly she got along with her mother. She did not want to have much to do with her. Yet to her it was obvious and normal to ask her mother to take care of her children and she preferred asking her to asking her sister, with whom she was on better terms. Close relatives can be asked without putting too much stress on good relations because it is not considered a service out of friendliness, but out of obligation towards family. In most other relations the factor of friendship is of crucial importance to be able to mobilize support. Asking a

---

[229] See for similar reactions of aged Koreans, Choong 1988.

neighbour with whom one is not on friendly terms is out of the question. But friendship may easily be overburdened and people shy away from taking that risk.[230]

Only rarely did we find people who claimed that even close relatives do not look after each other any more. In the few examples in which that was the case, there were no close relatives at all or at least not in the immediate proximity, or else the children had serious drug problems. In matters of daily support and cooperation the most important change from the camps to the neighbourhoods and over the past 30 years that Moluccans have lived in the neighbourhoods is a change in emphasis from a multiplicity of relationships towards an emphasis on the family. Today, there is an overwhelming reliance on relatives for daily services and cooperation, both at a normative level and at a practical level.

Dutch Moluccan Ceremonies

At more special occasions, such as baptism and confirmation for the Christians and at weddings and funerals for all Moluccans, many other relationships are invoked for participation and support. When people talk about trends towards individualism they usually do not mean these occasions which, on the contrary, are among the few examples where feelings of group-solidarity are still pronounced.

Every Moluccan is welcome to a funeral without invitation. The celebrations tend to be very large. People who have not seen each other for years, sometimes since time camp period, will meet again. People who do not participate much in neighbourhood activities or in Moluccan activities in general, rarely fail to come to funerals. Muslim funerals last longer than Christian funeral ceremonies. Not only the funeral itself, but the third, seventh, ninth, fortieth and hundredth day are also celebrated. As soon as one hears that a person has died, one goes to the house of the deceased. That means that meals have to be prepared for large numbers of guests. Most of the work is done by adult women who have no paid job: neighbours and close relatives, but also godchildren, *pela* and people from the same home-village as the deceased. The expenses are shared by all guests. Each one brings an envelope with a minimum of ƒ 10 for the younger and ƒ 25 for the older guests. But godchildren, *pela* and people from the same home-village are expected to, and will, contribute more. People who have a job will be selective in their physical contribution: if it concerns a distant relative who does not live in one's own neighbourhood, one will

---

[230] Bartels (1989: 161) mentions that Moluccans tend to entertain close friendships as much as possible among relatives. It could well be that in that way there is less stress because one can always ask for favours on the basis of family ties, instead of friendship.

go there after work, but for closer relatives or someone who lives in town, one may take a day off. Only for very close relatives are several days taken off. For the subsequent celebrations they only take a day off if it concerns a very close relative. The seventh day is a relatively small prayer-celebration, usually with close relatives and people from the neighbourhood only. The ninth and sometimes the fortieth day are big celebrations with many guests from outside. Among Christians only the funeral itself, which lasts three days and nights and the fortieth day are celebrated.

With weddings it is different. Here guest participation is basically upon invitation only. Thus families have to make a decision whether to have a small celebration within the immediate family circle or go for a full celebration which may involve several hundreds of guests. There is hardly anything in between, for it is impossible to be selective, unless one wants to risk serious conflicts. As with funerals, the guests share the costs by bringing envelopes with money, the content of which depends upon the relationship to the bride or groom. Godparents, *pela,* members of the same home village, and close relatives will pay more, sometimes up to hundreds of guilders. The others will pay a standard f 25. Most weddings end with a nice sum of money left over which the newlyweds can use to set up a household. Apart from the envelopes, the closer relatives and special relations will also give presents. Flowers are far less common than among the Dutch and it is considered highly inappropriate to give flowers only, even if a lot of money is spent on them.

The actual work is done by several working parties who are all explicitly invited. It takes days of work and is therefore mainly done by women who do not have a paid job. Married women form the cooking party, under the leadership of an elderly lady, who puts the menu together with the parents of the bride and groom. Every neighbourhood has a few women who are known for their ability to run such a large organization and who are frequently asked. They organize the shopping and the cooking. Cooking is mainly a task for women over 50 years old and they guard their position jealously. Only a few women between 43 and 49 have managed to participate fully. They will be the leaders of the next generation, the younger women do the more menial work of cutting vegetables, making tea and coffee and washing up. The formal meal is shared officially by a relatively small number of specially invited guests, including godparents, *pela,* close relatives from both sides, and the minister and his wife. The other guests are invited later and are offered elaborate snacks and drinks. Showing the guests their places and waiting upon them is done by unmarried women and men.[231] Christian weddings tend to be larger than Muslim weddings. This may have to do with the size of the Muslim community, which is

---

[231] See for a detailed description of a large Christian wedding ceremony, Strijbosch 1988.

only a fraction of the Christian community. Although Christian relatives and *pela* may be invited, they do not frequently participate in Muslim celebrations.

Confirmation and baptism take place around Easter time. If in any particular year many children in a neighbourhood are confirmed, then each one is likely to have a relatively small celebration, because the potential guests will have to divide their attention between the many. However, baptism and especially confirmation are often big occasions with large presents and many guests. Godparents have to be selected, which is a serious and problematic business because relationships may become seriously disturbed if someone is passed over (Bartels 1989: 155). In the *tangsi* and camp period they were chosen from among friends, patrol-mates, neighbours or relatives, but rarely from *pela*. Nowadays, they are often chosen from among very close relatives, for example an aunt or uncle. In the Moluccas, aunts and uncles were considered as substitutes for parents. Aunts from the mother's side are called little or big mother, depending on whether they are younger or older sisters of the mother. Likewise, uncles from father's side are called little or big father respectively. Godparents were sought outside this circle, because those who were already substitute parents on the basis of *adat*, were already responsible for their classificatory children.

These large celebrations are today a main focus of Moluccan culture and are therefore of great importance. People who complain that Moluccans have become too individualistic may tell you that these occasions are the only occasions at which a sense of group-solidarity arises. But what they do not seem to realize is that the size of the Moluccan community in the Netherlands has increased by a factor 4 and even today much time is involved in celebrations. Depending on age, family relationship and phase in time life-cycle, and type of occasion, a celebration may take up a few hours of their time for young unmarried youths, to time amounting to several weekends for married working women and the full ten days and another three days for the fortieth and hundredth day celebration for the middle-aged and elderly women who do most of the cooking. The fact that not every Moluccan participates in every big celebration does not necessarily mean that people spend far less time on such celebrations than the older generation used to do. It is part of their position as young unmarried youth that they do not do much. Several women whom we interviewed indicated that they had only started to frequent such celebrations when they were married and had children. As we shall see, the input of work in the Moluccas depends on the same factors.

Everyday Support in the Moluccas

In the years immediately following the Second World War and the Indonesian independence war, the economy in Moluccan villages on Ambon Lease and

Seram was mainly one of self-support. For most Moluccans there was enough land to live on. Those who did not have a paid job, the great majority of villagers, could make a living from the proceeds of their land. They grew vegetables and root crops in their gardens; sago, the main staple, was abundantly available on the island of Seram, if not in their own village on Ambon. There was plenty of fish in the sea. Some money was earned with cloves and nutmeg, although prices were very low at that time. Further money could be earned by sewing, washing clothes for wealthier families in government, and sometimes by making snacks or bread. Generally speaking, money played a relatively minor role in the village economy. Villages were traditionally the most important political units. They owned the uncultivated land up to the border of the adjacent villages. Most land within the boundaries of a village belonged to patrilineal clans.[232] Access to land was provided on the basis of patrilineal descent within a village and of bilateral inheritance. Part of the food production could be done with very little help from others. One could very well maintain a garden with vegetables, chili peppers and root crops alone. Usually husband and wife would have a garden, but widows and widowers often kept one on their own. As long as they were strong and healthy this was no problem. Sago production did require cooperation.[233] Small groups of three or four men, not necessarily close relatives, often friends, would grind the marrow from the sago palm, and wash the starch from the pulp. As a result of the land tenure and inheritance system, sago palms were usually owned communally by a number of people, all of whom would be entitled to a share. Thus the proceeds of every tree were usually distributed among a great number of people from various households. In effect, access to the staple food sago required a lot of cooperation. And if it was to be stored in an enduring form, women had to bake hard cakes from the flour, which often again involved cooperation and redistribution.

Houses were made from a stone foundation, with walls made from the huge leafstalks and thatched with leaves from the sago-palm. Some of the large family houses were built from chalk, burnt from the coral that was found on the beach, and also thatched with sago leaves. The building required the cooperation of large parties of men, who worked on the basis of mutual help, *masohi*, without payment, but on the understanding that the help would be returned when one needed to build a house oneself. They were provided with meals, tea and snacks. Feeding the working parties itself required quite a lot of cooperation, usually among the wives of the builders. Nowadays, many houses are built with concrete walls and corrugated iron roofs. The foundation is still laid in

---

[232] The actual land tenure system is very complicated. See F. von Benda-Beckmann 1990a. Apart from the indigenous Ambonese population, most villages had Butonese migrants, who had no political rights and could own land only under very restricted conditions. See F. von Benda-Beckmann 1990b.

[233] See for the different arrangements of cooperation around sago production and consumption F. von Benda-Beckmann 1990a.

masohi, but increasingly the rest of the house is being built by local experts and with the help of a handful of men who may be paid. These men are usually related to the owner of the house, but the relationship may be quite distant. Often a patron-client relationship exists between the workers and the owner of the house. Though friendship is usually the main basis for cooperation, people like to stress the kin ties in such a relationship. Houses from sago are still being built in *masohi,* but the working parties have become smaller. They are recruited from friends, neighbours and kin.

People at that time lived in two- or three-generation families. Although traditionally people lived in larger units in family houses, only a minority lived in this way in the 1940s. The trend to a living-pattern in which each married couple with their unmarried children had their own house was well on its way at that time. Living in one house did not and does not necessarily mean that all the people form one economic or consumption unit: there may be and frequently is more than one fireplace in a house. But even with separate kitchens, support of various kinds between those sharing a house would be more common than between people living in different houses.

As long as people are healthy and strong they could and can take care of themselves and require relatively little support in the middle of their life. But those who are old, sick or very young need help and care. Moluccans in the Netherlands like to think that back in the Moluccas these people are all taken care of 'by the whole community'. In actual fact that is not the case and has not been the case for generations. As long as one has parents or children with whom relations are not completely broken off, one is usually taken care of. Elderly people often stay with a child. According to *adat,* the youngest son and his wife will stay in the parental home and take care of their parents in old age, but parents often prefer to live with a daughter rather than a daughter-in-law. Most of the work is done by the daughter or daughter-in-law with whom the parents live, and not by the whole family, not even by all the children. Although families tend to have as many children as possible, child mortality is very high, and life expectancy low, which means that those who reach old age often do not have many children who can take care of them. The choice has become even smaller because of migration. Parents hope that at least one child will live in the village to care for them when they grow old. Of course, the Dutch Moluccans of the first generation are themselves such migrants who are unable to care for their parents personally, although some have brought their parents from Indonesia to stay with them. Those who have not often feel guilty and many send large sums of money to their parents and various other relatives, to make up for their absence.

Nowadays most families in Moluccan villages have at least one child who has left the village through entering the civil- or – preferably – military- or police-service, or becoming a teacher. Education is highly valued as a strategy to get children into jobs where they will be able to become brokers between their village relatives and all kinds of government services (F. and K. von Benda-Beckmann 1998). If the strategy is successful, this may mean an important source of financial support. But if a child does not find a job in town all the efforts have been for nothing: the child has become unwilling to take up farming and is in no position to support the parents. Education is thus a costly, risky, but nonetheless valued undertaking, for which high financial sacrifices may be made by parents, and also by siblings. This latter tradition started in the first half of this century, and was stronger in Christian than in Muslim villages. It was continued in the Netherlands, where older brothers and sisters have often also paid for the education of their younger siblings.

Most of the elderly are fairly well taken care of in the Moluccas, but for some, old age may be quite miserable. As most women who bear the bulk of the burden of help are already busy with their children, garden and other activities to make ends meet, they often have little time and little patience to attend to the old. It would hardly have been very different a few generations ago, especially not in the difficult years after the Japanese occupation and the early years of independence. Having children or parents is a pre-condition, but not a guarantee, that the daily care is good or even sufficient according to local standards.

For those who have neither children nor parents able or willing to help, life may he extremely hard. Muslims use one term for orphans and people without children: *yatim piatu.* We heard quite a number of cases of a shocking lack of help. In fact, during our fieldwork an orphaned youth of 17 died of undernourishment. Villagers felt uncomfortable about it but in no way were they under the impression that it had been the task of the village or even the wider circle of relatives to take care of this young man. It was seen as an unfortunate turn of fate. When I talked about it with Moluccans in the Netherlands they did not believe me at first. When I insisted that it had happened they started to think and admitted that they had heard of similar examples of neglect while visiting the Moluccas. It had been such a shock that they had not dared to talk about it upon their return, and had pushed it far back in their memory. However, old women considering whether they should go back and spend their old age in their home-village, often know what they may expect. It is not by chance that women are far more reluctant than their husbands to go hack. And indeed, it is a greater risk for them, because women are less easily taken up and cared for than men when they grow old and disabled. They know that it is not enough to have money. 'Money does not cook, money does not care', one woman retorted when her husband tried to convince me that nothing can go wrong as long as you have a (Dutch) pension. Such anxieties are not easily expressed, because they do not fit with the ideal image of the all-caring village community. Village life is harsh and has been harsh for generations. Family relationships are a basis for requesting support, but only very close relatives may be asked even where there is no additional basis, such as friendship. People might persist in asking favours, but they have also learned to say no to requests, much better in fact than have Dutch Moluccans (Pollmann, Seleky and Nienhuis 1982: 171).

Everyday support and help is only obligatory between close kin. This circle has become smaller, but it is difficult to say whether it was significantly larger forty years ago. Nowadays, grandparents, parents, children and siblings are expected to support each other under all conditions, but cousins may refuse help without being too much frowned upon. Outside the small circle of closest relatives, additional grounds are necessary. Friendship is the most important one. Neighbours may help, but only occasionally and where there is also a friendly relationship. Otherwise they will not help each other at all. On the other hand there are examples of elderly people without children being well looked after, but these are either especially liked for their gentle character, or else much respected for special reasons. There are some other substitutes for support between relatives, such as patron-client relationships, female prayer groups in Muslim villages, or sport clubs, the members of which support each other in many ways, but also come as a group to help at village activities. Van Paassen reports that in the harbour and market town of Tulehu many such associations, which operate on the basis of equality and reciprocity, have recently been set up and are increasingly taking the place of organizations based upon hierarchical principles which underlie kinship and government-initiated organizations (1987: 78). In addition, patron-client relationships between headmasters or headmistresses and villagers exist which are based in part upon kinship, though not necessarily so.

Apart from the physical work involved in daily support, there is also non-material care: giving attention, chatting, etc. In this respect there is an important difference from the situation in the Netherlands. Because of the tropical climate, people spend more time outside and thus meet neighbours and passers-by more frequently and more casually. In Moluccan villages people also walk in and out of houses far more easily than in the Netherlands. People do not get quite as lonely as in the Netherlands, although being blind or deaf may result in extreme loneliness even in Moluccan villages. In the Netherlands people have more respect for and patience with disabled persons than in the Moluccas.

Ceremonies in the Moluccas

Large celebrations such as big weddings and especially funerals are often still a matter for the village as a whole or at least a large part of it. They concern the whole village in the sense that all the men of the oldest generation, as representatives of their family, bring the dead to the grave and participate in the ceremonial meal and prayer session the night of the funeral. The women of the oldest generation have to be present at the cooking, also as representatives of their family. They sit, chat and chew *sirih-pinang* and comment on the cooking while they prepare the complicated snacks that take a lot of time, but are not strenuous. Middle-aged women do most of the heavier work and women with young children will come for a couple of hours only. Every woman who comes to cook also brings some money as well as vegetables or fruit from her garden. Thus the expenses are shared by all female participants. In addition, relatives and friends, both female and male, also pay extra amounts, depending on their status, the degree of relatedness, and wealth.

A circle of around 50 relatives or more will live for a number of days in the house of the deceased, in Muslim villages until the ninth day and in Christian villages until the third day. The women have to provide meals during this whole period until the large ceremonial meal on the 9th day. Relatives of the deceased may come from other villages, either by boat or by bus and stay for days. At the end of the main ceremonies the women are exhausted from the heavy work and lack of sleep.

In market towns, where the money economy plays a larger role than in the more isolated villages, the work is less strenuous; because much of the food can he bought at the market. There the amounts of money paid by relatives, neighbours and friends are much higher. What cannot be paid from these gifts is shared by the relatives up to the sixth degree, i.e. parents, siblings, adult children, aunts and uncles and cousins (Van Paassen 1987: 124 ff).

Wedding ceremonies vary greatly in scope. Traditionally there are two types of wedding: wedding by elopement and wedding by proposal. The first seems to have become the normal variant in some Christian villages: hardly any girl marries as a virgin and usually girls marry when they are pregnant. For that reason, and to save the costs of a wedding by proposal, they usually opt for a wedding by elopement (Wessels 1986: 92 ff). In Muslim villages many girls also marry by elopement, again because they are pregnant or cannot afford the full ceremony. But official proposals are still quite common. In many families it is a matter of status to have a large wedding and the largest wedding parties are celebrated by the children of civil servants or (ex)-military and police officers.

As in the Netherlands, one has to be invited to take part in a wedding celebration. One does not go and cook unless one is invited. But being invited, it is difficult to refuse. In that case, the women also have to bring some money, vegetables and fruit. Very large weddings have a reception in the evening, followed by a dancing party for the youth. Relatives, friends and neighbours, and in the Christian villages the godparents, will share in the costs of the feast, but *pela* hardly play any role of significance. The main reason is that villages who maintain *pela*-relationships usually lie far apart. In Moluccan villages *pela* meet each other only on rare occasions. The parents themselves pay most, especially if the father is a civil servant or a pensioned soldier or policeman. Guests invited to the reception are also expected to bring presents. Bride prices are still paid and may be quite substantial for women with higher education. But such women do not usually marry a villager and the bride price is paid by the groom himself. Guests from outside will stay for several days and have to be attended to by village women. However, these occasions tend to be less strenuous than funerals.

There is little information about the scope of baptism and confirmation celebrations and who participates and shares in the expenses. In Moluccan Muslim villages there is no such ceremony as *Chatam al Quoran,* which is more or less the Muslim counterpart to a Christian confirmation in West Sumatra. Circumcision is a rather sober ritual. A boy will choose a man whom he trusts and respects to hold him during the circumcision. There is usually a small celebration, with prayers and a meal for a group of invited men.

During wedding celebrations and funerals the prayer groups mentioned above, or the members of sports clubs or groups of clients of the same patron often work together. The prayer groups come as a working party to cook and the members of sports clubs may also help to put up roofs, collect chairs, fetch water or wood. The members of such groups will also make a point of coming to offer their help in case of death or weddings in the family of one of their members.

Taking Stock

Are Moluccans becoming increasingly individualistic and is this trend as disastrous as some fear? This paper is not a full analysis of all sectors of Moluccan social life. The focus lies on one crucial sector: informal social security. I have distinguished between everyday care and support and support for ceremonies and large celebrations. In both respects there have been changes towards individualism, but not very dramatic ones.

In the Moluccas, the main material basis for earning a living is shared property. Except for gardening and some forms of fishing, which may be done on a strictly individual basis, food production, as well as the production of cloves and nutmeg, and house building require a certain amount of cooperation. These activities are tied into elaborate systems of obligations of mutual help and redistribution. Rice, today nearly as important as sago, and modern building materials such as cement and corrugated iron, have to be bought. Moreover, education and health services cost considerable amounts of money. Even in the more remote villages money plays a more important role today than 40 years ago. Some of the old redistributive mechanisms have become somewhat obsolete and have been replaced by paid labour. New cooperation arrangements have been developed, taking the form of patron-client relationships, with their own obligations and redistribution. However, in cases of economic hardship people fall back on sago and old forms of cooperation.

In the Netherlands, Moluccan migrants, who rarely have their own private business, earn their living on an individual basis. Though many find a job through relatives or friends, the work itself does not require the cooperation of other Moluccans. Depending on whether one has a family to support or not, wages are all or in part spent on the family. Even unmarried children who live on their own contribute considerably to the household of their parents. Over the years, contributions from adult children have changed from obligation to more or less free disposition. Many young people are quite sensitive in this respect and develop ways to contribute in such a way that every appearance of coercion is avoided.

Life in the Moluccas in the 1940s was not nearly as communal as Dutch Moluccans like to believe. Support was and is a matter between close relatives, but the circle to which this applies has become narrower, both in the Moluccas and in the Netherlands. The persons who, according to local norms, are primarily responsible for each other in the Moluccas are parents, grandparents and children. Adult siblings do have a strong moral obligation, but may refuse help without all too serious social pressure. In the 1940s the circle probably extended to siblings and cousins, but there is no clear evidence that it was indeed the case. If they lived together in one house, which was more common than it is now, they participated in the care of an aged uncle or aunt, as they do today.

The composition of the group of persons who are responsible for each other and will potentially take care of each other has developed differently in the Moluccas and in the Netherlands. The Moluccan community in the Netherlands has developed from a rather homogeneous group of people who mostly lacked a full set of kindred, towards a far less homogeneous group with far more social and economic differentiation, with each individual having a full set of kindred. Substitutes that were developed because of the extraordinary situation of migration have decreased in importance. People have, as it were, gone back to normal.

Against this increase in the composition of kin-relationships stands a decrease in the size of nuclear families over the past three generations. Bartels points to the problem of recruiting godparents from among very close relatives. It concentrates the responsibility and financial load for children in cases of adversity on too small a group. The danger that such a group may not be able to bear the burden becomes even greater with the contracting size of families (Bartels 1989: 156). However, the number of persons primarily responsible for help and support was not very large in the Moluccas either, because of high rates of child mortality and low life expectancy, as well as migration. The result is a relatively small circle of primarily responsible adults who are healthy and strong enough to support the old, the sick and small children. Among Dutch Moluccans life expectancy is much higher and infant mortality is as low as among the Dutch. It is therefore not clear whether the net result is all that negative. The circle of primary responsibility in case of adversity is rather small and vulnerable both in the Moluccas and in the Netherlands. One important difference is that in the Moluccas the actual work is shared by a larger number of women than in the Netherlands, where the sick and aged are often cared for mainly by one or two women with whom they happen to live.

In the Moluccas a number of organizations based upon equality are replacing more hierarchically structured forms of cooperation, to some extent providing a substitute for kinship. In the Netherlands, kinship has in many ways regained its position as the primary source of support, although other forms of cooperation exist. Kinship has fundamentally changed in character in the Netherlands, however. There has been a dramatic change from a commanding structure to one of discussion and negotiation, very similar to the changes in Dutch society one or two generations earlier (De Swaan 1982). Young Dutch Moluccans are highly sensitive to their right to participate in decisions on an equal footing, although the oldest generation often denies them that right. But that does not mean that they feel free to refuse care and support. Though the social setting is far less hierarchical, these norms concerning mutual support are still strong and compelling. The main difference from a decade or so ago is that they have obtained a say in the precise kind and form it takes.

When it comes to large celebrations, Dutch Moluccans are on the whole no less individualistic than their relatives in the Moluccas, though the variation there is perhaps greater. In some Christian villages and certainly in the larger towns where the money economy has obtained dominance, large feasts are rarely celebrated by the whole community. In more isolated villages such celebrations are still common. They involve a tremendous amount of work and time, depending on the stage in the life cycle, gender, status, wealth and available time.

Those who regret the disintegration of the Dutch Moluccan community scarcely realize that the community is four times as large as it was 40 years ago. For that reason alone it is impossible to celebrate with the whole Moluccan community. Elderly and middle-aged women who have no job spend hardly less time on these activities than in past decades, or than they would have spent in a Moluccan village. There is one important difference with participation in the Moluccas, however. In the Netherlands many women of the age and position to do the main work, cannot fully participate because they have paid jobs. However, a remarkable number of them spend a lot of time in the evenings and weekends, as far as their jobs allow them to, on these activities. They comply as much as they can with the norms of cooperation at large celebrations.

All in all, if one considers the time and energy spent on support and cooperation, both in everyday care and in large celebrations, the fear that after one or two generations hardly anything will be left of traditional Moluccan forms of support is hardly realistic.

Chapter 11
Law, Violence and Peace Making on the Island of Ambon*

Keebet von Benda-Beckmann

On January 19, 1999 an Ambonese[234] taxi driver got into a fight with a Buginese tricycle rider in Ambon town. Similar fights often occur in the tough neighbourhood of Batu Merah, where people from many different, ethnic and religious backgrounds live closely packed. Emotions run high, often resulting in one or more wounded and sometimes even death. But usually as quickly as a fight flares up, it cools down again, but not this time. This was to be the beginning of a long period of intense fighting and rioting that has developed into something dose to civil war. At first it was confined to Ambon-Lease, the central Moluccan islands with Ambon as the provincial capital, but it has spread to the North Moluccan islands and to the Southeast Moluccas around Key and Tanimbar. Many people have died, more have lost their homes and fled, houses have been burnt down and mosques and churches have been burnt to ashes.[235] For almost a year the only road to the northern part of the island of Ambon was literally blocked by a brick wall, and nobody, especially not Christians, was allowed to pass. After the road over the hills was opened again, transport from Ambon town to the northern part of the island by road remained difficult. Only Muslims live behind the wall, both Ambonese and Butonese, though the number of Butonese has decreased. All Christians have fled the area, after the *kampong Kristen* in Hila/Kaitetu was attacked and set up in flames. The oldest Protestant church in Eastern Indonesia was destroyed, a beautiful building with a tiled

---

* Published 2004 in: M.-C. Foblets, and T. von Trotha (eds.), *Healing the Wounds. Essays on the Reconstruction of Societies after War*, pp. 221-239. Oxford and Portland Oregon: Hart Publishing. An earlier version of this paper appeared in Dutch: K von Benda-Beckmann 2000.

[234] I use the term Ambonese for someone who belongs to the autochthonous population of Ambon-Lease, which includes the islands Ambon, Haruku, Saparua, Nusa Laut and Eastern Ceram, in order to distinguish them from other ethnic groups on the island of Ambon. In the Dutch literature the term Moluccan is more current. However, strictly speaking this term would also refer to people from the Northern Moluccas (Ternate, Tidore, Halmahera) and South-Eastern Moluccas (Key and Tanimbar). On Ambon, these groups would not be considered autochthonous inhabitants: for them other *adat*, i.e. customs and customary law, would be applicable.

[235] Manuhutu 2000: 16 reports that 1,200 deaths and 160,000 displaced have been registered, but that estimates are a lot higher.

floor vaguely showing the symbols of the ancient and long abandoned secret male societies. The centre of marine studies, a research site of Universitas Pattimura, in which a number of Christians worked, was also attacked and looted and the Christians chased away. Many Butonese, though Muslim, have fled as well. Other Butonese, who used to live peacefully in Christian villages, fled to the Muslim northern part of the island, where they felt safer. Nobody knows exactly how many moved in and out of the area, and it is not quite clear where they went. Some went back to Buton, their land of origin on the southeast tip of Sulawesi, where a meagre existence is waiting in an overcrowded, barren area. Others have gone to other parts of Sulawesi, notably Macassar. The rest lead a quiet but uncertain life alongside their Ambonese Muslim neighbours largely cut off from the rest of Ambon. The north coast of Ambon no longer obtains its products through Ambon city, but directly through Macassar. Hitu, until recently a small, sleepy and insignificant harbour, is booming and expanding rapidly.

Plate 11.1: The 18th century Emanuel church in Hila, the oldest church in the Moluccas, before its destruction

Many have attempted to create peace and reconciliation: religious leaders – both Christian and Muslim – local leaders, influential intellectuals, and high politicians and even former president Abdulrahman Wahid and the current president Megawati Sukaronoputri, but all in vain.[236] Moluccans in the Netherlands are also trying to think of ways to de-escalate the violence and create reconciliation. Some look to *adat* procedures as a way of creating peace. Others have more faith in the rule of law: the military should return to the barracks, take a neutral position in the conflict, and refrain from infiltration, and a public administration together with a judiciary that have been cleansed of corruption must reinstall good governance. Still others hope the 'international community' might play an enabling role. And finally there is a small group that believes violence and armed force is the only way to reach any solution. In fact, nobody really knows what to do and most people are rather desperate for creative ideas.

Over the past years there have been several periods in which there was hope that the riots belonged to the past, but this hope was shattered over and over again. Every time, violence flares up, only to settle down and continue smouldering beneath the ashes. Since it has become clear that agitators from outside have been active, probably with support from high political circles, there are voices that say that the troubles are externally initiated and are not really an internal problem within the Moluccan community. This is very unlikely. Troublemakers from outside may have intensified violence; it would not have reached the level and intensity in the Moluccas if there had not been serious problems in the region. However, agitation and the import of weapons have definitely increased the level of violence. During the first months people fought with knives and home made weapons. Nowadays a large number of guns and highly modern automatic weapons is in the hands of civilians, bought or 'borrowed' from the armed forces, and illegally imported from outside. The navy has confiscated many transports, but many manage to get into the area.

The Moluccas are in a situation where peace has not yet been re-established. Unfortunately it is still impossible to know when and how peace will be achieved. To say something about the peace-making process is therefore necessarily somewhat speculative. We can only look at the process while it is taking place, without knowing for sure which direction developments are taking. Yet I believe it is of crucial importance to document and analyse the process as well as possible while it is going on, and see where things go wrong and where there may be an inroad towards possible peace. Explaining the process leading to peace with hindsight, when peace has been established, runs the risk of overlooking with what hopes, expectations, information and (mis)understanding of what is going on, people search for possible ways out of a dreadful situation.

I hope to contribute to understanding a process the outcome of which is still completely unclear. I do not pretend to be able to look into all factors, but shall confine myself to two points, which I consider to be of vital importance. I shall try to unravel the various constellations of parties in which the conflict is

---

[236] See also Manuhutu 2000: 14.

situated and I shall look at how state law and *adat* law play a part in the conflict. What is often presented as an inter-ethnic or an inter-religious conflict is in fact a vastly complex set of overlapping conflicts that are expressed in different constellations of parties.[237] I shall discuss the main constellations, describe the dividing lines along which the parties have been formed and ask what role various kinds of law play in the formation of parties. Then I shall describe what constitutes the conflict in each of these constellations. I shall draw attention to the lack of traditional institutions that reach beyond the level of villages. Furthermore, it is of crucial importance to understand the role of the youth in the processes of violence, and I shall argue that traditional mechanisms to break through cycles of violence have disintegrated. Finally I shall discuss to what extent the various legal systems carry possibilities for re-establishing peace. I shall suggest that *adat* and a common religious past might be re-activated as an important symbolic support to other methods of establishing trust between Ambonese Muslims and Christians. However, in constellations with other parties, such as Butonese or Buginese migrants, *adat* is unlikely to serve for peace making. Too strong an emphasis on *adat* may even deepen the conflict.

My analysis does not apply to the whole region, but will be confined to the island of Ambon. The situation there is complicated enough in itself. Besides, the problems and causes of violence and riots in the North- and Southeast Moluccas differ from those in the Central Moluccas and require different explanations and perhaps different modes of peace making than Ambon-Lease, which forms a single socio-political region.

Region and Centre

Since Indonesia became independent, the Moluccas have played a special role within the Indonesian state. Attempts to found the independent state of the South Moluccas after Independence have not been forgotten, let alone forgiven. The wish for an independent state was especially strong among Christian Moluccans, who feared the Muslim dominance from Western Indonesia. But it was by no means an entirely Christian dream. Many Muslim leaders backed the struggle for independence. These plans were supported by the Dutch government, who distrusted Sukarno and his political supporters and had been in favour of a Federal Indonesia in the first place. Besides, the Dutch government promised its support for an independent South Moluccan state in recognition of the loyalty of the Moluccan soldiers in its colonial army. When it became clear that the Netherlands would lose the Dutch Indies, it put the majority of the Moluccan section of its army together with their families on transports to the Netherlands, where they should await more peaceful and secure times to return

---

[237] For a similar analysis of 'ethnic conflicts' in the Transcaucasia, see Yamskov 1991.

to the Moluccas. Things turned out differently. The Moluccas did not obtain independence and Indonesia quickly turned into a centralist state and they never did return to the Moluccas. The dream of an independent state was kept alive in the Netherlands for many decades, reaching its summit in the mid seventies, when violent outbursts and train hijacking symbolised the frustration at broken promises by the Dutch government and poor integration in Dutch economy and society. During that whole period, connections with the Moluccas were very infrequent. It was only from the 1980s on that it became possible for Dutch Moluccans to travel to Indonesia and the Moluccas on a regular basis. And it was only then that people started to realise how much had changed, and how far they had grown apart from their relatives on the Moluccas, The political struggle for an independent state was not abandoned, but it lost much of its overall support and rallying power. Instead, people started to think of other ways of supporting their relatives and home communities.

This history was in part Dutch history, a history of a particular migrant community in the Netherlands, but it also remained part of Indonesian history. Despite the fact that the Christian church and the Christian public at large had supported the unitary Indonesian state from the very beginning of the Republic,[238] the Moluccas continued to be regarded as potentially disloyal to the Indonesian state and its unity and therefore needed special control. It was not by chance that Ambon became the most important naval port of Eastern Indonesia, from where it defended its territory towards the Pacific. This way the navy could also keep control over this unruly province. Besides, the navy, together with the civil government, created quite a lot of jobs. Jobs were scarce in that area of the archipelago and the central government hoped it would keep the population satisfied. Of course, it overruled its own policy by reserving the lucrative clove trade for one of Suharto's sons, who had secured for himself a monopoly on the trade and owned one of the largest cigarette factories producing clove cigarettes. Thus, the government took with one hand what it had given with the other: the possibility of making a decent living.

The unrest in Ambon is therefore part of the overall political developments in Indonesia. The struggles for power that started between the new civilian government of President Wahid and the military elites, who are divided amongst themselves, continued under President Megawati. It is reported that disloyal high officers try to create unrest to enhance their position with the help of *preman*, semi-militia and groups of militant youths trained and led by high politicians or military officers, who enter regions of unrest stirring up trouble and violence.[239] While the police is reported to be siding with the Christians and the military with Muslims, the navy stays in contact with both and seems to have had a mitigating effect on the conflicting parties. The reports about armed

---

[238] Bartels 2003
[239] Meuleman 2000: 22

forces who are kindling the fire and support or even send infiltrating militia, refer to the military and the police, not to the navy. The navy has remained remarkably reserved in the present conflict and managed to maintain an independent position among the parties.[240]

These are all part of the general political developments that are going on in Indonesia, with its decentralising policies and the development towards a more federal structure. Different parts of the state apparatus and different political groups have different interests and try to use these local upheavals to their own ends. These ends have only partially to do with regional politics, and are primarily inspired by what is going on in Jakarta, at the centre of power. But they do have a deep impact on the political constellation and the development of the struggles in the region. Unless this struggle at central level cools down, there will be no peace in the region. Whether the new law on decentralisation that allows for more regional autonomy is going to help in this process remains to be seen.

This is also part of a struggle between those who want to establish a nation state based on Islam, and those who are in favour of a secular state. The three presidents Indonesia has had since the demise of the Suharto regime have all strongly supported a secular state that offers room for all religions. However, militant Muslims from Java, belonging to the organisation of *Laskar Jihad,* have entered the Moluccas and call for a *jihad,* in the sense of a religious war. And they propagate a Muslim Indonesian state. Below, we shall come back to the religious factor in the conflict.

The situation escalated so much during the months of May and June 2002 that President Wahid decided to withdraw the Muslim commander of the army and substitute him with a Hindu, who was expected to take a more neutral position than his predecessor. He announced a state of civil emergency on 26 June 2000, on the basis of the Law of National Security.[241] Since May 2000, the situation has worsened, and the army has played a central role in this disintegration. While locally-made weapons were predominantly used in the initial phase, from May 2000, more and more professional weapons were imported into the region. There are strong indications that the army has provided Muslim groups with arms. It certainly has done little to de-escalate the conflict or to contain the import of weapons. Some politicians are calling for intervention by the UN, though it is unclear what such an intervention at this moment could do to reestablish order and peace. In the meantime, several international donor agencies have sent experts in peace making to the region. It is not clear yet whether these attempts have had any success.

---

[240] Manuhutu 2000: 13
[241] *Keputusan President* (Presidential Decree) 88, 26 June 2000. See Jakarta Post, 27 June 2000.

Citizens and Government

One of the greatest problems in the central Moluccas is great dissatisfaction with a failing, corrupt government. It is beyond the scope of this chapter to explain every way in which the government fails. But some factors are specific to the Moluccas, and they deserve to be mentioned here. The Moluccas have no industry of any importance. Economically they depend to a large extent on the production of spices, especially cloves for the cigarette and pharmaceutical industries, and nutmeg. Because of the monopoly in the hands of the inner circle around the former president Suharto, possibilities to sell these spices are very limited. Income from spices has been insecure throughout history, as a result of great fluctuations on the world market and, in addition, as a result of these monopolies. In the middle of the 1980s there was an economic boom in the Moluccas due to high prices and good harvests. Since that time, prices have dropped dramatically and no longer compensate price increases in rice and other basic food products that have to be imported into the region. The economic and monetary crisis has exacerbated the problems. The 1990s were a period of economic stress. The feelings of dejection were enhanced by a civil government that after a long period of expansion for the first time had to cut down. Till then, the government had managed to accommodate the majority of the young high school and university graduates with a good education, but this became increasingly difficult towards the end of the decade. The prospects of these well-educated youths who had completely turned away from the agriculture and horticulture of their parents, had crumbled. Going back to the village and the life of a peasant would mean disillusionment, loss of face and dissatisfaction. Many opted for an equally unsatisfactory attempt to survive in Ambon town on odd jobs. This development increased feelings of resentment towards the government.

The armed forces also no longer offered these youths the prospect of a job. The old ideal, to have at least one child in every family with the armed forces, no longer was a viable option. This increased the criticism on the side of the population, who had until then had a somewhat ambivalent attitude towards the armed forces. Those who had secured the protection of the armed forces because they had close relatives in its service tempered their critique. But those who had no relatives with the military or police voiced their criticism more freely.

There is a general feeling of dejection, and great distrust towards the government and towards 'Jakarta', which does too little for the Moluccas, is capricious and authoritarian and which creams off the profits from the spices through patronage and corruption. Growing youth unemployment especially under the better educated, and a town that is splitting at its seams with a very diverse population highlight these developments. The new regime has not managed to change this. Habibie was still identified with the Suharto regime and did not bring any real change to the situation. Only one thing really changed: it became possible to express one's discontent openly without having to fear the police, and people have done so increasingly and loudly. Under these conditions former President Habibie's attempt at reconciliation was bound to fail. The short visits by President Wahid and by President Megawati were not able to produce any results either, and the present government has not managed to gain the trust of the local population. Much more radical change is needed. The longer the conflict lasts, and the more people die, the longer the process leading to conciliation is going to last. The road from honesty to corruption is a lot shorter than the other way around.

Village against Village

It is remarkable that most reports and debates on the Moluccas conflict do not mention the age-old tensions between neighbouring villages. What is involved is more than ordinary rivalry between neighbours. Three centuries of colonial government and fifty years of centralist Indonesian government have not fully erased pre-colonial structures. The VOC, the Dutch East Indies Company, at the beginning of the seventeenth century forcibly resettled the population that lived in the mountains on the coast, in order to make them easier to control. 'What today are regarded as *adat* structures and *adat* positions, in fact were largely fabricated by the colonial government for these new settlements.'[242] Often, families who under the old structure had occupied little land and a lower position, and now were willing to cooperate with the Dutch and to take the lead in resettling on the coast, were rewarded with more land and leading positions. In this restructuring, the territory was redistributed, leading to disputes over land between neighbouring villages that have lasted until the present. The Dutch seizure of hegemony in the region aborted the fragile political structures that surpassed the village level and that might have been the first steps towards state formation in a region of autonomous villages. From then on *adat* structures were confined to the village level. Beyond that, there was colonial authority and later state authority, but no *adat* authority that could intervene in case of disputes. The colonial literature is full of lamentations of colonial officers whose attempts to settle quarrels and disputes between neighbouring villages remained unsuccessful. They complained about lacking clarity and the impossibility to reach a definitive settlement.

In the course of the nineteenth century Butonese migrants were encouraged to settle in the border regions between villages, and to act as a buffer between the rivalling parties. Below we shall come back to the position of the Butonese to discuss the tensions and conflicts of these migrants with the Am-

---

[242] F. von Benda-Beckmann 1999: 138 ff.

bonese population. Here it is important to note that these old rivalries have continued to exist even today. They are as vicious between neighbouring villages of the same religion as among those of different religions.[243] The quarrels and disputes are largely a result of the confrontation of colonial laws and *adat*, despite the fact that *adat* itself has been deeply affected by the colonial administration. But there are hardly any *adat* procedures and structures beyond the village level that could be called upon to deal with the larger issues we are confronted with today. And that is an immediate inheritance of the Dutch colonial experience.

Christian and Muslim Ambonese

Christianity and Islam came to the Central Moluccas around the same time in the late sixteenth and early seventeenth century. It was a period of great turmoil in the region, during which several trading powers tried to gain control over the profitable spice trade. Islam came from Ternate and Tidore in the Northern Moluccas, who were attempting to expand their hegemony to Ambon, Ceram and further. The Portuguese at first profited from these hegemonic claims, by supporting the local leaders who were in a process of state formation themselves and established themselves as the main traders. When the Portuguese became too greedy, the Dutch saw an opportunity to get rid of their rivals and to take their place as partners in the clove trade. Those who supported the Dutch became Christians, while their rivals, who lived mainly on the north coast of Ambon, opted for Islam, though the old religion was never fully abandoned. Throughout the colonial period this division of the Ambonese population into a Christian and a Muslim section continued to exist.[244] This resulted in a highly skewed access to positions in the colonial administration and colonial education. Upon Independence only children of the *rajas* and other *adat* officials had been able to follow Dutch education in Muslim villages, while Dutch education was far more common in Christian villages. The Indonesian state inherited an administration that was almost exclusively Christian. This advantage continued long after Independence. Only in the 1980s a growing Muslim self-consciousness allowed for pressure, with support from Jakarta, to appoint more Muslims in the provincial administration. From the mid 1980s onwards this policy was strongly implemented. Schulte Nordholt reports that from 1992 onwards members of the Islamic Organisation of Muslim Intellectuals (ICMI) were systematically appointed to all vacant high positions of the provincial ad-

---

[243] Historically, the choice for Christianity or Islam was always made by a whole village. There have been a few cases where the village was split and one half became Christian, while the other opted for Islam. As a result, two villages by the same name were founded, such as Siro Sori Serani (Christian) and Siri Sori Islam.
[244] Chauvel 1990

ministration.[245] But contrary to what Schulte Nordholt seems to suggest, replacement by Muslims had started many years before. This policy created a strong sense of insecurity among Christians, a feeling that was enhanced by reports that 'Christian capital' was disadvantaged in the financial world and was running the risk of being confiscated, while it became increasingly difficult for Christian companies to attract capital. Muslims point out that the new policy was only a long overdue correction to the imbalance that was an artefact of colonial policy. The issue is still very sensitive on both sides and each side reacts passionately to policy changes. President Abdurrahman Wahid was strongly opposed to the replacement policy, but was unable to prevent it. The substitution of Christian civil servants by Muslim has continued under President Megawati.

The conflict here is in part a socio-economic and political conflict over access to profitable positions in the state administration. These positions are all the more profitable because of all the extra income made possible by a corrupt administration. Of the local population only ethnic Ambonese are eligible for a position in the administration. Other local communities are barred due to a common unwillingness on Ambonese side to let them in. In that respect there is great unity between Christian and Muslim Ambonese. To be sure, there are non-Ambonese civil servants, especially in higher positions. They are highly educated people from Java and Sumatra. The divisions run along religious and ethnic lines, each with its own alliances. But while Muslim and Christian Ambonese fight for a position in the administration, members of other ethnic groups hardly make any attempt to do so. They are focused on the private sector, where each ethnic group used to have its own economic niche.

During the year 2000 the conflict among the population groups has changed in character. There are several reasons for this change. In the first place people have started to vent their anger on buildings of worship: mosques and churches have been burnt. Secondly the role of the armed forces has become increasingly problematic. The army reportedly supports and even actively sends agitators from outside to increase religious tension. Whether or not the first churches and mosques were set on fire at the instigation of these agitators is unclear. What has become clear is that *preman,* semi-militia and groups of militant youths have encouraged these actions. With that, the conflict has obtained a new dimension. Setting fire to buildings of worship touches upon the heart of religion because it is a sign that one wants to destroy the religion. This is seen as something fundamentally different from harassing people of another religion. It has led to great frustration, anger and especially to immense fear. It has been an important reason why relatively simple fights have developed into armed conflict. A conflict in which the army and the police are increasingly taking sides, which at the end of June 2000 led the President to force the army to replace the

---

[245] Schulte Nordholt 2000: 36

divisions with other, hopefully more neutral divisions. Several attempts have been made to improve the situation by replacing the leadership.[246] But the army and the police are still accused of taking sides in the conflict and neither has been able to stop violence.

In such a constellation it is hardly suitable to attempt to create peace with a single conciliation mission from Jakarta, as happened in 2000 with the visit of the President and the Vice-President. In order to decrease the mutual fear among Christians and Muslims, several conditions must be met. First and foremost the armed forces have to maintain a neutral position instead of taking sides. They also must stop providing arms to the civilian population. Secondly, the current appointing policy of the government has to be replaced by one based on meritocratic principles, where religion and ethnic background are not relevant features for an appointment. A credible beginning needs to be made to do away with corruption. Meeting each of these conditions on their own is difficult enough. In combination the task is truly formidable.

The question is what legal instruments are available. In principle, state law could provide the measures to deal with these issues. However, the practice of the Indonesian legal system is not promising. The judiciary, itself thoroughly demoralised, poorly salaried and highly corrupt,[247] is, under the present conditions, not capable of redressing the current discriminatory policies. The armed forces are even more problematic. The President, though perhaps in theory having supreme authority, does not seem to have the necessary control over them. This is primarily a political battle the outcome of which is highly uncertain.

Some have suggested that *adat* might play an important part in recreating peace. Possibilities seem rather limited, however, because this problem has to do with a realm of social life where traditionally *adat* had no role to play. There were no viable *adat* institutions to deal with such serious conflicts beyond the village level. Public administration has always been beyond the reach of *adat* and will continue to be that way.

However, there might be a role for *adat* as a symbolic universe to find a way out of violence. In a recent publication, Bubandt has called attention to the force of symbolic discourse as a stimulus for starting and continuing violence.[248] As in the North Moluccas, narratives of violence and of super-human invulnerability have a long tradition on Ambon as well. But it seems that they may not point as unequivocally towards violence between Muslims and Christians as in the North Moluccas. In the Central Moluccas these narratives of violence seem not to have been associated with clashes between Muslims and Christians, but rather with clashes of Muslims and Christians jointly against the colonial oppressor and against the central state. Moreover, as Bartels suggests,

---

[246] Tempo, 10 July 2000; Tempo, 11 July 2000; Antara, 11 July 2000(1)
[247] Bedner 2000
[248] Bubandt 2000: 17

Muslims and Christians share a common religious past.[249] Symbolically, this unity has been represented by the institution of *pela,* old alliances between villages that established ritual blood relationships, also between villages of different religions. Though such alliances are of limited practical value, symbolically they may serve as a possible way out of violence among Muslims and Christians. Since the outburst of violence, Muslims and Christians have forgotten that it was not long ago that they recognised each other's God.[250] Nevertheless the joint religious past and *adat* could symbolically be reactivated and help Muslims and Christians find peace together.

Ambonese and Urban Migrants: Buginese, Macassarese and Torajas

The fight between the taxi driver and the *becak* driver was a fight between an Ambonese and a Buginese. The Ambonese happened to be Christian, while the Buginese was Muslim, but religion in that particular constellation was of marginal importance. Like the conflict mentioned above, this conflict, too, is a socio-economic conflict, but now between an autochthonous population and a group of relatively recent migrants living in a densely populated neighbourhood in Ambon, Batu Merah, where most of the *becak* drivers live. Until violence broke out, Buginese and Macassarese dominated this economic sector, while Muslim and Christian Torajas occupied the furniture sector. Torajas are considered to be less aggressive and threatening. The differences are no less, but they are more moderate and perhaps economically less important.

But in contrast to the conflict between Christian and Muslim Ambonese mentioned above, we are here dealing with a conflict over access to sectors in the private economy, not to government positions and the related patronage-economy. The economic depression certainly has exacerbated the conflict. While in the past the economic sectors in which different ethnic groups dominated were rather sharply separated, the boundaries have recently begun to dissolve because Ambonese have tried to enter into these sectors and claim a dominant position for themselves. Manuhutu points out that Ambonese who until recently looked down upon a *becak* driver, now want to drive one themselves to make a living.[251]

State law can do little here as long as the economic situation remains problematic and as long as the police have little authority and remain corrupt. For this type of conflict in an urban setting, *adat* has little to offer. On the contrary, *adat* enhances some of the conflicts in so far as it gives only Ambonese people a position of full citizenship placing migrants in a subordinate position.

---

[249] Bartels 1978 and 2003
[250] Bartels 2003
[251] Manuhutu 2000: 12

Ambonese and Rural Migrants: Butonese

In rural Ambon there is another ethnic conflict, but this time between Ambonese and Butonese people.[252] Since the second half of the nineteenth century there has been a constant stream of Butonese migrants to the central Moluccas. This migration is spontaneous and has nothing to do with transmigration programs of the government. As mentioned before, these Butonese were welcomed and were assigned a place at the border between neighbouring villages where they acted as a buffer between rivalling village communities. They remained second-rate citizens, which throughout history repeatedly led to violent conflicts. Until the beginning of the 1980s they were prevented from participating in the *raja* elections for the traditional village head who at the same time has the position of mayor in the state administration. But more important was that their second rate position also put them at an economic disadvantage. They were not allowed to own land or trees – especially not the profitable clove and nutmeg trees. An exception was made in the case of land for housing and only for old migrant families. As a result, Butonese people could not participate in the production of the most profitable crops of cloves and nutmeg and could only partake in the profits in sharecropping relationships. During the boom years of clove prices in the 1980s this led to serious disturbances between Ambonese and Butonese inhabitants in dispute over the division of the harvest and trees. The trees had been planted by migrants who thought they would acquire half of the trees as soon as they started to produce. In this conflict several people died, among them a police officer.

Because they were not allowed to own land and trees, many Butonese were forced to grow annual or biannual crops. Many have become successful vegetable growers, while commercial coastal fishing is largely in the hands of Butonese fishermen. When clove prices dropped dramatically in the late 1980s, many Ambonese also turned to growing vegetables. They became dependent on the knowledge and seeds of Butonese experts.

The struggle around the spices also had another economic background. Planting a clove or nutmeg tree, which only starts to produce after at least six years, means a long-term commitment of the land on which the trees stand. The Ambonese feared that planting trees would after some time result in a claim to the land. Ambon a*dat* recognises a division of ownership between the land and what is on the land, but this rule has been contested throughout history. There is an inherent tension between the formal legal division and the economic unity of land and tree ownership. This tension has resulted in violence many times in the past, especially when prices on the world market happened to be high.

---

[252] See F. von Benda-Beckmann and Taale 1992, 1996 and F. and K. von Benda-Beckmann 1999 for a detailed analysis of the relationships between Ambonese and Butonese in Hila, on the north coast of Ambon.

In this constellation of parties within the conflict *adat* appears to be as much part of the problem as a way to solving it. It is not by chance that Butonese people always have called for state law to defend their position. They base their claims on civil rights laid down in state legislation. But in practice things have been different. They have had to submit to the dominant position regarding land and administration, as embedded in *adat*.

Ambonese on Ambon and the Moluccan Community in the Netherlands

As the upheavals on Ambon acquired a more and more religious character, this came as a great shock to the Moluccan community in the Netherlands. For more than forty years they had lived with the idea that relationships between Muslims and Christians were good on the Moluccas. Relations in the Netherlands had been strained in the beginning. Muslims had been tormented so badly during the initial period in which they lived in camps that a Muslim camp had been created. And during the first years in which they had started to live in Moluccan neighbourhoods, there had been fights among Christians and Muslims in Waalwijk and Ridderkerk, where Muslim Moluccans were concentrated. But overall there was the idea that there were no real contradictions and that the religions lived peacefully side-by-side, because of their common pre-Christian and pre-Muslim religion.[253] The fierce battles that have driven Christians and Muslims on the Moluccas apart came as a great surprise and meant an enormous blow to the image they had of themselves. This image had been symbolised by their common ancient religion and by the institute of *pela*. These features were important markers of their ethnic identity. It is clear to most Moluccans in the Netherlands that *pela* is not sufficient to help bring the parties together.[254] What might help, but only as one element in a much larger process of reconciliation, is a reference to the common ancient religion, as a way of emphasising commonality in otherwise diverse religions. This could offer a symbolic support for other and more difficult means necessary to re-establish mutual trust.

Many Dutch Moluccans have lost relatives or friends. And almost everyone has been asked for help by relatives and village members on Ambon, either through relatives or through *kumpulan*, organisations based on common descent from the same village. These requests create grave dilemmas for them. For in as far as support is asked for food, clothing, housing, medical treatment, and rebuilding religious centres, people are eager to help and large amounts of money are sent. But requests for money to buy arms are an entirely different matter. They are faced with the question whether to help relatives defend them-

---

[253] Bartels 1978
[254] Bartels 1978, 1989; Strijbosch 1986; Manuhutu 2000: 11

selves, at the risk of encouraging violence. There is only a minute, but radical minority that is prepared to support armed defence. The large majority is radically against any support for arms. But the pressure is high and heated debates are going on over the question as to what support from the Netherlands could be most effective. There are many initiatives and ideas floating around, but the situation on the Moluccas does not allow for any concrete projects yet.

The Moluccan Historical Museum started an initiative to provide information on Internet and E-mail. At first, the Moluccan community thought that the upheavals were all initiated from outside the Moluccas. They could believe that violence among Christians and Muslims was an external thing. However, it turned out that more was at stake and that the violence had become an internal issue that cannot be fully explained by infiltration. The Dutch Moluccans find it difficult to get a proper insight into what is going on. In part this is due to the internal structure of the conflict itself: the more rigid the religious divide and the more segregated society on Ambon is becoming, the more difficult it is to get reliable information on all sides. The Muslim Moluccan community in the Netherlands is small and by far the most information comes from the side of Christian Moluccans. The Moluccan Historical Museum is doing its utmost to develop initiatives that bind people from both religions together.

Support from the Netherlands is complicated by the historical distrust on the side of the Indonesian government towards the Free South Moluccan movement. This is particularly the case in military circles, though President Wahid did not seem to be much intimidated by this history. Laskar Jihad and other radical Muslim organisations continue to stress that Christians are seeking an independent state. This history does hinder the Dutch community from contributing to reconciliation.

The Moluccan community in the Netherlands is not the only Moluccan migrant community. There are many Moluccan migrants in Jakarta employed in government service and in private companies, well educated and with a high income. They have also organisations that resemble the *kumpulan* in the Netherlands. However, their relationships with Ambon seem to be far less emotionally loaded than those of the Dutch Moluccans. Much material support is provided to relatives, but it is unclear in what way and to what extent there are attempts to de-escalate the conflict.

Youth and Leadership

One of the aspects that have received relatively little attention is that the actual violence is predominantly committed by young, usually unmarried men. In small groups they plan raids, make weapons and go out every time there is a rumour that a mosque or church has been burned down. They operate independently and seem to be living in a restricted awareness where they can only think of the next operation, how to get hold of arms and who or what to attack next. Some speak of 'tunnel vision', typical of such violent groups of young men who increasingly become incapable of thinking about the wider issues involved. Of course there is nothing new to this fact. But there is little known about the social field in which these youth operate. It is not quite clear who these young people are, whether they are largely unemployed, what their level of education is, etc. There are rumours of bandleaders who have gathered groups of youth around them. Some even talk about 'war lords'. However, there is very little inside information and what can be said is necessarily somewhat speculative. Though there are some strong leaders, group formation seems to be very loose and youths seem to operate predominantly in shifting ad hoc associations.

Some of the violence that is occurring now resembles a traditional pattern of violent conflict management. If a close relative is wounded, for instance in a traffic accident, brothers and cousins set out to catch the presumed perpetrator. If they succeed, he will be severely beaten, sometimes even to death, whereupon a counterattack may follow. But if the perpetrator is not immediately caught, violent retaliation will no longer be sought and another mode of conflict regulation takes its place: negotiation and reconciliation by elderly relatives. This form of violence is very common, and the practice of immediate violent reaction is constrained as elderly men and women take over. But in the present violence the social restrictions and constraints that prevent serious escalation of the conflict seem to be failing. Youths still follow more or less classical patterns of immediate violent reactions to real or presumed violence against their relatives. But there are three important differences. The amount and quality of available weapons have raised the violence to a previously unknown level. The military leadership claims that the weapons used by civilians are often of higher quality than the weapons of the army itself. Besides, there seems to have been an extension of the classical pattern in the sense that not only relatives and village members, but also all members of the religious community have to be defended. But rather than having undergone the same extension, traditional constraining mechanisms seem to be rapidly disintegrating. The elderly would not know whom to talk to in order to negotiate a solution and they are totally at loss as to how peace might be re-created.

Conclusions

One of the biggest problems is how to find a way out of violence that is increasing at a frightening speed. The government, being the only structure of authority that surpasses the village level, is too much part of the problems to be an acceptable independent third party. It is very doubtful whether the substitution of the military commanders will be sufficient, though it is an important first step.

Most ideas and attempts to create peace start out from the assumption that the parties should be reconciled in order to establish mutual trust so that they can start building up their society again. But how should one envisage this? The above analysis shows how complex the conflict is, or rather, that what is presented as one conflict in reality is a complex of related conflicts with different constellations and alliances of parties. This complicates the task of identifying the parties that should be re-conciliated. Yet this may turn out to be the easiest part of the problem. Far more problematic is the fact that many attempts hinge on the idea that there is a clear leadership, while in reality there is a striking lack of leadership. As explained before, there are no *adat* structures beyond the village level. Furthermore the religious structures on Ambon make it difficult to find religious leaders with sufficient authority.[255] Islam on Ambon-Lease is virtually exclusively locally organised. In rural areas, mosque functionaries are appointed locally and are intimately tied up in *adat* positions. They have rarely received religious training outside their village, nor do they form part of a wider hierarchy of authority beyond the village.

Christian church organisations show different characteristics. There is a more centralised authority with a synod and pastors have received church-related training. The problem here is that the embedding in *adat* has only partially taken place. Many pastors are considered to be outsiders in villages where they have been appointed, because they usually have not been born there and therefore have no position in *adat*. Though there is clearer religious leadership in Ambon than in the Islamic community, the church structure is also a problematic basis for solving the kind of complex problems we are dealing with here.

This means that all attempts to re-establish the kind of trust necessary to finish violence have to start out from an extremely diffuse social field with many conflicting interests and a complex of conflicts with many and diverse features. Attempts to come up with solutions within a short period of time with a relatively small number of leaders are bound to fail. Far more is needed than the mere promise of greater autonomy. Much time, energy, patience and careful listening to all involved must be invested in order to find modes and procedures that cannot be directly derived from one set of norms, regulations and institutions, be it *adat,* religion, or the state.

Trust has to be built at many levels. An interesting approach has been suggested by a former village head, who, besides trying to set up some overall Ambon projects that explicitly link Muslims and Christians, pleads for an incremental approach, in which neighbouring village leaders, together with groups of young people start discussing and doing things together. Once they

---

[255] F. and K. von Benda-Beckmann 1988, 1993

have built up some trust and common projects, the next village has to be approached to collaborate. What makes the approach interesting is that it is not confined to one single level, but operates at different levels at the same time. In bringing Ambonese Muslims and Christians together again, reactivating their common religious background, symbolised by the institution of *pela* may help, as a powerful symbol of unity, to lead the way out of violence.

Many other laudable initiatives are going on by local and international organisations for peace making. One of the problems is the lack of co-ordination between these projects and initiatives. This again is a feature that shows remarkable persistence throughout history: projects are started but rarely reach a state of permanence and co-ordination that makes them viable over a longer period of time.

Change is needed in so many ways: the civilian government has to make a credible start to banning corruption, so that people can begin to believe that its government and legal system has something valuable to offer. The military has to take a neutral position instead of encouraging unrest and start collecting arms instead of providing the civilian population with arms. People from different religions have to start collaborating in providing help to the dislocated refugees and create forums of common discussion, while the calls and support for *jihad* from Java have to be stopped emphatically. The fact that Laskar Jihad has finally been forced to withdraw from the region is a welcome beginning. Additionally, all initiatives have to take the younger generation seriously, both in binding it into immediate tasks and projects, as well as providing it with prospects for a meaningful existence instead of a future as marginal horticulturists for which young people have not received an education and in which they do not believe. It is indeed a formidable task to establish the beginning of trust that is needed to finish the state of terror. The signs at this moment are not promising. Violence is still rampant, the import and spreading of arms are not under control. And there is still a great distrust in the police and the military and civilian leadership.

References

Abdullah, T. 1966. Adat and Islam: An Examination of Conflict in Minangkabau. *Indonesia* 2: 1-24.
——. 1972. Modernization in the Minangkabau World. In: C. Holt. (ed.), *Culture and Politics in Indonesia*, pp. 179-245. Ithaca: Cornell University Press.
Agarwal, B. 1991. Social Security and the Family: Coping with Seasonality and Calamity in Rural India. In: E. Ahmad, J. Drèze, J. Hills, and A. Sen (eds.), *Social Security in Developing Countries*, pp. 171-244. Oxford: Clarendon Press.
Ahmad, E., J. Drèze, J. Hills, and A. Sen (eds.). 1991. *Social Security in Developing Countries*. Oxford: Clarendon Press.
Al Buny, D. D. 1983. *Problematika Harta dan Zakat*. Surabaya: Bina Ilmu.
Alexander, J., and P. Alexander. 1982. Shared Poverty as Ideology: Agrarian Relationships in Colonial Java. *Man (N.S.)* 17: 597-619.
Alderson-Smith, G. 1984. Confederations of Households: Extended Domestic Enterprises in Cities and Country. In: N. Long, and B. Roberts (eds.), *Miners, Peasants and Entrepreneurs; Regional Development in the Central Highlands of Peru*, pp. 217-234. London and New York: Cambridge University Press.
Anders, G. 2005. *Civil Servants in Malawi: Cultural Dualism, Moonlighting and Corruption in the Shadow of Good Governance*. PhD Thesis. Rotterdam: Erasmus University Rotterdam.
Anon. n.d. *USAID Report on Zakat as a Means of Combating Poverty in Egypt*.
Appadurai, A. 1986. Introduction: Commodities and the Politics of Value. In: A. Appadurai (ed.), *The Social Life of Things*, pp. 3-63. Cambridge: Cambridge University Press.
Arndt, H. W., and R. M. Sundrum. 1979. Civil Service Compensation in Indonesia: A Comment. *BIES* 15: 114-124.
Azer, A. 1988. Dilemmas of Formal and Informal Social Security in Third World Countries: The Case of Egypt. In: F. von Benda-Beckmann, K. von Benda-Beckmann, E. Casiño, F. Hirtz, G. R. Woodman, and H. F. Zacher (eds.), *Between Kinship and the State: Social Security and Law in Developing Countries*, pp. 419-436. Dordrecht: Foris.
Azis, I. J. 1996. Eastern Indonesia in the Current Policy Environment. In: C. Barlow, and J. Hardjono (eds.), *Indonesia Assessment: Development in Eastern Indonesia*, pp. 75-122. Singapore: Institute of Southeast Asian Studies.
Baert, P. J. N. 1989. The Creation of an Invented Future: An Inquiry into G. H. Mead's Relatively-Open Future with Special Reference to Sociological Theory. *International Philosophical Quarterly* 29(3): 319-338.

Bambang Ismawan dan D. E. Susapto (ed.). 1994. *Program IDT: Kelompok Masyarakat dan Pendampingannya.* Jakarta: P.T. Penebar Swadaya.
Bambang Ismawan dan Otok S. Pamuji (ed.). 1994. *LSM dan Program IDT.* Jakarta: P.T. Penebar Swadaya.
Bappenas. 1995. *IDT Program Action-Research.* Yogyakarta: Adiya Media.
Bardhan, P. K. 1988. *The Economic Theory of Agrarian Institutions.* Oxford: Clarendon Press.
Barlow, C., and J. Hardjono (eds.). 1996. *Indonesia Assessment: Development in Eastern Indonesia.* Singapore: Institute of Southeast Asian Studies.
Barraclough, S. L. 1986. National Food Policies in Developing Countries: Research Needs and Priorities. In: A. P. Smits (ed.), *Food Security in Developing Countries*, pp. 11-20. The Hague: RAWOO.
Bartels, D. 1978. *Guarding the Invisible Mountain: Intervillage Alliances, Religious Syncretism and Ethnic Identity among Ambonese Christians and Moslems in the Moluccas.* Ithaca: Cornell University Press.
——. 1989. *Moluccans in Exile. A Struggle for Ethnic Survival. Socialization, Identity Formation, and Emancipation among an East-Indonesian Minority in the Netherlands.* Leiden: Centrum voor Oderzoek naar Maatschappelijke Tegenstellingen.
——. 2003. Your God is no Longer Mine: Moslem-Christian Fratricide in the Central Moluccas (Indonesia) after a Half-Millennium of Tolerant Co-Existence and Ethnic Unity. In: S. Pannell (ed.), *Proceedings of the 5th Maluku Conference*, pp. 128-153. Darwin: NTU Press.
Beck, U. 1988. *Gegengifte. Die organisierte Unverantwortlichkeit.* Frankfurt am Main: Suhrkamp.
Bedner, A. 2000. *Administrative Courts in Indonesia: A Socio-Legal Study.* Leiden: University of Leiden.
Benda-Beckmann, F. von. 1979. *Property in Social Continuity: Continuity and Change in the Maintenance of Property Relationships through Time in Minangkabau, West Sumatra.* The Hague: Martinus Nijhoff.
——. 1986. Leegstaande Luchtkastelen: Over de Pathologie van Grondenrechtshervormingen in Ontwikkelingslanden. In: W. Brussaard, P. de Visser, B. Dam, and G. M. F. Snijders (eds.), *Recht in Ontwikkeling: Tien Agrarisch-Rechtelijke Opstellen*, pp. 91-109. Deventer: Kluwer.
——. 1987. De Ijsjes van de Rechter: Een Verkenning van Complexe Sociale Zekerheidssystemen. *Recht der Werkelijkheid* 1: 69-82.
——. 1988. Islamic Law and Social Security in an Ambonese Village. In: F. von Benda-Beckmann, K. von Benda-Beckmann, E. Casiño, F. Hirtz, G. R. Woodman, and H. F. Zacher (eds.), *Between Kinship and the State: Social Security and Law in Developing Countries*, pp. 339-365. Dordrecht: Foris, Berlin: Walter de Gruyter.
——. 1989. Scapegoat or Magic Charm: Law in Development Theory and Practice. *Journal of Legal Pluralism* 28: 129-148.

——. 1990a. Sago, Law and Food Security on Ambon. In: J. I. H. Bakker (ed.), *Food Security versus Economic Development. The World Food Crisis: Food Security in Comparative Perspective*, pp. 157-199. Toronto, Ontario: Canadian Scholars' Press Inc.

——. 1990b. Ambonese Adat as Jurisprudence of Insurgency and Oppression. In: R. Kuppe, and R. Potz (eds.), *Law and Anthropology, International Yearbook for Legal Anthropology, Volume 5*, pp. 25-42. The Hague, Boston, London: Martinus Nijhoff.

——. 1990c. On Social Units and Relationships. Paper presented at the EIDOS/Erasmus Summer School on Development Sociology and Anthropology, 19-23 June. Amsterdam.

——. 1993a. Recht, Tijd en Maatschappij. In: G. van den Bergh, C. Lorenz, and R. Pieterman (eds.), *Het Recht van de Geschiedenis: Historische Dimensies in Sociaal-Wetenschappelijk Onderzoek van Recht*, pp. 135-160. The Hague: Vuga.

——. 1993b. Le Monopole d'Etat de la Violence dans la Perspective de l'Anthropologie Juridique. In: E. Le Roy, and T. von Trotha (eds.), *La Violence et l'Etat: Formes et Evolution d'un Monopole*, pp. 35-57. Paris: L'Harmattan.

——. 1999. Multiple Legal Constructions of Socio-Economic Spaces: Resource Management and Conflict in the Central Moluccas. In: M. Rösler, and T. Wendl (eds.), *Frontiers and Borderlands: Anthropological Perspectives*, pp. 131-158. Frankfurt am Main, Berlin, Bern, New York, Wien: Lang.

Benda-Beckmann, F. von, and K. von Benda-Beckmann. 1978. Residence in a Minangkabau Nagari. *Indonesia Circle* 15: 6-17.

——, ——. 1984. Recht en Sociale Zekerheid op Ambon. *Nieuwsbrief voor Nederlandstalige Rechtssociologen, Rechtsantropologen en Rechtspsychologen* 5(2): 262-281.

——, ——. 1985. Preliminary Final Report on the Research on Law and Mutual Help and Social Security on Ambon. Hila.

——, ——. 1987a. Verwantschap tussen Dorp en Staat. Paper presented at the 6th Conference on Tropical Asia (KOTA), June 1987. Amsterdam.

——, ——. 1987b. De Testamenten van Hasan Suleiman: Grondenrechtenkwesties op Islamitisch Ambon. *Bijdragen tot de Taal-, Land- en Volkenkunde* 143: 237-266.

——, ——. 1988. Adat and Religion in Minangkabau and Ambon. In: H. J. M. Claessen, and D. S. Moyer (eds.), *Time Past, Time Present, Time Future. Essays in Honour of Professor P. E. de Josselin de Jong*, pp. 195-212. Dordrecht: Foris.

——, ——. 1991. Law in Society: From Blindman's-Bluff to Multilocal Law. *Living Law in the Low Countries.* Special Issue *Recht der Werkelijkheid* 1: 119-139.

——, ——. 1993. Eine turbulente Geschichte im Verhältnis zwischen Religion und Volksrecht: Die Molukker in Indonesien und den Niederlanden. In: W. Krawietz, L. Pospisil, and S. Steinbrich (eds.), *Sprache, Symbole und Symbolverwendungen in Ethnologie, Kulturanthropologie, Religion und Recht. Festschrift für Rüdiger Schott zum 65. Geburtstag*, pp. 141-157. Berlin: Duncker & Humblot.

——, ——. 1994a. Property, Politics, and Conflict: Ambon and Minangkabau Compared. *Law and Society Review* 28(3): 589-607.

——, ——. 1994b. Coping with Insecurity. In: F. von Benda-Beckmann, K. von Benda-Beckmann, and H. Marks (eds.), *Coping with Insecurity: An 'Underall' Perspective on Social Security in the Third World. Special Issue Focaal 22/23*, pp. 7-31. Nijmegen: Focaal.

——, ——. 1995. Rural Populations, Social Security, and Legal Pluralism in the Central Moluccas of Eastern Indonesia. In: J. Dixon, and R. P. Scheurell (eds.), *Social Security Programs: A Cross-Cultural Perspective*, pp. 75-107. Westport: Greenwood.

——, ——. 1998. Where Structures Merge: State and Off-State Involvement in Rural Social Security on Ambon, Eastern Indonesia. In: S. Pannell, and F. von Benda-Beckmann (eds.), *Old World Places, New World Problems: Exploring Resource Management Issues in Eastern Indonesia*, pp. 143-180. Canberra: The Australian National University, Centre for Resource and Environmental Studies, CRES Publications.

——, ——. 1999. A Functional Analysis of Property Rights, with Special Reference to Indonesia. In: T. van Meijl, and F. von Benda-Beckmann (eds.), *Property Rights and Economic Development: Land and Natural Resources in Southeast Asia and Oceania*, pp. 15-56. London, New York: Kegan Paul International.

Benda-Beckmann, F. von, K. von Benda-Beckmann, E. Casiño, F. Hirtz, G. R. Woodman, and H. F. Zacher (eds.). 1988a. *Between Kinship and the State: Social Security and Law in Developing Countries*. Dordrecht: Foris, Berlin: Walter de Gruyter.

Benda-Beckmann, F. von, K. von Benda-Beckmann, B. O. Bryde, and F. Hirtz. 1988b. Introduction: Between Kinship and the State. In: F. von Benda-Beckmann, K. von Benda-Beckmann, E. Casiño, F. Hirtz, G. R. Woodman, and H. F. Zacher (eds.), *Between Kinship and the State: Social Security and Law in Developing Countries*, pp. 7-20. Dordrecht: Foris.

Benda-Beckmann, F. von, A. van Eldijk, J. Spiertz, and F. Huber. 1989. Interface or Janus-Faces: A Critical Assessment of the Interface Approach in Development Sociology from a Socio-Legal Perspective. In: N. Long (ed.), *Encounters at the Interface*, pp. 205-220. Wageningen: Pudoc.

——, and T. Taale. 1992. The Changing Laws of Hospitality: Guest Labourers in the Political Economy of Rural Legal Pluralism. In: F. von Benda-

Beckmann, and M. van der Velde (eds.), *Law as a Resource in Agrarian Struggles*, pp. 61-87. Wageningen: Pudoc.

——, and T. Taale. 1996. Land, Trees, and Houses: Changing (Un)Certainties in Property Relationships on Ambon. In: D. Mearns, and C. Healey (eds.), *Remaking Maluku: Social Transformation in Eastern Indonesia*, pp. 39-63. Darwin: Northern Territory University, Centre for Southeast Asian Studies.

——, R. Kirsch, and J. Freiberg-Strauss. 1997. *The Capacity of Social Security Systems in Southern Africa: Conditions, Constellations and Sociopolitical Relevance*. Eschborn: GTZ.

Benda-Beckmann, K. von. 1984. *The Broken Stairways to Consensus: Village Justice and State Courts in Minangkabau*. Dordrecht, Cinnaminson: Foris, Leiden: KITLV Press.

——. 1987. Overheidskoöperaties als Partikuliere Ondernemingen: Sociale Zekerheid op Islamitisch Ambon. *Recht der Werkelijkheid* 1: 54-68.

——. 1988. Social Security and Small-Scale Enterprises in Islamic Ambon. In: F. von Benda-Beckmann, K. von Benda-Beckmann, E. Casiño, G. R. Woodman, and H. F. Zacher (eds.), *Between Kinship and the State: Social Security and Law in Developing Countries*, pp. 451-472. Dordrecht, Cinnaminson: Foris.

——. 1991a. Developing Families: Moluccan Women and Changing Patterns of Social Security in the Netherlands. In: H. Claessen, M. van den Engel, and D. Plantenga (eds.), *Het Kweekbed Omheind: Opstellen Aangeboden aan Els Postel ter Gelegenheid van haar Afscheid als Hoogleraar*, pp. 35-60. Leiden: Vakgroep Culturele Antropologie en VENA.

——. 1991b. Development, Law and Gender-Skewing: An Examination of the Impact of Development on the Socio-Legal Position of Indonesian Women, with Special Reference to Minangkabau. *Journal of Legal Pluralism* 30/31: 87-120.

——. 1991c. Plural Forms of Social Security in the Central Moluccas, Indonesia. Paper presented at the Conference of the Law and Society Association, Amsterdam, 26-29 June 1991.

——. 1992. Joint Brokerage of Spouses on Islamic Ambon. In: S. van Bemmelen, M. Djajadiningrat-Nieuwenhuis, E. Locher-Scholten, and E. Touwen-Bouwsma (eds.), *Women as Mediators in Indonesia*, pp. 13-32. Leiden: KITLV Press.

——. 1994. Social Security in Developing Countries: A Mixed Blessing. In: M. T. W. Meereboer. *Social (In)Security and Poverty as Global Issues*, pp. 10-26. The Hague: Ministry of Foreign Affairs, Development Information Department.

——. 1996. The Practice of Care: Social Security in Moslem Ambonese Society. In: D. Mearns, and C. Healey (eds.), *Remaking Maluku: Social*

Transformation in Eastern Indonesia, pp. 121-139. Darwin: Northern Territory University, Centre for Southeast Asian Studies.

——. 2000. Recht en Geweld op Ambon. In: H. Elffers (ed.), *Libris Satiari Nequeo. Afscheidsbundel voor Kees Boender. 9 Juni 2000*, pp. 7-20. Rotterdam: Juridische Faculteit EUR.

——, R. Latumahina, and F. Leatemina. 1990. Rapport Positie Molukse Vrouwen in Nederland.

——, and F. Leatemia-Tomatala 1992. *De Emancipatie van Molukse Vrouwen in Nederland*. Utrecht: Jan van Arkel.

Bender, D. R. 1967. A Refinement of the Concept of Household, Families, Coresidence and de jure Hoseholds in Onde. *American Anthropologist* 73: 223-241.

Berg, A. van den. 1994. Land and Marriage: Women's Strategy in the Extreme North of Cameroon. In: F. von Benda-Beckmann, K. von Benda-Beckmann, and H. Marks (eds.), *Coping with Insecurity: An 'Underall' Perspective on Social Security in the Third World. Special Issue Focaal 22/23*, pp. 65-81. Nijmegen: Focaal.

——. 1997. *Land Right-Marriage Left: Women's Management of Insecurity in North Cameroon*. Leiden: CNWS Publications.

Biezeveld, R. 2002. *Between Individualism and Mutual Help: Social Security and Natural Resources in a Minangkabau Village*. Delft: Eburon.

Böcker, A. 1990. Social Security among Turkish Immigrant Families in the Netherlands. Paper presented at the EIDOS/Erasmus Summer School on Development Sociology and Anthropology, 19-23 June 1990. Amsterdam.

——. 1994. *Turkse Migranten en Sociale Zekerheid: Van Onderlinge Zorg naar Overheidszorg?* Amsterdam: Amsterdam University Press.

Boissevain, J. 1969. Patrons as Brokers. *Sociologische Gids* 16: 379-386.

Boland, B. J., and I. Farjon. 1983. *Islam in Indonesia. A Bibliographical Survey*. Dordrecht, Providence: Foris Publications.

Boos, C., L. Geleijnse, R. Muffels, and J. Berghman. 1993. *Omvang van de Sociale Zekerheid. Een Ondezoek naar de Omvang en Samenstelling van Sociale Zekerheidsuitgaven in Nederland 1988 op Basis van een Ruim Begrip van Sociale Zekerheid, Report Nr. 41*. Tilburg: Commissie Onderzoek Sociale Zekerheid.

Bossert, A. 1985. *Traditionelle und moderne Formen sozialer Sicherung in Tanzania*. Berlin: Duncker & Humblot.

Bourdieu, P. 1990. *The Logic of Practice*. Stanford: Stanford University Press.

Bowen, J. R. 1996. On the Political Reconstruction of Tradition: Gotong Royong in Indonesia. *Journal of Asian Studies* XLV(3): 545-559.

——. 2003. *Islam, Law and Equality in Indonesia: An Anthropology of Public Reasoning*. Cambridge: Cambridge University Press.

Breman, J. 1971. Over Oude en Nieuwe Afhankelijkheden. In: *Buiten de Grenzen: Sociologische Opstellen Aangeboden aan Prof. Dr. W. F. Wertheim, 25 Jaar Amsterdams Hoogleraar*. Meppel: Boom.
Brouwer, A. R. 1990. *Science, Social Security and Sago*. Wageningen: Agricultural University of Wageningen.
——. 1996. Natural Resources, Sustainability and Social Security: Simplifying Discourses and the Complexity of Actual Resource Management in a Central Moluccan Village. In: D. Mearns, and C. Healey (eds.), *Remaking Maluku: Social Transformation in Eastern Indonesia*, pp. 64-79. Darwin: Northern Territory University, Centre for Southeast Asian Studies.
——. 1998. From Abundance to Scarcity: Sago, Crippled Modernization and Curtailed Coping. In: S. Pannell, and F. von Benda-Beckmann (eds.), *Old World Places, New World Problems: Exploring Resource Management Issues in Eastern Indonesia*, pp. 336-387. Canberra: The Australian National University, Centre for Resource and Environmental Studies.
Bruijn, M. de. 1994. The Sahelian Crisis and the Poor: The Role of Islam in Social Security among Fulbe Pastoralists, Central Mali. In: F. von Benda-Beckmann, K. von Benda-Beckmann, and H. Marks (eds.), *Coping with Insecurity: An 'Underall' Perspective on Social Security in the Third World. Special Issue Focaal 22/23*, pp. 47-64. Nijmegen: Focaal.
——, and H. van Dijk. 1995. *Arid Ways, Cultural Understandings of Insecurity in Fulbe Society, Central Mali*. Amsterdam: Thela Publishers.
Buchholt, H. 1990. *Kirche, Kopra, Bürokraten: Gesellschaftliche Entwicklung und strategisches Handeln in Nord Sulawesi, Indonesien*. Saarbrücken, Fort Lauderdale: Breitenbach Publishers.
Bubandt, N. 2000. Conspiracy Theories, Apocalyptic Narratives and the Discursive Construction of 'the Violence in Maluku'. *Antropologi Indonesia* 63: 15-32.
Burgess, R., and N. Stern. 1991. Social Security in Developing Countries: What, why, who, and how? In: E. Ahmad, J. Drèze, J. Hills, and A. Sen (eds.), *Social Security in Developing Countries*, pp. 41-80. Oxford: Clarendon Press.
Buysse, F. 1984. *De Zeeuwse Gemeenschap van Holanda, Brazilie 1858-1982: Een Antropologische Studie over Integratie en Identiteit. Bijdragen tot de Geschiedenes van West-Zeeuws-Vlaanderen 13. Heemkundige Kring West-Zewuws-Vlaanderen*. Nijmegen.
Castells, M. 1998. *End of Millenium*. Oxford: Blackwell.
Chauvel, R. 1980. Ambon's other Half: Some Preliminary Observations on Ambonese Moslem Society and History. *Review of Indonesian and Malayan Affairs* 14: 40-80.
——. 1981. Stagnatie, Exodus en Frustratie. *Intermediair* 17(8): 29, 31, 33, 35.

——. 1990. *Nationalists, Soldiers and Separatists: The Ambonese Islands from Colonisation to Revolt 1880 – 1950*. Leiden: KITLV Press.
Chhabra, H. R. 1980. National Strategies for the Provision of Rural Social Security in Developing Countries in Asia. In: ISSA (ed.), *Report of the Asian Regional Round Table Meeting on Social Security of the Rural Population in Developing Countries*. Kuala Lumpur: Social Security Documentation Series No. 5.
Clark, D. H., and M. Oey-Gardiner. 1991. How Indonesian Lecturers Have Adjusted to Civil Service Compensation. *BIES* 27(3): 129-141.
Cohen, M. L. 1976. *House United, House Divided: The Chinese Family in Taiwan*. New York: Columbia University Press.
Commission on Human Security. 2003. *Human Security now*. New York: Commission on Human Security.
Conkling, R. 1979. Authority and Change in the Indonesian Bureaucracy. *American Ethnologist* 6: 543-554.
Conn, S., and S. J. Langdon. 1988. Retribalization as a Strategy for Achievement of Group and Individual Social Security in Alaska Native Villages – with a Special Focus on Subsistence. In: F. von Benda-Beckmann, K. von Benda-Beckmann, E. Casiño, F. Hirtz, G. R. Woodman, and H. F. Zacher (eds.), *Between Kinship and the State: Social Security and Law in Developing Countries*, pp. 437-450. Dordrecht: Foris.
Connolly, P. 1985. The Politics of the Informal Sector: A Critique. In: N. Redclift, and E. Mingione (eds.), *Beyond Employment. Households, Gender and Subsistence*, pp. 55-95. Oxford, New York: Basil Blackwell.
Cooley, F. L. 1961. *Altar and Throne in Central Moluccan Societies: A Study of the Relationship between the Institutions of Religion and the Institutions of Local Government in a Traditional Society Undergoing Rapid Social Change*. New Haven: Yale University, Southeast Asian Studies.
——. 1962. *Ambonese Adat: A General Description*. New Haven: New York University.
——. 1967. Allang: A Village on Ambon Island. In: Koentjaraningrat (ed.), *Villages in Indonesia*, pp. 129-156. New York and Ithaca: Cornell University Press.
Choong Soon Kim. 1988. An Anthropological Perspective on Final Piety versus Social Security. In: F. von Benda-Beckmann, K. von Benda-Beckmann, E. Casiño, F. Hirtz, G. R. Woodman, and H. F. Zacher (eds.), *Between Kinship and the State: Social Security and Law in Developing Countries*, pp. 125-135. Dordrecht: Foris.
Damsté, H. T. 1908. Een 'Reglement voor de Regeling van de Mohammedaansche Kerkelijke Zaken in de Residentie Palembang' uit 1832. *Tijdschrift Binnenlands Bestuur* 34: 213-221.
Dassen, M. H. 1848. *De Nederlanders in de Molukken*. Utrecht: Van Heijningen.

Deinum, H. 1948. Sago. In: C. J. J. van Hall, and C. van de Koppel (eds.), *De Landbouw in de Indische Archipel*, vol. 2, pp. 604-621. The Hague: Van Hoeve.
Departemen Dalam Negeri 1981/1982. *Petunjuk Lapangan Pembinaan Lembaga Ketahanan Masyarakat Desa* (L.K.M.D.).
Department of Social Affairs/ Republic of Indonesia. 1984. *Basic Design for Social Welfare Development*. Jakarta.
Departement Pekerjaan Umum/Direktorat Cipta Karya/Direktorat Tata Kota dan Tata Daerah 1983. *Proyek Pemgembangan Regional Maluku*. Jakarta.
Dijk, H. van. 1994. Livestock Transfers and Social Security in Fulbe Society in the Hayre, Central Mali. In: F. von Benda-Beckmann, K. von Benda-Beckmann, and H. Marks (eds.), *Coping with Insecurity: An 'Underall' Perspective on Social Security in the Third World. Special Issue Focaal 22/23*, pp. 97-112. Nijmegen: Focaal.
Dirkse, J.-P., F. Hüsken, and M. Rutten (eds.). 1993. *Development and Social Welfare: Indonesia's Experiences under the New Order*. Leiden: Royal Institute of Linguistics and Anthropology [VKI 161].
Dobbin, C. 1983. *Islamic Revivalism in a Changing Peasant Economy: Central Sumatra, 1784-1847*. London, Malmö: Curzon Press.
Dove, M. R. 1986. The Ideology of Agricultural Development in Indonesia. In: C. MacAndrews (ed.), *Central Government and Local Development in Indonesia*, pp. 221-247. Singapore: Oxford University Press.
Drèze, J., and A. Sen. 1991. Public Action for Social Security: Foundations and Strategy. In: E. Ahmad, J. Drèze, J. Hills, and A. Sen (eds.), *Social Security in Developing Countries*, pp.1-40. Oxford: Clarendon Press.
Dwyer, D. H., and J. Bruce. 1988. *A Home Divided: Women and Income in the Third World*. Stanford: Stanford University Press.
Effendi, S. 1984. *Hukum Perburuhan di Indonesia: Kumpulan Lengkap Undang-Undang dan Peraturan-Peraturan No. 4*. Jakarta: Ghalia Indonesia.
Eliade, M. 1966. *Kosmos und Geschichte – Der Mythos der ewigen Wiederkehr*. Reinbeck: Rowohlt.
Elias, N. 1982. *Über den Prozess der Zivilisation: Soziogenetische und psychogenetische Untersuchungen*. Frankfurt am Main: Suhrkamp.
Ellen, R. F. 1978. *Nuaulu Settlement and Ecology. An Approach to the Environmental Relations of an Eastern Indonesian Community*. Verhandelingen KITLV 83. The Hague: Martinus Nijhoff.
——. 1979. Sago Subsistence and the Trade in Spices: A Provisional Model of Ecological Succession and Imbalance in Moluccan History. In: P. C. Burnham, and R. F. Ellen (eds.), *Social and Ecological Systems*, pp. 43-74. London and New York: Academic Press.
Ellis, F. 1988. *Peasant Economics: Farm Households and Agrarian Development*. Cambridge: Cambridge University Press.

Elwert, G. 1980a. Die Elemente der traditionellen Solidarität. Eine Fallstudie in Westafrika. *Kölner Zeitschrift für Soziologie und Sozialpsychologie* 32: 681-704.

———. 1980b. Überleben in Krisen, kapitalistische Entwicklung und traditionelle Solidarität: Zur Ökonomie und Sozialstruktur eines westafrikanischen Bauerndorfes. *Zeitschrift für Soziologie* 9(4): 343-365.

———. 1991. Gabe, Reziprozität und Warentausch: Überlegungen zu einigen Ausdrücken und Begriffen. In: E. Berg, J. Lauth, and A. Wimmer (eds.), *Ethnologie im Widerstreit: Kontroversen über Macht, Geschäft, Geschlecht in fremden Kulturen. Festschrift für Lorenz G. Löffler*, pp. 159-177. München: Trickster Verlag.

Emrich, K. R. 1982. *Review of Social Development in the ESCAP Region: Emerging Trends and Perspectives*, pp. 1-33. Bangkok: ESCAP.

ESCAP 1985. *Poverty, Productivity and Participation: Contours of an Alternative Strategy for Poverty Eradication.* Bangkok.

Esmara, H., and P. Tjiptoherijanto. 1986. The Social Security System in Indonesia. *ASEAN Economic Bulletin* 3(July 1986): 53-69.

Evers, H.-D., W. Clauss, and D. Wong. 1984. Subsistence Reproduction. A Framework for Analysis. In: J. Smith, I. Wallerstein, and H.-D. Evers (eds.), *Households and the World-Economy*, pp. 23-36. Beverly Hills, London, New Delhi: Sage.

———, and T. Schiel. 1988. *Strategische Gruppen: Vergleichende Studien zu Staat, Bürokratie und Klassenbildung in der Dritten Welt.* Berlin: Reimer.

Fabian, J. 1983. *Time and the Other: How Anthropology Makes its Object.* New York: Columbia University Press.

Fapohunda, E. 1988. The Nonpooling Household: A Challenge to Theory. In: D. Dwyer, and J. Bruce (eds.), *A Home Divided: Women and Income in the Third World*, pp. 143-154. Stanford: Stanford University Press.

Ferman, L. A., S. Henry, and M. Hoyman. 1987. Issues and Prospects for the Study of Informal Economies: Concepts, Research Strategies and Policy. *Annals of AAPSS* 493(1): 154-172.

Field, M. J. 1960. *Search for Security: An Ethno-Psychiatric Study of Rural Ghana.* New York: Norton.

Finch, J. 1989. *Family Obligations and Social Change.* Cambridge: Polity Press.

Flach, M. 1983. *The Sago Palm: The Domestication of the Sago Palm. The Exploitation of Sago Forests, and Sago Palm Products Technology. A Development Paper.* Rome: FAO.

———, and H. A. Luning. 1983. *LTA-72: Maluku Development Project: Final Report of a Technical Mission on Agricultural Research an Extension Aspects.* Wageningen.

Folbre, N. 1988. The Black Four of Hearts: Toward a New Paradigm of Household Economics. In: D. Dwyer, and J. Bruce (eds.), *A Home Divided: Women and Income in the Third World*, pp. 248-262. Stanford: Stanford University Press.
Fraassen, C. F. van. 1972. *Ambon-Rapport*. Leiden: Stichting Werkgroep Studiereizen Ontwikkelingslanden.
Freiberg-Strauss, J., and D. Jung. 1988. Social Security in the Peasant Society of Boyacá, Columbia. In: F. von Benda-Beckmann, K. von Benda-Beckmann, E. Casiño, F. Hirtz, G. R. Woodman, and H. F. Zacher (eds.), *Between Kinship and the State: Social Security and Law in Developing Countries*, pp. 229-267. Dordrecht: Foris.
——, and K. Meyer (eds.). 1999. *The Real World of Social Policy*. Eschborn: GTZ.
Fuchs, M. 1985. *Soziale Sicherheit in der Dritten Welt – Zugleich eine Fallstudie Kenia*. Baden-Baden: Nomos.
——. 1988. Social Security in Third World Countries. In: F. von Benda-Beckmann, K. von Benda-Beckmann, E. Casiño, F. Hirtz, G. R. Woodman, and H. F. Zacher (eds.), *Between Kinship and the State: Social Security and Law in Developing Countries*, pp. 39-51. Dordrecht: Foris.
Getubig, I. P. 1992. Social Security and the Poor. In: I. P. Getubig, and S. Schmidt (eds.), *Rethinking Social Security: Reaching out to the Poor*, pp. 1-17. Kuala Lumpur: APDC, Eschborn: GTZ.
——, and S. Schmidt (eds.). 1992. *Rethinking Social Security: Reaching out to the Poor*. Kuala Lumpur: APDC, Eschborn: GTZ.
Giddens, A. 1981. *A Contemporary Critique of Historical Materialism*. London: Macmillan.
——. 1984. *The Constitution of Society*. Oxford: Polity Press.
——. 1985. *The Nation State and Violence*. Cambridge: Polity Press.
——. 1991. *Modernity and Self-Identity*. Oxford: Polity Press.
Gilbert, N. 1976. Alternative Forms of Social Protection for Developing Countries. *Social Service Review* 50(3): 363-387.
Ginneken, W. van. 2003 *Extending Social Security: Policy for Developing Countries. ESS Paper No. 13*. Geneva: International Labour Office, Social Security and Development Branch.
Glick Schiller, N. 2002. Transborder Citizenship: Legal Pluralism within a Transnational Social Field. Paper presented at the Workshop on Mobile People, Mobile Law: Expanding Legal Relations in a Contracting World, Max Planck Institute for Social Anthropology, Halle/Saale, Germany, 7-9 November 2002.
Goldschmidt, W. 1966. *Comparative Functionalism*. Berkeley: University of California Press.

Goodall, K. 1990. 'Public and Private' in Legal Debate. *International Journal of the Sociology of Law* 18: 445-458.

Goody, J. 1986. *The Logic of Writing and the Organization of Society.* Cambridge: Cambridge University Press.

Gray, C. 1979. Civil Service Compensation in Indonesia. *BIES* 15: 85-113.

Guyer, J. I. 1988. Dynamic Approaches to Domestic Budgeting: Cases and Methods from Africa. In: D. Dwyer, and J. Bruce (eds.), *A Home Divided: Women and Income in the Third World*, pp. 155-172. Stanford: Stanford University.

———, and P. Peters. 1987. Conceptualizing the Household: Issues of Theory and Policy in Africa. *Development & Change* 18(2): 197-213.

Hansen, G. E. 1973. *The Politics and Administration of Rural Development in Indonesia*. Berkeley: University of California, Center for South and Southeast Asian Studies.

Hardjono, J. 1983. Rural Development in Indonesia: The Top-Down Approach. In: D. A. M. Lea, and D. P. Chauduri (eds.), *Rural Development and State: Contradictions and Dilemmas in Developing Countries*, pp. 38-65. London: Methuen.

Hassan, F. 1981. *The Concept of State and Law in Islam*. Lanham: University Press of America.

Held, D. 1989. *Political Theory and the Modern State.* Oxford: Polity Press.

Hirtz, F. 1989. *Managing Insecurity: State Social Policy and Family Networks in the Rural Philippines, Past and Present.* Bielefeld: University of Bielefeld.

———. 1994. Issues and Authors in the Field of Social Security in the Third World. In: F. von Benda-Beckmann, K. von Benda-Beckmann, and H. Marks (eds.), *Coping with Insecurity: An 'Underall' Perspective on Social Security in the Third World. Special Issue Focaal 22/23*, pp. 231-236. Nijmegen: Focaal.

———. 1995. *Managing Insecurity: State Social Policy and Family Networks in the Rural Philippines.* Saarbrücken: Verlag für Entwicklungspolitik.

Hoëvell, G. W. W. C. Baron van. 1875. *Ambon en Meer Bepaaldelijk de Oeliassers*. Dordrecht: Van Blussee and Van Braam.

Holleman, F. D. 1923. *Het Adat-Grondenrecht van Ambon en de Oeliasers*. Delft: Molukken Instituut.

Hooker, M. B. (ed.). 1983. *Islam in South-East Asia.* Leiden: Brill.

Hospes, O. 1996. *People that Count. Changing Savings and Credit Practices in Ambon, Indonesia.* Amsterdam: Thesis Publishers.

Hüsken, F. 1989. *Een Dorp op Java: Sociale Differentiatie in een Boerengemeenschap, 1850-1950.* Amsterdam: ACASEA.

———, and J. Koning. 2006. Between two Worlds: Social Security in Indonesia. In: F. Hüsken, and J. Koning (eds.), *Ropewalking and Safety Nets: Lo-*

cal Ways of Meaning – Inseciruties in Indonesia, pp. 1-26. Leiden, Boston: Brill.

ILO 1984. *Introduction to Social Security*. Geneva: International Labour Office.

———. 1985. *Report to the Government of Indonesia on the Planning and Administration of Social Security: Project Findings and Recommendations*. Geneva: International Labour Office.

Joenoes, M. 1982. *Reading in Social Security: The Indonesian Case*. Jakarta.

Johnson, N. 1987. *The Welfare State in Transition: The Theory and Practice of Welfare Pluralism*. Brighton: Wheatsheaf Books.

Jong, W. de, C. Roth, F. Badini-Kinda, and S. Bhagyanath. 2005. *Ageing in Insecurity: Case Studies of Social Security and Gender in India and Burkina Faso*. Münster: LIT Verlag.

Junus, U. 1966. The Payment of Zakat al-Fitrah in a Minangkabau Community. *BKI* 122: 447-454.

Juynboll, T. W. 1925. *Handleiding tot de Kennis van de Mohammedaansche Wet volgens de Leer der Sjâfi'itische School*, 3rd edn. Leiden: Brill.

Kaesberry, I. 2002. Elder Care, Old-Age Security and Social Change in Rural Yogyakarta, Indonesia. PhD Thesis, Agricultural University of Wageningen.

Kanbur, R. 1987. The Standard of Living: Uncertainty, Inequality and Opportunity. In: G. Hawthorn (ed.), *The Standard of Living*, pp. 59-69. Cambridge: Cambridge University Press.

Kaufmann, F.-X. 1973. *Sicherheit als soziologisches und sozialpolitisches Problem*. Stuttgart: Enke.

Kennedy, R. 1955. *Fieldnotes on Indonesia: Ambon and Ceram, 1949-1950*. New Haven: HRAF.

Kloek, E. 1981. *Gezinshistorici over Vrouwen; een Overzicht van het Werk van Gezinshistorici en de Betekenis daarvan voor de Vrouwengeschiedenis*. Amsterdam: Sua.

Knaap, G. J. 1981a. De Komst van de Kruidnagel. *Intermediair* 17(5): 23, 25, 27, 45.

———. 1981b. Monopolie en Monocultuur. *Intermediair* 17(6): 45, 49, 51.

———. 1987a. *Kruidnagelen en Christenen: De Verenigde Oost-Indische Compagnie en de Bevolking van Ambon 1656-1696*. Dordrecht: Foris.

———. (ed.). 1987b. *Memoires van Overgave van Gouverneurs van Ambon in de Zeventiende an Achttiende Eeuw*. Bewerkt door G. J. Knaap. The Hague: Martinus Nijhoff.

Knorr-Cetina, K. D. 1988. The Micro-Social Order: Towards a Reconception. In: N. G. Fielding (ed.), *Actions and Structure: Research Method in Social Theory*, pp. 21-53. London: Sage.

Köhler, P. A. 1977. Entstehung der Sozialversicherung: Ein Zwischenbericht. In: H. F. Zacher (ed.), *Bedingungen für die Entstehung und Entwicklung von Sozialversicherung*, pp. 19-88. Berlin: Duncker & Humblot.

Koninck, R. de. 1983. Getting them to Work Profitably: How the Small Peasants Help the Large Ones, the State and Capital. *Bulletin of Concerned Asian Scholars* 15: 32-41.
Koning, J. 2006. Fishermen and Farmers: Entrepreneurs in Risks, Resources and Resource-Risks? In: J. Koning, and F. Hüsken (eds.), *Ropewalking and Safety Nets: Local Ways of Managing Insecurities in Indonesia*, pp. 147-173. Leiden, Boston: Brill.
——, and F. Hüsken (eds.) 2006. *Ropewalking and Safety Nets: Local Ways of Managing Insecurities in Indonesia.* Leiden, Boston: Brill.
Kopytoff, I. 1986. The Cultural Biography of Things: Commoditization as Process. In: A. Appadurai (ed.), *The Social Life of Things*, pp. 64-91. Cambridge: Cambridge University Press.
Krause-Katerla, H.-J. 1986. *Die Gewürznelkenproduktion auf den Molukken: Soziale Auswirkungen langfristiger Weltmarktintegration.* Bielefeld: University of Bielefeld.
Leach, E. R. 1961. *Rethinking Anthropology.* London: The Athlone Press.
Leirissa, R. Z., Z. J. Manusama, A. B. Lapian, and P. R. Abdurrachman (eds.). 1982. *Maluku Tengah di Masa Lampau: Gambaran Sekilas Lewat Arsip Abad Sembilan Belas.* Jakarta: Arsip Nasional.
Leliveld, A. 1994. The Impact of Labour Migration on the Swazi Rural Homestead as Solidarity Group. In: F. von Benda-Beckmann, K. von Benda-Beckmann, and H. Marks (eds.), *Coping with Insecurity: An 'Underall' Perspective on Social Security in the Third World. Special Issue Focaal 22/23*, pp. 177-197. Nijmegen: Focaal.
Lev, D. S. 1972. *Islamic Courts in Indonesia: A Study in the Political Bases on Legal Institutions.* Berkeley, Los Angeles: University of California Press.
Lipsky, M. 1980. *Street-Level Bureaucracy: Dilemmas of the Individual in Public Services.* New York: Russell Sage Foundation.
Long, N. (ed.). 1989. *Encounters at the Interface.* Wageningen: Pudoc.
Lont, H. 1999. Mutual Associations and the Indonesian Monetary Crisis: Crisis and Stability. Paper presented at the Conference on Crises in the World, Crises in Understanding. Fredericton, New Brunswick.
——. 2002. Juggling Money in Yogyakarta. Financial Self-Help Organisations and the Quest for Security. Thesis. University of Amsterdam
——. 2006. Managing Money: Urban Self-Help Organisations in Yogyakarta. In: J. Koning, and F. Hüsken (eds.), *Ropewaling and Safety Nets: Local Ways of Managing Insecurities in Indonesia*, pp. 125-146. Leiden, Boston: Brill.
LTA 72. 1983. *Draft Development Framework for the Moluccan Province.* Ambon.
Lundström-Burghoorn, W. 1981. *Minahasa Civilization: A Tradition of Change.* Göteborg: Acta Universitatis Gothoburgensis.

MacAndrews, C. 1986a. Central Government and Local Development in Indonesia. An Overview. In: C. MacAndrews (ed.), *Central Government and Local Development in Indonesia*, pp. 6-19. Singapore, Oxford, New York: Oxford University Press.

——. 1986b. The Structure of Government in Indonesia. In: C. MacAndrews (ed.), *Central Government and Local Development in Indonesia*, pp. 20-41. Singapore, Oxford, New York: Oxford University Press.

Macarov, D. 1980. *Work and Welfare: The Unholy Alliance*. London: Sage.

MacPherson, S., and J. Midgley. 1987. *Comparative Social Policy and the Third World*. New York: St. Martin's Press.

Manuhutu, W. 2000. Een Jaar Geweld op de Molukken: Een Terugblik. In: W. Manuhutu, J. H. Meuleman, H. G. Schulte Nordholt, and J. Willemse (eds.), *Maluku Manis, Maluku Menangis: De Molukken in Crisis*, pp. 7-17. Utrecht: Moluks Historisch Museum.

Manusama, Z. J. 1977. *Hikayat Tanah Hitu*. Leiden: Leiden University.

Marianti, R. 2002. Surviving Spouses. Support for Widows in Malang, East Java. Thesis. University of Amsterdam.

——. 2006. Precarious Safety Nets: Family Support for Widows in Malang. In: J. Koning, and F. Hüsken (eds.), *Ropewalking and Safety Nets: Local Ways of Meaning – Insecirities in Indonesia*, pp. 79-105. Leiden, Boston: Brill.

Marks, H. 2000. *Knechten Knechten: De Ervaring en Verbeelding van Sociale Ongelijkheid in de Baksteenindustrie, 1920-1970*. Deventer: Gouda Quint.

Marris, P. 1968-69. The Social Barriers of African Entrepreneurship. *Journal of Development Studies* 5: 29-38.

Mboi, B. 1996. The Socio-Economic Development in Eastern Indonesia. In: C. Barlow, and J. Hardjono (eds.), *The Role of Government. Indonesia Assessment: Development in Eastern Indonesia*, pp. 123-140. Singapore: Institute of Southeast Asian Studies.

McGillivray, W. R. 1980. Observations on the Provision of Social Security to Rural Workers and their Dependants. In: ISAA (ed.), *Report of the Asian Regional Round Table Meeting on Social Security of the Rural Population in Developing Countries*. Kuala Lumpur: Social Security Documentation Series No. 5.

McLeod, R. H. 1993. Workers' Social Security in Indonesia. In: C. Manning, and J. Hardjono (eds.), *Indonesia Assessment 1993. Labour: Sharing in the Benefits of Growth?* Singapore, Canberra: Australian National University, Institute of Southeast Asian Studies.

Melossi, D. 1990. *The State of Social Control*. Cambridge: Polity Press.

Mesa-Lago, C. 1978. *Social Security in Latin America: Pressure Groups, Stratification and Inequality*. Pittsburgh: University of Pittsburgh Press.

———. 1991. Social Security in Latin America and the Caribbean: A Comparative Assessment. In: E. Ahmad, J. Drèze, J. Hills, and A. Sen (eds.), *Social Security in Developing Countries*, pp. 356-394. Oxford: Clarendon Press.

Meuleman, J. H. 2000. Islam in het Hedendaagse Indonesië. In: W. Manuhutu, J. H. Meuleman, H. G. Schulte Nordholt, and J. Willemse (eds.), *Maluku Manis, Maluku Menangis: De Molukken in Crisis*, pp. 19-27. Utrecht: Moluks Historisch Museum.

Midgley, J. 1984. *Social Security, Inequality, and the Third World*. Chichester: John Wiley & Sons.

———. 1994. Social Security Policy in Developing Countries: Integrating State and Traditional Systems. In: F. von Benda-Beckmann, K. von Benda-Beckmann, and H. Marks (eds.), *Coping with Insecurity: An 'Underall' Perspective on Social Security in the Third World. Special Issue Focaal 22/23*, pp. 219-229. Nijmegen: Focaal.

———, and E. Kaseke. 1996. Challenges to Social Security in Developing Countries: Coverage and Poverty in Zimbabwe. In: J. Midgley, and M. B. Tracy (eds.), *Challenges to Social Security: An International Exploration*, pp. 103-122. Westport, Conn., London: Auburn House.

———, and M. B. Tracy (eds.). 1996. *Challenges to Social Security: An International Exploration*. Westport, Conn., London: Auburn House.

———, and M. Sherraden (eds.). 1997. *Alternatives to Social Security: An International Inquiry*. Westport-London: Auburn House.

Moore, S. F. 1973. Law and Social Change: The Semi-Autonomous Social Field as an Appropriate Subject of Study. *Law & Society Review* 7(4): 719-746.

———. 1978a. *Law as Process: An Anthropological Approach*. London: Routledge and Kegan Paul.

———. 1978b. Uncertainties in Situations, Indeterminacies in Culture. In: S. F. Moore (ed.), *Law as Process: An Anthropological Approach*, pp. 32-53. London: Routledge and Kegan Paul.

———. 1994. Law in Unstable Settings: The Dilemma of Migration. In: F. von Benda-Beckmann, K. von Benda-Beckmann, and H. Marks (eds.), *Coping with Insecurity: An 'Underall' Perspective on Social Security in the Third World. Special Issue Focaal 22/23*, pp. 141-152. Nijmegen: Focaal.

Morfit, M. 1986. Strengthening the Capacities of Local Government: Policies and Constraints. In: C. MacAndrews (ed.), *Central Government and Local Development in Indonesia*, pp. 56-76. Singapore: Oxford University Press.

Morse, B. W., and G. R. Woodman (eds.). 1988. *Indigenous Law and the State*. Dordrecht: Foris, Berlin: Walter de Gruyter.

Mouton, P. 1975. *Social Security in Africa: Trends, Problems and Prospects*. Geneva: ILO.
Mubyarto. 1994. *Profil Desa Tertinggal Indonesia 1994*. Yogyakarta: Adiya Media.
Mulder, K. 1987. Reserve-Arbeid in een Reserve-Kolonie: Immigratie en Kolonisatie van de Javanen in Suriname 1890-1950. Unpublished Master Thesis, Rotterdam: Erasmus University Rotterdam.
——. 1994. The Javanese Celebrations in Surinam: Social Security through an Alliance of Costs and Culture. In: F. von Benda-Beckmann, K. von Benda-Beckmann and H. Marks (eds.), *Coping with Insecurity: An 'Underall' Perspective on Social Security in the Third World. Special Issue Focaal 22/23*, pp. 113-138. Nijmegen: Focaal.
Nader, L. 1969. Introduction. In: L. Nader (ed.), *Law in Culture and Society*, pp. 1-11.Chicago: Aldine.
NEI (Nederlandsch Ekonomisch Instituut) 1982. *Maluku Regional Development Framework (Provisional)*. Ambon and Rotterdam.
Ngwira, A. 1995. An Appraisal of Social Security in Rural Food Security: A Case of Central Malawi. Unpublished contribution to the 1995 GTZ Conference on The Capacity of Social Security Systems in Southern Africa.
Niehof, A. 1985. Women and Fertility in Madura. PhD Thesis, University of Leiden.
——. 1994. Het Duveltje uit de Zwarte Doos: De Ongemakkelijke Relatie tussen Gender en Huishouden. Inaugural Lecture. Wageningen: Agricultural University of Wageningen.
Nooteboom, G. 1999. Buruh Patik Jadi Boss, Pak Sutip Jadi Buruh. Indonesia in Crisis. A Tale of two Families, Patron-Client relations and Social Security. Paper presented at the Conference on the Crisis in Indonesia. Berg en Dal, Nijmegen.
Oosterwijk, M. 1994. Review on Anita Böcker, Turkse Migranten en Sociale Zekerheid: Van Onderlinge Zorg naar Overheidszorg. Amsterdam: University Press, 1994. In: F. von Benda-Beckmann, K. von Benda-Beckmann, and H. Marks (eds.), *Coping with Insecurity: An 'Underall' Perspective on Social Security in the Third World. Special Issue Focaal 22/23*, pp. 238-239. Nijmegen: Focaal.
Paassen, A. van. 1987. *Sociale Zekerheid: Recht op Bestaan in Tulehu*. Wageningen: Agricultural University of Wageningen.
Pahl, R. E. 1984. *Divisions of Labour*. Oxford: Basic Blackwell.
Palmer, I. 1978. *The Indonesian Economy since 1965: A Case Study of Political Economy*. London: Frank Cass.
Palriwala, R., and C. Risseeuw (eds.). 1996. *Shifting Circles of Support: Contextualising Kinship and Gender in South Asia and Sub-Saharan Africa*. Delhi, London: Sage Publications.

Parkin, D. J. 1972. *Palms, Wine and Witnesses: Public Spirit and Private Gain in an African Farming Community*. London: Intertext Books.
Partsch, M. 1983. *Prinzipien und Formen sozialer Sicherung in nichtindustriellen Gesellschaften*. Berlin: Duncker & Humblot.
Paulus, J., D. G. Stibbe, and S. de Graaff (eds.). 1917-1939. *Encyclopedie van Nederlandsch Indië*. Leiden: Brill.
Pearse, A. 1980. *Seeds of Plenty – Seeds of Want*. Oxford: Clarendon Press.
Pengadilan Tinggi Maluku 1981. *Pembinaan Hukum/Yurisprudensi di Maluku, Tahun 1978-1979*. Buku III, Perdata. Hasil Kerjasama Pengadilan Tinggi Maluku Dengan Fakultas Hukum Universitas Pattimura. Ambon: Percetakan Negara R.I.
Pine, F., and H. Haukanes. 2005. Introduction. In: F. Pine, and H. Haukanes (eds.), *Generations, Kinship and Care: Gendered Provisions of Social Security in Central Eastern Europe*, pp. 1-22. Bergen: University of Bergen.
Platteau, J.-P. 1991. Traditional Systems of Social Security and Hunger Insurance: Past Achievements and Modern Challenges. In: E. Ahmad, J. Drèze, J. Hills, and A. Sen (eds.), *Social Security in Developing Countries*, pp. 112-170. Oxford: Clarendon Press.
Poensen, C. 1874. Djakat en Pitrah. *Mededelingen van het Nederlandschzendingsgenootschap* 18: 1-16.
Polanyi, K. 1966. *Dahomey and the Slave Trade*. Seattle: University of Washington Press.
Pollmann, T., J. Seleky, and B. Nienhuis. 1982. *Terug op de Molukken*. Amsterdam: Uitgeverij de Arbeiderspers.
Polman, K. 1983. *The Central Moluccas. An Annotated Bibliography*. Dordrecht: Foris.
Popkin, S. L. 1979. *The Rational Peasant*. Berkeley: University of California Press.
Prawotosoediro, P. 1982. *Pegawai Negeri Sipil*. Jakarta: Pradnya Paramita.
Quarles van Ufford, P. (ed.). 1987. *Local Leadership and Programme Implementation in Indonesia*. Amsterdam: Free University Press.
Radwan, S. 1994. Outlook on Employment and Poverty: Challenges and Scope for Employment-intensive Growth Strategy. In: M.-T. W. Meereboer (ed.), *Social (In)security and Poverty as Social Issues. Pre-conference Reader*. Conference in preparation of the UN World Summit on Social Development, Copenhagen, pp. 42-81. The Hague: Development Cooperation Information Department.
Ravallion, M. 1988. Inpres and Inequality: A Distributional Perspective on the Centre's Regional Disbursements. *BIES* 24(3): 53.
Read, R., and T. Thelen. 2007 (in print). Social Security and Care after Socialism: Reconfigurations of Public and Private. *Focaal* 2007(2).

Redclift, N., and E. Mingione (eds.). 1985. *Beyond Unemployment: Households, Gender and Subsistence.* Oxford: Basil Blackwell.

Redmond, G., and S. Hutton. 2000. Poverty in Transition Economies: An Introduction to the Issues. In: S. Hutton, and G. Redmond (eds.), *Poverty in Transition*, pp. 1-13. London, New York: Routledge.

Reidy, E. 1980. Welfarists and the Market: A Study of the Self-Employment Assistance Programme in the Philippines. *Development & Change* 11: 297-312.

Risseeuw, C. 1980. *The Wrong End of the Rope: Women Coir Workers in Sri Lanka.* Colombo, Leiden: Research Project Women and Development.

Risseeuw, C., and K. Ganesh (eds.). 1998. *Negotiation and Social Space: A Gendered Analysis of Changing Kin and Security Networks in South Asia and Sub-Saharan Africa.* New Delhi: Sage Publications.

Robison, R. J. 1982. The Transformation of State in Indonesia. *Bulletin of Concerned Asian Scholars* 14: 48-60.

——. 1986. *Indonesia: The Rise of Capital.* Sidney: Allen and Unwin.

Rodman, W. L. 1983. Gaps, Bridges and Levels of Law: Middlemen as Mediators in a Vanuatu Society. In: W. L. Rodman, and D. A. Counts (eds.), *Middlemen and Brokers in Oceania*, pp. 69-96. Lanham, New York, London: University Press of America.

Rohregger, B. A. 2006. *Shifting Boundaries. Social Security in the Urban Fringe of Lilongwe City, Malawi.* Aachen: Shaker Verlag.

Rose, N. 1987. Beyond the Public/Private Division: Law, Power and the Family. *Journal of Law and Society* 14(1): 61-76.

Rose, R. 1989. *Ordinary People in Public Office: A Behavioural Analysis.* London: Sage.

Rosenthal. E. 1965. *Islam in the Modern National State.* Cambridge: Cambridge University Press.

Ruinen, W. 1921. Sagopalmen en Hunne Beteekenis voor de Molukken. *Adatrechtbundel* 24: 235-243.

Rumphius, G. E. 1910. De Ambonsche Historie (deel 1 en 2), *BKI* 64.

Sahlins, M. 1974a. *Stone Age Economics.* London: Tavistock.

——. 1974b. On the Sociology of Primitive Exchange. In: M. Sahlins (ed.), *Stone-Age Economics*, pp. 185-275. London: Tavistock.

Sahri, M. 1982. *Pengembangan Zakat & Infak Dalam Usaha Meningkatkan Kesejahteraan Masyarakat.* Malang: Avecina.

Savy, R. 1972. *Social Security in Agriculture.* Geneva: ILO.

Schmidt, S. 1992. Social Security in Developing Countries. Basis Tenets and Fields of State Intervention. In: I. P. Getubig, and S. Schmidt (eds.), *Rethinking Social Security: Reaching out to the Poor*, pp. 18-40. Kuala Lumpur and Eschborn: APDC and GTZ.

Schott, R. 1988. Traditional Systems of Social Security and their Present-Day Crisis in West Africa. In: F. von Benda-Beckmann, K. von Benda-

Beckmann, E. Casiño, F. Hirtz, G. R. Woodman, and H. F. Zacher (eds.), *Between Kinship and the State: Social Security and Law in Developing Countries*, pp. 89-107. Dordrecht: Foris.
Schrijvers, J. 1985. *Mothers for Life: Motherhood and Marginalization in the North Central Province of Sri Lanka*. Delft: Eburon.
Schulte Nordholt, H. G. 1985. Het Transformatieproces in Indonesie in een Crisis. *Internationale Spectator* 24: 355-363.
——. 2000. De Molukken als Oefenterrein voor de Machsstrijd in Jakarta. In: W. Manuhutu, J. H. Meuleman, H. G. Schulte Nordholt, and J. Willemse (eds.), *Maluku Manis, Maluku Menangis: De Molukken in Crisis*, pp. 33-44. Utrecht: Moluks Historisch Museum.
Schwitters, R. J. S. 1991. Riskante Aansprakelijkheid. *Recht en Kritiek* 17(1): 5-39.
Scott, J. C. 1972. The Erosion of Patron-Client Bonds and Social Change in Rural South East Asia. *Journal of Asian Studies* 32: 5-37.
——. 1976. *The Moral Economy of the Peasant: Rebellion and Subsistence in Southeast Asia*. New Haven and London: Yale University Press.
——. 1985. *Weapons of the Weak: Everyday Forms of Peasant Resistance*. New Haven and London: Yale University Press.
——, and B. Kerkvliet. 1973. The Politics of Survival: Peasant Response to 'Progress' in Southeast Asia. *Journal of Southeast Asian Studies* 4(2): 241-268.
Seidman, A., and R. B. Seidman. 1984. The Political Economy of African Customary Law in the Former British Territories in Africa. *Journal of African Law* 28: 44-55.
Sen, A. 1981. *Poverty and Famines: An Essay on Entitlement and Deprivation*. Oxford: Oxford University Press.
——. 1987a. The Standard of Living. Lecture I and II. In: G. Hawthorn (ed.), *The Standard of Living*, pp. 1-38. Cambridge: Cambridge University Press.
——. 1987b. Reply. In: G. Hawthorn (ed.), *The Standard of Living*, pp. 103-112. Cambridge: Cambridge University Press.
Siddieqy, T. M. 1981. *L'Edoman Zakat*. Jakarta: Bulan Bintang.
Siddique, S. 1972. *Some Malay Ideas on Modernization, Islam and Adat*. Singapore: University of Singapore.
Simanjuntak, P. J. 1979. Civil Service Compensation in Indonesia. A Further Comment. *BIES* XI(3): 123-126.
Skocpol, T. 1986. Bringing the State back in: Strategies of Analysis in Current Research. In: P. Evans, T. Skocpol, and D. Rueschemeyer (eds.), *Bringing the State back in*, pp. 3-37. Cambridge: Cambridge University Press.
Slaats, H. M. C., and M. K. Portier. 1988. Changing Traditional Patterns of Social Security: Access to Land in Karo-Batak Society. In: F. von Benda-

Beckmann, K. von Benda-Beckmann, E. Casiño, F. Hirtz, G. R. Woodman, and H. F. Zacher(eds.), *Between Kinship and the State: Social Security and Law in Developing Countries*, pp. 137-151. Dordrecht: Foris.
Smits, A. P. (ed.). 1986. *Food Security in Developing Countries: Research Needs and Priorities*. The Hague: RAWOO.
Snouck Hurgronje, C. 1893/94. *De Atjehers*. Leiden: Brill.
Sondakh, L. 1996. Agricultural Development in Eastern Indonesia: Performance, Issues, and Policy Options. In: C. Barlow, and J. Hardjono (eds.), *Indonesia Assessment: Development in Eastern Indonesia*, pp. 141-162. Singapore: Institute of Southeast Asian Studies.
Sousa Santos, B. de. 1985. On Modes of Production of Law and Social Power. *International Journal of the Sociology of Law* 13: 299-336.
Stamboel, I. 1986. The National Experience of Indonesia in the Field of Social Security Protection for the Rural Population. ISSA Paper.
Steinmetz, S. K. 1988. Parental and Filial Relationships: Obligation, Support, and Abuse. In: S. K. Steinmetz (ed.), *Family and Support Systems across the Life Span*, pp. 165-182. New York and London: Plenum Press.
Strijbosch, F. 1985. The Concept of Pèla and its Social Significance in the Community of Moluccan Immigrants in the Netherlands. *Journal of Legal Pluralism* 23: 177-208.
———. 1986. Het Pèlarecht van Molukkers in Nederland. *Nederlands Juristenblad* 63(6): 177-183.
———. 1988. Informal Social Security among Moluccan Immigrants in the Netherlands, In: F. von Benda-Beckmann, K. von Benda-Beckmann, E. Casiño, F. Hirtz, G. R. Woodman, and H. F. Zacher (eds.), *Between Kinship and the State: Social Security and Law in Developing Countries*, pp. 169-185. Dordrecht: Foris.
Swaan, A. de 1982. *De Mens is de Mens een Zorg*. Amsterdam: Meulenhof.
———. 1989. *Zorg en de Staat: Welzijn, Onderwijs en Gezondheidszorg in Europa en de Verenigde Staten in de Nieuwe Tijd*. Amsterdam: Bert Bakker.
Swartz, M. J. 1983. Bridges, Metaphors and Theories: A Commentary. In: W. L. Rodman, and D. A. Counts (eds.), *Middleman and Brokers in Oceania*, pp. 267-286. Lanham, New York, London: University Press of America.
Taale, T. 1988. *Ambon tussen Kruidnagel en Sago: Een Onderzoek naar de Relatie tussen Handelslandbouw en Voedselfvoorziening ca. 1450 -1863*. Wageningen: Agricultural University of Wageningen.
———. 1991. Looking for a Livelihood in Hila: Continuity and Change in Land Use and its Implications for Social Security in an Ambonese Village. Unpublished Master Thesis, Wageningen: Agricultural University of Wageningen.

Takaya, Y. 1984. Two Sago Villages in South Sulawesi. In: Narifumi Maeda, and Mattulada (eds.), *Transformation of the Agricultural Landscape in Indonesia*, pp. 85-108. Kyoto: Kyoto University, Center for South East Asian Studies.

———. 1986. Sago Production at Desa Tanjung, Riau, Sumatra: Its Past and Future Prospects. In: T. Kato, M. Lufti, and N. Maeda (eds.), *Environment, Agriculture and Society in the Malay World*, pp. 87-101. Kyoto: Kyoto University, Center for Southeast Asian Studies.

Tang, M. 1996. *Aneka Ragam Pengaturan Sekuritas Sosial di Bekas Kerajaan Berru Sulawesi Selatan, Indonesia*. Wageningen: Agricultural University of Wageningen.

Thelen, T., and A. Baerwolf. 2007 (in press) Navigating Kinship Relations in Eastern Germany: Love, Care and Limits. In: P. Heady, and T. Schweitzer (eds.), *Eighteen Localities: Family, Kinship and Community at the Start of the 21st Century*, pp. 174-210. Cheltenham (UK), Northampton (USA): Edwars Elgar.

Thomas, C. 2000. *Global Governance, Development and Human Security: The Challenge of Poverty and Inequality*. London, Sterling, Va.: Pluto Press.

Tigar, M. E., and M. R. Levy. 1977. *Law and the Rise of Capitalism*. New York, London: Monthly Review Press.

Tilly, C. 1986. War Making and State Making as Organized Crime. In: P. Evans, T. Skocpol, and D. Rueschemeyer (eds.), *Bringing the State back in*, pp. 169-191. Cambridge: Cambridge University Press.

Tjadens, F. L. J., and C. L. Woldringh. 1989. *Informele Zorg in Nederland: Zelfzorgproblemen, Behoefte aan Zorg en Praktisch-Instrumentele Onderlinge Hulp*. Nijmegen: Instituut voor Toegepaste Sociale Wetenschappen.

Unang Sunarjo. 1984. *Tinjauan Singkat Tentang Pemerintahan Desa dan Kelurahan*. Bandung: Tarsito.

Veenman, J., and T. Mual-Bakarbessy. 1986. *Rondom het Heimwee. Een Probleeminventariserend Onderzoek onder Molukse Ouderen*. Rotterdam: ISEO.

Vel, J. A. C. 1994a. Manu Wolu and the Birds' Nests. The Consequences of a Deviant Way to Cope with Insecurity. In: F. von Benda-Beckmann, K. von Benda-Beckmann, and H. Marks (eds.), *Coping with Insecurity: An 'Underall' Perspective on Social Security in the Third World. Special Issue Focaal 22/23*, pp. 35-46. Nijmegen: Focaal.

———. 1994b. The Uma-Economy. Indigenous Economics and Development Work in Lowanda, Sumba (Eastern-Indonesia). PhD Thesis. Agricultural University of Wageningen.

Ven, J. van de. 1994. Members Only: Time-sharing Rice Fields and Food Security in a Sumatran Valley. In: F. von Benda-Beckmann, K. von Benda-

Beckmann, and H. Marks (eds.), *Coping with Insecurity: An 'Underall' Perspective on Social Security in the Third World. Special Issue Focaal 22/23*, pp. 85-96. Nijmegen: Focaal.
Verkerk Pistorius, A. W. P. 1871. *Studiën over de Inlandsche Huishouding in de Padangsche Bovenlanden*. Zaltbommel: Noman en Zoon.
Veth, P. J. 1871. De Djakat. *Tijdschrift Nederlandsch-Indië* 5: 451-477.
Volker, T. 1920. Adatrecht op Hitoe. *Adatrechtbundel* 24: 359-371.
——. 1925. Het Recht van Sasi in de Molukken. *Adatrechtbundel* 24: 296-313.
Walsum, S. van. 1994. Mixed Metaphors: The Nation and the Family. In: F. von Benda-Beckmann, K. von Benda-Beckmann, and H. Marks (eds.), *Coping with Insecurity: An 'Underall' Perspective on Social Security in the Third World. Special Issue Focaal 22/23*, pp.199-215. Nijmegen: Focaal.
——. 2000. *De Schaduw van de Grens: Het Nederlandse Vreemdelingenrecht en de Sociale Zekerheid van Javaanse Surinamers*. Deventer: Gouda Quint.
Weber, M. 1922. *Wirtschaft und Gesellschaft*. Tübingen: Mohr.
Weintraub, J. 1997. The Theory and Politics of the Public/Private Distinction. In: J. Weintraub, and K. Kumar (eds.), *Public and Private in Thought and Practice. Perspectives on a Grand Dichotomy*, pp. 1-42. Chicago, London: The University of Chicago Press.
Wessels, A. 1986. *Ik Rijg de Kralen: Traditie en Protestantisme in Kaibobo, een Dorp op Ceram*. Amsterdam: Free University of Amsterdam.
Wheelock, J. 1990. *Husbands at Home: The Domestic Economy in a Post-Industrial Society*. London: Routledge.
Whitehead, A. 1990. Food Crisis and Gender Conflict in Africa. In: H. Bernstein (ed.), *The Food Question: Profit versus People?* pp. 54-68. London: Earthscan.
Wolf, D. L. 1990. Daughters, Decisions and Domination: An Empirical and Conceptual Critique of Household Strategies. *Development & Change* 21(1): 43-74.
——. 1992. *Factory Daughters: Gender, Household Dynamics, and Rural Industrialization in Java*. Berkeley, Los Angeles, Oxford: University of California Press.
Wolff van Westerrode, W. de. 1901. Rapport Omtrent de Perdikan-Dessa's in de Afdeeling Poerwokerto, Residentie Banjoemas. *Tijdschrift Binnenlandsch Bestuur* 21: 355-394.
Wolters, W. 1979. Staatsvorming, Klassevorming en Patronage in Zuidoost-Azie. In: M. Vellinga, and D. Kruijt (eds.), *Afhankelijkheid en Onderontwikkeling. Special Issue Sociologische Gids* 26: 191-208.
Wong, D. 1984. The Limits of Using the Household as a Unit of Analysis. In: J. Smith, I. Wallerstein, and H.-D. Evers (eds.), *Households and the*

World-Economy, pp. 56-63. Beverly Hills, London, New Delhi: Sage Publications.

——. 1987. *Peasants in the Making: Malaysia's Green Revolution*. Singapore: Institute of Southeast Asian Studies.

Woodman, G. R. 1988. The Decline of Folk-Law Social Security in Common-Law Africa. In: F. von. Benda-Beckmann, K. von Benda-Beckmann, E. Casiño, F. Hirtz, G. R. Woodman, and H. F. Zacher (eds.), *Between Kinship and the State: Social Security and Law in Developing Countries*, pp. 69-88. Dordrecht: Foris Publications.

World Bank 1990. *World Development Report: Poverty*. Oxford: Oxford University Press.

Yamskov, A. N. 1991. Ethnic Conflict in the Transcaucasus: The Case of Nagorny-Karabakh. *Theory and Society* 20(5): 631-660.

Yanagisako, S. J. 1979. Family and Household: The Analysis of Domestic Groups. *Annual Review of Anthropology* 8: 161-205.

Zacher, H. F. 1977. Vorfragen zu den Methoden der Sozialrechtsvergleichung. In: H. F. Zacher (ed.), *Methodische Probleme des Sozialrechtsvergleichs*, pp. 21-74. Berlin: Duncker & Humblot.

——. 1988. Traditional Solidarity and Modern Social Security: Harmony or Conflict? In: F. von Benda-Beckmann, K. von Benda-Beckmann, E. Casiño, F. Hirtz, G. R. Woodman, and H. F. Zacher (eds.), *Between Kinship and the State: Social Security and Law in Developing Countries*, pp. 21-38. Dordrecht: Foris Publications.

——. (ed.). 1979. *Bedingungen für die Entstehung und Entwicklung von Sozialversicherung*. Berlin: Duncker & Humblot.

The Journal of Legal Pluralism and Unofficial Law
published by the Foundation for the Journal of Legal Pluralism
Editor in Chief: Gordon R. Woodman (Professor of Comparative Law, University of Birmingham)

Franz von Benda-Beckmann; Keebet von Benda-Beckmann (Eds.)
Dynamics of Plural Legal Orders
This volume examines dynamics of legal pluralism and explores the varied ways in which constellations of legal pluralism play out in social life. It aims to bridge the social and theoretical space between small-scale case studies and abstract generalisation. The introduction provides an overview of developments in the field of legal pluralism and offers an analytical perspective on the dynamics of the maintenance of and change in constellations of legal pluralism. Contributions examine situations in which the state is seen as remote from local settings and others in which local populations are actively engaged in widening the scope and validity of state law. By focusing on historical developments and the fault-lines of rapid political change in both post-socialist and post-authoritarian states, the volume shows that legal legacies of the past continue to have an impact. Authors look at the social significance of the various, and sometimes competing, types of law which religious and secular transnational actors introduce into local settings.
Bd. 53/54, 2006, 296 S., 29,90 €, br., ISBN 3-8258-9898-9

LIT Verlag Berlin – Hamburg – London – Münster – Wien – Zürich
Fresnostr. 2 48159 Münster
Tel.: 0251 / 620 32 22 – Fax: 0251 / 922 60 99
e-Mail: vertrieb@lit-verlag.de – http://www.lit-verlag.de

Market, Culture and Society
edited by Hans-Dieter Evers, Rüdiger Korff, Gudrun Lachenmann, Joanna Pfaff-Czarnecka, Günther Schlee, and Heiko Schrader

> Market, Culture and Society
>
> Luise Steinwachs
>
> ## Die Herstellung sozialer Sicherheit in Tanzania
>
> Prozesse sozialer Transformation und die Entstehung neuer Handlungsräume
>
> LIT

Luise Steinwachs
Die Herstellung sozialer Sicherheit als gesellschaftliches Verhandlungsfeld in Tanzania
Prozesse sozialer Transformation und die Entstehung neuer Handlungsräume
In Tanzania wird derzeit eine Diskussion um die Erweiterung sozialer Sicherheit geführt, wobei es meist um formale Ansätze geht. Die Autorin analysiert darüber hinaus – basierend auf empirischer Forschung in Tanzania – die Herstellung sozialer Sicherheit im Alltagshandeln und entwickelt das Konzept *soziale Sicherheit* weiter. Die wesentlichen Handlungsfelder, anhand derer sie gesellschaftlichen Wandel im Kontext sozialer Sicherheit aufzeigt, sind Familiennetzwerke, ökonomische Zusammenarbeit und Selbstorganisation. Speziell fokussiert sie auf den Gesundheitsbereich und diskutiert Ansätze einer integrierten Gesundheitsfinanzierung.
Bd. 15, 2006, 296 S., 25,90 €, br., ISBN 3-8258-8293-4

LIT Verlag Berlin – Hamburg – London – Münster – Wien – Zürich
Fresnostr. 2 48159 Münster
Tel.: 0251 / 620 32 22 – Fax: 0251 / 922 60 99
e-Mail: vertrieb@lit-verlag.de – http://www.lit-verlag.de